JUMP Math 6.1

Book 6 Part 1 of 2

T0302621

Contents

jump math™

MULTIPLYING POTENTIAL.

JUMP Math
One Yonge Street, Suite 1014
Toronto, Ontario M5E 1E5
Canada
www.jumpmath.org

Writers: Dr. John Mighton, Dr. Sindi Sabourin, Dr. Anna Klebanov, Dr. Sohrab Rahbar, Julie Lorinc
Editors: Dimitra Chronopoulos, Debbie Davies-Wright, Ewa Krynski
Layout and Illustrations: Linh Lam, Gabriella Kerr
Cover Design: Blakeley Words+Pictures
Cover Photograph: © iStockphoto.com/Grafissimo

ISBN 978-1-927457-06-1

Fourth printing July 2020

Printed and bound in Canada

A note to educators, parents, and everyone who believes that numeracy is as important as literacy for a fully functioning society

Welcome to JUMP Math

Entering the world of JUMP Math means believing that every child has the capacity to be fully numerate and to love math. Founder and mathematician John Mighton has used this premise to develop his innovative teaching method. The resulting resources isolate and describe concepts so clearly and incrementally that everyone can understand them.

JUMP Math is comprised of teacher's guides (which are the heart of our program), interactive whiteboard lessons, student assessment & practice books, evaluation materials, outreach programs, and teacher training. The Common Core Editions of our resources have been carefully designed to cover the Common Core State Standards. All of this is presented on the JUMP Math website: **www.jumpmath.org**.

Teacher's guides are available on the website for free use. Read the introduction to the teacher's guides before you begin using these resources. This will ensure that you understand both the philosophy and the methodology of JUMP Math. The assessment & practice books are designed for use by students, with adult guidance. Each student will have unique needs and it is important to provide the student with the appropriate support and encouragement as he or she works through the material.

Allow students to discover the concepts by themselves as much as possible. Mathematical discoveries can be made in small, incremental steps. The discovery of a new step is like untangling the parts of a puzzle. It is exciting and rewarding.

Students will need to answer the questions marked with a in a notebook. Grid paper notebooks should always be on hand for answering extra questions or when additional room for calculation is needed.

Contents

PART 1

Unit 1: Ratios and Proportional Relationships: Ratio Tables

Unit 2: The Number System: Fractions

Unit 3: Expressions and Equations: Variables and Equations

Unit 4: The Number System: Decimals

Unit 5: Ratios and Proportional Relationships: Equivalent Ratios and Percentages

Unit 6: Geometry: Area

PART 2

Unit 1: The Number System: Fractions and Decimals

Unit 6: Expressions and Equations: Algebraic Equations

Unit 7: Statistics and Probability: Mean and Dot Plots

Unit 8: Geometry: Volume and Surface Area

Unit 9: Statistics and Probability: Distribution

RP6-1 Sequences

In an **increasing sequence**, each number is greater than the one before it.

Deborah wants to continue the number sequence: 6 , 8 , 10 , 12 , ____

She finds the **difference** between the first two numbers:

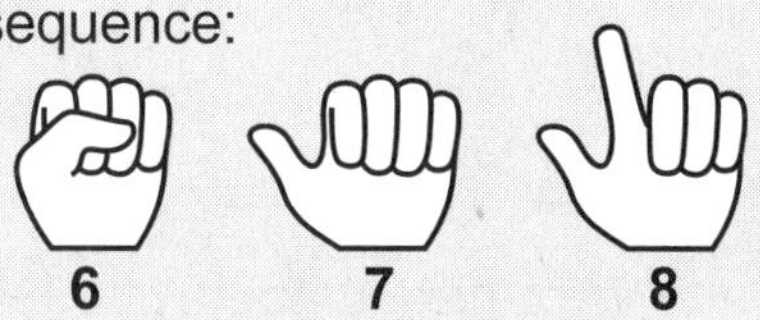

(2) 6 , 8 , 10 , 12 , ____

She finds that the difference between the other numbers in the sequence is also 2. So the sequence was made by adding 2:

(2) (2) (2) 6 , 8 , 10 , 12 , ____

To continue the sequence, Deborah adds 2 to the last number in the sequence.

The next number in the sequence is 14:

(2) (2) (2) (2) 6 , 8 , 10 , 12 , 14

1. Extend the sequence. Start by finding the gap between the numbers.

a) 2 , 5 , 8 , ____ , ____ , ____

b) 1 , 7 , 13 , ____ , ____ , ____

c) 2 , 7 , 12 , ____ , ____ , ____

d) 4 , 8 , 12 , ____ , ____ , ____

e) 1 , 6 , 11 , ____ , ____ , ____

f) 4 , 10 , 16 , ____ , ____ , ____

g) 2 , 12 , 22 , ____ , ____ , ____

h) 7 , 15 , 23 , ____ , ____ , ____

i) 31 , 34 , 37 , ____ , ____ , ____

j) 92 , 98 , 104 , ____ , ____ , ____

k) 12 , 23 , 34 , ____ , ____ , ____

l) 0 , 8 , 16 , ____ , ____ , ____

2. A plant that is 17 cm tall grows 2 cm each day.

a) How tall will the plant be after three days? ____________

b) In how many days will the plant be 27 cm tall? ____________

In a **decreasing sequence**, each number is less than the one before it.

Faraz wants to continue the number sequence: 25 , 23 , 21 , ____

He finds the **difference** between the first two numbers:

25 , 23 , 21 , ____ (−2)

He finds that the difference between the other numbers in the sequence is also 2. So the sequence was made by subtracting 2.

25 , 23 , 21 , ____ (−2) (−2)

The next number in the sequence is 19:

25 , 23 , 21 , 19 (−2) (−2) (−2)

3. Extend the sequence.

a) 18 , 15 , 12 , ____ , ____ , ____

b) 32 , 26 , 20 , ____ , ____ , ____

c) 52 , 47 , 42 , ____ , ____ , ____

d) 34 , 30 , 26 , ____ , ____ , ____

e) 51 , 46 , 41 , ____ , ____ , ____

f) 84 , 80 , 76 , ____ , ____ , ____

g) 62 , 51 , 40 , ____ , ____ , ____

h) 97 , 89 , 81 , ____ , ____ , ____

i) 71 , 64 , 57 , ____ , ____ , ____

j) 62 , 58 , 54 , ____ , ____ , ____

k) 82 , 73 , 64 , ____ , ____ , ____

l) 84 , 72 , 60 , ____ , ____ , ____

4. Use a decreasing sequence to solve each problem:

a) Judi has $49. She spends $8 each day. How much money does she have left after 5 days?

b) Huang has a roll of 74 stamps. He uses 7 stamps each day for 4 days. How many stamps are left?

RP6-2 Extending a Sequence

1. Add the number given to continue the sequence.

   a) (add 4) 41, 45, ________, ________, ________

   b) (add 8) 60, 68, ________, ________, ________

   c) (add 3) 74, 77, ________, ________, ________

   d) (add 11) 20, 31, ________, ________, ________

   e) (add 8) 61, 69, ________, ________, ________

   f) (add 11) 31, 42, ________, ________, ________

2. Subtract the number given to continue the sequence.

   a) (subtract 3) 25, 22, ________, ________, ________

   b) (subtract 2) 34, 32, ________, ________, ________

   c) (subtract 6) 85, 79, ________, ________, ________

   d) (subtract 12) 89, 77, ________, ________, ________

   e) (subtract 8) 57, 49, ________, ________, ________

   f) (subtract 7) 57, 50, ________, ________, ________

BONUS ▶ Create a sequence of your own. After writing the sequence in the blanks, say what you added or subtracted each time.

______ , ______ , ______ , ______ , ______ My rule: ______________________________

3. Which one of the following sequences was made by adding 7? Circle it.
   Hint: Check all the numbers in the sequence.

   4, 10, 18, 21 4, 11, 16, 21 3, 10, 17, 24

4. 72, 61, 50, 39, 28, ...
   Brenda says this sequence was made by subtracting 12 each time.
   Rajiv says it was made by subtracting 11.

   Who is right? __________ Explain how you know. ______________________________

RP6-3 Tables

Claude creates an **increasing pattern** with squares. He records the number of squares in each figure in a T-table. He also records the number of squares he adds each time he makes a new figure.

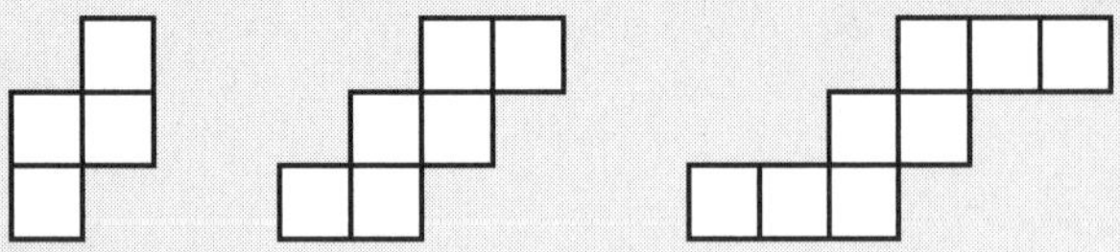

Figure	# of Squares
1	4
2	6
3	8

(2) (2) ← Number of squares added each time

The number of squares in the figures are 4, 6, 8, ….

Claude writes a **rule** for this number pattern:

Start at 4 and add 2 each time.

1. Claude makes other *increasing patterns* with squares.

How many squares does he add to make each new figure?

Write your answer in the circles. Then write a rule for the pattern.

a)

Figure	Number of Squares
1	2
2	8
3	14

Rule:

b)

Figure	Number of Squares
1	3
2	9
3	15

Rule:

c)

Figure	Number of Squares
1	1
2	6
3	11

Rule:

d)

Figure	Number of Squares
1	1
2	8
3	15

Rule:

e)

Figure	Number of Squares
1	5
2	13
3	21

Rule:

f)

Figure	Number of Squares
1	11
2	22
3	33

Rule:

g)

Figure	Number of Squares
1	3
2	12
3	21

Rule:

h)

Figure	Number of Squares
1	6
2	13
3	20

Rule:

i)

Figure	Number of Squares
1	7
2	13
3	19

Rule:

2. Extend the number pattern. How many squares would be used in Figure 6?

a)

Figure	Number of Squares
1	2
2	10
3	18

b)

Figure	Number of Squares
1	4
2	9
3	14

c)

Figure	Number of Squares
1	7
2	11
3	15

3. After making Figure 3, Claude has only 35 squares left. Does he have enough squares to complete Figure 4? Circle your answer.

a)

Figure	Number of Squares
1	4
2	13
3	22

Yes No

b)

Figure	Number of Squares
1	6
2	17
3	28

Yes No

c)

Figure	Number of Squares
1	9
2	17
3	25

Yes No

4. Make a T-table to show how many shapes will be needed to make the 5th figure in each pattern.

a) 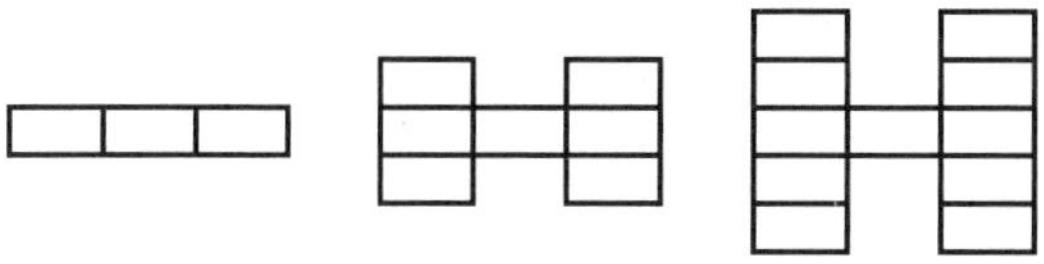

b) 

5. a) The snow is 17 cm deep at 5 p.m. Each hour, 4 cm of snow falls. How deep is the snow at 9 p.m.?

Time	Depth of Snow
5 p.m.	17 cm

b) Philip had $42 in savings by the end of July. Each month he saves $9. How much will he have by the end of October?

Month	Savings
July	$42

6. Sarah's fish tank is leaking.
At 6 p.m. there are 21 L of water in the tank.
At 7 p.m. there are 18 L, and at 8 p.m. there are 15 L.

a) How many liters of water leak out each hour?

____

b) How many liters will be left in the tank at 10 p.m.?

____

c) How many hours will it take for all the water to leak out?

____

Time	Amount of Water in the Tank
6 p.m.	21 L
7 p.m.	18 L
8 p.m.	15 L
9 p.m.	
10 p.m.	

7. A store rents snowboards at $7 for the first hour and $5 for every hour after that. How much does it cost to rent a snowboard for 6 hours?

8. a) How many triangles would Marco need to make a figure with 10 squares?

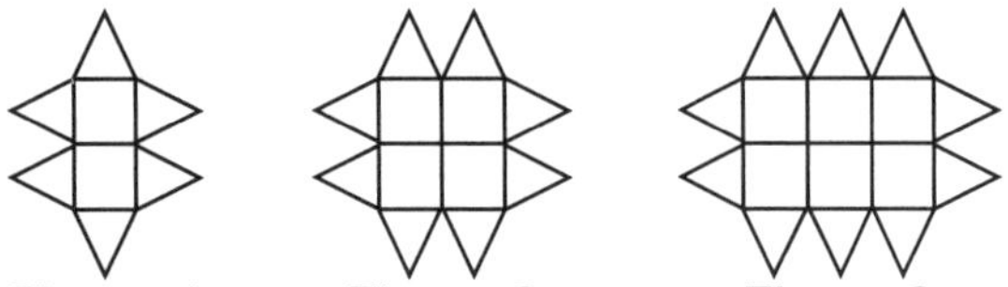

Figure 1 Figure 2 Figure 3

b) April says that she needs 15 triangles to make the sixth figure. Is she correct?

9. Merle saves $55 in August. She saves $6 each month after that.
Alex saves $42 in August. He saves $7 each month after that.
Who will have saved the most money by the end of January?

RP6-4 Multiplying and Dividing by Skip Counting

Amy finds the product of **3** and **5** by skip counting on a number line. She counts off three 5s. From the picture, Amy can see that the **product** of 3 and 5 is 15.

$3 \times 5 = 5 + 5 + 5 = 15$

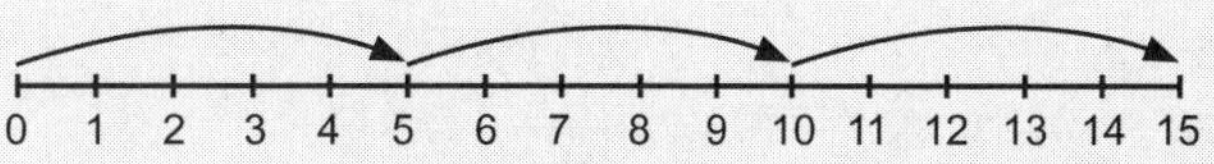

1. Draw arrows to find the product by skip counting.

a) **4** × **2** =

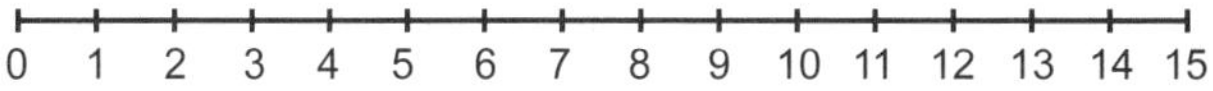

b) **3** × **4** =

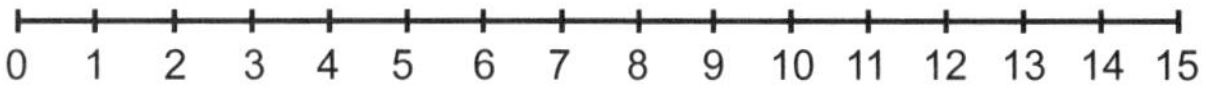

2. Use the number line to skip count by 4s, 6s, and 7s. Fill in the boxes below as you count.

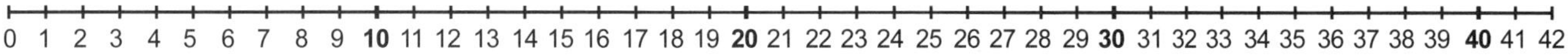

a)

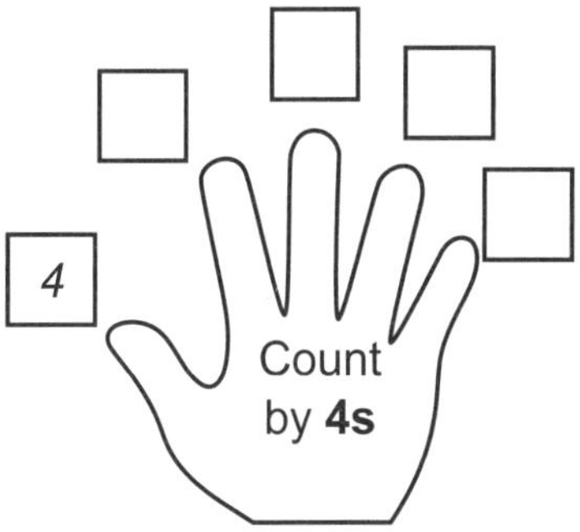

b)

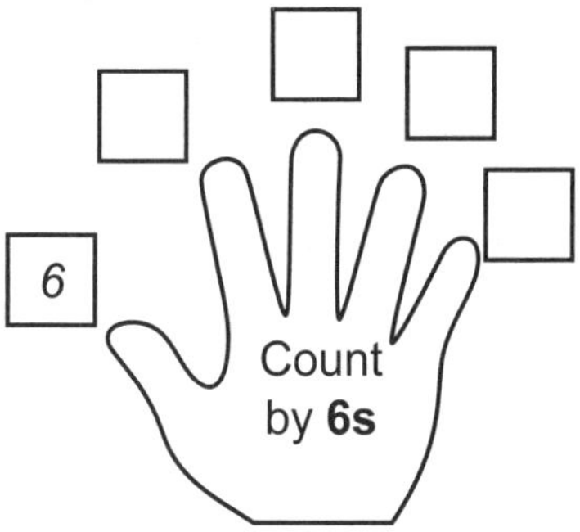

c)

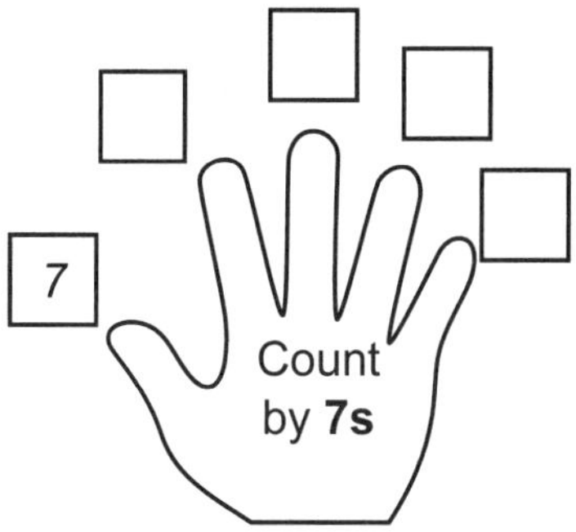

3. Find the product by skip counting on your fingers. Use the hands from Question 2 to help:

a) 3 × 5 =	b) 5 × 2 =	c) 3 × 4 =	d) 3 × 6 =	e) 1 × 7 =
f) 3 × 7 =	g) 3 × 3 =	h) 6 × 1 =	i) 2 × 7 =	j) 5 × 5 =
k) 2 × 2 =	l) 7 × 1 =	m) 4 × 4 =	n) 4 × 6 =	o) 1 × 6 =

4. Find the number of items in each picture. Write a multiplication statement for each picture.

a)

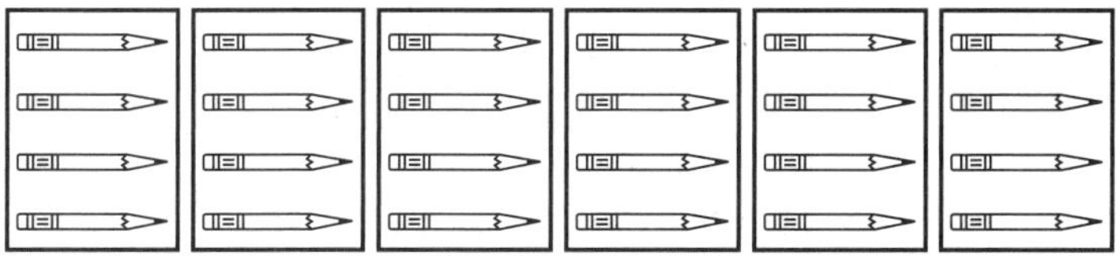

____

b)

____

You can solve the division problem **12 ÷ 4 = ?** by skip counting on a number line.

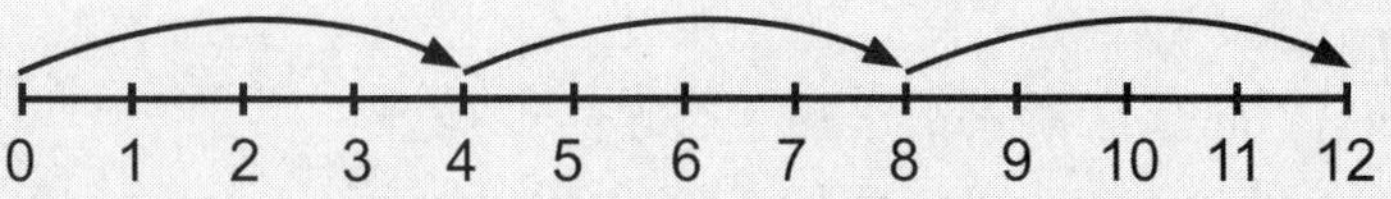

The number line shows that it takes three skips of size 4 to get 12.

4 + 4 + 4 = 12 so **12 ÷ 4 = 3**

5. Use the number line to find the answer to the division problem. Be sure to draw arrows to show your skip counting.

a)

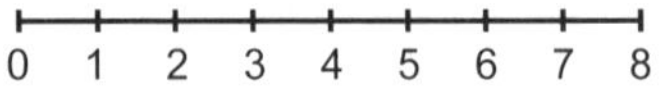

$8 \div 2 =$ ________

b)

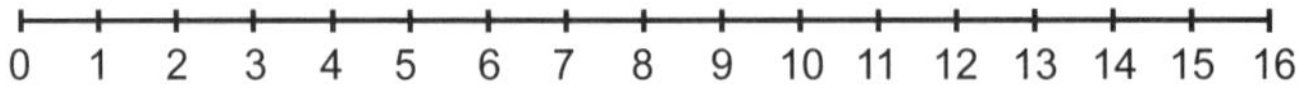

$16 \div 8 =$ ________

6. What division equation does the picture represent?

a)

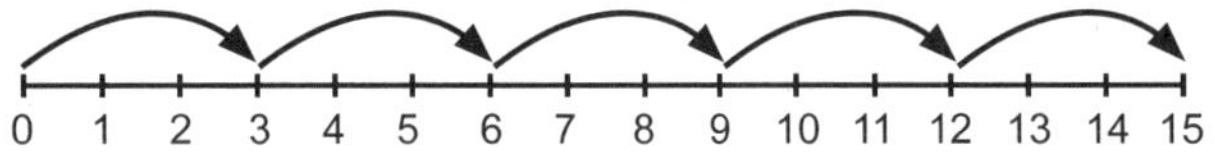

____

b)

____

You can also find the answer to a division question by skip counting on your fingers.

For example, to find **45 ÷ 9**, count by 9s until you reach 45. The number of fingers you have up when you say "45" is the answer.

So **45 ÷ 9 = 5**

7. Find the answer by skip counting on your fingers.

a) $35 \div 5 =$ _____ b) $12 \div 6 =$ _____ c) $32 \div 8 =$ _____ d) $21 \div 7 =$ _____ e) $45 \div 5 =$ _____

f) $36 \div 4 =$ _____ g) $25 \div 5 =$ _____ h) $42 \div 6 =$ _____ i) $27 \div 3 =$ _____ j) $16 \div 2 =$ _____

k) $36 \div 6 =$ _____ l) $35 \div 7 =$ _____ m) $18 \div 3 =$ _____ n) $21 \div 3 =$ _____ o) $40 \div 8 =$ _____

8. There are 24 flowers in 6 bouquets. How many flowers are in each bouquet? ________________

9. 36 trees are in 9 rows. How many trees are in each row? ________________

10. Amy uses 8 pencils in a month. How many months will she take to use 32 pencils? ________________

RP6-5 Mental Math and the Standard Method for Multiplication

This is how Leela multiplies **4 × 22**:

She rewrites 22 as a sum: 22 = 20 + 2

She multiplies 4 by 20: 4 × 20 = 80

She multiplies 4 by 2: 4 × 2 = 8

She adds the two results: 80 + 8 = 88

Leela concludes that **4 × 22 = 88.**

This picture shows why Leela's method works:

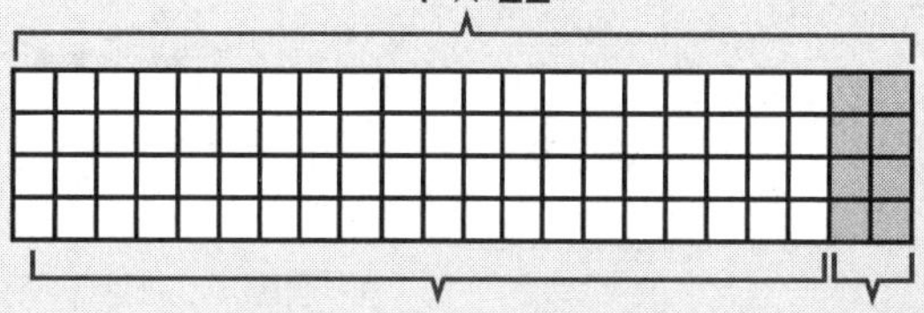

4 × 22 = (4 × 20) + (4 × 2) = 80 + 8 = 88

1. Use the picture to write the multiplication expression as a sum.

a)

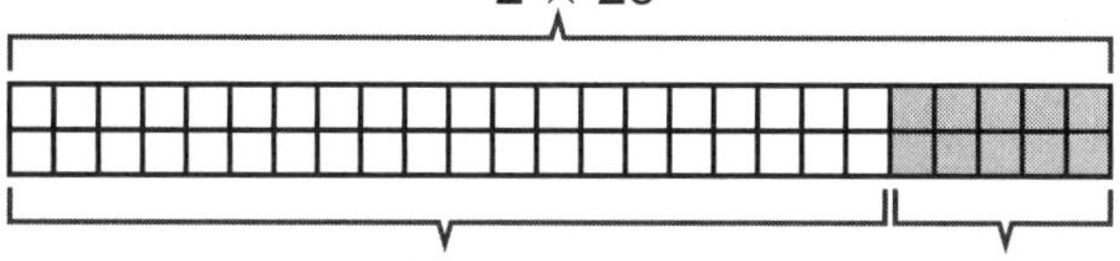

2 × 20 ______ *2 ×* ______

2 × 25 = (*2 ×* ______) + (*2 ×* ______)

b)

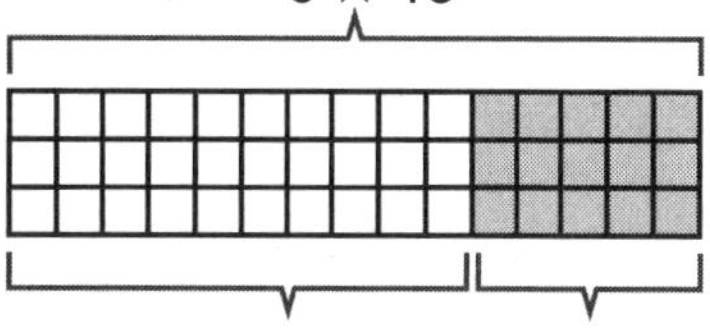

______ ______

3 × 15 = (______) + (______)

2. Multiply using Leela's method.

a) 5 × 13 = *5 × 10* + *5 × 3* = *50 + 15* = *65*

b) 4 × 21 = ______ + ______ = ______ = ______

c) 3 × 43 = ______ + ______ = ______ = ______

d) 2 × 432 = *2 × 400* + *2 × 30* + *2 × 2* = *800 + 60 + 4* = *864*

e) 3 × 312 = ______ + ______ + ______ = ______ = ______

f) 4 × 321 = ______ + ______ + ______ = ______ = ______

3. Multiply in your head by multiplying the digits separately.

a) 3 × 12 = ______ b) 3 × 52 = ______ c) 6 × 31 = ______ d) 7 × 21 = ______

e) 5 ×31 = ______ f) 3 × 42 = ______ g) 6 × 51 = ______ h) 2 × 44 = ______

i) 4 × 521 = ______ j) 3 × 621 = ______ k) 5 × 411 = ______ l) 2 × 444 = ______

m) 3 × 632 = ______ n) 4 × 422 = ______ o) 4 × 212 = ______ p) 2 × 421 = ______

4. a) Stacy placed 821 books in each of 4 bookshelves. How many books did she place altogether?

b) David put 723 pencils in each of 3 boxes. How many pencils did he put in the boxes?

How to solve $3 \times 42 = 3 \times 40 + 3 \times 2$

$= 3 \times 4 \text{ tens} + 3 \times 2 \text{ ones}$

Step 1:

Multiply the ones digit by 3 (3×2 ones $= 6$ ones).

	4	2
×		3
		6

ones

Step 2:

Multiply the tens digit by 3 (3×4 tens $= 12$ tens).

Regroup 10 tens as 1 hundred.

	4	2
×		3
1	**2**	**6**

hundreds tens

5. Use **Steps 1** and **2** to find the product.

a) 94×2 b) 83×3 c) 74×2 d) 63×2 e) 92×3

How to solve $7 \times 53 = 7 \times 50 + 7 \times 3$

$= 7 \times 5 \text{ tens} + 7 \times 3 \text{ ones}$

Step 1:

Multiply 3 ones by 7 ($7 \times 3 = 21$).

Step 2:

Regroup 20 ones as 2 tens.

	2	
	5	3
×		7
		1

6. Complete **Steps 1** and **2** of the multiplication.

a) 27×5 (regrouped: 3; ones: 5) b) 15×6 c) 25×3 d) 16×3 e) 49×5

f) 36×4 g) 47×2 h) 58×3 i) 47×6 j) 97×8

Step 3:

Multiply 5 tens by 7
(7 × 5 tens = 35 tens).

	2	
	5	3
×		7
		1

Step 4:

Add 2 tens to the result
(35 + 2 = 37 tens).

	2	
	5	3
×		7
3	**7**	1

7. Complete **Steps 3** and **4** of the multiplication.

a)

	1	
	2	4
×		3
	7	2

b)

	4	
	3	5
×		9
		5

c)

	2	
	1	5
×		5
		5

d)

	1	
	7	3
×		5
		5

e)

	4	
	8	9
×		5
		5

8. Complete **all steps** of the multiplication.

a) 35×9

b) 35×6

c) 15×7

d) 25×8

e) 24×5

9. Multiply by regrouping ones as tens.

a) 227×3

b) 116×5

c) 224×3

d) 119×5

e) 328×3

10. Multiply by regrouping when you need to.

a) 237×5

b) 756×3

c) 528×2

d) 532×7

e) 213×8

11. A dog is 13 years old. Multiply that by 7 to estimate the dog's age in human years.

12. Anna borrowed a library book for 21 days. She reads 9 pages each day. If the book is 165 pages long, will she need to renew the book?

RP6-6 Introduction to Ratios

A **ratio** is a comparison of two quantities.

1. 

a) The ratio of moons to circles is _2_ : _6_

b) The ratio of triangles to moons is ____ : ____

c) The ratio of stars to squares is ____ : ____

d) The ratio of squares to circles is ____ : ____

e) The ratio of squares to moons is ____ : ____

f) The ratio of squares to figures is ____ : ____

2. Write the number of vowels compared to the number of consonants in the following words.

a) apple _2_ : _3_

b) banana ____ : ____

c) orange ____ : ____

d) pear ____ : ____

3. Write the ratio of the lengths.

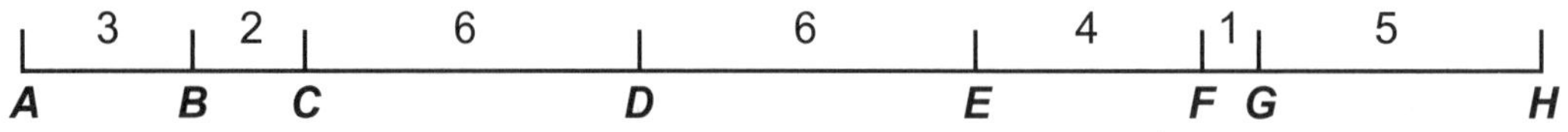

a) *AB* to *DE* ____ : ____

b) *BC* to *CD* ____ : ____

c) *EF* to *FG* ____ : ____

d) *EF* to *BC* ____ : ____

e) *AB* to *GH* ____ : ____

BONUS ▶ *AB* to *EG* ____ : ____

4. To make fruit salad, you need 4 cups of apples, 2 cups of oranges, and 3 cups of bananas.

a) How many cups do you need in total? ____

b) What is the ratio of cups of apples to cups of fruit salad? ____ : ____

5. 

a) In the above pattern, what does the ratio 2 : 3 describe?

____

b) What does the ratio 5 : 10 describe?

____

6. Build a model or draw a picture that could be described by the ratio 3 : 4.

RP6-7 Introduction to Ratio Tables

1. Each column was made by skip counting by a number. Complete each column.

a)

4
8
12

b)

5
10

c)

3
9

d)

2
8

e)

7
21

f)

12
24

Michael makes orange paint by mixing 1 cup of red paint for every 3 cups of yellow paint. He records the number of cups in a **ratio table**.

Cups of Red	Cups of Yellow
1	3
2 (×2)	6 (×2)
3 (×3)	9 (×3)
4 (×4)	12 (×4)

In a ratio table, you must multiply the numbers in the **first row** by the same number to get another row.

2. Use skip counting or multiplication to complete a ratio table for each ratio.

a) 4 : 1

4	1
8	*2*
12	*3*
16	*4*

b) 1 : 2

1	2
2	*4*

c) 3 : 1

3	1

d) 1 : 7

1	7

e) 2 : 3

2	3

f) 5 : 2

5	2

g) 6 : 4

6	4

h) 3 : 5

3	5

3. Find the missing number(s) in each ratio table.

a) 2 : 7

2	7
4	14
6	

b) 4 : 1

4	1
8	2
	3

c) 3 : 2

3	2
	4
9	

BONUS ▶ 6 : _____

6	
12	10
18	15

4. Jackie created an increasing pattern with squares and recorded the number of squares in a table.

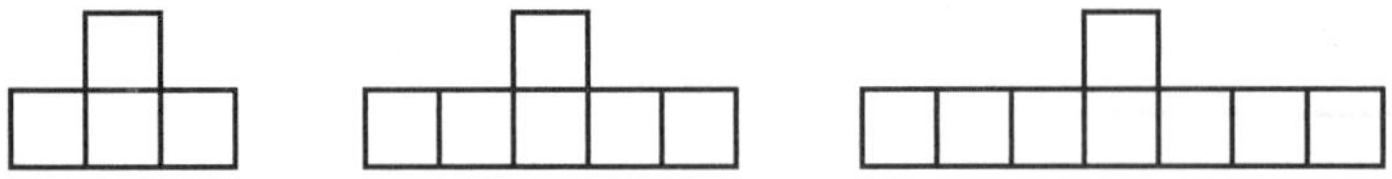

Figure 1 Figure 2 Figure 3

Figure	# of Squares
1	4
2	6
3	8

Is this a ratio table? _____ Explain how you know. ____

____

____

5. Circle the table(s) that is/are a ratio table.

7	3
14	6
21	9
28	12

4	2
8	5
12	8
16	11

6	5
12	10
18	15
24	20

1	5
2	6
3	7
4	8

6. Don makes punch. He needs 5 cups of ginger ale for every 3 cups of cranberry juice. Use the following ratio table to find out how many cups of ginger ale he needs for 9 cups of cranberry juice.

Cups of Ginger Ale	Cups of Cranberry Juice
5	*3*

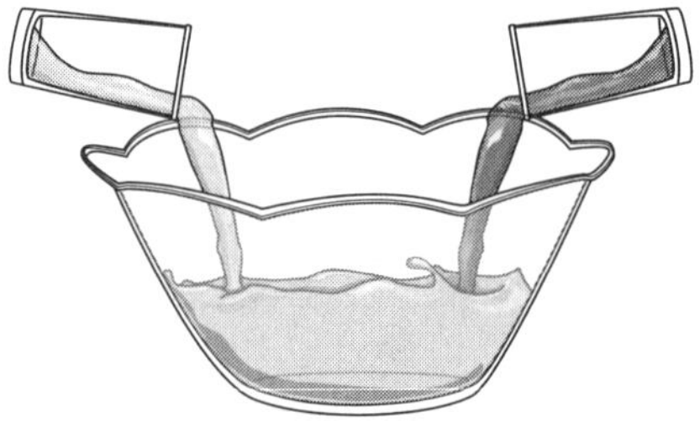

BONUS ▶ In Question 6, how many cups each of ginger ale and cranberry juice does Don need to make 40 cups of punch? Use the following ratio table to find out.

Cups of Ginger Ale	Cups of Cranberry Juice	Cups in Total
5	*3*	*8*

RP6-8 Unit Rates

In a **unit rate**, one quantity is equal to 1.

For example, "30¢ for each apple" is a unit rate.

1. Complete the table for each rate.

a) Each ticket costs $4.

# of Tickets	Cost ($)
1	4
2	8
3	12

b) 3 hours of practice every day

Time (h)	# of Days
3	1
6	2

c) 25 students in each class

# of Students	# of Classes

d) Each girl has 5 flowers.

# of Girls	# of Flowers

e) 60 miles every hour

Time (h)	Distance (mi)
1	60

f) 6 cards for each boy

# of Cards	# of Boys

2. A blue whale typically travels 12 miles every hour. Use the following table to find out how long it takes for a blue whale to travel 48 miles.

Distance (mi)	Time (h)
12	1

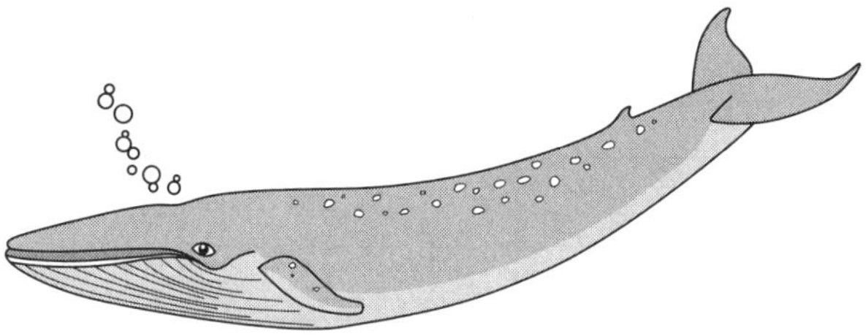

3. Multiply to find the missing information.

a) 1 book costs $5
×4 → 4 books cost *$20* ← ×4

b) 3 miles in 1 hour
______ miles in 5 hours

c) 1 teacher for 25 students
3 teachers for ______

4. Measure the height of each picture. Then find the height of each animal in real life if 1 cm in the picture represents 50 cm in real life.

a) Height of picture _____ cm
Height of animal _____ cm

b) Height of picture _____ cm
Height of animal _____ cm

c) Height of picture _____ cm
Height of animal _____ cm

5. Find the missing information.

a) $15 allowance in 1 week

______ allowance in 4 weeks

b) 60 miles in 1 hour

______ miles in 5 hours

6. David earns $11 per hour for mowing lawns. How much will he earn in 6 hours?

7. The fuel economy of a car (how far it can go with a unit of gas) is reported in miles per gallon (MPG). Car A has a fuel economy of 30 MPG and Car B has a fuel economy of 40 MPG.

a) Complete the tables to find out which car uses less gas for a 120-mile trip.

Car A

Gas Used (gal)	**Distance (mi)**
1	*30*

Car B

Gas Used (gal)	**Distance (mi)**
1	*40*

b) Suppose gas costs $4 for every gallon. How much will the gas for the trip cost?

For Car A: ______________________

For Car B: ______________________

c) Which car has a better fuel economy? ______ Explain how you know. ______________________

____

RP6-9 Finding Unit Rates

1. Divide to find the missing information.

a) 6 mangoes cost $18
÷6
1 mango costs _______

b) 4 cakes cost $16
1 cake costs _______

c) 5 pears cost $20
1 pear costs _______

d) 3 notebooks cost $24
1 notebook costs _______

e) 2 jackets cost $20
1 jacket costs _______

BONUS ▶ 150 miles per 5 gallons
_______ miles per 1 gallon

John paid $10 for 5 hot dogs. He wants to know how much 1 hot dog costs.

Step 1: He makes a chart showing the cost for each quantity of hot dogs.
He writes a question mark (?) for the missing quantity.

Hot Dogs	Costs ($)
5	10
1	?

Step 2: He finds the number being divided by in the first column.
Then he divides by that number in the second column to find the missing number.

	Hot Dogs	Costs ($)	
	5	10	
÷5	1	2	÷5

John finds that 1 hot dog costs $2.

2. a) Ron earns $66 babysitting for 6 hours.
How much does he earn in an hour?

b) Tina earns $75 cutting lawns for 5 hours.
How much does she earn in an hour?

3. Find the unit rate.

a) 4 kg of rice for 24 cups of water
1 kg of rice for _____ cups of water

b) 36 miles in 3 hours
_____ miles in 1 hour

4. Find the unit rate from each table.

# of Tickets	Cost ($)
3	15
4	20
5	25

a) *$5* for each ticket

Time (h)	Distance (mi)
2	50
3	75
4	100

b) ☐ miles every hour

# of Buses	# of Students
2	40
4	80
8	160

c) ☐ students in each bus

Double Number Line Diagrams

Rose uses 3 eggs for each cup of flour to make a cake. Instead of using a table, she records the number of eggs and cups of flour on a horizontal **double number line diagram**.

Flour (cups)	Eggs
1	3
2	6
3	9
4	12

×2 ×3 ×4

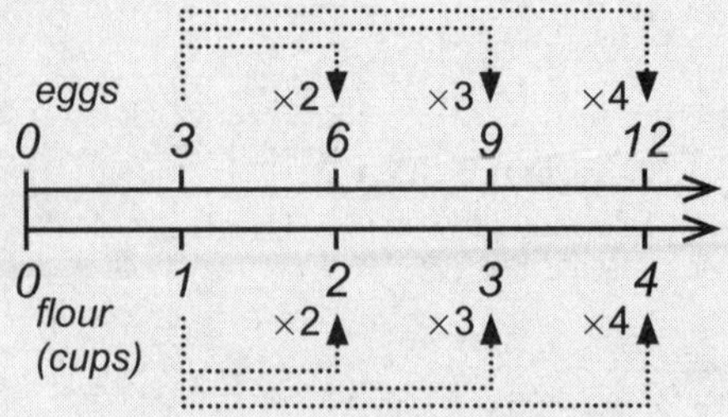

1. Make a double number line diagram for each table.

a)

2	5
4	10
6	15
8	20

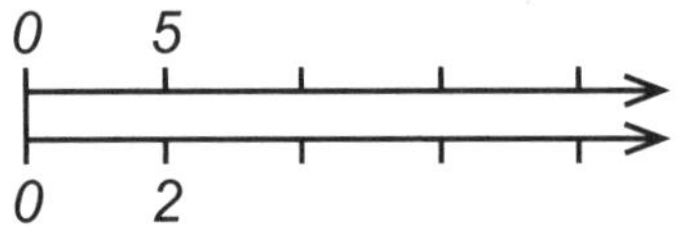

b)

4	3
8	6
12	9
16	12

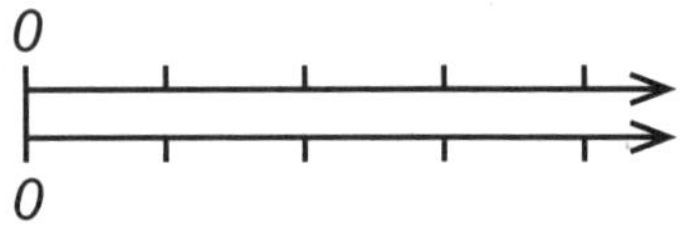

2. Find the missing numbers in each double number line diagram.

a)

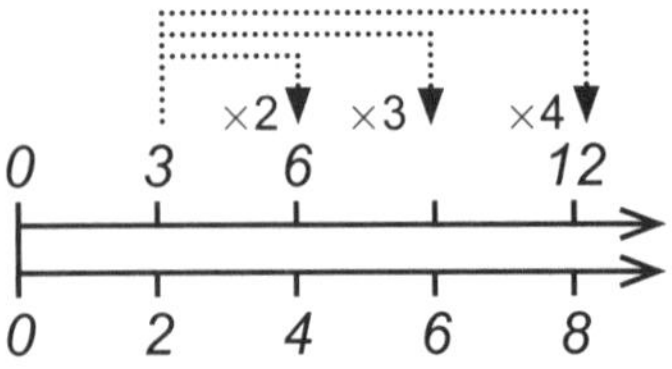

b)

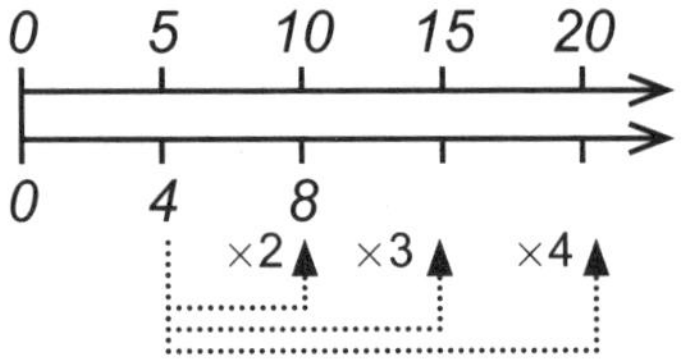

c)

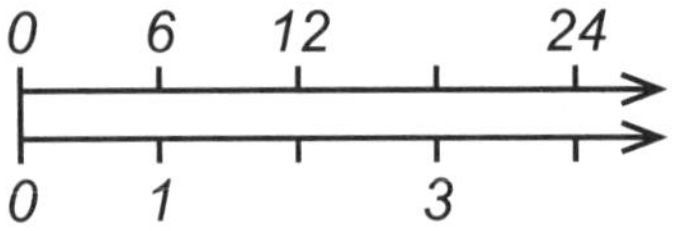

d)

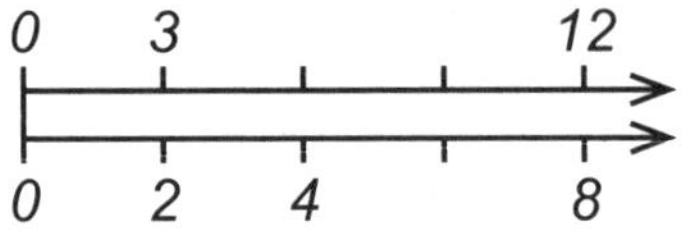

e)

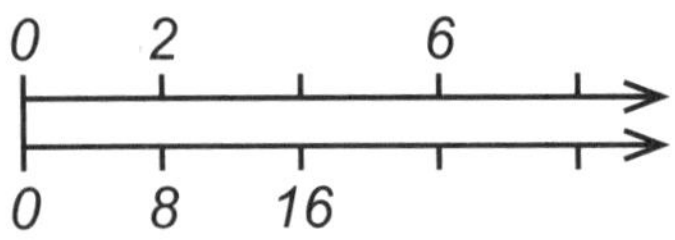

BONUS ▶

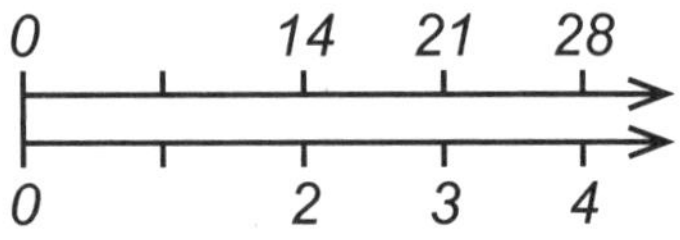

3. Sam drives 60 miles every hour. He is driving to his uncle's house 300 miles away.
Use the following double number line diagram to find out how long it takes to get there.

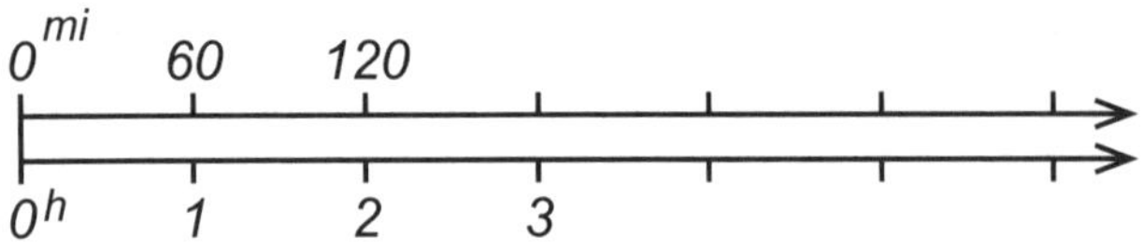

NS6-1 Place Value

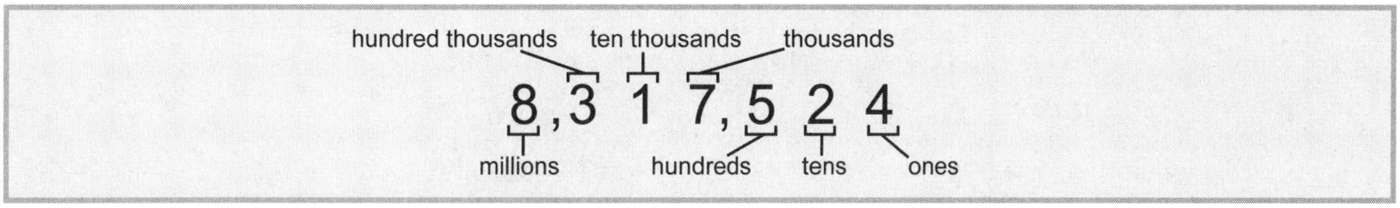

1. Write the place value of the underlined digit.

a) 56,2$\underline{3}$6 *tens*

b) $\underline{1}$,956,336 ______

c) 8,$\underline{2}$56,601 ______

d) 7,103,25$\underline{6}$ ______

e) 2,5$\underline{8}$9,143 ______

f) 3,$\underline{9}$21,052 ______

g) 903,$\underline{7}$46 ______

h) 2,6$\underline{0}$5,416 ______

2. Write the place value of the digit 5 in each of the numbers below.
Hint: First underline the 5 in each number.

a) 3$\underline{5}$,689 *thousands*

b) 5,308,603 ______

c) 36,905 ______

d) 512 ______

e) 2,542 ______

f) 3,451,628 ______

g) 43,251 ______

h) 152,776 ______

i) 1,543,001 ______

j) 5,704,021 ______

k) 7,305 ______

l) 9,695,000 ______

3. Write each number into the place value chart.

	Millions	Hundred Thousands	Ten Thousands	Thousands	Hundreds	Tens	Ones
a) 2,316,953							
b) 62,507							
c) 5,604,891							
d) 1,399							
e) 17							
f) 998,260							
g) 5,002,008							

The number 784,523 is a **6-digit number**.

- The **digit** 7 stands for 700,000—the **value** of the digit 7 is 700,000.
- The digit 8 stands for 80,000—the value of the digit 8 is 80,000.
- The digit 4 stands for 4,000—the value of the digit 4 is 4,000.
- The digit 5 stands for 500—the value of the digit 5 is 500.
- The digit 2 stands for 20—the value of the digit 2 is 20.
- The digit 3 stands for 3—the value of the digit 3 is 3.

4. Write the **value** of each digit.

a) 654,872

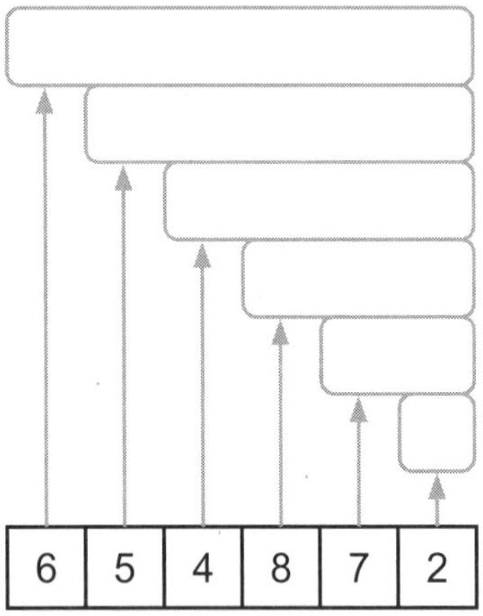

b) 128,537

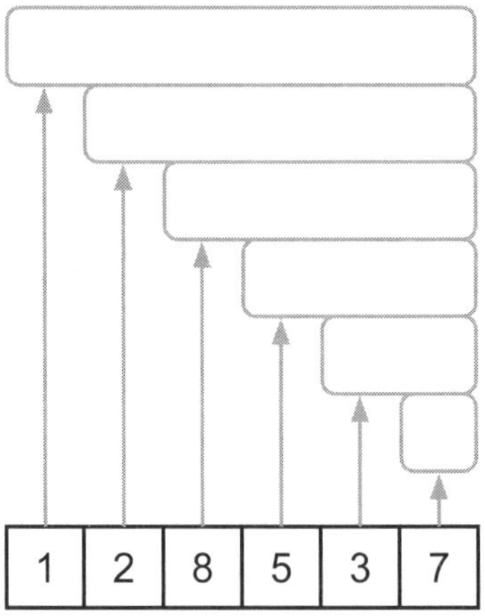

5. What does the digit 7 stand for in each number?

a) 8,476 *70*

b) 38,725

c) 93,726

d) 730,025

e) 7,250

f) 64,297

g) 43,075

h) 382,457

6. Fill in the blank.

a) In the number 4,523, the digit 5 stands for ______________ .

b) In the number 34,528, the digit 3 stands for ______________ .

c) In the number 420,583, the value of the digit 8 is ______________ .

d) In the number 723,594, the digit _______ is in the ten thousands place.

Number words for the tens place: ten twenty thirty forty fifty sixty seventy eighty ninety

7. Say whether the underlined numbers represent **thousands** or **millions**.

a) 327,510,210 *millions* b) 216,772,015 ____ c) 5,321,859 ____

d) 879,054,815 ____ e) 129,000,307 ____ f) 2,500,623 ____

8. Write the value of the underlined digits.

a) 375,231,872 *three hundred seventy-five million*

b) 287,036,253 ____

c) 79,253,812 d) 3,770,823 e) 22,306,235

9. Write numerals for the number words.

a) Seventy-three million, fifty-seven thousand, one hundred four

b) Nine hundred seven million, four hundred three thousand, twenty-one

10. Write number words for the numerals.

a) 275,381,210 b) 89,023,100 c) 998,325,593

11. Write how many years ago each period started, using words and then numerals. (Note: "mya" means millions of years ago.)

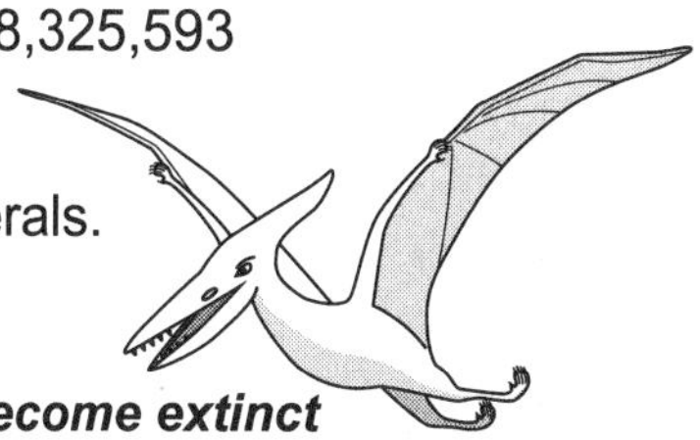

Dinosaurs evolve	*Birds evolve*	*Dinosaurs become extinct*
Triassic Period	Jurassic Period	Cretaceous Period

248 mya 199 mya 145 mya 65 mya

12. a) Write the distance from each planet to the Sun using words.

Planet	Distance from Sun (km)
Mercury	57,600,000
Venus	107,520,000
Earth	148,640,000

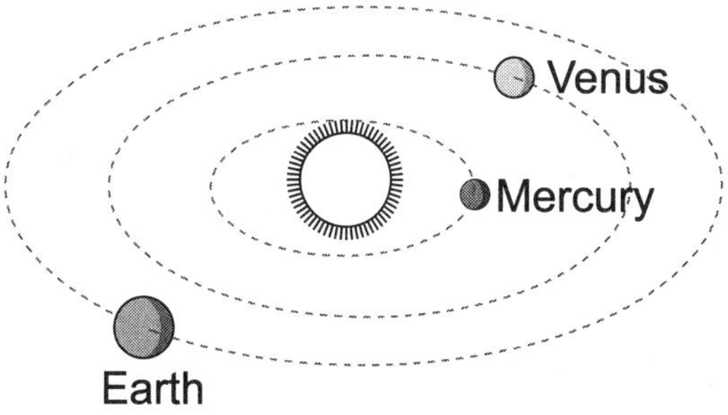

b) **Billions** come after millions.
The planet Neptune is 4,468,640,000 km from the Sun.
Write this number in words.

NS6-2 Representation in Expanded Form

1. Write the number in expanded form. Then draw a base ten model.

Example: 3,152 = *3,000 + 100 + 50 + 2*

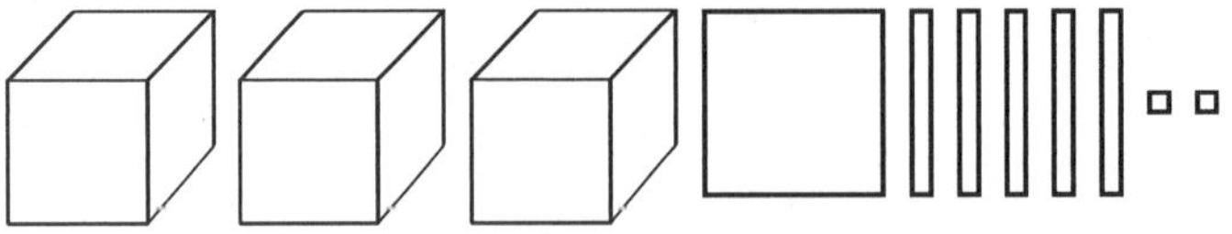

a) 4,354 = ____________________

b) 2,604 = ____________________

2. Expand the number using numerals and words.

a) 2,536,784 = *2 millions + 5 hundred thousands + 3 ten thousands + 6 thousands + 7 hundreds + 8 tens + 4 ones*

b) 6,235,401 = ____________________

c) 3,056,026 = ____________________

3. Write the number in expanded form (using numerals).

a) 72,613 = *70,000 + 2,000 + 600 + 10 + 3*

b) 36 = ____________________

c) 12,052 = ____________________

d) 526 = ____________________

e) 56,384 = ____________________

f) 2,493 = ____________________

g) 3,082,385 = ____________________

4. Write the number for each expanded form.

a) 6,000 + 700 + 40 + 5 = __________

b) 800 + 60 + 8 = __________

c) 3,000 + 30 + 2 = __________

d) 50,000 + 6,000 + 400 + 90 + 3 = __________

e) 30,000 + 2,000 + 500 = __________

f) 90,000 + 3,000 + 600 + 8 = __________

g) 70,000 + 700 + 7 = __________

h) 10,000 + 6,000 + 200 + 30 + 4 = __________

BONUS ▶ 300,000 + 2,000,000 + 5 + 70,000 + 200 = ____________________

5. Find the missing numbers.

a) 2,000 + 600 + _____ + 5 = 2,645

b) 4,000 + 200 + _____ + 5 = 4,285

c) 40,000 + 3,000 + _____ + 10 + 5 = 43,715

d) 80,000 + 5,000 + _____ + 60 + 3 = 85,263

e) 20,000 + 6,000 + 300 + _____ = 26,302

f) _____ + 400 = 9,400

g) 6,000 + _____ = 6,080

h) 80,000 + _____ + _____ = 87,005

i) 300,000 + 90,000 + _____ + _____ = 390,702

6. How many thousands blocks would you need to represent a million?

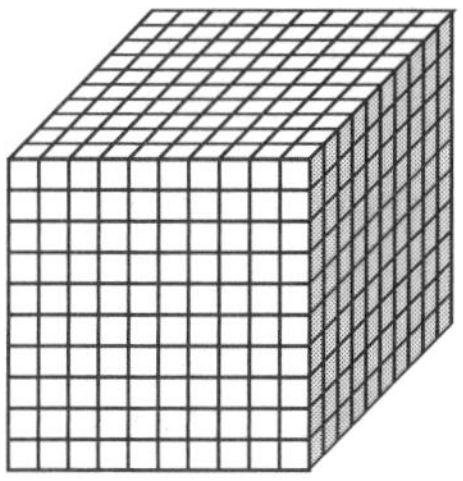

7. In the number 38,562, what is the sum of the tens digit and the thousands digit?

8. a) How many two-digit numbers have digits that add to 12?

b) How many two-digit numbers have digits that add to 10?

c) How many two-digit numbers have digits that add to 8?

9. Using only 5 base ten blocks, make (or draw) a model of a number such that…

a) the number is odd.

b) there are twice as many thousands blocks as hundreds blocks.

10. Represent the number 8,564 in four different ways.

- by sketching a base ten model
- as a word
- in expanded form (2 ways)

NS6-3 Integers

The height above sea level and the depth below sea level are recorded on a scale that includes zero (0), **positive whole numbers** (1, 2, 3, …), and **negative whole numbers** (–1, –2, –3, …).

These numbers are called **integers**.

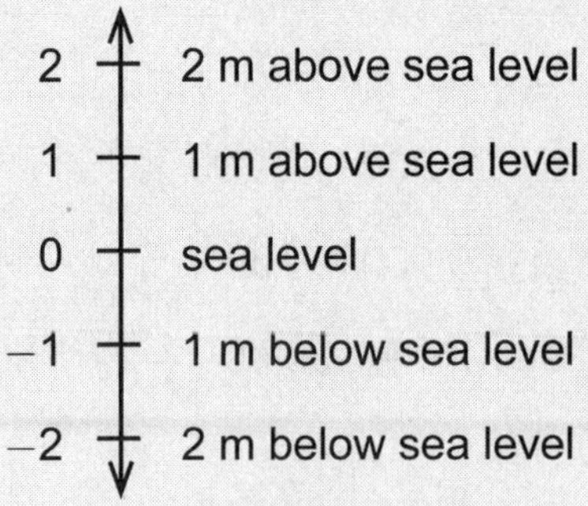

1. a) Write an integer for the level at which each animal typically flies or swims.

Falcon 100 m

Seagull 50 m above

sea level

Dolphin 50 m below

Mackerel 100 m below

Stingray 150 m below

Stingray	Mackerel	Dolphin	Seagull	Falcon
–150	______	______	______	______

b) Which animal swims above the other, the dolphin or the mackerel? ____________________

One integer is **greater than** another if it is

- higher up on a vertical number line or
- further right on a horizontal number line.

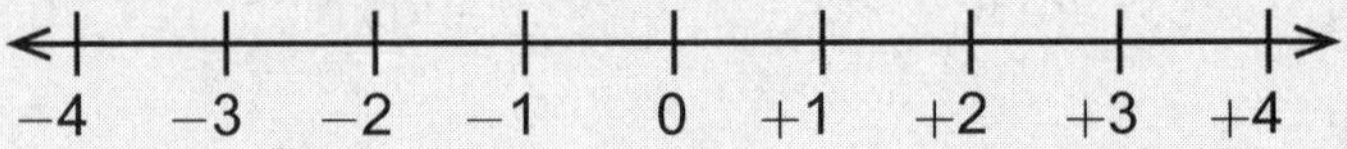

The inequality sign > means "is greater than" and < means "is less than."

c) Write an integer inequality to show your answer in part b): ______ < ______

Integers that are **greater than 0** are called **positive integers**. Integers that are **less than 0** are called **negative integers**.

Positive integers are sometimes written with a "+" sign in front. Example: 3 can be written as 3 or +3, but −3 is only written as −3.

2. Label the following numbers on the number line with their letters.

E. 6 **O.** − 3 **G.** −7 **L.** −5 **B.** 3

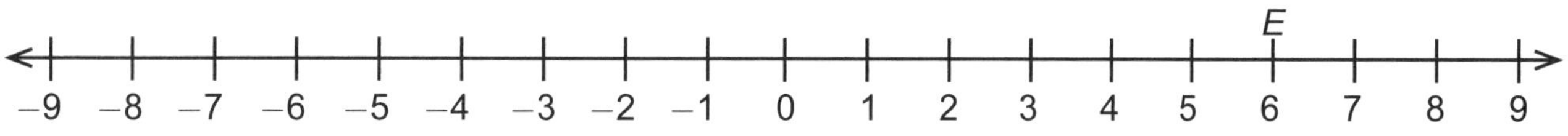

3. Write the integers on the number line.

A. −3 **B.** +3 **C.** −4 **D.** +7 **E.** −2

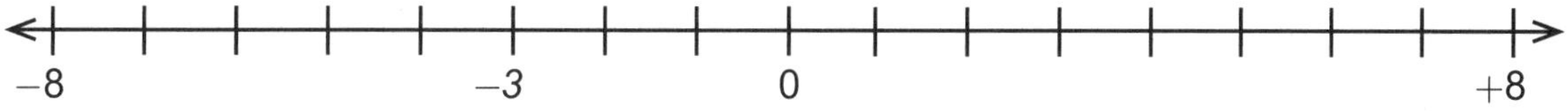

4. Circle the greater integer in each pair. Hint: Use the number line from Question 2.

a) −3 or +5 b) +7 or −2 c) +8 or +3 d) −5 or −4

5. a) Circle the integers on the number line: 3 −4 −8 −1 7

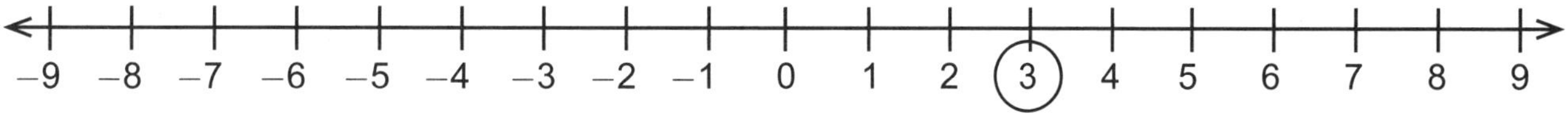

b) Order the integers you circled from least to greatest.

_______ < _______ < _______ < _______ < _______

6. Write < (is less than) or > (is greater than) in the box.

a) +3 ☐ +7 b) −5 ☐ +4 c) +7 ☐ −2 d) −4 ☐ −6

7. Put the integers into the boxes in order, from greatest to least.

+5, −3, +10, −7, −2 ⟶ ☐ > ☐ > ☐ > ☐ > ☐

8. Use any of the number lines above to answer these questions.

a) How many negative integers are greater than (to the right of) −4? ________

b) Write 3 integers that are less than −5. ________, ________, ________

c) How many integers are between −4 and +2? ________

d) Which integers are closer together, −3 and +3 or −4 and +4? ________

Temperature is also recorded using integers. Some places on Earth, and on other planets, are cold enough to have negative temperatures.

9. Write “warmer” or “colder,” then write $>$ or $<$ to show your answer.

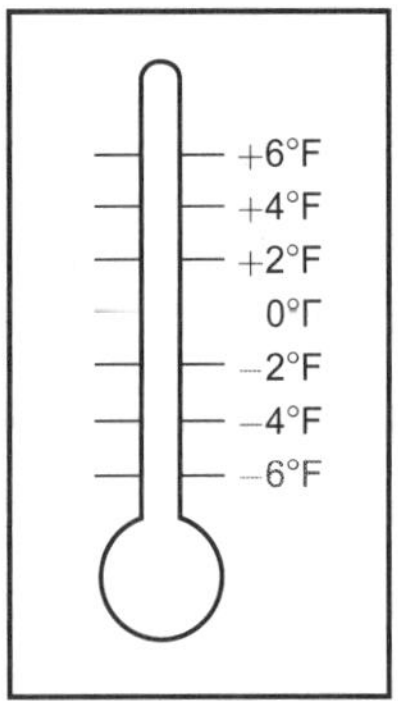

a) $+3$°F is ________________ than -4°F, so $+3$ ☐ -4.

b) -5°F is ________________ than -2°F, so -5 ☐ -2.

c) -3°F is ________________ than -6°F, so -3 ☐ -6.

10. The graph shows the average temperature on the planets in our solar system.

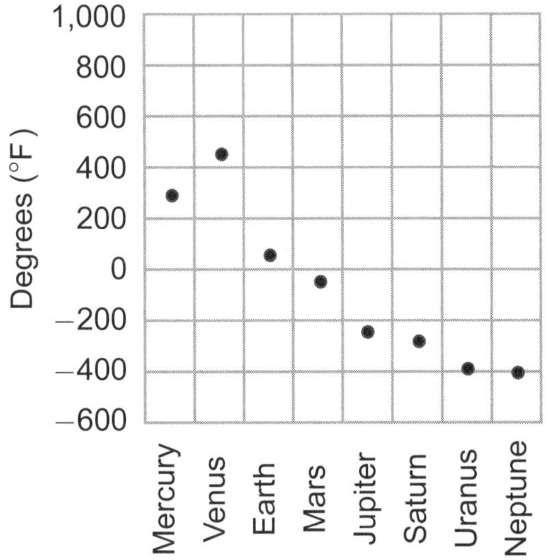

a) What is the warmest average temperature?

About _______ °F

b) What is the coldest average temperature?

About _______ °F

BONUS ▶ What is the difference between the coldest average temperature and the warmest average temperature?

About _______ °F

11. The temperature in Deadhorse, Alaska, was -8°F on Monday and -11°F on Tuesday.

Which day was warmer? ____________________

Integers can be used to describe quantities having opposite directions from a given point.

Examples: temperatures above (+) and below (−) zero, golf scores above (+) and below (−) par, hours ahead of (+) or behind (−) London, England.

12. Write an integer to represent each quantity.

a) A temperature of fifty-two above zero _________

b) A depth of two hundred meters below sea level _________

c) A golf score of 5 shots above par _________

d) A height of three hundred meters above sea level _________

e) 5 hours behind London, England _________

NS6-4 Opposite Integers

When two integers are the same distance from 0, but in opposite directions, they are called **opposite** integers. Example: +3 and −3 are opposite integers.

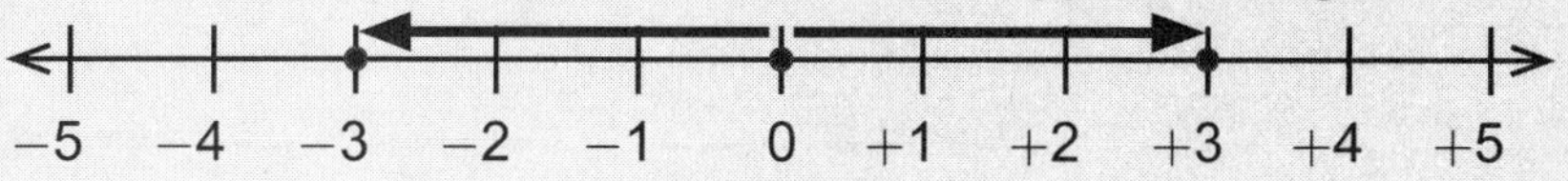

1. Use the number line above to write the opposite integer.

a) +4 ________ b) −2 ________ c) +5 ________ d) −1 ________

The opposite of an integer has the same whole number part, but the opposite sign (+ or −).

Example: The opposite of −100 is +100.

2. The opposite of 429 is _______.

3. Circle the number that is closer to 0.

a) −3 or −7 b) 3 or 7 c) −2 or +5 d) +2 or −5

4. Label each integer with its letter. What US state do the letters spell?

E. the opposite of −6
A. halfway between −1 and −5
M. on the same side of 0 as −3, but twice as far from 0 as −3
N. halfway between +1 and +5
I. an equal distance from +4 and −4

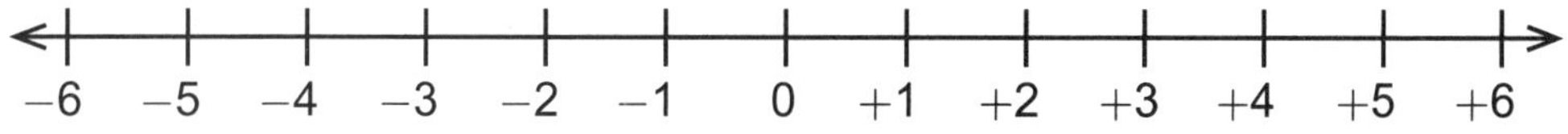

5. The integer 0 is halfway between…

a) −2 and ________ b) −5 and ________ c) −12 and ________ d) −573 and ________

6. a) Use the number line to compare the positive numbers and their opposite negative numbers. Write $<$ or $>$.

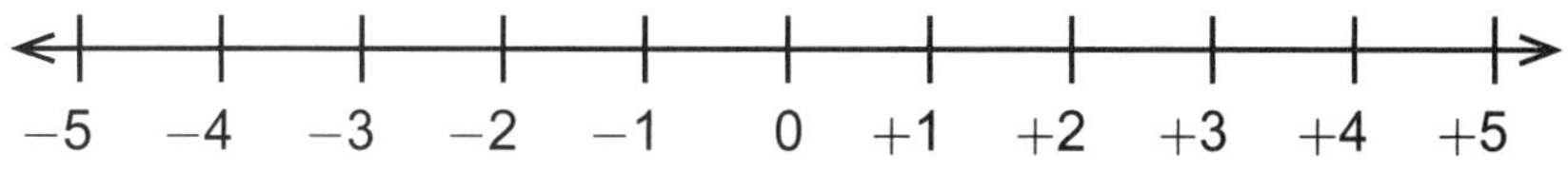

i) 2 ☐ 5 and −2 ☐ −5 ii) 4 ☐ 3 and −4 ☐ −3

iii) 3 ☐ 1 and −3 ☐ −1 iv) 2 ☐ 4 and −2 ☐ −4

b) Predict using the pattern from part a): since $235 < 246$, then −235 ☐ −246.

BONUS ▶ What integer is equal to its opposite? Explain.

NS6-5 Comparing Multi-Digit Integers

1. Write each number in expanded form. Then complete the sentence.

a) 725 = 700 + 20 + 5

735 = 700 + 30 + 5

735 is greater than 725

b) 512 = _______ + _______ + _______

412 = _______ + _______ + _______

_______ is greater than _______

c) 608 = _______ + _______ + _______

618 = _______ + _______ + _______

_______ is greater than _______

d) 769 = _______ + _______ + _______

768 = _______ + _______ + _______

_______ is greater than _______

2. Circle the pair of digits that is different in each pair of numbers.
Then write the greater number in the box.

a) 8 3 7 5 2
8 3 7 6 2
[83,762]

b) 2 7 3 6 0 5
2 7 2 6 0 5
[ ]

c) 6 1 4 8 5 2
6 1 4 8 5 8
[ ]

d) 3 8 3 2 5
4 8 3 2 5
[ ]

3. Read the numbers from left to right. Circle the first pair of digits you find that is different. Then write the greater number in the box.

a) 6 4 1 5 8 3
6 4 1 5 9 7
[641,597]

b) 3 8 4 6 0 7
3 8 9 5 8 3
[ ]

c) 5 7 6 9 8 6
6 0 3 4 7 0
[ ]

d) 6 1 4 9 2
6 1 4 8 3
[ ]

4. Write the correct inequality sign (> or <) in the box.

a) 8,653 [>] 8,486

b) 15,332 [ ] 16,012

c) 9,000 [ ] 7,999

d) 2,382 [ ] 589

e) 323,728 [ ] 323,729

f) 24,489 [ ] 38,950

g) 642,103 [ ] 642,097

h) 52,305 [ ] 61,302

i) 3,289 [ ] 10,104

j) 1,572,306 [ ] 1,573,306

REMINDER ▶ Two integers are opposite integers if they are the same distance from 0, but in opposite directions.

If you can compare positive integers, you can compare their opposite negative integers too.

Example: 32 is **less than** 500, so −32 is **greater than** −500.

5. Compare the positive integers, then compare the negative integers.

a) +5,421 [$<$] +5,432
so −5,421 [$>$] −5,432

b) +25,453 ☐ +23,674
so −25,453 ☐ −23,674

c) +7,000 ☐ +5,982
so −7,000 ☐ −5,982

d) 13,000 ☐ 14,000
so −13,000 ☐ −14,000

e) 72,516 ☐ 75,216
so −72,516 ☐ −75,216

f) +30,407 ☐ +3,407
so −30,407 ☐ −3,407

6. Compare the negative integers by imagining their opposite positive integers.

a) −652 ☐ −1,538   b) −809,417 ☐ −796,583   c) −6,000 ☐ −40,000

7. Do you need to compare the numbers 38 and 27 to compare −38 to +27? _______

Explain. ____

____

8. Write “greater than” or “less than” in the blank.

A negative integer is always ______________________ a positive integer.

9. Compare the integers. Write $<$ or $>$.

a) −200 ☐ 100   b) 750 ☐ −4,000   c) −800 ☐ −1,000

d) −6,000 ☐ 5,000   e) 72,413 ☐ −5,000   f) +853,416 ☐ +872,503

g) 751,602 ☐ 83,917   h) −615,893 ☐ −1,000,000   i) −983,417 ☐ 785,392

j) −62,953 ☐ 304,502   k) −621,419 ☐ +583,742   l) −8,217,354 ☐ −8,216,493

10. Use the digits 4,5,6, and 7 to create…

a) the greatest integer possible.

b) the least integer possible.

c) the greatest negative integer possible.

d) a number between −6,456 and −6,576.

NS6-6 Models of Fractions

A **fraction** names a part of a whole.

The pie is cut into 4 equal parts.
3 parts out of 4 are shaded.

So $\frac{3}{4}$ of the pie is shaded.

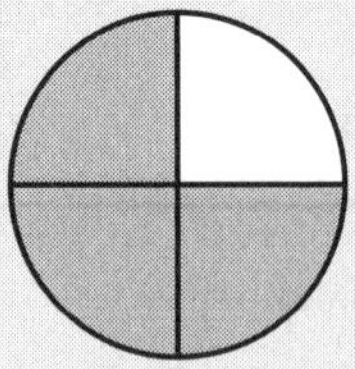

$\frac{3}{4}$

The **numerator** (3) tells you how many equal parts are shaded.

The **denominator** (4) tells you how many equal parts are in a whole.

1. Name the fraction.

a) 

b) 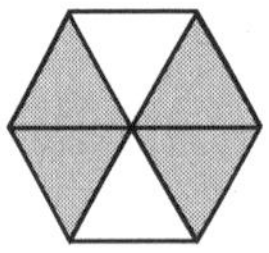

c) 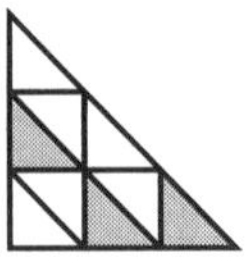

d) 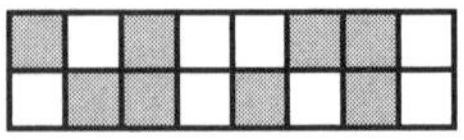

2. Use a centimeter ruler to divide the box into equal parts.

a) 3 equal parts 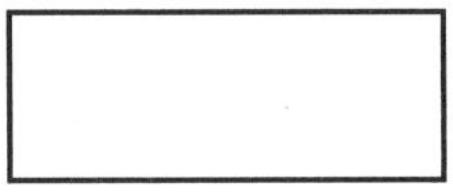

b) 10 equal parts 

3. Using a centimeter ruler, find what fraction of the box is shaded.

a) 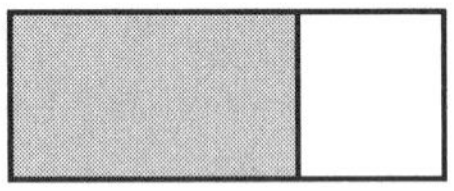

is shaded.

b) 

is shaded.

4. Using a centimeter ruler, complete the figure to make a whole.

a) 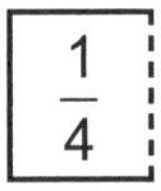

b) 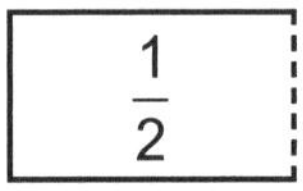

c) 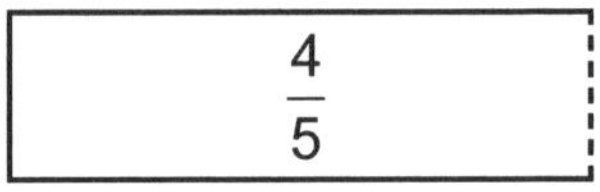

5. You have $\frac{5}{8}$ of a pie.

a) What does the denominator (bottom) of the fraction tell you?

b) What does the numerator (top) of the fraction tell you?

6. Which pictures show $\frac{1}{4}$ and which do not show $\frac{1}{4}$? Explain.

a) 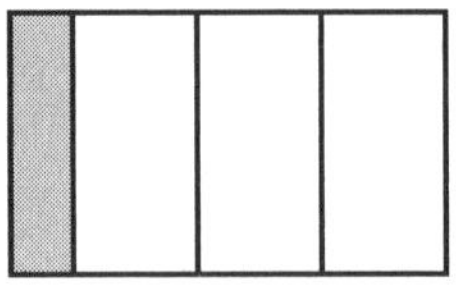

b) 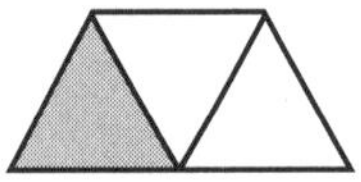

c) 

d) 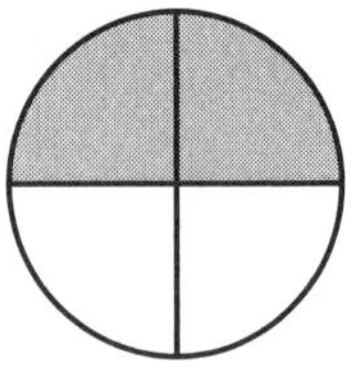

Fractions can name parts of a set: $\frac{1}{5}$ of the figures are squares, $\frac{1}{5}$ are circles, and $\frac{3}{5}$ are pentagons.

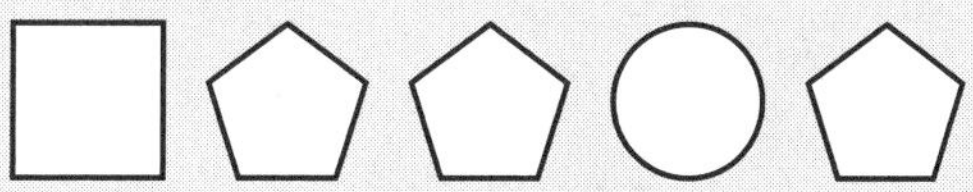

7. Fill in the blank.

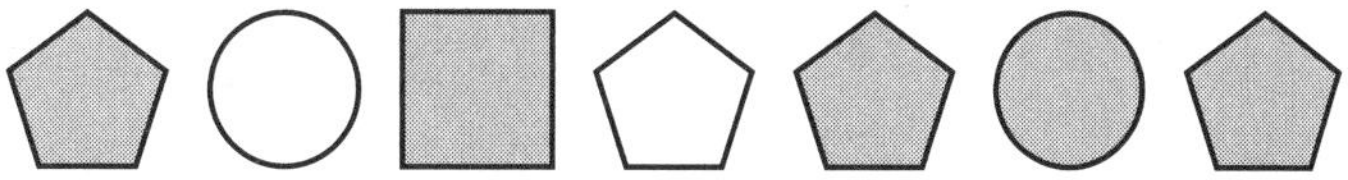

a) ________ of the figures are circles.

b) ________ of the figures are white.

c) ________ of the figures are white circles.

d) ________ of the figures are shaded pentagons.

e) $\frac{4}{7}$ of the figures are ____________________.

f) $\frac{5}{7}$ of the figures are ____________________.

BONUS ▸ $\frac{0}{7}$ of the figures are ____________________.

8. Describe this set in two different ways using the fraction $\frac{3}{5}$.

a) $\frac{3}{5}$ of the figures are ____________________.

b) $\frac{3}{5}$ of the figures are ____________________.

9. A hockey team wins 6 games, loses 4 games, and ties one game.

What fraction of the games did the team …

a) win?

b) lose?

c) tie?

10. A box contains 2 blue marbles, 3 red marbles, and 4 yellow marbles.

What fraction of the marbles are *not* blue?

11. There are 23 children in a class. Each child chose to do a science project on animals or on plants.

The chart shows the number who chose each topic.

a) Fill in the missing numbers in the chart.

b) What fraction of the children chose to study animals?

c) What fraction of the girls chose to study plants?

	Animals	**Plants**
Boys	7	4
Girls		
Children	12	

12. What fraction of the squares are on the outside of the figure?

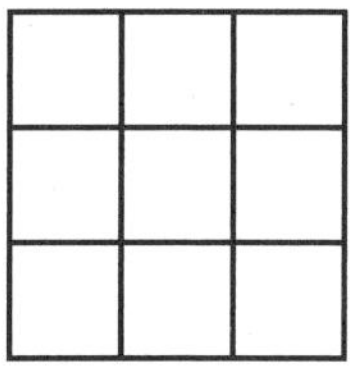

NS6-7 Comparing Positive and Negative Fractions

1. Circle the greater fraction in each pair. Use the number line.

a) i) $\frac{5}{8}$ or $\frac{3}{8}$ ii) $\frac{2}{8}$ or $\frac{7}{8}$ iii) $\frac{4}{8}$ or $\frac{6}{8}$ iv) $\frac{5}{8}$ or $\frac{1}{8}$

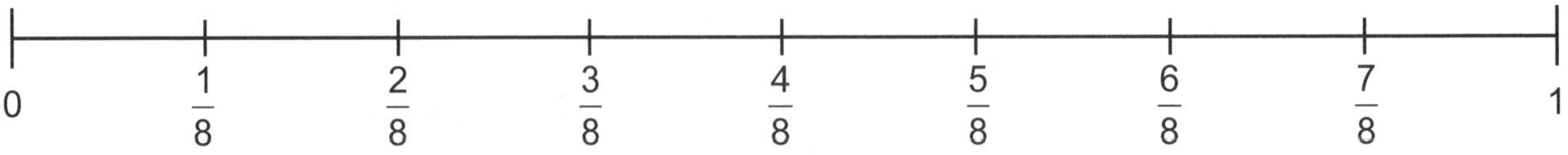

b) i) $\frac{3}{10}$ or $\frac{8}{10}$ ii) $\frac{4}{10}$ or $\frac{1}{10}$ iii) $\frac{7}{10}$ or $\frac{6}{10}$ iv) $\frac{5}{10}$ or $\frac{9}{10}$

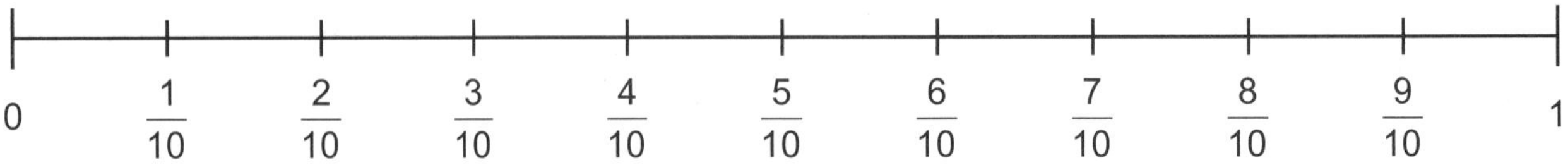

2. Circle the greater fraction in each pair.

a) $\frac{1}{5}$ or $\frac{3}{5}$ b) $\frac{4}{9}$ or $\frac{2}{9}$ c) $\frac{5}{11}$ or $\frac{8}{11}$ d) $\frac{9}{31}$ or $\frac{6}{31}$

3. Two fractions have the same denominators (bottoms) but different numerators (tops). How can you tell which fraction is greater?

____

4. Order the fractions from least to greatest.

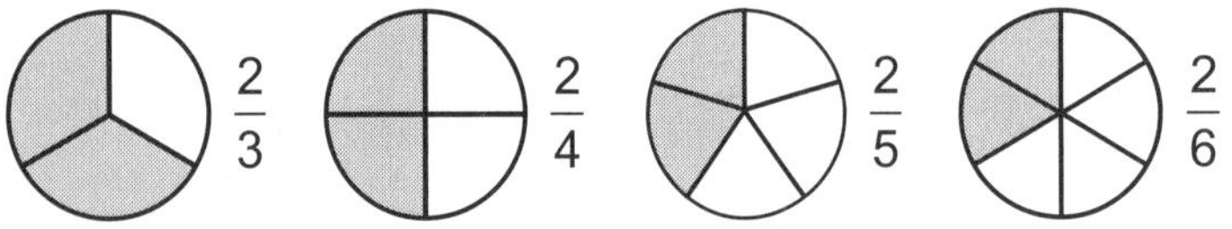

☐ < ☐ < ☐ < ☐

5. Which fraction is greater, $\frac{1}{2}$ or $\frac{1}{100}$? Use the picture to justify your answer.

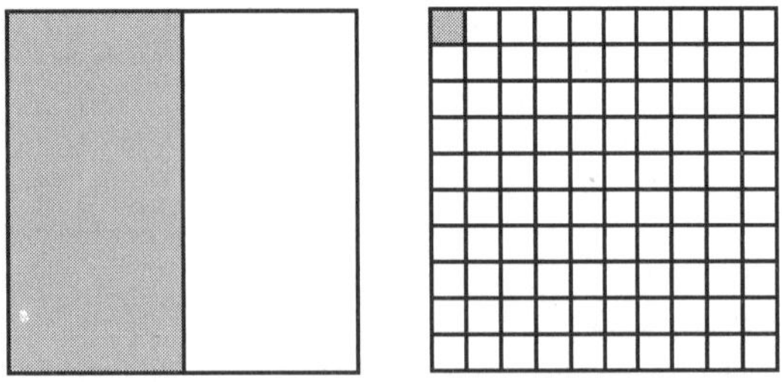

6. Two fractions have the same numerators (tops) but different denominators (bottoms). How can you tell which fraction is greater?

____

Fractions can be negative too!

The mosquito is $\frac{3}{4}$ inch above the surface of the water.

The larva is $\frac{1}{4}$ inch below the surface of the water.

Using the water surface as 0, you can record the mosquito's position as $+\frac{3}{4}$ and the larva's position as $-\frac{1}{4}$.

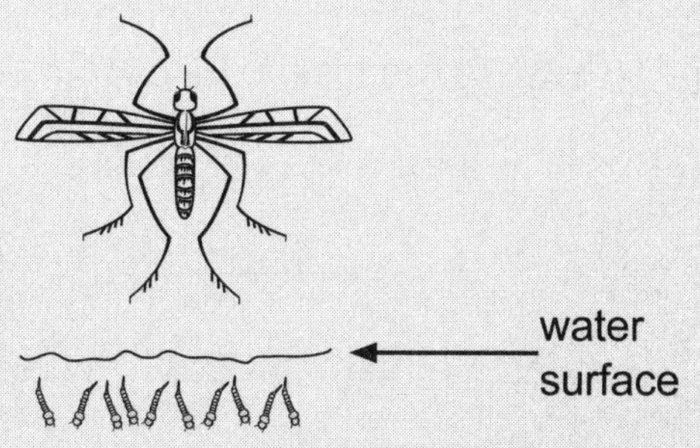

7. Use the number line to compare the fractions. Write $<$ or $>$.

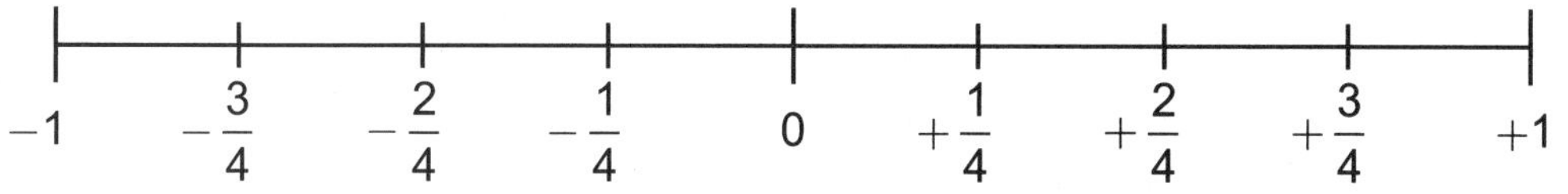

a) $+\frac{3}{4} \square +\frac{1}{4}$ and $-\frac{3}{4} \square -\frac{1}{4}$

b) $+\frac{1}{4} \square +\frac{2}{4}$ and $-\frac{1}{4} \square -\frac{2}{4}$

c) $+1 \square +\frac{1}{4}$ and $-1 \square -\frac{1}{4}$

d) $0 \square +\frac{2}{4}$ and $0 \square -\frac{2}{4}$

Two fractions are **opposite** fractions if they are the same distance from 0, but in opposite directions.

Example: The opposite of $+\frac{3}{4}$ is $-\frac{3}{4}$.

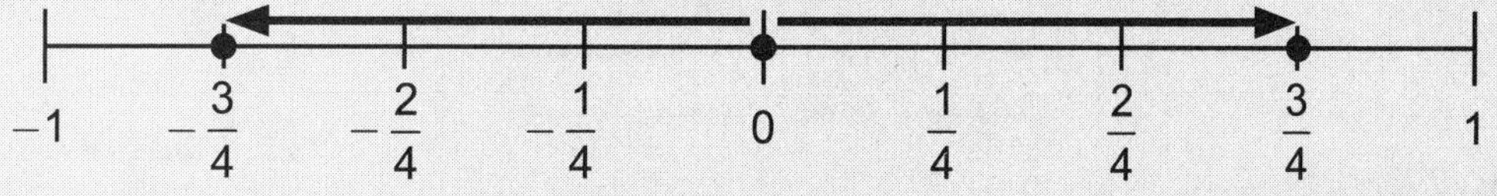

8. Compare the positive fractions, then compare their opposite negative fractions. Write $<$ or $>$.

a) $\frac{2}{5} \square \frac{4}{5}$ so $-\frac{2}{5} \square -\frac{4}{5}$

b) $\frac{7}{9} \square \frac{2}{9}$ so $-\frac{7}{9} \square -\frac{2}{9}$

c) $\frac{3}{8} \square \frac{3}{11}$ so $-\frac{3}{8} \square -\frac{3}{11}$

d) $\frac{7}{12} \square \frac{7}{10}$ so $-\frac{7}{12} \square -\frac{7}{10}$

REMINDER ▶ A positive number is always greater than a negative number.

9. Compare each pair of fractions. Write $<$ or $>$.

a) $+\frac{1}{8} \square -\frac{1}{9}$

b) $-\frac{1}{7} \square \frac{1}{10}$

c) $-\frac{2}{5} \square +\frac{2}{7}$

d) $\frac{4}{7} \square -\frac{4}{9}$

e) $-\frac{1}{3} \square -\frac{2}{3}$

f) $\frac{5}{8} \square \frac{3}{8}$

g) $-\frac{1}{4} \square -\frac{3}{4}$

h) $\frac{3}{10} \square -\frac{7}{10}$

NS6-8 Mixed Numbers and Improper Fractions

Mattias and his friends ate the amount of pie shown.

They ate two and three quarter pies

altogether (or $2\frac{3}{4}$ pies).

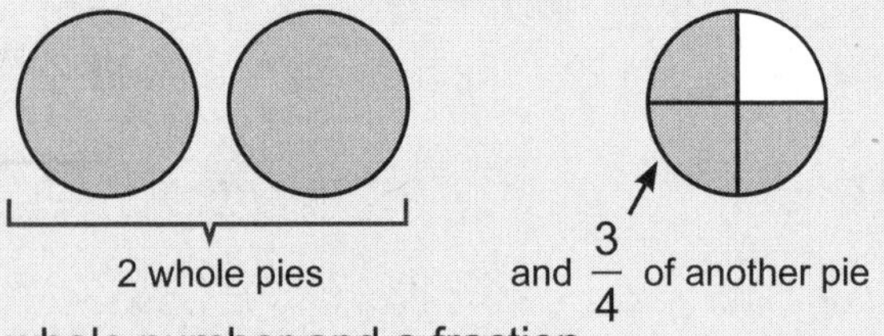

$2\frac{3}{4}$ is called a **mixed number** because it is a mixture of a whole number and a fraction.

1. Find the mixed number for each picture.

a) 

_2_ whole pies and $\frac{1}{3}$ of another pie = $2\frac{1}{3}$ pies

b) 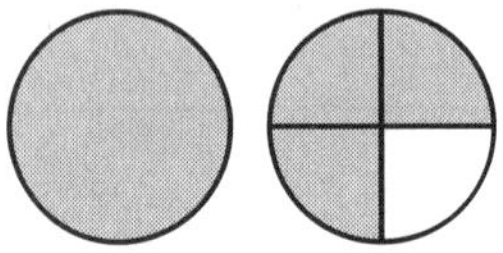

_____ whole pie and of another pie = pies

c) 

_____ whole pies and of another pie = pies

2. Find the mixed number for each picture.

a) 

b) 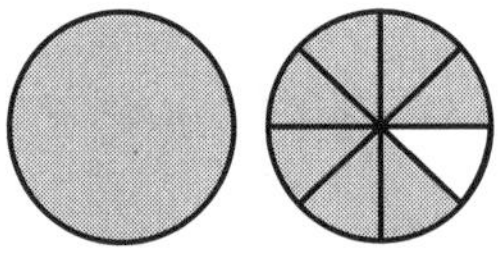

c) 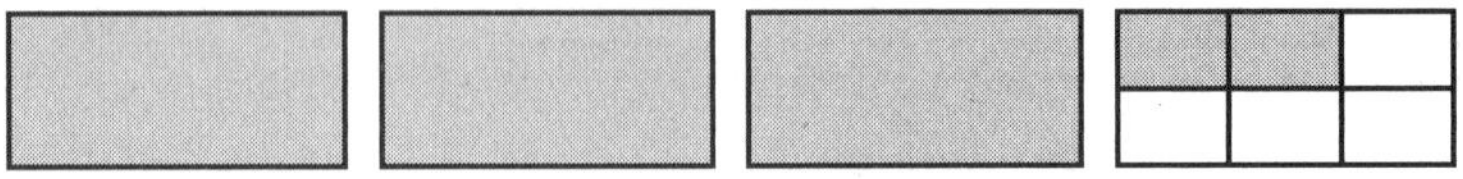

d) 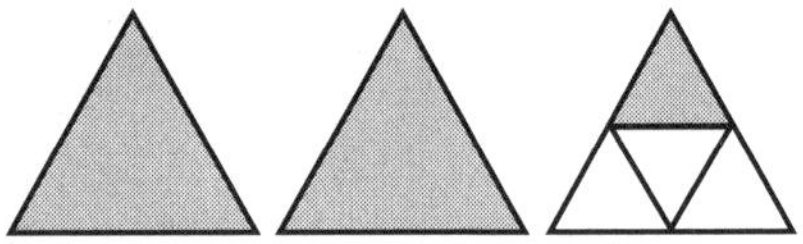

3. Shade the area given by the mixed number. Note: There may be more figures than you need.

a) $2\frac{1}{3}$ 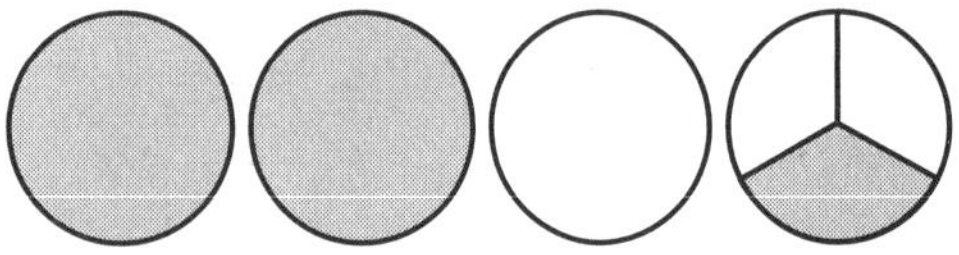

b) $3\frac{1}{4}$ 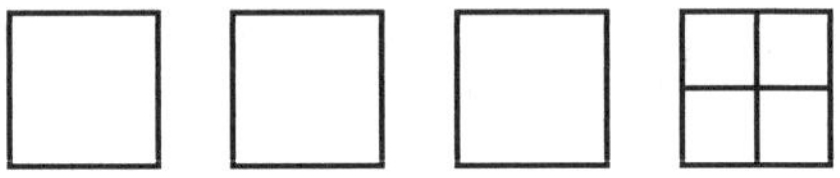

c) $1\frac{5}{6}$ 

d) $2\frac{4}{5}$ 

4. Sketch.

a) $3\frac{3}{4}$ pies b) $2\frac{1}{3}$ pies c) $2\frac{5}{6}$ pies d) $3\frac{7}{8}$ pies

5. Which fraction represents more pie: $3\frac{2}{3}$, $4\frac{1}{4}$, or $4\frac{3}{4}$? How do you know?

6. Is $5\frac{3}{4}$ closer to 5 or 6?

Huan-Yue and her friends ate 9 quarter-sized pieces of pizza.

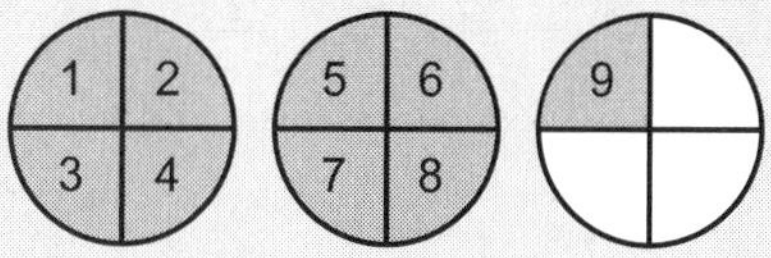

$\frac{9}{4} = 2\frac{1}{4}$

improper fraction ↗ mixed number ↖

Altogether, they ate $\frac{9}{4}$ pizzas.

When the numerator of a fraction is greater than the denominator, the fraction represents **more than a whole**. Such fractions are called **improper fractions**.

7. Write the fraction as an improper fraction.

a) 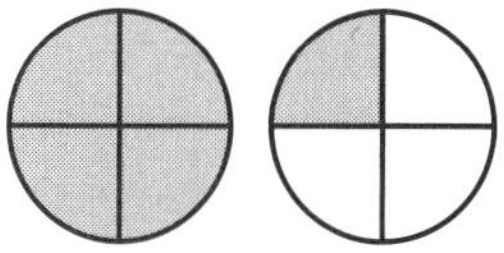

b) 

c) 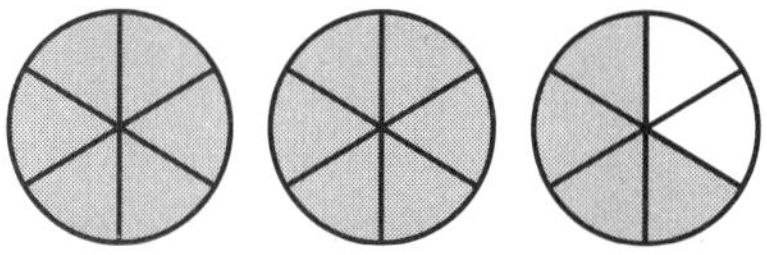

d) 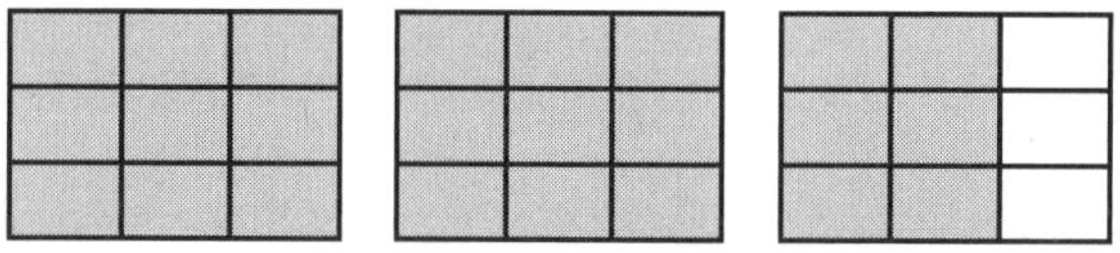

e) 

f) 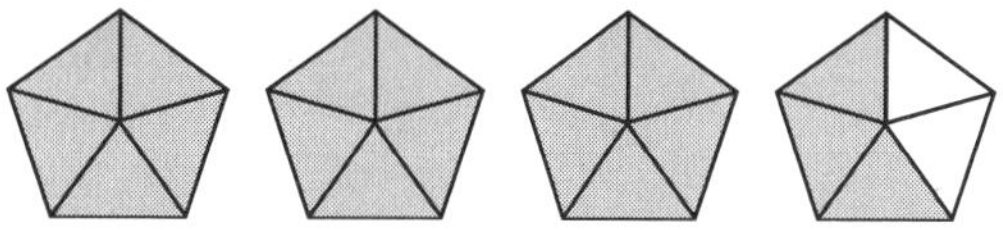

8. Shade one piece at a time until you have shaded the amount of pie given by the improper fraction.

a) $\frac{7}{2}$ 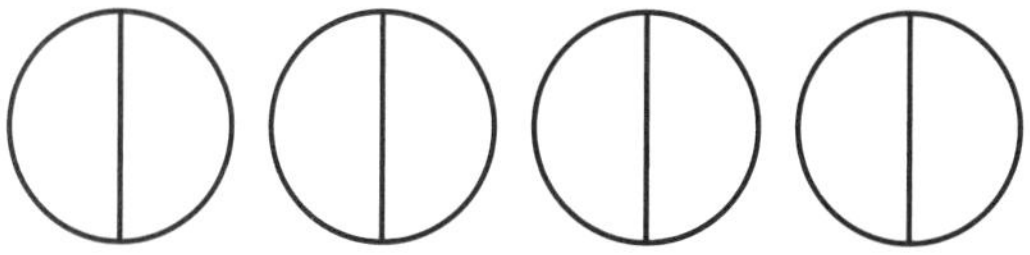

b) $\frac{9}{4}$ 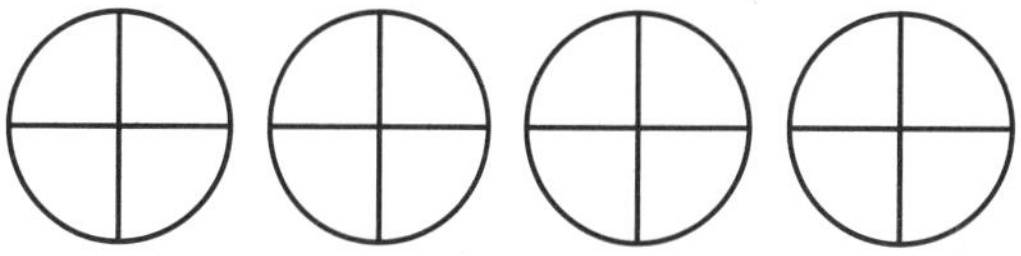

c) $\frac{8}{3}$ 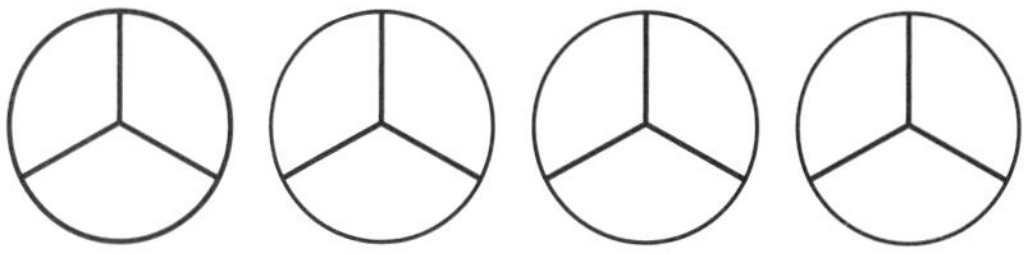

d) $\frac{15}{5}$ 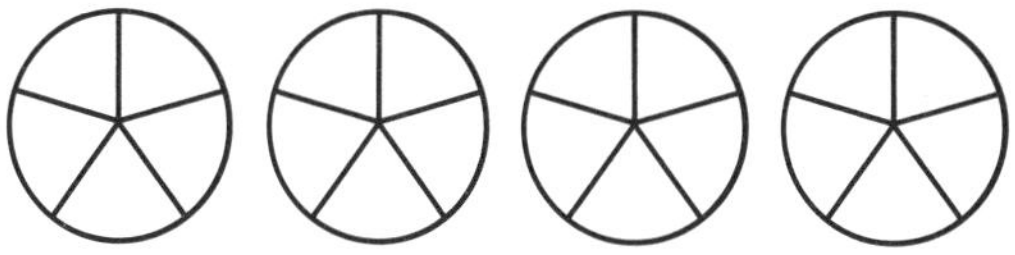

9. Sketch.

a) $\frac{13}{4}$ pies b) $\frac{7}{3}$ pies c) $\frac{9}{2}$ pies d) $\frac{11}{6}$ pies

10. Which fraction represents more pie: $\frac{7}{4}$, $\frac{9}{4}$, or $\frac{9}{3}$? Justify your answer with a picture.

11. Is the fraction an improper fraction? How do you know?

a) $\frac{5}{7}$ b) $\frac{9}{8}$ c) $\frac{13}{11}$ d) $\frac{11}{13}$

12. Find the mixed number for each picture.

a) 

$\underline{\ 2\ }$ whole pies and

$\frac{1}{4}$ of another pie

$= 2\frac{1}{4}$ pies

b) 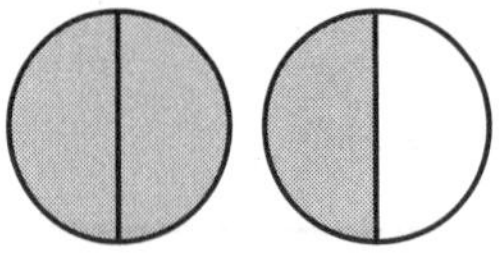

____ whole pies and

of another pie

= pies

c) 

____ whole pies and

of another pie

= pies

13. Write the fraction as a mixed number and as an improper fraction.

a) 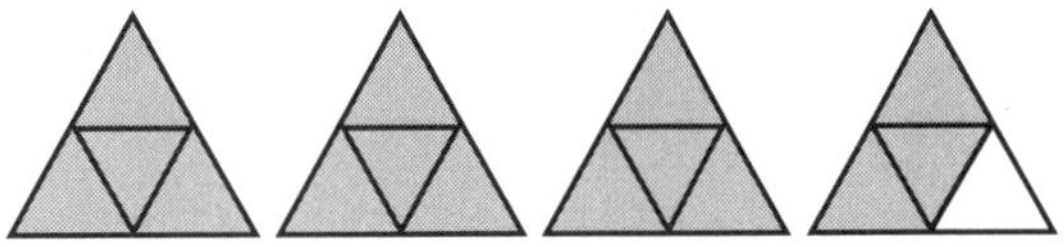

=

b) 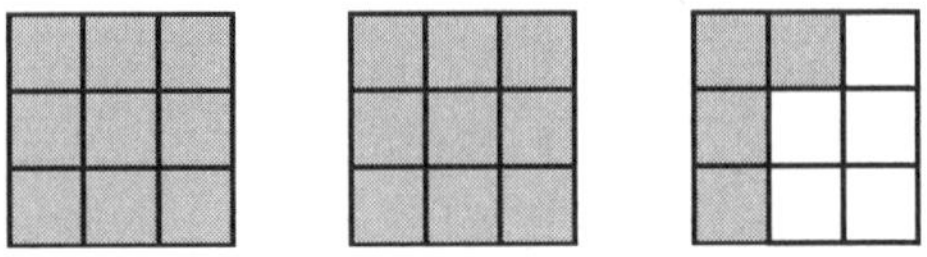

=

14. Shade the amount of pie given by the mixed number. Then write an improper fraction for the amount.

a) $3\frac{1}{2}$ 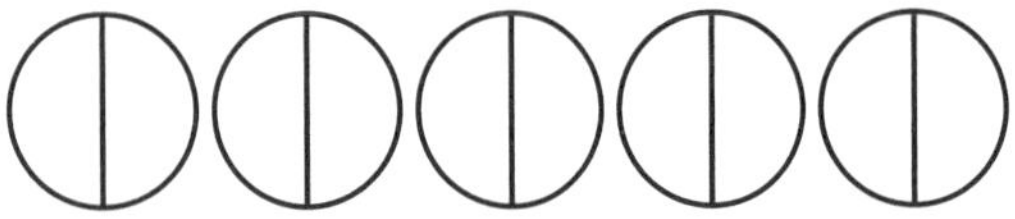

Improper fraction:

b) $4\frac{3}{4}$ 

Improper fraction:

15. Shade the area given by the improper fraction. Then write a mixed number for the shaded area.

a) $\frac{7}{3}$ 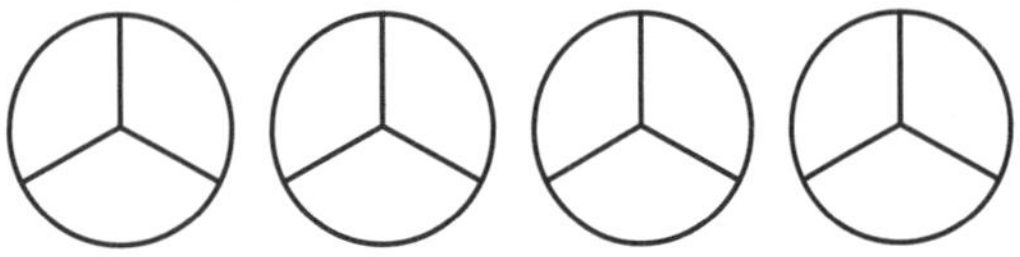

Mixed number:

b) $\frac{17}{6}$ 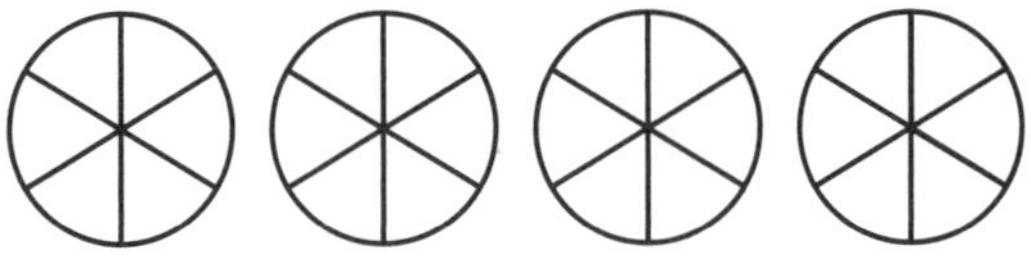

Mixed number:

c) $\frac{13}{5}$ 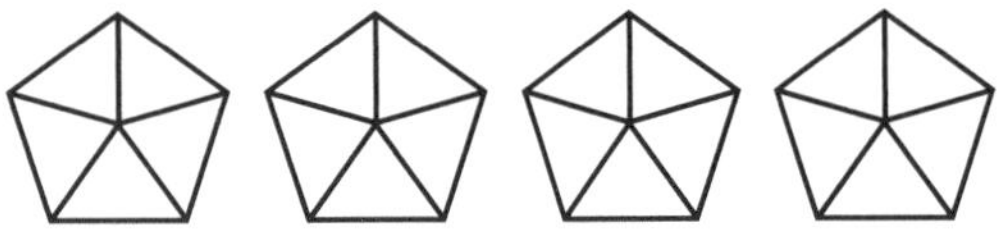

Mixed number:

d) $\frac{21}{8}$ 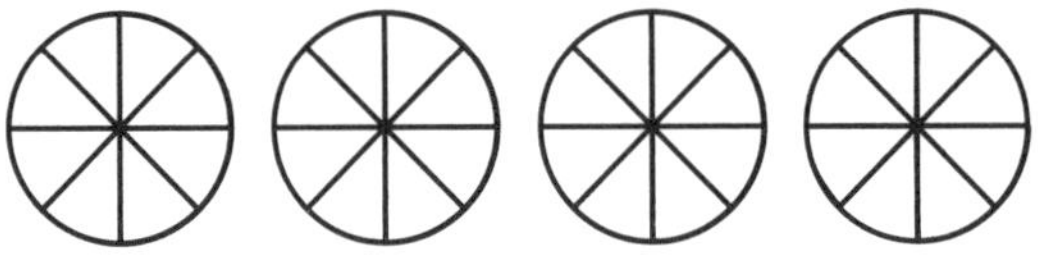

Mixed number:

16. Draw a picture to find out which number is greater.

a) $3\frac{1}{2}$ or $\frac{5}{3}$ b) $1\frac{4}{5}$ or $\frac{11}{5}$ c) $\frac{15}{8}$ or $\frac{7}{3}$ d) $\frac{13}{4}$ or $2\frac{2}{3}$

17. How could you use division to find out how many whole pies are in $\frac{13}{5}$ of a pie? Explain.

NS6-9 Fractions on a Number Line

REMINDER ▶ Numbers on the right are **greater** than numbers on the left.

1. a) Mark the opposite of the improper fraction on each number line.

i)

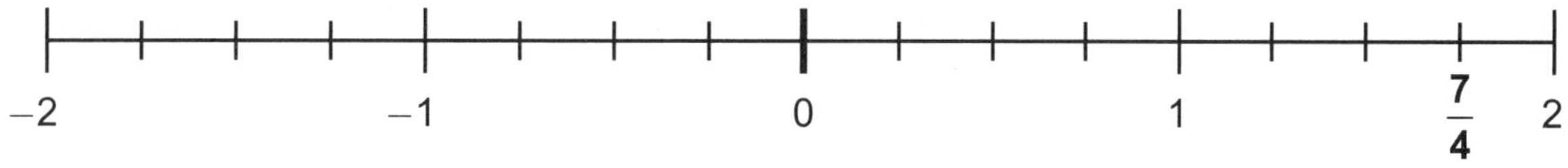

ii)

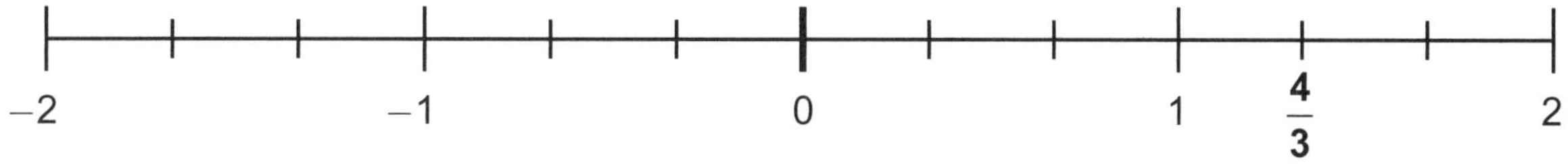

iii)

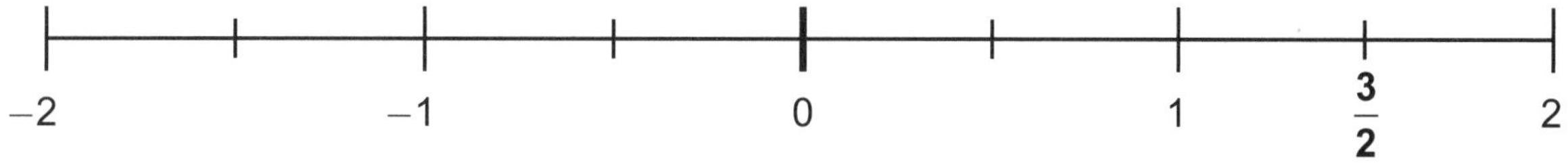

b) Order the fractions from least to greatest: $-\frac{7}{4}, -\frac{4}{3}, -\frac{3}{2}$. $\square < \square < \square$

Since $1\frac{2}{3}$ is $\frac{2}{3}$ of the way from 1 to 2, $-1\frac{2}{3}$ is $\frac{2}{3}$ of the way from −1 to −2.

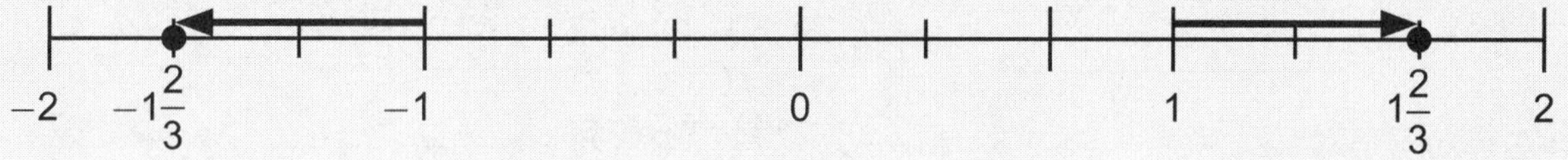

2. Mark the opposite of the boldface number on the number line.

a)

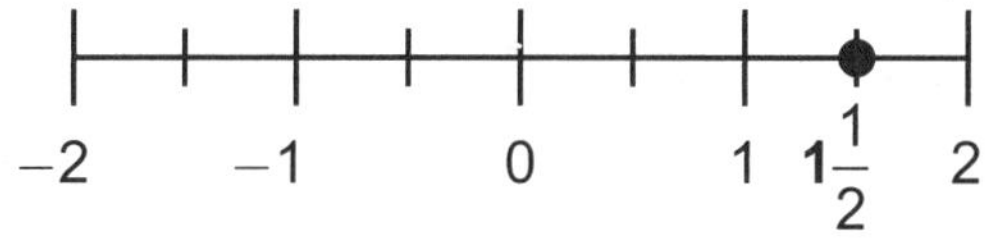

b)

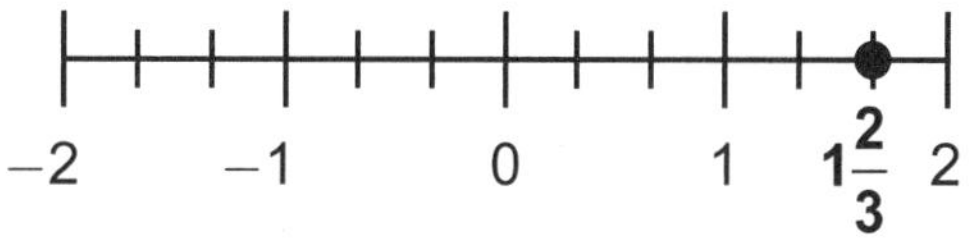

3. Write a fraction or mixed number for each labeled point.

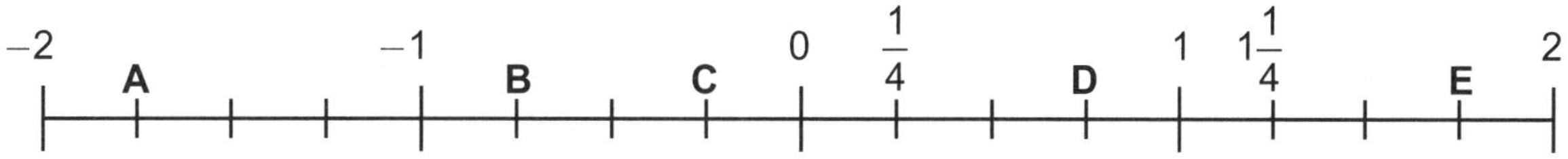

A: **B:** **C:** **D:** **E:**

4. Use the number line to decide which fraction is greater. Write $<$ or $>$.

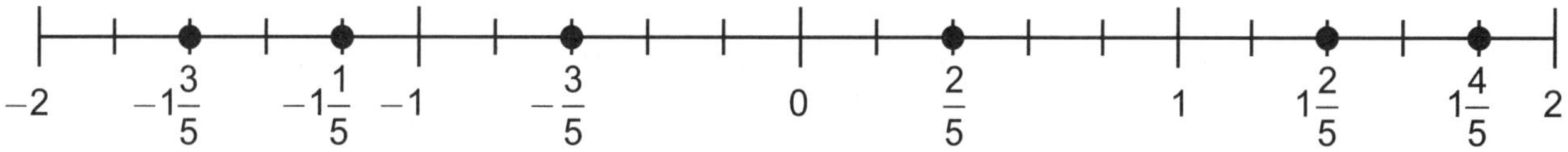

a) $-1\frac{3}{5} \square \frac{2}{5}$ b) $-\frac{3}{5} \square -1\frac{1}{5}$ c) $1\frac{4}{5} \square 1\frac{2}{5}$ d) $1\frac{2}{5} \square -1\frac{1}{5}$

NS6-10 More Mixed Numbers and Improper Fractions

How many quarter pieces are in $2\frac{3}{4}$ pies?

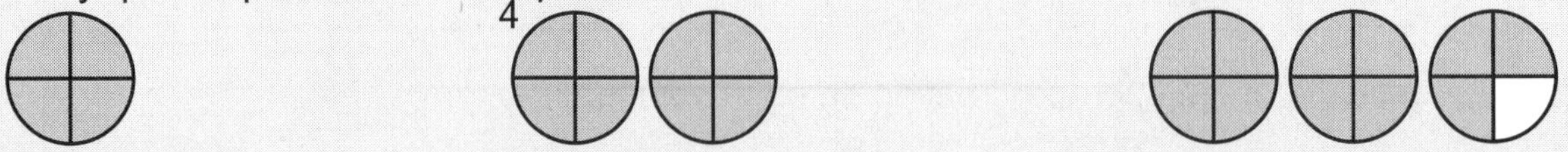

There are 4 quarter pieces in 1 pie.

There are 2×4 quarters in 2 pies.

8 pieces (2×4) + 3 extra pieces = 11

$2\frac{3}{4} = \frac{11}{4}$

So there are 11 quarter pieces altogether.

1. Find the number of **halves** in each amount.

a) 1 pie = ______ halves

b) 2 pies = ______ halves

c) 4 pies = ______ halves

d) $3\frac{1}{2}$ pies = ______ halves

e) $4\frac{1}{2}$ pies = ______ halves

f) $5\frac{1}{2}$ pies = ______________________

2. Each pie has 3 pieces, so each piece is a third. Find the number of **thirds** in each amount.

a) 1 pie = ___*3*___ thirds

b) 2 pies = ______ thirds

c) 4 pies = ______ thirds

d) $1\frac{1}{3}$ pies = ______ thirds

e) $2\frac{2}{3}$ pies = ______________________

f) $5\frac{2}{3}$ pies = ______________________

3. A box holds 4 cans, so each can is a fourth. Find the number of cans each amount holds.

a) 2 boxes hold ______ cans.

b) $2\frac{1}{4}$ boxes hold ______ cans.

c) $3\frac{3}{4}$ boxes hold ______ cans.

d) $2\frac{3}{4}$ boxes hold ______ cans.

4. If a bag holds 12 peas, then …

a) $1\frac{1}{12}$ bags hold ______ peas.

b) $2\frac{7}{12}$ bags hold ______ peas.

5. Write the mixed numbers as improper fractions.

a) $2\frac{1}{3} = \frac{\quad}{3}$

b) $5\frac{1}{2} = \frac{\quad}{2}$

c) $4\frac{2}{5} = \frac{\quad}{5}$

d) $7\frac{1}{4} = \frac{\quad}{4}$

6. Envelopes come in packs of 6. Alice used $2\frac{5}{6}$ packs. How many envelopes did she use? ______

7. Maia and her friends ate $4\frac{3}{4}$ pizzas. How many quarter-sized pieces did they eat? ______

BONUS ▶ How many quarters are in $4\frac{1}{2}$ dollars? ______

Win-Chi has 13 party gifts to give out at his birthday party. He packs 3 gifts in each bag.

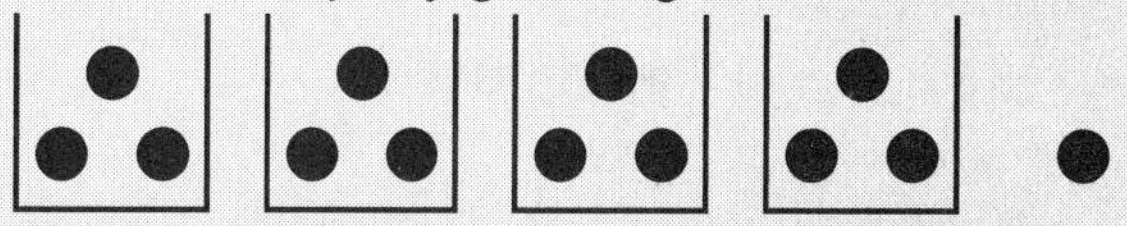

Win-Chi can give out 4 bags, but there is one party gift left over. The leftover gift is called the **remainder**.

$13 \div 3 = 4$ Remainder 1 OR **$13 \div 3 = 4$ R 1**

"R" means "Remainder"

8. Can 9 party gifts all be packed into bags of 2? Show your work with a picture.

9. Put as many gifts as you can into bags. Show your work with a picture.

a) 11 gifts altogether; 3 gifts in each bag

_____ bags; _____ gifts remaining

b) 17 gifts altogether; 4 gifts in each bag

_____ bags; _____ gifts remaining

10. Put as many dots as you can into circles. Draw a picture and write a division equation.

a) 2 dots in each circle; 11 dots altogether

11 ÷ *2* = _____ R _____

b) 5 dots in each circle; 23 dots altogether

_____ ÷ _____ = _____ R _____

11. How many whole pies are there and how many leftover pieces?
Draw a picture and write a division equation to show your answer.

a) Pies are each cut into four pieces. There are 14 pieces of pie in total.

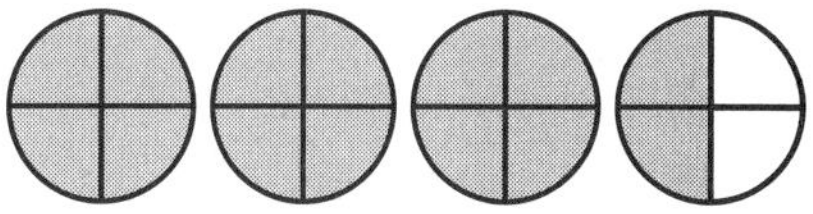

14 ÷ 4 = _____ R _____
(whole pies) (leftover pieces)

b) Pies are each cut into six pieces. There are 17 pieces of pie altogether.

How many whole pies are in $\frac{13}{4}$ pies?

There are 13 pieces altogether, and each pie has 4 pieces: **13 ÷ 4 = 3 Remainder 1**

There are 3 whole pies and 1 quarter left over: 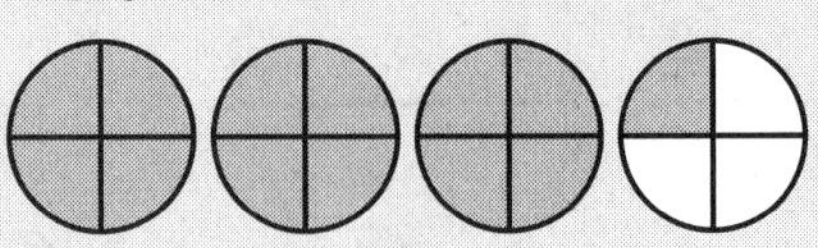 $\frac{13}{4} = 3\frac{1}{4}$

12. Find the number of whole pies in each amount by dividing.

a) $\frac{4}{2}$ pies = _____ whole pies b) $\frac{15}{3}$ pies = _____ whole pies c) $\frac{8}{4}$ pies = _____ whole pies

13. Find the number of whole pies and the number of pieces remaining by dividing.

a) $\frac{5}{2}$ pies = ___2___ whole pies and ___1___ half pie = $2\frac{1}{2}$ pies

b) $\frac{9}{2}$ pies = _______ whole pies and _______ half pie = pies

c) $\frac{10}{3}$ pies d) $\frac{15}{4}$ pies e) $\frac{18}{5}$ pies f) $\frac{17}{9}$ pies **BONUS ▸** $\frac{70}{9}$ pies

14. Divide the numerator by the denominator to write each improper fraction as a mixed number.

a) $\frac{13}{3}$ 13 ÷ 3 = __4__ R __1__ So $\frac{13}{3} = 4\frac{1}{3}$

b) $\frac{13}{6}$ 13 ÷ 6 = ____ R ____ So $\frac{13}{6} =$

c) $\frac{15}{4}$ 15 ÷ 4 = ____ R ____ So $\frac{15}{4} =$

d) $\frac{3}{2} =$ e) $\frac{8}{3} =$ f) $\frac{22}{5} =$

15. Write a mixed number and an improper fraction for the total number of liters.

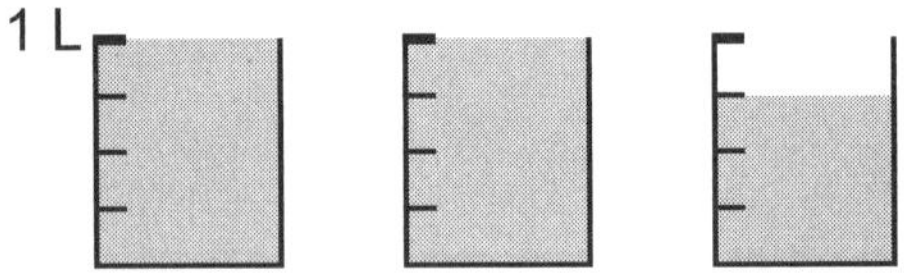

16. Write a mixed number and an improper fraction for the length of the rope.

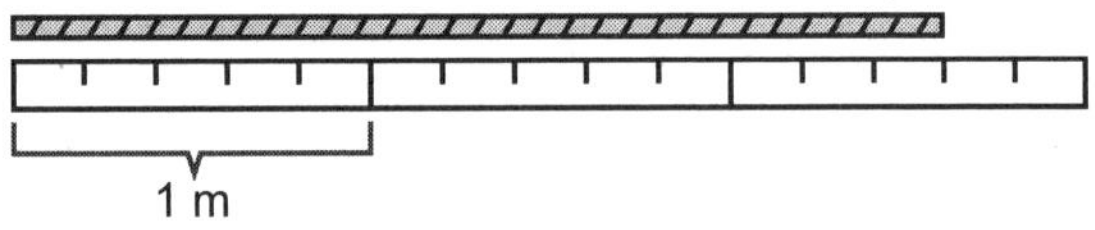

Since $\frac{7}{4} = 1\frac{3}{4}$, their opposites are equal too: $-\frac{7}{4} = -1\frac{3}{4}$.

17. Complete the chart.

Mixed Number	$-2\frac{3}{4}$	$-3\frac{2}{5}$		$-4\frac{1}{2}$				$-1\frac{3}{8}$
Improper Fraction	$-\frac{11}{4}$		$-\frac{7}{5}$		$-\frac{8}{3}$	$-\frac{9}{4}$	$-\frac{11}{3}$	

NS6-11 Comparing Fractions on a Number Line

1. Use the number line to complete the chart.

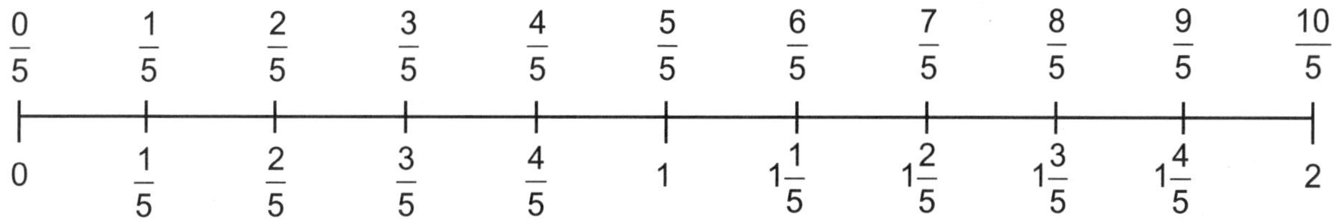

Mixed Number	$1\frac{4}{5}$			$1\frac{1}{5}$		
Improper Fraction		$\frac{7}{5}$	$\frac{10}{5}$		$\frac{8}{5}$	$\frac{5}{5}$

2. Fill in the number line, then compare the mixed number to the improper fraction.
Write <, >, or = in the box.

a)

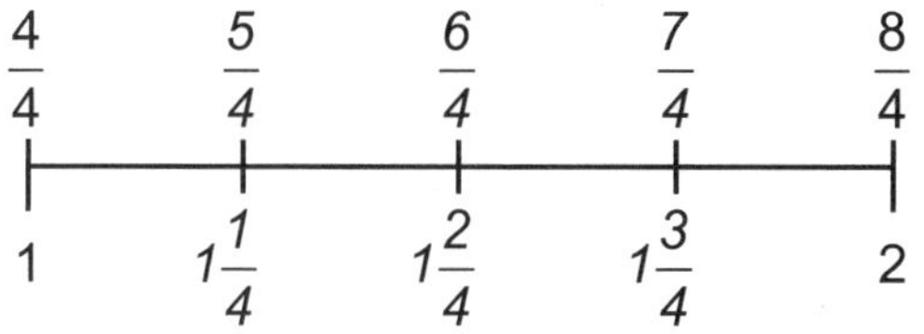

$1\frac{3}{4}$ [>] $\frac{5}{4}$

b)

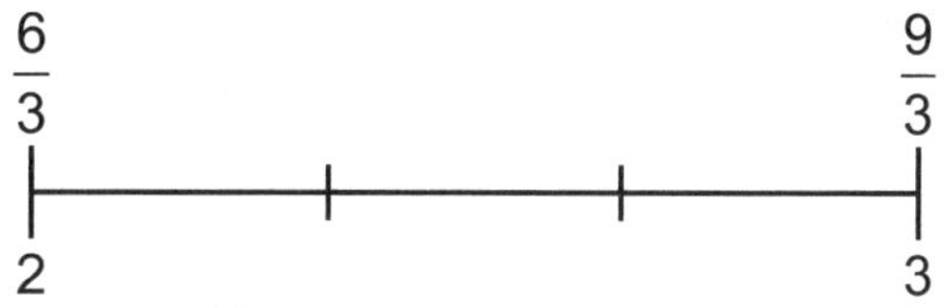

$2\frac{1}{3}$ [ ] $\frac{8}{3}$

c)

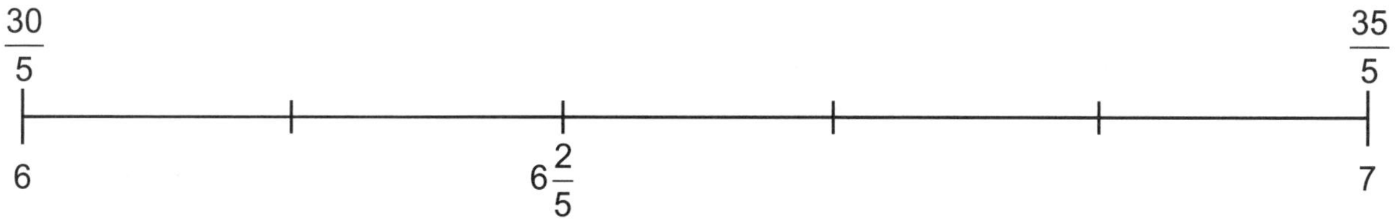

i) $6\frac{2}{5}$ [ ] $\frac{34}{5}$ ii) $6\frac{3}{5}$ [ ] $\frac{30}{5}$ iii) $6\frac{1}{5}$ [ ] $\frac{31}{5}$ iv) $6\frac{4}{5}$ [ ] $\frac{35}{5}$

d)

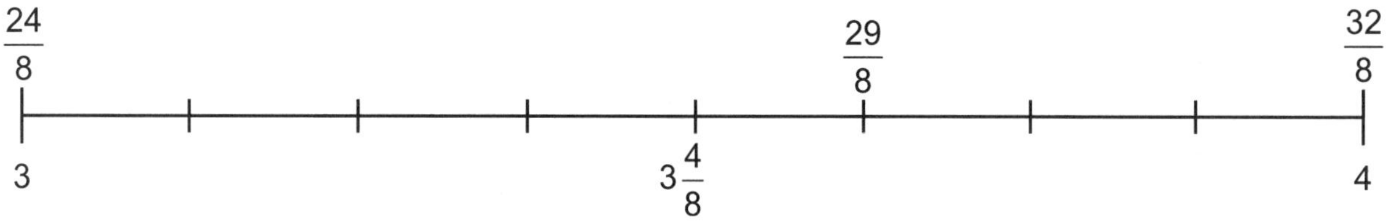

i) $3\frac{7}{8}$ [ ] $\frac{29}{8}$ ii) $3\frac{3}{8}$ [ ] $\frac{27}{8}$ iii) $3\frac{5}{8}$ [ ] $\frac{27}{8}$ iv) 4 [ ] $\frac{32}{8}$

3. What two whole numbers is $\frac{32}{9}$ between? Draw a number line to show your answer.

4. Ari's party guests ate $\frac{34}{6}$ pies. Ari had less than 1 pie left over. How many pies did he bake?

5. Use the number line to complete the chart.

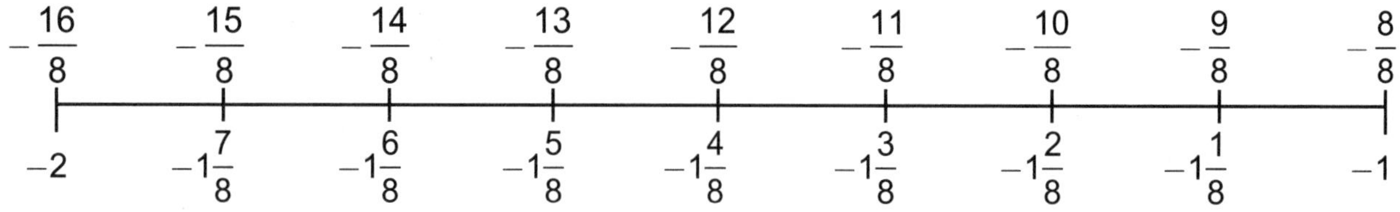

Mixed Number	$-1\frac{5}{8}$			$-1\frac{2}{8}$		$-1\frac{6}{8}$	
Improper Fraction		$-\frac{15}{8}$	$-\frac{8}{8}$		$-\frac{11}{8}$		$-\frac{9}{8}$

6. Fill in the number line, then compare the mixed number to the improper fraction. Write $<$, $>$, or $=$ in the box.

a)

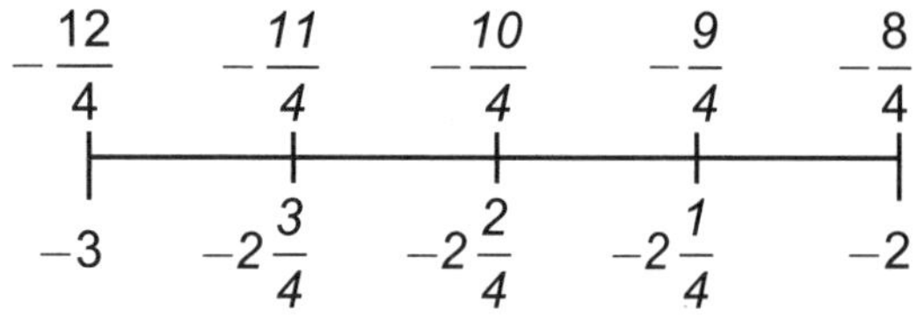

$-2\frac{1}{4}$ [=] $-\frac{9}{4}$

b)

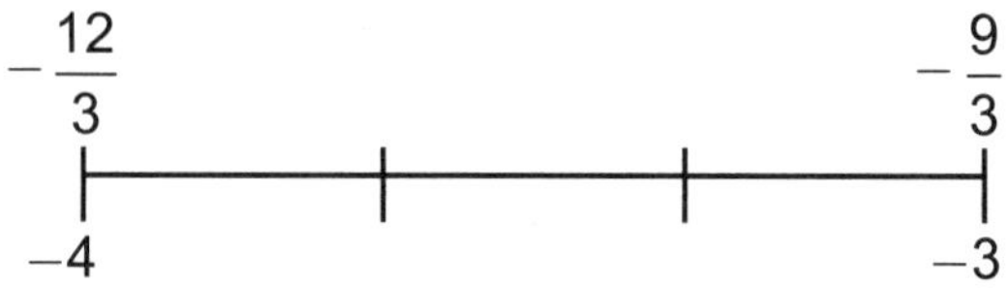

$-3\frac{1}{3}$ [ ] $-\frac{10}{3}$

c)

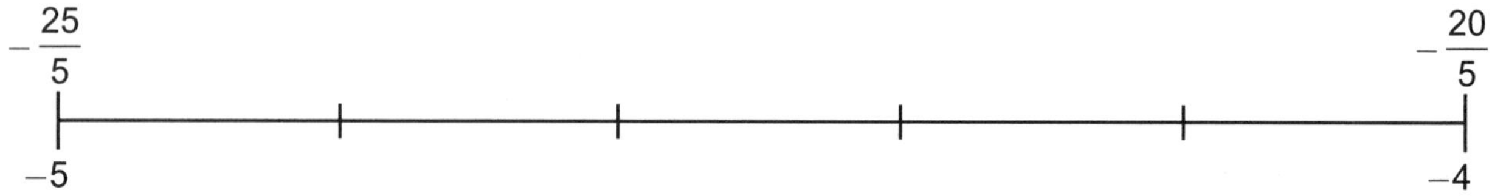

i) $-4\frac{2}{5}$ [ ] $-\frac{24}{5}$ ii) $-4\frac{3}{5}$ [ ] $-\frac{22}{5}$ iii) $-4\frac{1}{5}$ [ ] $-\frac{23}{5}$ iv) $-4\frac{4}{5}$ [ ] $-\frac{25}{5}$

d)

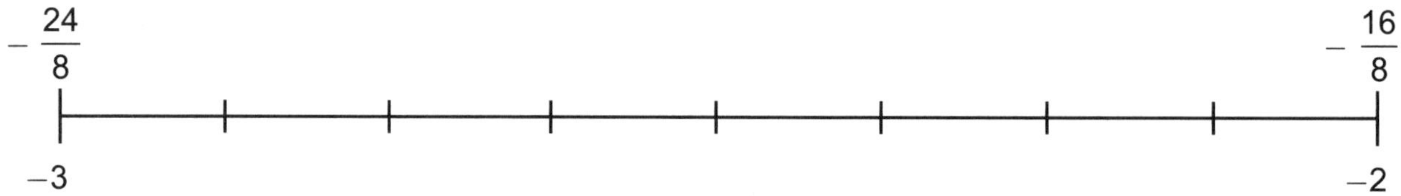

i) $-2\frac{7}{8}$ [ ] $-\frac{23}{8}$ ii) $-2\frac{3}{8}$ [ ] $-\frac{22}{8}$ iii) $-2\frac{5}{8}$ [ ] $-\frac{19}{8}$ iv) -2 [ ] $-\frac{16}{8}$

7. What two integers is $-\frac{35}{6}$ between? Draw a number line to show your answer.

8. What temperature is colder, $-\frac{22}{5}$ °F or $-4\frac{3}{5}$ °F ? Show your answer on a number line.

NS6-12 Equivalent Fractions

Two or more fractions are **equivalent** if they can be shown by the same part of the same whole.

Example: $\frac{2}{3}$ and $\frac{4}{6}$ are equivalent fractions.

$\frac{2}{3} =$ 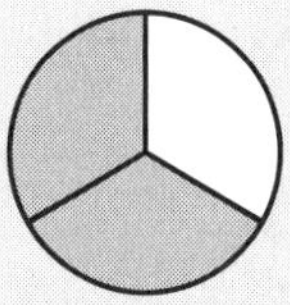 $\frac{4}{6} =$ 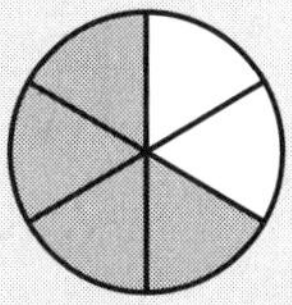

1. What equivalent fractions do these pictures show?

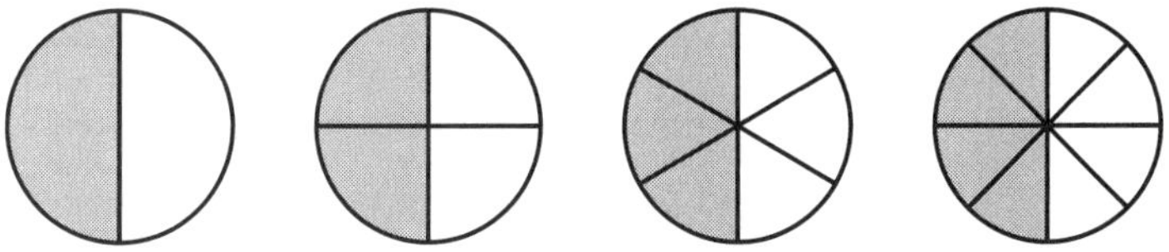

$\frac{1}{2}$ = ___ = ___ = ___

2. Shade the same part to find a fraction equivalent to the first fraction.

a) 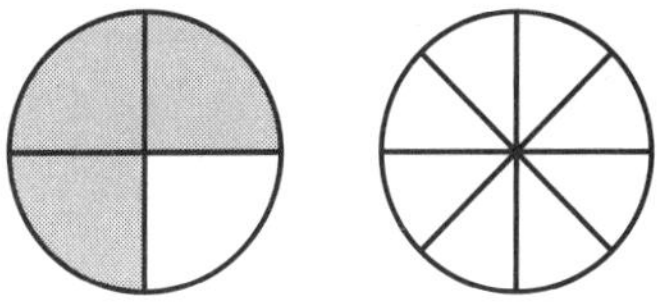

$\frac{3}{4}$ =

b) 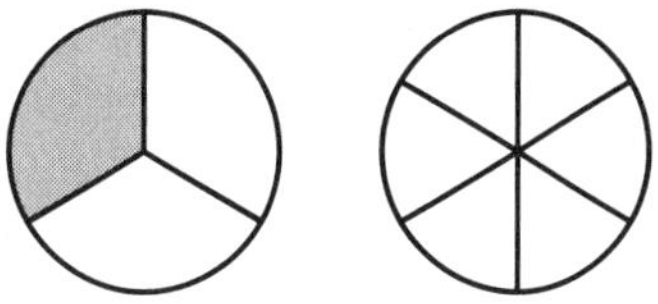

$\frac{1}{3}$ =

c) 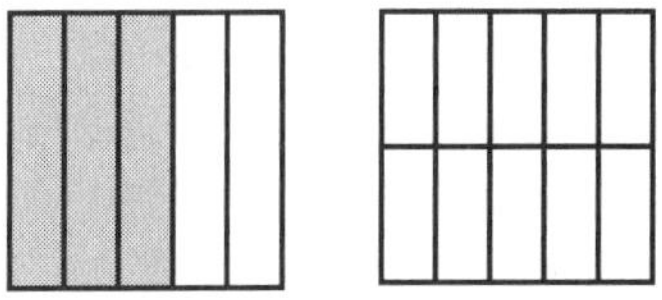

$\frac{3}{5}$ =

d) 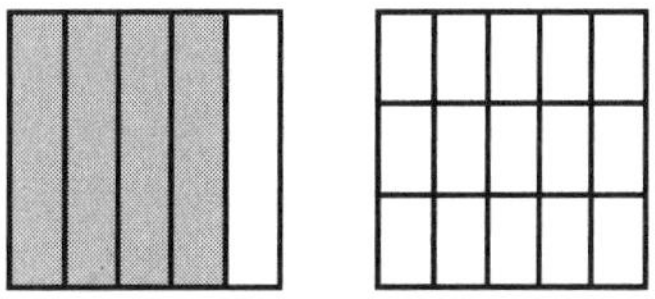

$\frac{4}{5}$ =

3. How many times as many parts?

a)  has ________ times as many parts as 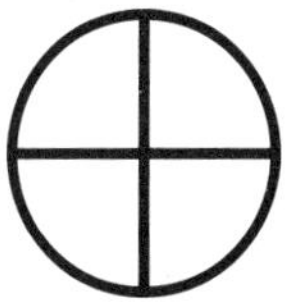

b)  has ________ times as many parts as 

c)  has ________ times as many parts as 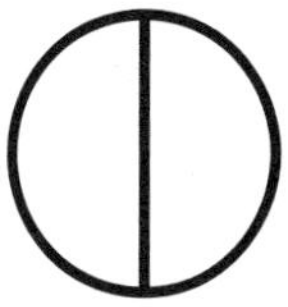

4. Fill in the blanks.

A B

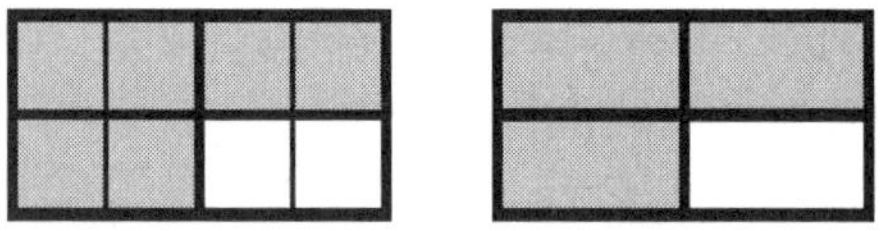

a) A has _______ times as many parts as B.

A has _______ times as many shaded parts as B.

A B

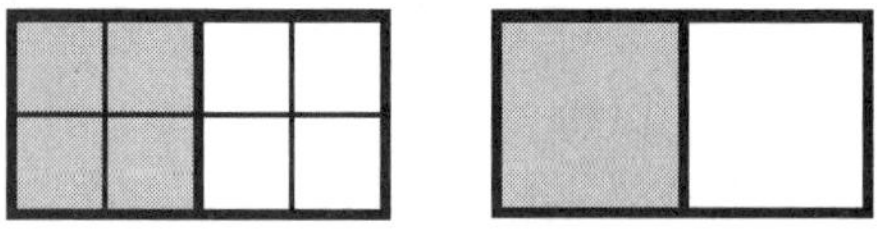

b) A has _______ times as many parts as B.

A has _______ times as many shaded parts as B.

A B

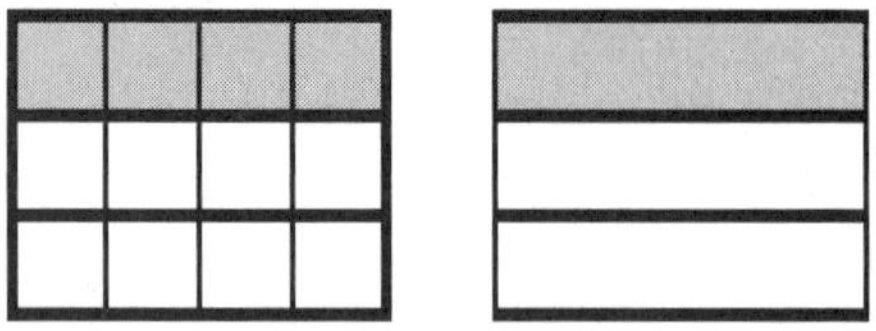

c) A has _______ times as many parts as B.

A has _______ times as many shaded parts as B.

5. The picture shows two equivalent fractions. How many times as much as the first numerator and denominator are the second numerator and denominator?

a) 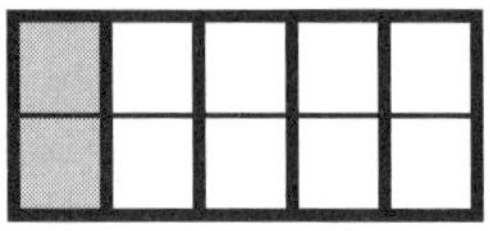 $\frac{1}{5}$ and $\frac{2}{10}$

2 is _______ times as much as 1.

10 is _______ times as much as 5.

b) 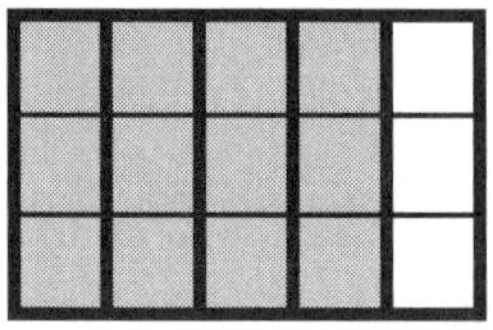 $\frac{4}{5}$ and $\frac{12}{15}$

12 is _______ times as much as 4.

15 is _______ times as much as 5.

6. Write another equivalent fraction for each picture. Then write how many times as much as the first numerator and denominator the second numerator and denominator are.

a) 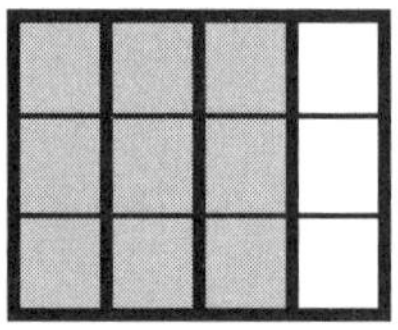 $\frac{3}{4} = \boxed{\frac{9}{12}}$

_______ times as much

b) 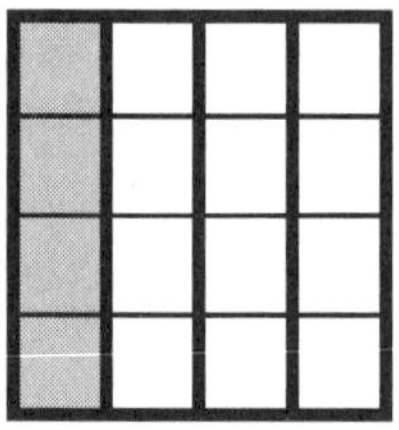 $\frac{1}{4} = \square$

_______ times as much

c) 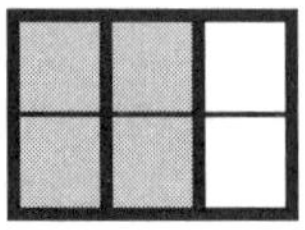 $\frac{2}{3} = \square$

_______ times as much

BONUS ▶

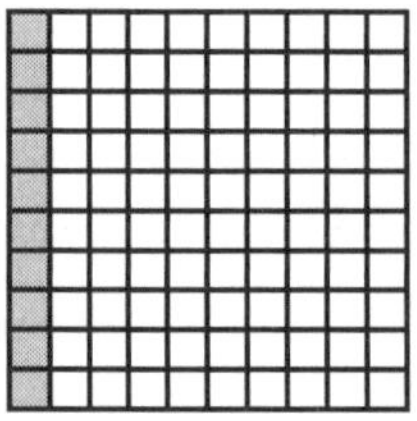 $\frac{1}{10} = \square$

_______ times as much

You can multiply the numerator and denominator by the same number to get an equivalent fraction.

Example: Picture A

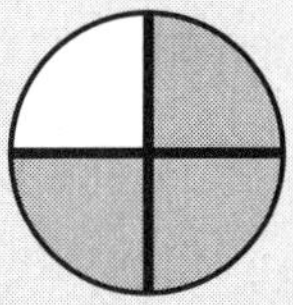

$$\frac{3}{4} \xrightarrow{\times 2} \frac{6}{8}$$

Picture B

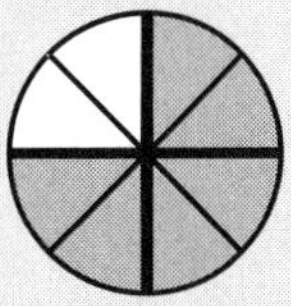

Picture B has twice as many **parts** as Picture A.
Picture B has twice as many **shaded parts** as Picture A.

7. Draw lines to cut the pies into more pieces. Then fill in the numerators of the equivalent fractions.

a)

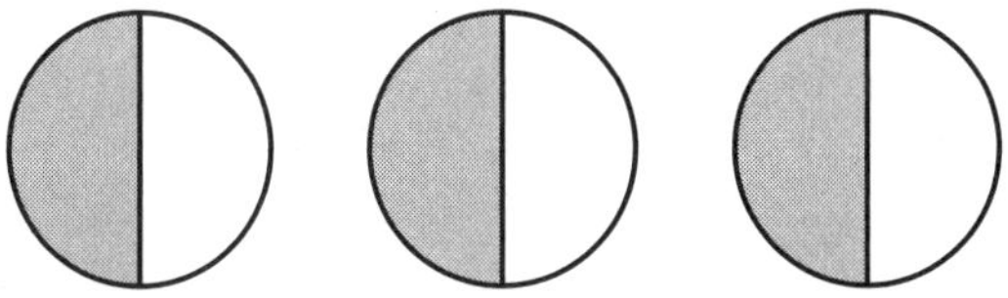

4 pieces 6 pieces 8 pieces

$\frac{1}{2} = \frac{\_\_}{4} = \frac{\_\_}{6} = \frac{\_\_}{8}$

b)

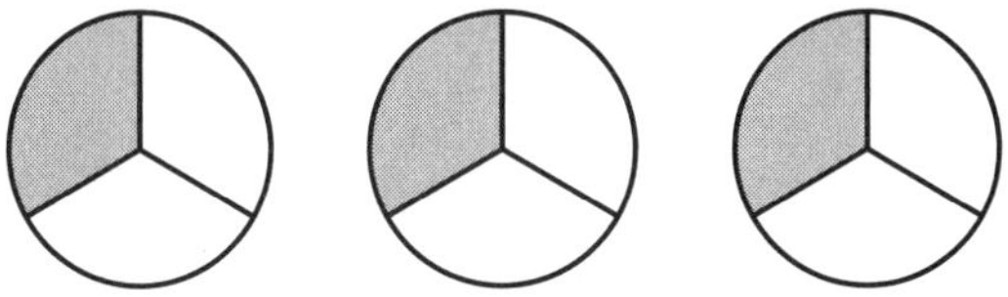

6 pieces 9 pieces 12 pieces

$\frac{1}{3} = \frac{\_\_}{6} = \frac{\_\_}{9} = \frac{\_\_}{12}$

8. Cut each pie into more pieces. Then fill in the missing numbers.

a)

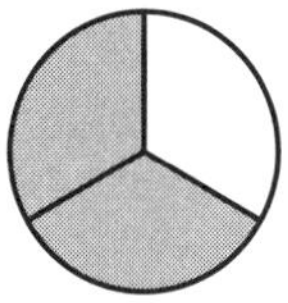

$\frac{2}{3} \xrightarrow{\times 2} \frac{\_\_}{6}$ (× 2 on both numerator and denominator)

↑ This number tells you how many pieces to cut each slice into.

b)

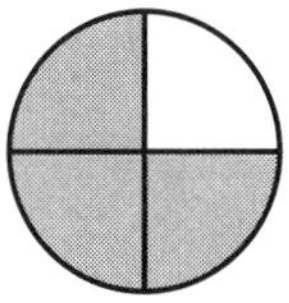

$\frac{3}{4} \xrightarrow{\times 2} \frac{\_\_}{8}$ (× 2 on both numerator and denominator)

c)

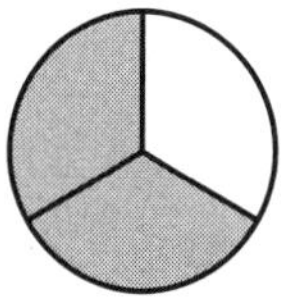

$\frac{2}{3} \xrightarrow{\times \_\_} \frac{\_\_}{9}$ (× on both numerator and denominator)

9. Use multiplication to find the equivalent fraction.

a) $\frac{1 \times 2}{3 \times 2} = \frac{\_\_}{6}$

b) $\frac{1 \times \_\_}{2 \times \_\_} = \frac{\_\_}{10}$

c) $\frac{2}{5} = \frac{\_\_}{10}$

d) $\frac{3}{4} = \frac{\_\_}{8}$

e) $\frac{1}{4} = \frac{\_\_}{12}$

f) $\frac{4}{5} = \frac{\_\_}{15}$

g) $\frac{5}{6} = \frac{\_\_}{12}$

h) $\frac{3}{10} = \frac{\_\_}{100}$

i) $\frac{5}{9} = \frac{\_\_}{72}$

10. Write five fractions equivalent to $\frac{7}{10}$.

$\frac{7}{10} = \square = \square = \square = \square = \square$

NS6-13 Equivalent Negative Fractions

1. a) Use the positive fractions to label the negative fractions on the number lines.

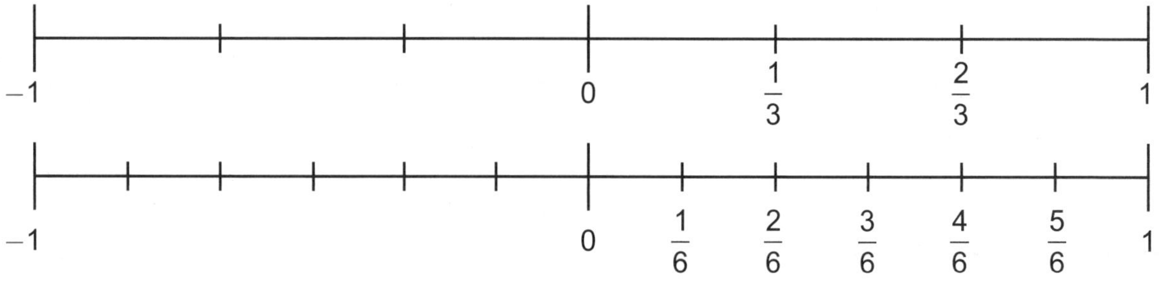

b) Name the equivalent positive fraction and the equivalent negative fraction.

i) $\frac{1}{3} = \frac{}{6}$ and $-\frac{1}{3} = -\frac{}{6}$ ii) $\frac{2}{3} = \frac{}{6}$ and $-\frac{2}{3} = -\frac{}{6}$

If two fractions are equivalent, their opposites are equivalent too.

Example: $\frac{2}{3} = \frac{4}{6}$, so $-\frac{2}{3} = -\frac{4}{6}$

2. Use the equivalent positive fraction to find the equivalent negative fraction.

a) $\frac{1}{3} = \frac{4}{12}$, so $-\frac{1}{3} = -\frac{}{12}$ b) $\frac{3}{4} = \frac{9}{12}$, so $-\frac{3}{4} = -\frac{}{12}$

c) $\frac{5}{6} = \frac{10}{12}$, so $-\frac{5}{6} = -\frac{}{12}$ d) $\frac{1}{2} = \frac{6}{12}$, so $-\frac{1}{2} = -\frac{}{12}$

REMINDER ▶ You can multiply the numerator and denominator by the same number to get an equivalent fraction.

$\frac{2}{5} \xrightarrow{\times 4} \frac{8}{20}$ (numerator $2 \times 4 = 8$, denominator $5 \times 4 = 20$)

3. Find the equivalent positive fraction, then find the equivalent negative fraction.

a) $\frac{2}{3} = \frac{}{9}$, so $-\frac{2}{3} =$ b) $\frac{3}{8} = \frac{}{40}$, so $-\frac{3}{8} =$

c) $\frac{4}{3} = \frac{}{12}$, so $-\frac{4}{3} =$ d) $\frac{7}{10} = \frac{}{40}$, so $-\frac{7}{10} =$

e) $\frac{9}{10} = \frac{}{100}$, so $-\frac{9}{10} =$ f) $3\frac{1}{2} = \frac{}{2}$, so $-3\frac{1}{2} =$

4. Write 5 fractions equivalent to $-\frac{3}{5}$.

$-\frac{3}{5} = \square = \square = \square = \square = \square$

NS6-14 Lowest Common Multiples (LCMs)

The **whole numbers** are the numbers 0, 1, 2, 3, and so on. The **multiples** of a whole number are the numbers you get by multiplying the number by another whole number.

Examples:

The multiples of 2 are $2 \times 0 = \mathbf{0}$ $2 \times 1 = \mathbf{2}$ $2 \times 2 = \mathbf{4}$ $2 \times 3 = \mathbf{6}$ $2 \times 4 = \mathbf{8}$ ...

The multiples of 3 are $3 \times 0 = \mathbf{0}$ $3 \times 1 = \mathbf{3}$ $3 \times 2 = \mathbf{6}$ $3 \times 3 = \mathbf{9}$ $3 \times 4 = \mathbf{12}$ ...

1. a) Skip count to write the multiples of 3 up to 3×10.

0, *3*, ____, ____, ____, ____, ____, ____, ____, ____, ____

b) Use your answers in part a) to circle the multiples of 3.

12 17 22 24 25 27

A number is a **common multiple** of two numbers if it is a multiple of both of them.

2. Mark the multiples of the two numbers on the number lines. Then write their common multiples.

a) Which numbers are common multiples of both 3 and 4?

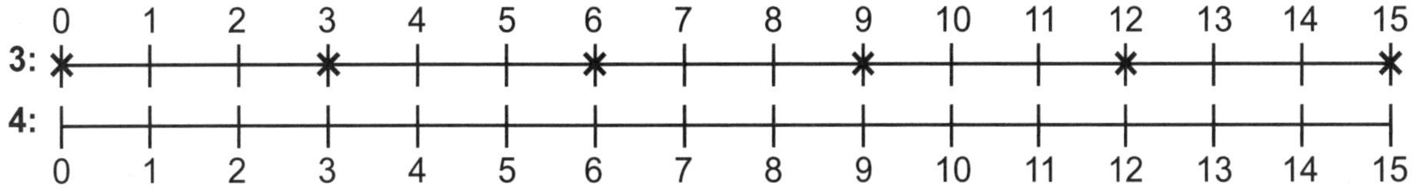

____ and ____

b) Which numbers are common multiples of both 2 and 3?

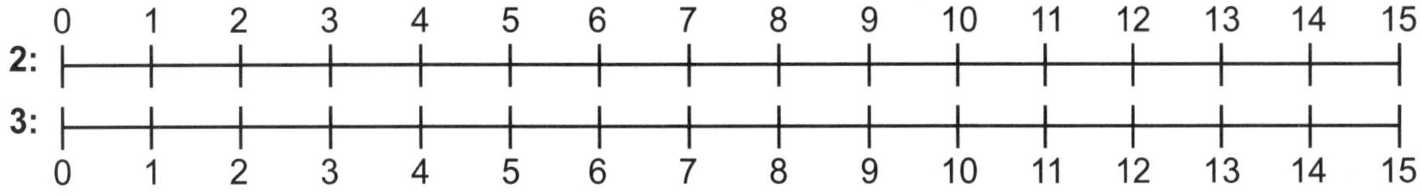

____, ____, and ____

c) Which numbers are common multiples of both 4 and 6?

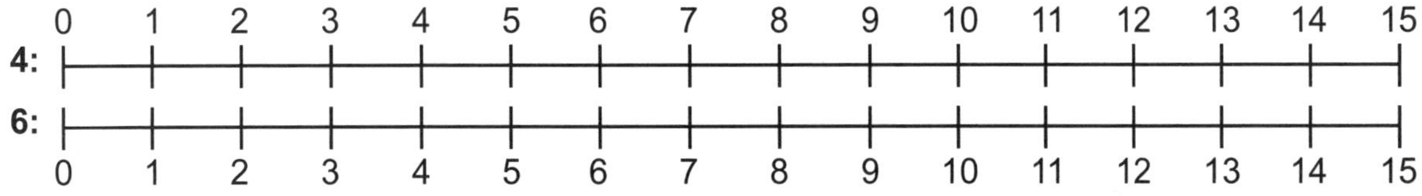

____ and ____

3. List the multiples of both numbers, up to 10 times each number.

Write the first two common multiples, not including 0.

a) 3 and 4

3: *0, 3, 6, 9, 12, 15, 18, 21, 24, 27, 30*

4: ______

The first two common multiples are ______ and ______.

b) 2 and 3

2: ______

3: ______

The first two common multiples are ______ and ______.

c) 3 and 5 d) 2 and 5 e) 2 and 4 f) 4 and 5

The number 0 is a multiple of every number. The **lowest common multiple (LCM)** of two numbers is the smallest whole number (not 0) that is a multiple of both numbers.

4. Find the lowest common multiple of each pair of numbers.

a) 4 and 10

4: *4, 8, 12, 16, 20*

10: *10, 20*

LCM = ______

b) 3 and 6

3:

6:

LCM = ______

c) 4 and 6

4:

6:

LCM = ______

d) 5 and 10

5:

10:

LCM = ______

e) 6 and 8

6:

8:

LCM = ______

f) 5 and 7

5:

7:

LCM = ______

g) 8 and 10 h) 8 and 12 i) 8 and 16

5. Find the LCM of each number and itself.

a) 3 and 3 ______ b) 4 and 4 ______ c) 5 and 5 ______

BONUS ▶ The LCM of 183 and 183 is ______.

To find the lowest common multiple of two numbers, write the first few multiples of the *larger* number until you see one that is also a multiple of the smaller number:

Example: Find the LCM of 3 and 5.

The first few multiples of 5 are 5, 10, 15. ⟵ Stop here because 15 is a multiple of 3.

6. Find the lowest common multiple.

a) 6 and 10

10, 20, 30

LCM = *30*

b) 9 and 12

LCM = ________

c) 7 and 10

LCM = ________

d) 6 and 9

LCM = ________

e) 6 and 15

LCM = ________

f) 8 and 9

LCM = ________

g) 5 and 8

LCM = ________

h) 3 and 6

LCM = ________

7. a) Write the LCM of each pair of numbers.

i) 2 and 3 ________ ii) 2 and 4 ________ iii) 2 and 5 ________ iv) 2 and 6 ________

v) 2 and 7 ________ vi) 2 and 8 ________ vii) 2 and 9 ________ viii) 2 and 10 ________

b) For which numbers in part a) is the LCM of 2 and the number equal to the number itself?

_____ , _____ , _____ , and _____

c) What is the LCM of 2 and 184? How do you know? ________________________________

____

Factors

There are only three ways to write 4 as a product of two whole numbers:

$1 \times 4 = 4 \quad 2 \times 2 = 4 \quad 4 \times 1 = 4$

The numbers that appear in the products are called the **factors** of 4.

The factors of 4 are the numbers 1, 2, and 4.

1. Write the number that makes the equation true. If no number makes the equation true, write "**X**" in the box.

a) 3 × [*4*] = 12   b) 4 × [**X**] = 14   c) 2 × [ ] = 16   d) 3 × [ ] = 10

2. Write "yes" or "no." Use your answers to Question 1 to explain your answer.

a) Is 3 a factor of 12? *yes* because *4 makes the equation true*.

b) Is 4 a factor of 14? *no* because *no number makes the equation true*.

c) Is 2 a factor of 16? ________ because ____________________.

d) Is 3 a factor of 10? ________ because ____________________.

3. Write the number that makes the equation true. If no number makes the equation true, write "**X**" in the box. Then list the factors of the number.

a) Find the factors of 6.

1 × [*6*] = 6
2 × [*3*] = 6
3 × [*2*] = 6
4 × [**X**] = 6
5 × [**X**] = 6
6 × [*1*] = 6

1, 2, 3, 6

b) Find the factors of 8.

1 × [ ] = 8
2 × [ ] = 8
3 × [ ] = 8
4 × [ ] = 8
5 × [ ] = 8
6 × [ ] = 8
7 × [ ] = 8
8 × [ ] = 8

____

c) Find the factors of 9.

1 × [ ] = 9
2 × [ ] = 9
3 × [ ] = 9
4 × [ ] = 9
5 × [ ] = 9
6 × [ ] = 9
7 × [ ] = 9
8 × [ ] = 9
9 × [ ] = 9

____

2 and 3 are a **factor pair** of 6 because $2 \times 3 = 6$.

4. List the factor pairs of each number. List each pair only once.

a) 6

1 and *6*

2 and *3*

b) 8

_______ and _______

_______ and _______

c) 9

_______ and _______

_______ and _______

5. Alana lists the factor pairs of 10 by using a chart. When a number is not a factor, she writes an "**✕**" in the second column.

First Factor	Second Factor
1	10
2	5
3	✕
4	✕
5	2
6	✕
7	✕
8	✕
9	✕
10	1

a) Why didn't Alana list 11 as a first factor?

____

b) Use Alana's chart to write the factors of 10.

_____ , _____ , _____ , _____

c) Use Alana's chart to write the factor pairs of 10.

_______ and _______ _______ and _______

6. a) Use Alana's method to find all the factor pairs of 12.

First Factor	Second Factor
1	
2	
3	
4	
5	
6	
7	
8	
9	
10	
11	
12	

Factor pairs of 12:

_______ and _______

_______ and _______

_______ and _______

b) Write "bigger" or "smaller" in the blanks:

As you go down the chart, the first factor gets

_____________________________ and the

second factor gets _____________________.

7. Use Alana's method to find all the factor pairs of each number.

a) 14 b) 15 c) 16 d) 18 e) 20 f) 24 g) 25

8. Use the top half of each chart to finish the bottom half.

a) 18

First Factor	Second Factor
1	18
2	9
3	6
6	3
	2
	1

b) 30

First Factor	Second Factor
1	30
2	15
3	10
5	6
	5
	3
	2
	1

c) 36

First Factor	Second Factor
1	36
2	18
3	12
4	9
6	6

To list all the factors of a given number, stop when you get a number that is already part of a factor pair.

9. Make a chart to find all the factor pairs. There might be more rows than you need in the chart.

a) 20

First Factor	Second Factor
1	*20*
2	*10*
4	*5*
5	*STOP*

b) 81

First Factor	Second Factor
1	*81*
3	*27*
9	*9*
STOP	

c) 28

First Factor	Second Factor

d) 42

First Factor	Second Factor

e) 36

First Factor	Second Factor

f) 99

First Factor	Second Factor

NS6-16 Greatest Common Factors (GCFs)

1. Place the numbers in the Venn diagram. Cross out the numbers as you place them.

a) ~~1~~ ~~2~~ ~~3~~ ~~4~~ ~~5~~ 6 7 8 9

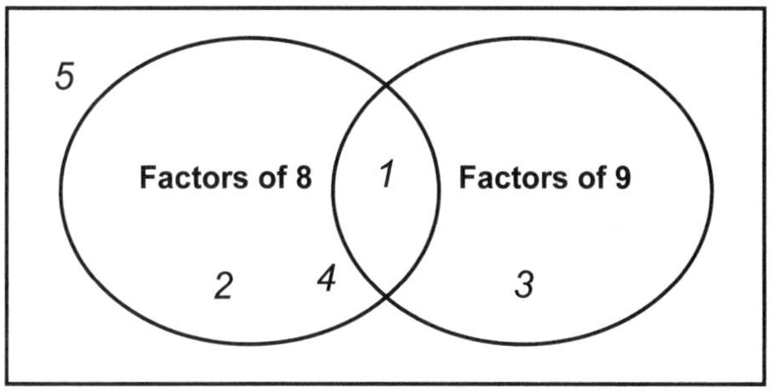

b) 1 2 3 4 5 6 7 8 9 10 11 12

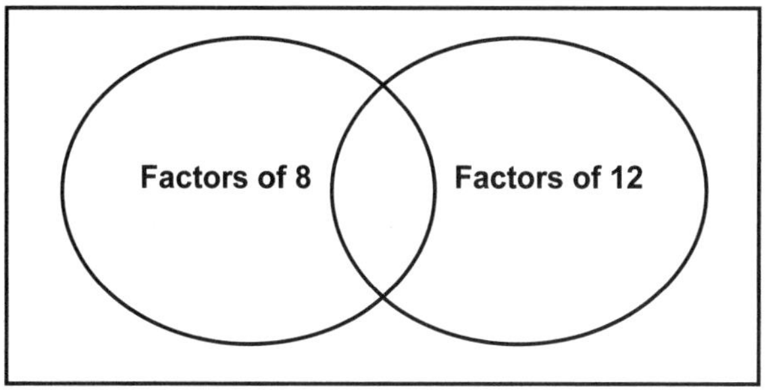

c) 1 2 3 4 5 6 7 8 9

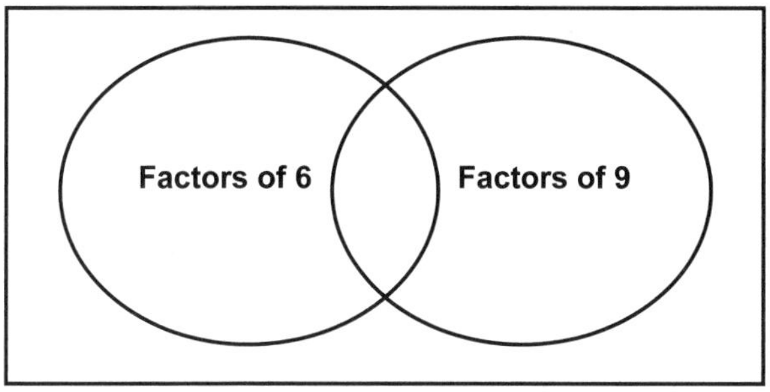

d) 1 2 3 4 5 6 7 8

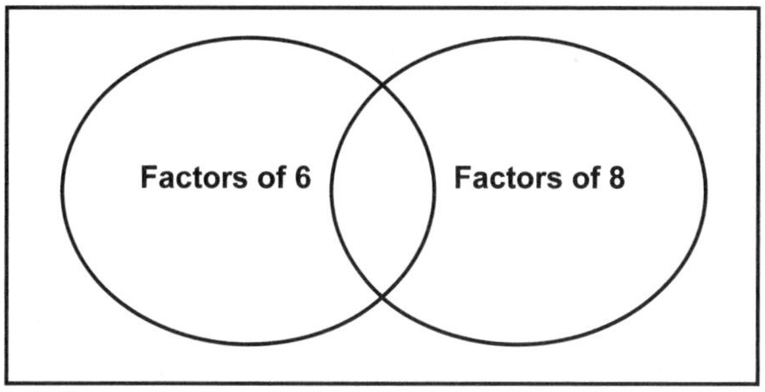

2. What number is a factor of every number? _______

The **greatest common factor (GCF)** of two numbers is the greatest number that is a factor of both numbers.

3. a) In what region of each Venn diagram above does the greatest common factor occur?

____

b) Find the greatest common factor of ...

i) 8 and 9 [ ] ii) 8 and 12 [ ] iii) 6 and 9 [ ] iv) 6 and 8 [ ]

4. a) Find and list all the factors of each number. You can make a chart if it helps.

i) 33 ii) 55 iii) 60

1, 3, 11, 33

b) Use your answers in part a) to find the greatest common factor of ...

i) 33 and 55 _______ ii) 33 and 60 _______ iii) 55 and 60 _______

5. a) Write "GCF" or "LCM."

i) 6 and 10

GCF = 2

LCM = 30

ii) 5 and 10

_______ = 5

_______ = 10

iii) 6 and 15

_______ = 3

_______ = 30

iv) 8 and 12

_______ = 4

_______ = 24

v) 5 and 8

_______ = 40

_______ = 1

vi) 15 and 20

_______ = 60

_______ = 5

vii) 12 and 14

_______ = 84

_______ = 2

viii) 20 and 30

_______ = 60

_______ = 10

6. a) List the factors of 6.

_____ , _____ , _____ , and _____

b) List the first four multiples of 6, not including 0.

_____ , _____ , _____ , and _____

c) What number is both a factor and a multiple of 6? _____

7. What number is both a factor and a multiple of the given number?

a) 8 [ ] b) 9 [ ] c) 10 [ ] d) 12 [ ]

BONUS ▶ 12,351 [ ]

8. a) List the factors of 12.

_____ , _____ , _____ , _____ , _____ , and _____

b) What numbers are both a multiple of 6 and a factor of 12? _____ and _____

c) Write "more" or "less." All the factors of 6 except for 6 itself are _____________ than 6.

d) Write "more" or "less." All the multiples of 12 except for 0 and 12 itself are _____________ than 12.

e) Are any numbers both a factor of 6 and a multiple of 12? How do you know?

____

____

BONUS ▶

a) What is the LCM of 10 and 10? _____

b) What is the GCF of 10 and 10? _____

NS6-17 Greatest Common Factors (Advanced)

You can draw arrays to show factors.

3 is a factor of 6 and 3 is a factor of 21. So 3 is a factor of 21 + 6, too!

$6 =$  $= 3 \times 2$

$21 =$ 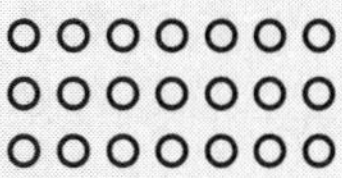 $= 3 \times 7$

$21 + 6 =$ 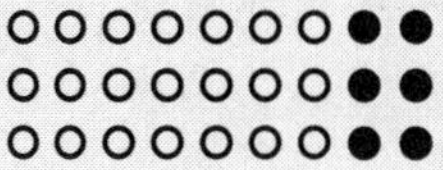 $= 3 \times 9$

1. Write what the white dots, the black dots, and the whole picture show.

	Picture	White dots show ...	Black dots show ...	Whole picture shows ...
a)	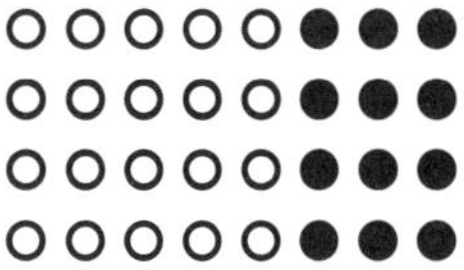	4 is a factor of _20_	4 is a factor of _12_	4 is a factor of _20_ + _12_ = _32_
b)	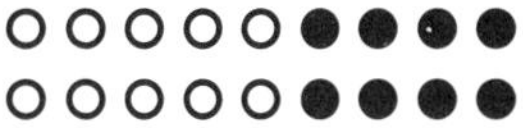	2 is a factor of ______	2 is a factor of ______	2 is a factor of ______ + ______ = ______
c)	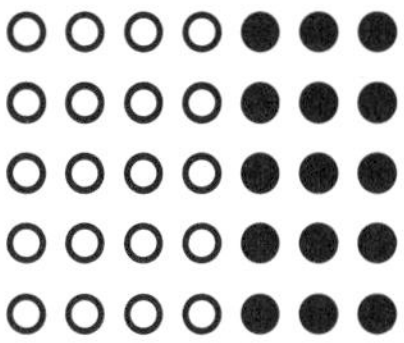	5 is a factor of ______	5 is a factor of ______	5 is a factor of ______ + ______ = ______
d)	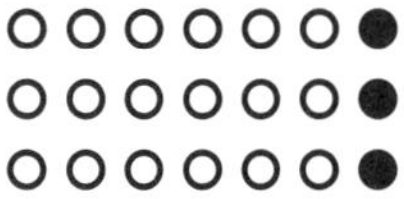	3 is a factor of ______	3 is a factor of ______	3 is a factor of ______ + ______ = ______

2. a) Draw black dots to show that 4 is a factor of 8. Draw white dots to show that 4 is a factor of 20.

$8 =$ $20 =$

b) Combine your pictures from part a) to show that 4 is a factor of $28 = 20 + 8$.

3. Fill in the blanks to say what the picture shows.

a) 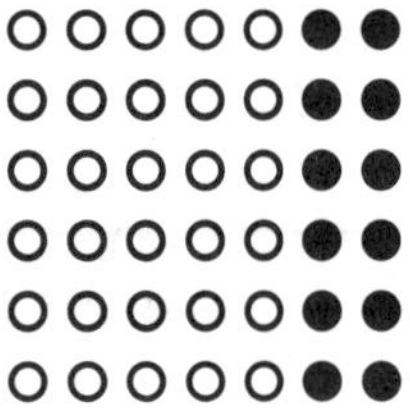

$30 = 6 \times \underline{\ 5\ }$ and $12 = 6 \times \underline{\ 2\ }$

so $30 + 12 = 6 \times (\underline{\ 5\ } + \underline{\ 2\ })$

$= 6 \times \underline{\ 7\ }$

b) 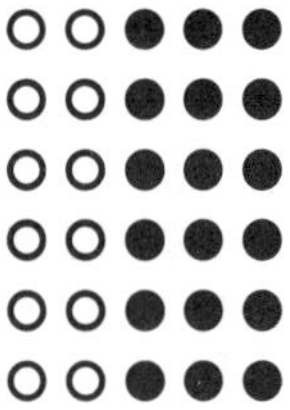

$12 = 6 \times$ _____ and $18 = 6 \times$ _____

so $12 + 18 = 6 \times$ (_____ + _____)

$= 6 \times$ _____

c) 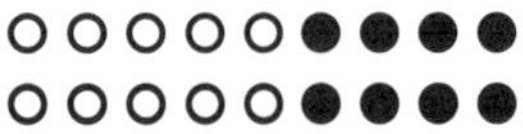

$10 + 8 = 2 \times$ (_____ + _____)

d) 

$4 + 14 = 2 \times$ (_____ + _____)

4. Imagine the picture to fill in the blanks.

a) $10 + 6 = 2 \times$ (_____ + _____)

b) $9 + 15 = 3 \times$ (_____ + _____)

c) $18 + 45 = 9 \times$ (_____ + _____)

d) $21 + 49 = 7 \times$ (_____ + _____)

BONUS ▸ $18 + 24 + 33 = 3 \times$ (_____ + _____ + _____)

5. Find the GCF of the two numbers. Then rewrite the sum using the GCF as one factor.

a) $18 + 24 =$ _____ (GCF) × (_____ + _____)

b) $25 + 35 =$ _____ (GCF) × (_____ + _____)

c) $9 + 12 =$ _____ (GCF) × (_____ + _____)

d) $6 + 30 =$ _____ (GCF) × (_____ + _____)

e) $16 + 40 =$ _____ (GCF) × (_____ + _____)

f) $18 + 30 =$ _____ (GCF) × (_____ + _____)

g) $28 + 35 =$ _____ (GCF) × (_____ + _____)

h) $42 + 60 =$ _____ (GCF) × (_____ + _____)

i) $40 + 64 =$ _____ (GCF) × (_____ + _____)

j) $42 + 54 =$ _____ (GCF) × (_____ + _____)

6. Ravi has 12 roses and 15 lilies. He wants to make bouquets so that:

- he uses all his flowers
- each bouquet has the same number of roses, and
- each bouquet has the same number of lilies.

What is the greatest number of bouquets that he can make?

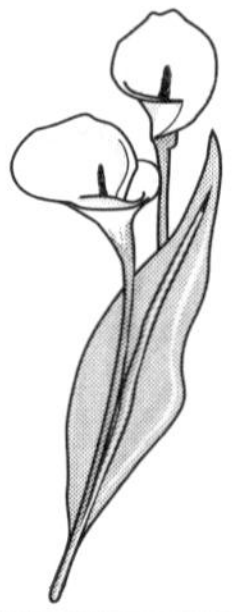

NS6-18 Counterexamples

1. Circle the picture that shows the claim is not true.

a) All circles are shaded.

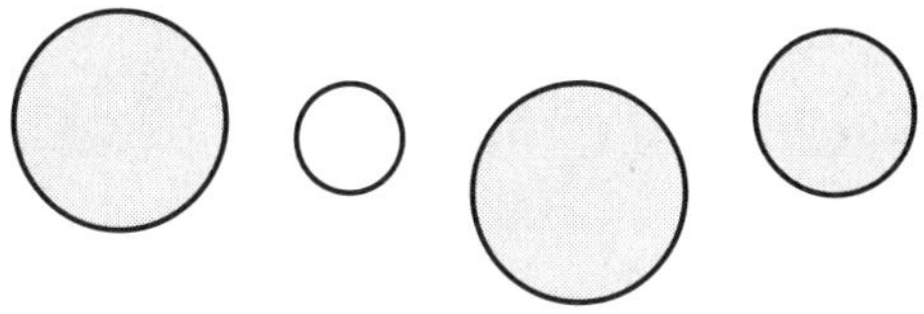

b) All squares are striped.

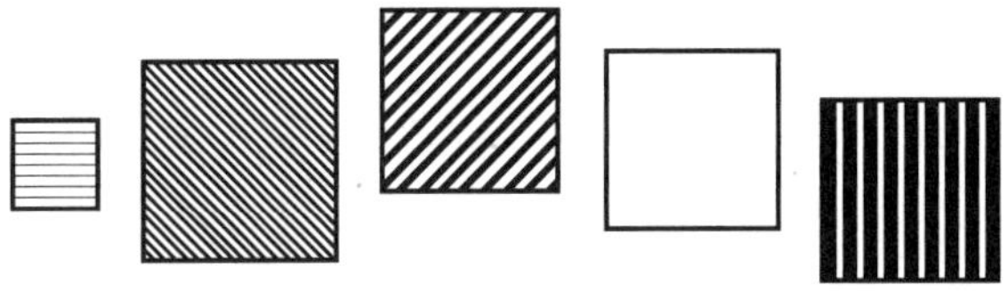

2. Which picture shows the claim is not true?

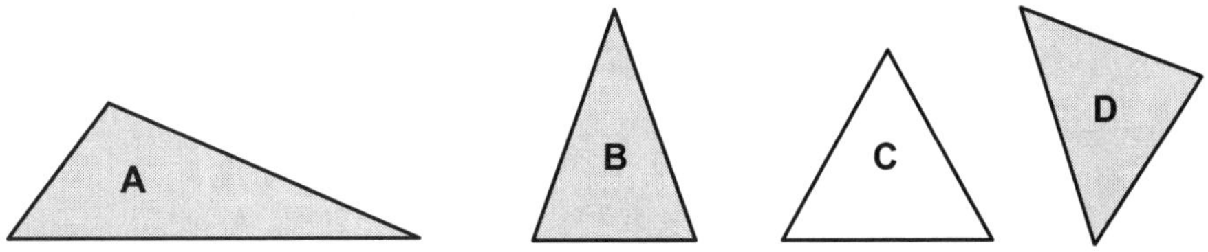

a) All triangles are shaded. ______

b) All triangles have a horizontal side. ______

3. Which letter in the list shows the claim is not true?

A R U i E O

a) All letters are vowels. ______

b) All letters are capital letters. ______

An example that shows a claim is not true is called a **counterexample**. To show that a claim is not true, you only need one counterexample.

4. Circle the *first* example, when reading from left to right, that shows the claim is not true.

a) All words have a letter “b.”

bed big buy globe stone

b) All names have five letters.

Jacob Mark Randy Sam Darya

Only circles can be counterexamples to this statement: All *circles* are shaded.

5. For each statement, circle the counterexample.

a) All circles in the set are shaded.

b) All triangles in the set are white.

c) All striped shapes in the set are circles.

d) All white shapes in the set are circles.

6. Circle the counterexamples. Some questions will have more than one counterexample.

a) All vehicles have four wheels.

b) All words have an "e."

person place thing object bcjxp bcjxe

c) All English sentences end with a period.

Who's there? No way! ¿Cual es tu nombre? My name is Ahmed.

7. In Question 6. a), why are the bananas not a counterexample?

All black shapes are circles.

This sentence is about black shapes, so a white shape cannot show the statement is false.
To prove the statement false, you need a black shape that is not a circle.

8. a) Write "F" in the box if the picture shows the statement is false.

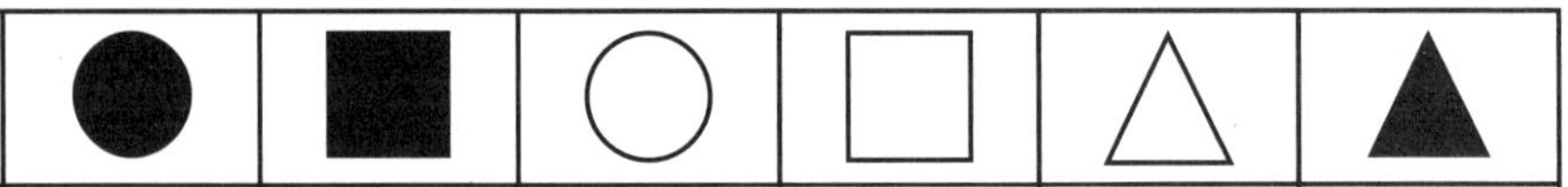

All black shapes are circles.						
All triangles are black.						
All white shapes are squares.						
All circles are black.						

b) Check your answers in part a). You should have written 6 Fs in total.

NS6-19 Problems and Puzzles (Advanced)

> To prove a statement is true, you need to **check all examples** to make sure there is no counterexample.

1. If the statement is true, write "true." If the statement is false, name a counterexample.

A. ▫ B. ⬜ C. ▪ D. ● E. ◯ F. ▵ G. △

a) All black shapes are small. _______________

b) All small shapes are black. _______________

c) All circles are black. _______________

d) All white shapes are big. _______________

e) All squares are white. _______________

f) All big shapes are white. _______________

BONUS ▶

All white circles are big. _______________

All white squares are small. _______________

> When there is a reason why something must always be true, you don't need to check all examples.

2. For each statement, either write "true" or give a counterexample.

a) All even numbers have an even digit. _______________

b) All even numbers have an odd digit. _______________

c) All odd numbers have an even digit. _______________

d) All odd numbers have an odd digit. _______________

e) All multiples of 3 are multiples of 6. _______________

f) All multiples of 6 are multiples of 3. _______________

g) All multiples of 10 have 3 digits. _______________

h) All multiples of 10 have ones digit 0. _______________

i) All multiples of 3 have a digit that is a multiple of 3. _______________

j) All multiples of 5 have a digit that is a multiple of 5. _______________

k) All multiples of 5 have ones digit 5. _______________

l) All odd multiples of 5 have ones digit 5. _______________

m) All even multiples of 5 have ones digit 0. _______________

BONUS ▶ Choose a statement that you said was true, and give a reason why it is true.

____

____

The **greatest common factor of three numbers** is the greatest number that is a factor of all three numbers.

3. List the factors of each number. Then find the GCF of all three numbers.

a) 6, 8, and 10

6: ______________

8: ______________

10: ______________

GCF = _______

b) 9, 15, and 33

9: ______________

15: ______________

33: ______________

GCF = _______

c) 42, 54, and 75

42: ______________

54: ______________

75: ______________

GCF = _______

BONUS ▶ You can find the GCF of four numbers, too! Find the GCF of 30, 50, 75, and 90.

4. a) For which statements is 10 a counterexample? ________________________________

A. All even numbers are multiples of 4.

B. All multiples of 3 are multiples of 6.

C. All factors of 12 are factors of 15.

D. All factors of 20 are factors of 25.

E. All multiples of 5 are multiples of 10.

b) All statements above are false. Write a counterexample (not 10!) for each.

A. _______ **B.** _______ **C.** _______ **D.** _______ **E.** _______

5. a) Write the LCM and GCF of each pair of numbers.

2 and 3 have LCM = _______ and GCF = _______

4 and 6 have LCM = _______ and GCF = _______

6 and 9 have LCM = _______ and GCF = _______

8 and 12 have LCM = _______ and GCF = _______

b) Predict:
10 and 15 have LCM = _______ and GCF = _______

c) Check your answers in part b). Are they correct?

d) Which pattern rules did you use to make your prediction in part b)?

LCM: start at _______ and add _______ each time

GCF: ____

NS6-20 Comparing Fractions Using Equivalent Fractions

1. Skip count to fill in the numerators of the equivalent fractions.

a) $\frac{2}{3} = \frac{\ }{6} = \frac{\ }{9} = \frac{\ }{12} = \frac{\ }{15}$

b) $\frac{3}{5} = \frac{\ }{10} = \frac{\ }{15} = \frac{\ }{20} = \frac{\ }{25}$

2. a) Use your answers from Question 1 to write two fractions with the same denominator.

$\frac{2}{3} = \square$ and $\frac{3}{5} = \square$

b) Which of the two fractions is greater, $\frac{2}{3}$ or $\frac{3}{5}$? $\square$ How do you know?

____

3. Draw lines to cut the left-hand pie into the same number of pieces as the right-hand pie. Write an equivalent fraction, then circle the greater fraction.

a)

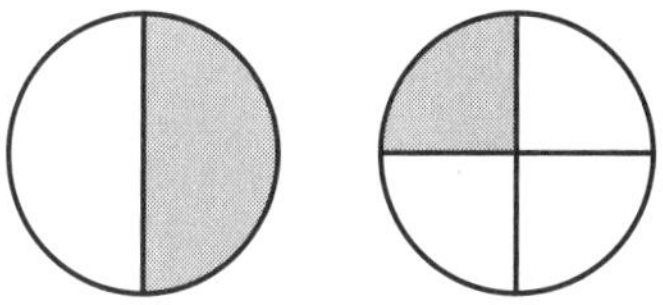

$\frac{1}{2} = \frac{\ }{4}$ $\qquad$ $\frac{1}{4}$

b)

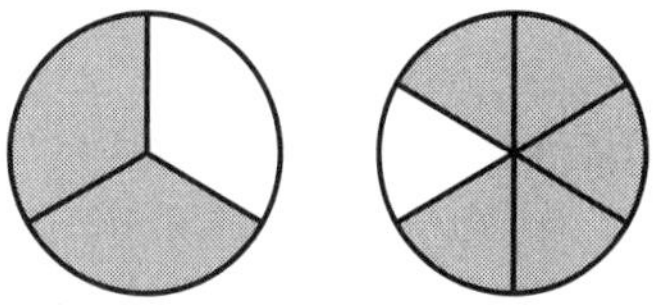

$\frac{2}{3} = \frac{\ }{6}$ $\qquad$ $\frac{5}{6}$

4. Turn each fraction on the left into an equivalent fraction with the same denominator as the fraction on the right. Then write < or > to show which fraction is greater.

a) $\frac{1 \times 3}{2 \times 3} = \frac{3}{6} \square \frac{4}{6}$

b) $\frac{1 \times}{2 \times} = \frac{\ }{8} \square \frac{5}{8}$

c) $\frac{1}{2} = \frac{\ }{\ } \square \frac{3}{4}$

d) $\frac{1}{3} = \frac{\ }{\ } \square \frac{4}{9}$

e) $\frac{1}{5} = \frac{\ }{\ } \square \frac{7}{10}$

f) $\frac{1}{4} = \frac{\ }{\ } \square \frac{7}{16}$

5. Write equivalent fractions with the same denominator. Then circle the greater fraction.

a) $\frac{1}{4} = \frac{\ }{20}$ and $\frac{2}{5} = \frac{\ }{20}$

b) $\frac{3}{8} = \frac{\ }{24}$ and $\frac{1}{3} = \frac{\ }{24}$

6. a) Create an equivalent fraction with denominator 12.

i) $\frac{2}{3} = \frac{\ }{12}$ ii) $\frac{5}{6} = \frac{\ }{12}$ iii) $\frac{3}{4} = \frac{\ }{12}$ iv) $\frac{1}{2} = \frac{\ }{12}$

b) Write the fractions from part a) from least to greatest. $\square < \square < \square < \square$

To compare $\frac{3}{4}$ and $\frac{7}{10}$, Rowan changes them into fractions with the same denominator.

Step 1: Rowan finds the lowest common multiple (LCM) of the denominators. The LCM of 4 and 10 is 20.

Step 2: Rowan changes both fractions into fractions with that denominator. Now the fractions are easy to compare!

$$\frac{3}{4} \xrightarrow{\times 5} \frac{15}{20} \qquad \frac{7}{10} \xrightarrow{\times 2} \frac{14}{20}$$

Since $\frac{15}{20} > \frac{14}{20}$, then $\frac{3}{4} > \frac{7}{10}$

7. Use Rowan's method to compare the fractions. Show your answer using $<$ or $>$.

a) $\frac{3}{4}$ and $\frac{5}{7}$ LCM of 4 and 7 is *28*

$\frac{3}{4} = \frac{21}{28}$ and $\frac{5}{7} = \frac{20}{28}$ so $\frac{3}{4}$ [>] $\frac{5}{7}$

b) $\frac{1}{2}$ and $\frac{2}{3}$ LCM of 2 and 3 is ____

$\frac{1}{2} =$ and $\frac{2}{3} =$ so $\frac{1}{2}$ ☐ $\frac{2}{3}$

c) $\frac{3}{4}$ and $\frac{5}{8}$ LCM of 4 and 8 is ____

$\frac{3}{4} =$ and $\frac{5}{8} =$ so $\frac{3}{4}$ ☐ $\frac{5}{8}$

d) $\frac{7}{9}$ and $\frac{5}{6}$ LCM of 9 and 6 is ____

$\frac{7}{9} =$ and $\frac{5}{6} =$ so $\frac{7}{9}$ ☐ $\frac{5}{6}$

8. Compare the positive fractions. Then compare the negative fractions.

a) $\frac{3}{4}$ and $\frac{5}{6}$ LCM of 4 and 6 is ____

$\frac{3}{4} =$ and $\frac{5}{6} =$

so $\frac{3}{4}$ ☐ $\frac{5}{6}$ and $-\frac{3}{4}$ ☐ $-\frac{5}{6}$

b) $\frac{2}{3}$ and $\frac{5}{9}$ LCM of 3 and 9 is ____

$\frac{2}{3} =$ and $\frac{5}{9} =$

so $\frac{2}{3}$ ☐ $\frac{5}{9}$ and $-\frac{2}{3}$ ☐ $-\frac{5}{9}$

9. Compare the fractions. Do the rough work in your notebook.

a) $\frac{2}{3}$ ☐ $\frac{5}{8}$ b) $-\frac{2}{3}$ ☐ $-\frac{5}{8}$ c) $-\frac{2}{3}$ ☐ $\frac{5}{8}$ d) $\frac{2}{3}$ ☐ $-\frac{5}{8}$

e) $-1\frac{2}{3}$ ☐ $-2\frac{3}{5}$ f) $1\frac{5}{8}$ ☐ $1\frac{7}{10}$ g) $\frac{7}{3}$ ☐ $\frac{12}{5}$ h) $-\frac{7}{3}$ ☐ $-\frac{12}{5}$

i) $-\frac{3}{4}$ ☐ $\frac{1}{10}$ j) $\frac{3}{5}$ ☐ $-\frac{3}{5}$ k) $-\frac{3}{4}$ ☐ $-\frac{5}{8}$ l) $-\frac{12}{5}$ ☐ $\frac{8}{7}$

10. Which temperature is warmer, $-\frac{3}{5}$°F or $-\frac{5}{8}$°F? Explain how you know.

NS6-21 Applying LCMs and GCFs to Fractions

1. Imagine moving the shaded pieces from pies A and B onto pie plate C.
   Show how much of C would be filled, then write a fraction for C.

A B C

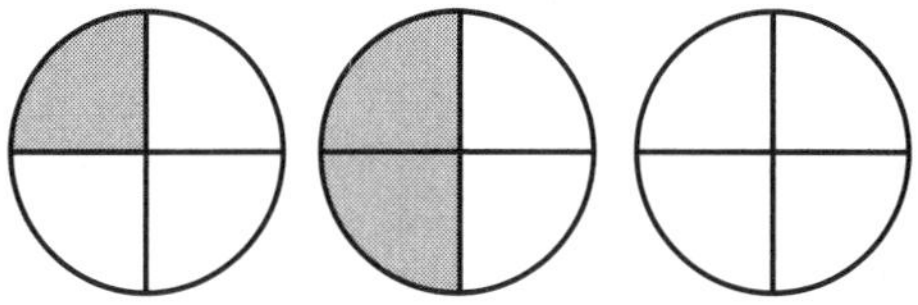

$\frac{1}{4} + \frac{2}{4} = \frac{\quad}{\quad}$

2. Imagine pouring the liquid from cups A and B into C. Shade the amount of liquid that would be in C. Then complete the addition equations.

a)

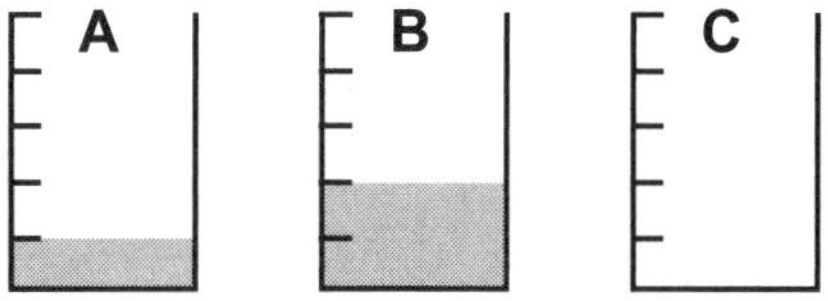

$\frac{\quad}{5} + \frac{\quad}{5} = \frac{\quad}{\quad}$

b)

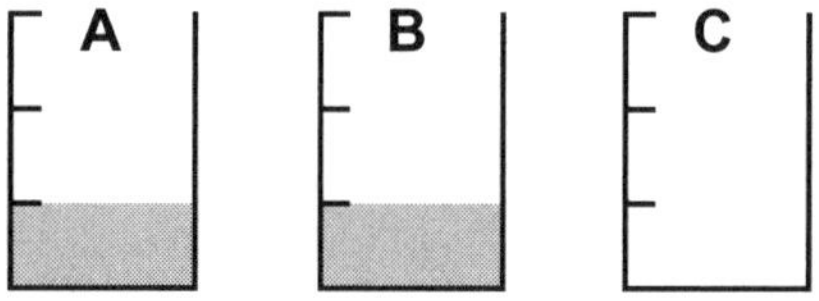

$\frac{\quad}{3} + \frac{\quad}{3} = \frac{\quad}{\quad}$

3. Add.

a) $\frac{3}{5} + \frac{1}{5} =$ b) $\frac{2}{4} + \frac{1}{4} =$ c) $\frac{3}{7} + \frac{2}{7} =$ d) $\frac{5}{8} + \frac{2}{8} =$

e) $\frac{3}{11} + \frac{7}{11} =$ f) $\frac{5}{17} + \frac{9}{17} =$ g) $\frac{11}{24} + \frac{10}{24} =$ h) $\frac{3}{57} + \frac{13}{57} =$

4. Show how much pie would be left if you took away the amount shown.
   Then complete the fraction statement.

a)

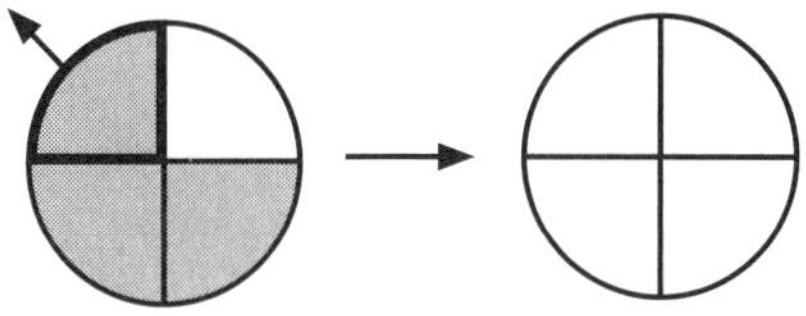

$\frac{3}{4} - \frac{1}{4} = \frac{\quad}{\quad}$

b)

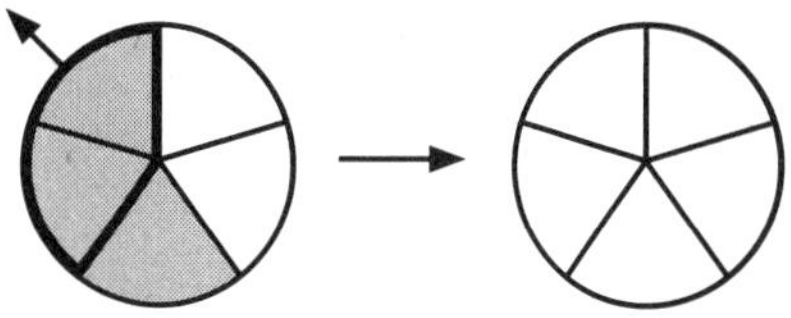

$\frac{3}{5} - \frac{2}{5} = \frac{\quad}{\quad}$

5. Subtract.

a) $\frac{2}{3} - \frac{1}{3} =$ b) $\frac{3}{5} - \frac{1}{5} =$ c) $\frac{6}{7} - \frac{3}{7} =$ d) $\frac{5}{8} - \frac{2}{8} =$

e) $\frac{9}{12} - \frac{2}{12} =$ f) $\frac{6}{19} - \frac{4}{19} =$ g) $\frac{9}{28} - \frac{3}{28} =$ h) $\frac{17}{57} - \frac{12}{57} =$

Follow the steps to add or subtract fractions with different denominators.

Example: $\frac{1}{3} + \frac{2}{5}$

Step 1: Find the **lowest common denominator (LCD)** of the fractions (the LCM of the denominators).
Example: The LCM of the denominators, 3 and 5, is 15.

Step 2: Create equivalent fractions with that denominator.

Example: $\frac{1}{3} + \frac{2}{5} = \frac{5 \times 1}{5 \times 3} + \frac{2 \times 3}{5 \times 3} = \frac{5}{15} + \frac{6}{15} = \frac{11}{15}$

6. Find the LCD of each pair of fractions. Then show what numbers you would multiply the numerator and denominator of each fraction by in order to add.

a) $\frac{3 \times 1}{3 \times 2} + \frac{2 \times 2}{3 \times 2}$ LCD = 6

b) $\frac{3}{4} + \frac{1}{8}$ LCD = ______

c) $\frac{1}{6} + \frac{2}{9}$ LCD = ______

d) $\frac{1}{4} + \frac{2}{3}$ LCD = ______

e) $\frac{1}{4} + \frac{1}{6}$ LCD = ______

f) $\frac{2}{5} + \frac{1}{10}$ LCD = ______

7. Add or subtract the fractions by changing them to equivalent fractions with denominators equal to the LCD of the fractions.

a) $\frac{2}{5} + \frac{1}{4}$

=

=

b) $\frac{4}{15} + \frac{2}{3}$

=

=

c) $\frac{5}{6} + \frac{3}{8}$

=

=

d) $\frac{1}{6} + \frac{11}{24}$

e) $\frac{5}{28} - \frac{1}{7}$

f) $\frac{4}{9} - \frac{1}{6}$

g) $\frac{3}{8} + \frac{7}{16}$

h) $\frac{7}{16} - \frac{3}{8}$

i) $\frac{7}{9} - \frac{3}{8}$

BONUS ▶ $\frac{4}{15} + \frac{1}{3} + \frac{2}{5}$

REMINDER ▶ To find the GCF (greatest common factor) of 6 and 8, list their factors:

The factors of 6 are 1, **2**, 3, 6
The factors of 8 are 1, **2**, 4, 8
} GCF = greatest number that appears on both lists

The GCF of 6 and 8 is 2.

8. Find the GCF of each pair of numbers.

a) 3 and 4 ______ b) 6 and 10 ______ c) 5 and 8 ______ d) 6 and 9 ______

A fraction is reduced to **lowest terms** when the GCF of its numerator and denominator is equal to 1.

Example: $\frac{3}{4}$ is in lowest terms, but $\frac{6}{8}$ is not.

9. Find the GCF of the numerator and denominator. Then decide if the fraction is in lowest terms.

Fraction	$\frac{3}{6}$	$\frac{2}{5}$	$\frac{4}{5}$	$\frac{5}{10}$	$\frac{6}{10}$	$\frac{7}{10}$	$\frac{15}{16}$	$\frac{9}{5}$
GCF	*3*							
Lowest terms?	*No*							

10. Reduce the fractions below by dividing the numerator and the denominator by their GCF.

a) $\frac{2 \div 2}{10 \div 2} = \frac{1}{5}$ b) $\frac{4 \div}{12 \div} =$ c) $\frac{6 \div}{9 \div} =$ d) $\frac{20 \div}{25 \div} =$

11. Add or subtract, then reduce your answer to lowest terms.

a) $\frac{5 \times 1}{5 \times 6} + \frac{1 \times 3}{10 \times 3}$ b) $\frac{13}{15} - \frac{1}{5}$ c) $\frac{5}{6} + \frac{3}{10}$ d) $\frac{25}{28} - \frac{1}{7}$

$= \frac{5}{30} + \frac{3}{30}$

$= \frac{8}{30}$

$= \frac{4}{15}$

NS6-22 Adding and Subtracting Mixed Numbers

$1 + 2\frac{5}{6} = \textcircled{3}\frac{5}{6}$ (circled 3 = $1 + 2$)

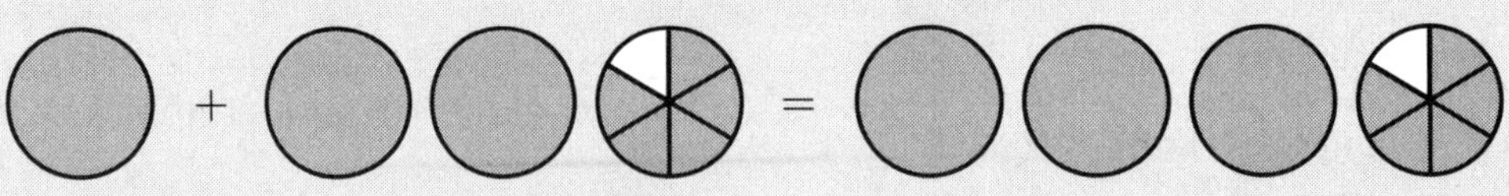

1. Add. Write your answer as a mixed number.

   a) $4 + 3\frac{2}{5} =$ b) $2 + 1\frac{2}{3} =$ c) $3 + 2\frac{1}{2} =$

2. Add by adding the parts and the wholes separately.

   a) $2\frac{1}{5} + 1\frac{3}{5} = 3\frac{4}{5}$ b) $2\frac{4}{7} + 3\frac{2}{7} =$ c) $3\frac{5}{9} + 1\frac{2}{9} =$

   d) $3\frac{2}{8} + 7\frac{5}{8} =$ e) $5\frac{2}{9} + 1\frac{6}{9} =$ **BONUS ▶** $5\frac{1}{8} + 9\frac{1}{8} + 3\frac{1}{8} =$

3. Sarah biked 4 miles to school and then $5\frac{3}{4}$ miles to the library.

   How far did she bike altogether? ______

Remember: A mixed number is made up of a whole number and a proper fraction.

When you add mixed numbers, the fraction part of the sum is sometimes an improper fraction (greater than 1). Example: $1\frac{3}{6} + 2\frac{4}{6} = 3\frac{7}{6}$ ← $\frac{7}{6} > 1$

You can change the fraction part to a proper fraction. Example: $3\frac{7}{6} = 3 + 1\frac{1}{6} = 4\frac{1}{6}$

4. Change the improper fraction to a mixed number.

   a) $\frac{11}{8} = 1\frac{}{8}$ b) $\frac{9}{7} = 1\frac{}{7}$ c) $\frac{5}{3} = 1\frac{}{3}$

   d) $\frac{9}{5} =$ e) $\frac{10}{9} =$ f) $\frac{13}{8} =$ g) $\frac{7}{5} =$ **BONUS ▶** $\frac{835}{833} =$

5. Each mixed number includes an improper fraction. Change each of them so it includes a proper fraction.

   a) $3\frac{7}{5} = 3 + 1\frac{2}{5} = 4\frac{2}{5}$ b) $2\frac{5}{4} =$ c) $5\frac{10}{7} =$

   d) $4\frac{8}{5} =$ e) $6\frac{11}{6} =$ f) $5\frac{7}{4} =$

6. Add. You will need to change the fraction part of the sum to a proper fraction.

a) $2\frac{3}{5} + 1\frac{4}{5} = 3\frac{7}{5} = 3 + 1\frac{2}{5}$
$= 4\frac{2}{5}$

b) $2\frac{3}{7} + 1\frac{5}{7}$

c) $2\frac{5}{8} + 4\frac{6}{8}$

7. Make the mixed numbers have a denominator equal to the LCD (lowest common denominator) of the fractions. Add the wholes and the parts separately.

a) $2\frac{2}{7} + 4\frac{1}{2}$
$= 2\frac{4}{14} + 4\frac{7}{14} = 6\frac{11}{14}$

b) $2\frac{1}{2} + 1\frac{1}{3}$

c) $4\frac{2}{3} + 1\frac{2}{9}$

8. Add. You will need to change the fraction part of the sum to a proper fraction.

a) $1\frac{1}{2} + 2\frac{2}{3}$

b) $2\frac{3}{5} + \frac{2}{3}$

c) $3\frac{1}{4} + 3\frac{5}{6}$

9. Add. Write your answer in lowest terms.

a) $3\frac{3}{5} + 2\frac{9}{10}$

b) $3\frac{5}{6} + 4\frac{1}{4}$

c) $2\frac{1}{6} + 4\frac{8}{15}$

10. Subtract.

a) $2\frac{3}{4} - \frac{3}{4} = 2$

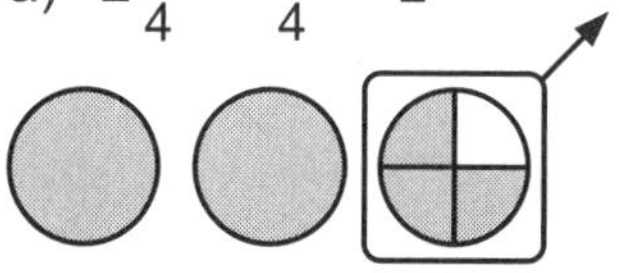

b) $3\frac{1}{4} - 2\frac{1}{4} =$

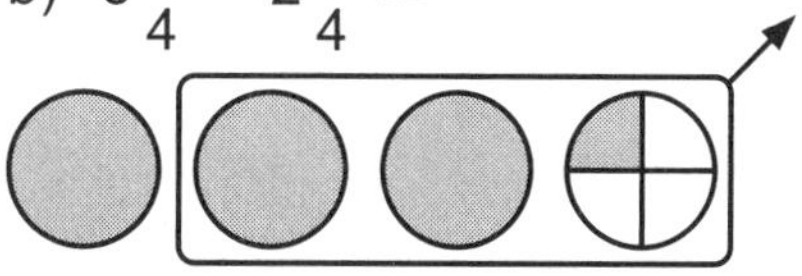

c) $2\frac{1}{2} - 1\frac{1}{2} =$

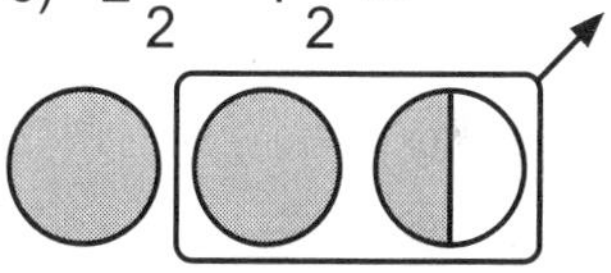

d) $2\frac{3}{4} - 1\frac{1}{4} = 1\frac{2}{4}$

e) $3\frac{5}{8} - 1\frac{2}{8} =$

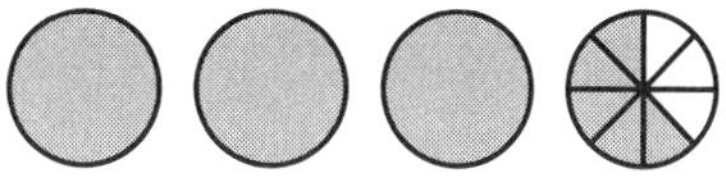

f) $3\frac{7}{8} - 2 =$

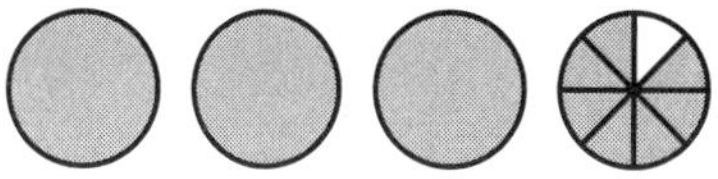

11. Subtract by separating the wholes and the parts.

a) $7\frac{4}{5} - 5\frac{1}{5} = 2\frac{3}{5}$

$7 - 5$ $\qquad$ $\frac{4}{5} - \frac{1}{5}$

b) $7\frac{3}{4} - 5\frac{2}{4} =$

c) $7\frac{5}{8} - 5\frac{2}{8} =$

d) $10\frac{5}{9} - 4\frac{1}{9} =$

e) $9\frac{6}{7} - 4\frac{2}{7} =$

To subtract $9\frac{1}{4} - 5\frac{3}{4}$,

Step 1: Regroup $9\frac{1}{4}$ by subtracting 1 from 9 and adding 1 to $\frac{1}{4}$: $9\frac{1}{4} = 8 + 1\frac{1}{4} = 8\frac{5}{4}$

Step 2: Now you can subtract the wholes and parts separately: $9\frac{1}{4} - 5\frac{3}{4} = 8\frac{5}{4} - 5\frac{3}{4} = 3\frac{2}{4}$

12. Regroup the mixed number by subtracting 1 from the whole number and making an improper fraction.

a) $4\frac{2}{5} = 3\frac{\boxed{7}}{\boxed{5}}$ b) $2\frac{1}{8} = 1\frac{\square}{\square}$ c) $6\frac{3}{7} = 5\frac{\square}{\square}$

d) $7\frac{4}{5} =$ e) $3\frac{2}{7} =$ f) $3\frac{5}{8} =$

13. Subtract by regrouping.

a) $6\frac{1}{3} - 2\frac{2}{3} = 5\frac{4}{3} - 2\frac{2}{3}$

$= 3\frac{2}{3}$

b) $3\frac{2}{5} - 1\frac{4}{5}$ c) $7\frac{1}{8} - 3\frac{6}{8}$

d) $3\frac{4}{6} - 2\frac{5}{6}$ e) $8 - 3\frac{5}{7}$

14. Make the mixed numbers have a denominator equal to the LCD of the fractions. Then subtract the wholes and the parts separately.

a) $5\frac{2}{3} - 3\frac{1}{2} = 5\frac{4}{6} - 3\frac{3}{6}$

$= 2\frac{1}{6}$

b) $7\frac{5}{6} - 2\frac{3}{8}$ c) $5\frac{3}{4} - 4\frac{7}{12}$

d) $7\frac{3}{4} - 5\frac{1}{3}$ e) $8\frac{7}{8} - 3\frac{4}{5}$

15. Subtract. You will need to regroup.

a) $3\frac{1}{5} - 1\frac{3}{4} = 2\frac{6}{5} - 1\frac{3}{4}$

$= 2\frac{24}{20} - 1\frac{15}{20}$

$= 1\frac{9}{20}$

b) $4\frac{2}{5} - 1\frac{5}{8} =$ c) $2\frac{3}{7} - 1\frac{3}{5} =$

16. Add or subtract. Write your answer in lowest terms.

a) $3\frac{1}{2} - 2\frac{3}{4}$ b) $4\frac{2}{5} + 1\frac{9}{10}$ c) $5\frac{3}{8} - 2\frac{13}{24}$

17. Ron made 8 pies for a bake sale. He has $2\frac{3}{8}$ pies left. How many pies did he sell?

18. Niki made 12 pies for a bake sale. She and some friends ate $\frac{3}{4}$ of a pie before the bake sale and then sold $9\frac{7}{8}$ pies. How much pie did they have left?

NS6-23 More Problems and Puzzles

1. Rima needs $\frac{2}{3}$ of a cup of flour for a recipe. She only has $\frac{1}{5}$ of a cup. How much flour is she missing?

2. A recipe for soup calls for $\frac{2}{3}$ of a can of tomatoes. A recipe for spaghetti sauce calls for $\frac{5}{6}$ of a can of tomatoes. Which recipe uses more tomatoes?

3. Find two fractions with different denominators that add to $\frac{11}{12}$.

4. Write five fractions equivalent to -1.

5. Explain the mistake Fatima made in her addition: $\frac{1}{4} + \frac{1}{3} = \frac{2}{7}$.

6. Do you need to compare $\frac{1}{4}$ and $\frac{2}{9}$ in order to compare $-6\frac{1}{4}$ and $-5\frac{2}{9}$? Explain.

7. a) Add $1\frac{1}{3} + 3\frac{1}{2}$ by adding the wholes and parts separately.

b) Complete the fractions: $\frac{4}{3} + \frac{7}{2} = \frac{\quad}{6} + \frac{\quad}{6} = \frac{\quad}{6}$

c) Write your answer to part b) as a mixed number.
Are your answers to parts a) and b) the same?
Why is this the case?

8. Draw a number line from -10 to $+10$ and mark the following numbers on it.

A. 2 less than 0

B. 3 less than 4

C. 3 greater than -1

D. 5 greater than -2

E. halfway between $+2$ and $+6$

F. an equal distance from -8 and -2

G. the same distance from 0 as -9

H. twice as far from 0 as -4, but positive

9. How many negative integers are greater than -6? ____________

10. Circle the temperature that is further from -3°F.

a) -5°F or 5°F

b) 7°F or 10°F

c) 2°F or -9°F

d) 5°F or -10°F

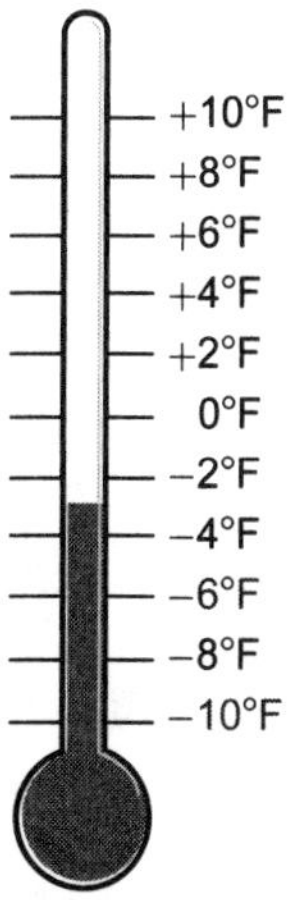

11. a) What fraction of the walls was painted green?

b) What color was used to paint one-fifth of the walls?

c) What color was used to paint one-half of the walls?

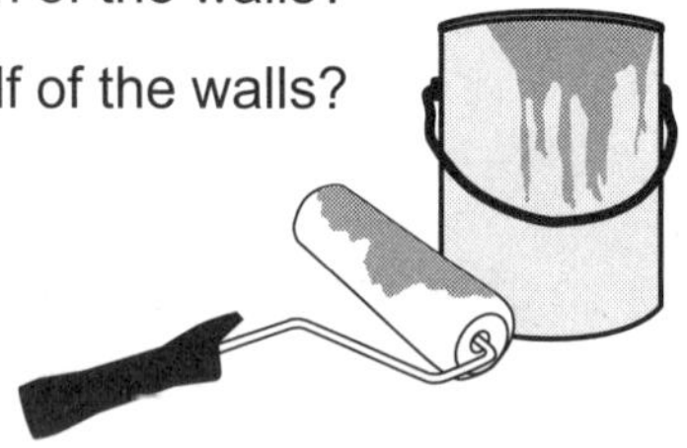

Color	Number of Walls Painted
White	10
Yellow	5
Blue	4
Green	1

12. John, Brian, Eldad, and Ahmed bought some pizzas. They ate the following fractions of a pizza (in no particular order):

$\frac{2}{10}, \frac{2}{5}, \frac{7}{10}, \frac{6}{5}$

There were 5 slices from one pizza left over.

a) How many pizzas did the boys buy?

b) Eldad ate $\frac{1}{5}$ of a pizza. Ahmed ate $\frac{7}{10}$, which was 3 more slices than Brian. John ate more than one pizza. How many slices did each boy eat?

13. The number line shows how many hours the time in each city is ahead of (+) or behind (−) the time in London, England.

Time Zone Number Line

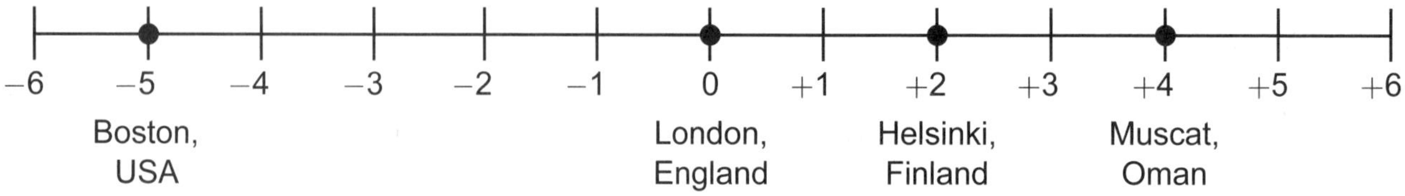

a) How many hours behind London is Boston? __________

b) It is 11 a.m. in London. Use the number line below to find the time in Boston. __________

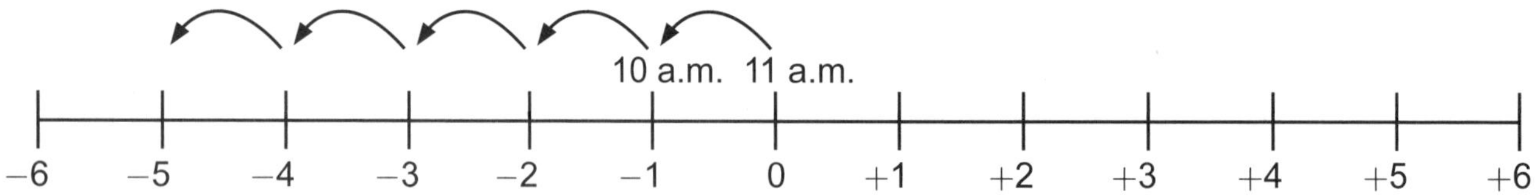

c) It is 1 p.m. in London. Draw a number line to find the time in Muscat.

d) There is a figure skating event being held in Helsinki at 8 p.m. Brian lives in Boston. What time should he turn on his television to watch the event live?

EE6-1 Numerical Expressions

A **numerical expression** is a combination of numbers, operation signs, and sometimes brackets that represents a quantity.

Example: These numerical expressions all represent 10:

$7 + 3$ $\quad$ $12 - 2$ $\quad$ $100 \div 10$ $\quad$ $(4 + 1) \times 2$

1. Calculate each numerical expression.

a) $1 + 3 + 4$ _____ b) 3×4 _____ c) $2 \times 2 \times 2$ _____

d) $(1 + 3) \times 4$ _____ e) $3 + (4 \div 2)$ _____ f) $(4 \times 3) \div 2$ _____

An **equation** is a statement that has two equal expressions separated by an equal sign.

Example: $12 - 2 = 100 \div 10$

2. a) Circle two expressions in Question 1 that represent the same number.

b) Write an equation using those two expressions.

_______________ = _______________

3. Verify that each equation is true.

a) $(4 + 3) \times 2 = (5 \times 3) - 1$

$(4 + 3) \times 2$ and $(5 \times 3) - 1$

$= 7 \times 2$ $\quad$ $= 15 - 1$

$= 14$ $\quad$ $= 14$

b) $3 \times 4 \times 5 = 6 \times 10$

c) $5 + 12 = (5 + 1) + (12 - 1)$

d) $5 + 12 = (5 + 2) + (12 - 2)$

BONUS ▶ Add brackets where necessary to the equation to make it true.

a) $6 - 2 \times 2 = 8$

b) $6 - 2 \times 2 = 2$

c) $5 \times 4 - 3 = 5$

d) $16 \div 2 \times 2 = 4$

e) $8 - 4 \times 2 = 0$

f) $6 \times 4 \div 2 = 12$

EE6-2 Unknown Quantities

1. Some apples are inside a box and some are outside the box. The total number of apples is shown. Draw the missing apples in the box. The first one is done for you.

a) 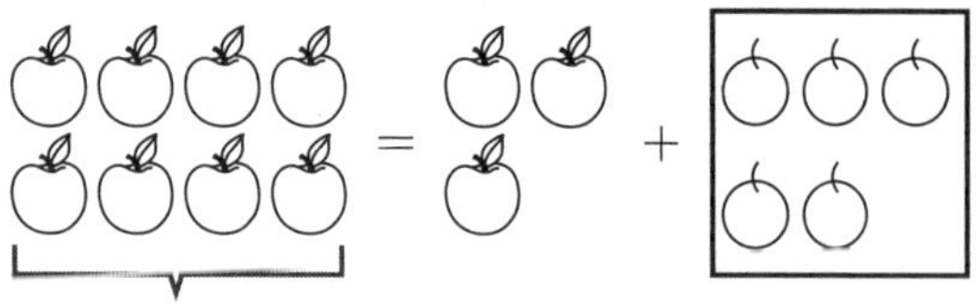

total number of apples

b) 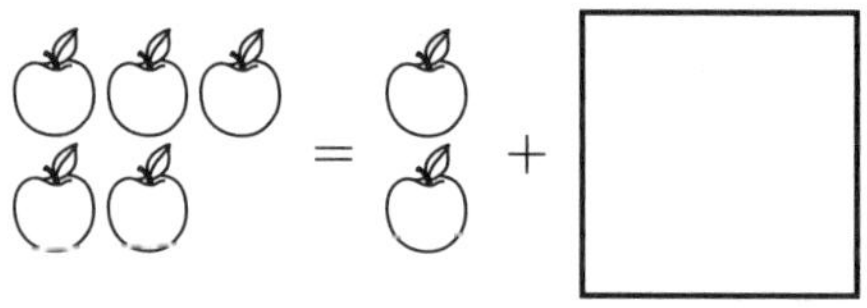

c) 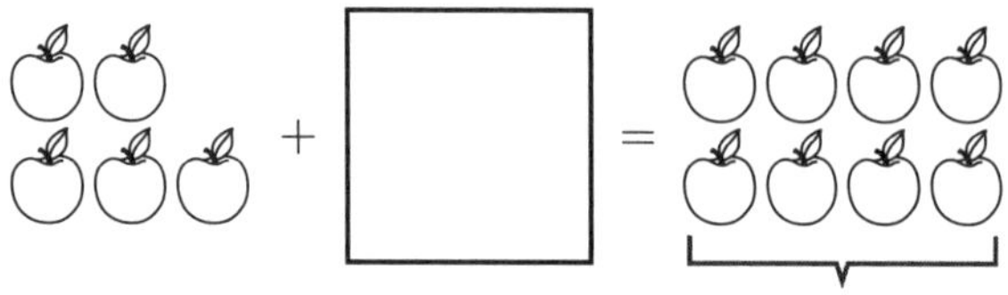

total number of apples

d) 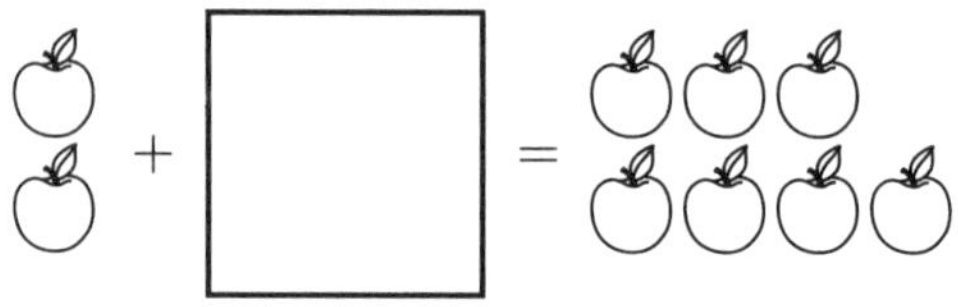

2. Draw the missing apples in the box. Then write an equation (with numbers) to represent the picture.

a) 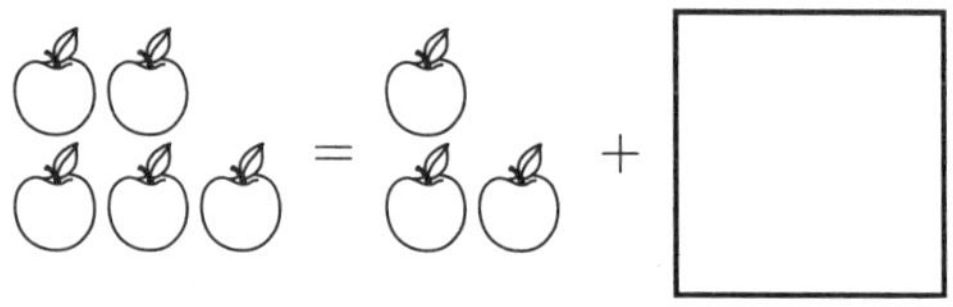

$\underline{\ 5\ } = \underline{\ 3\ } + \square$

b) 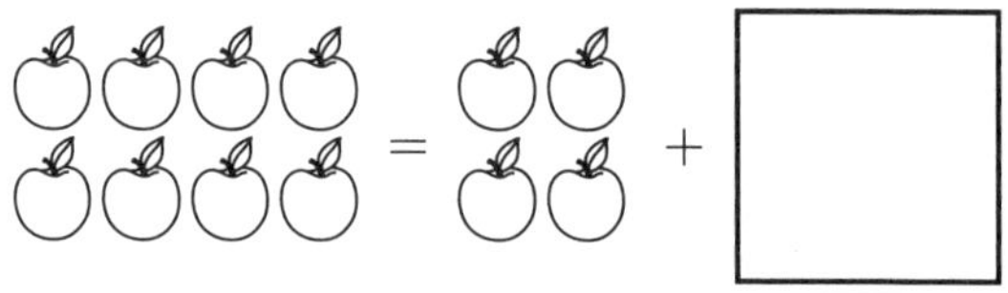

$\underline{\qquad} = \underline{\qquad} + \square$

c) 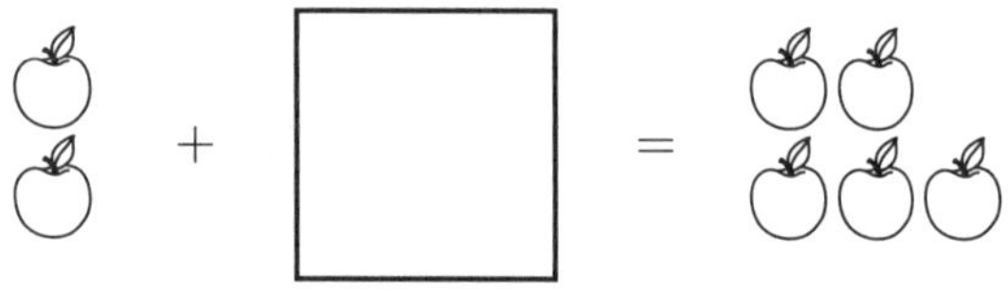

$\underline{\qquad} + \square = \underline{\qquad}$

d) 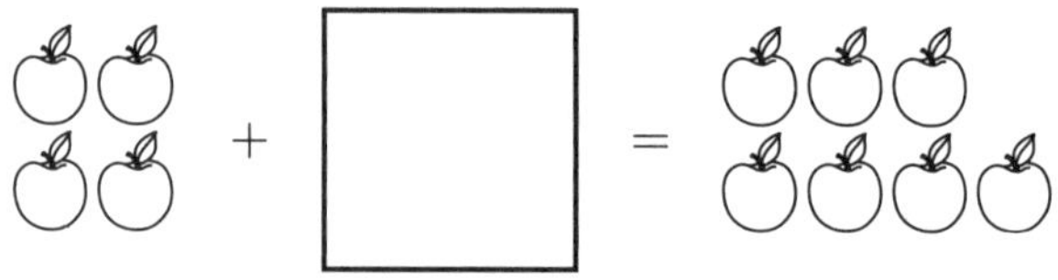

$\underline{\qquad} + \square = \underline{\qquad}$

3. Write an equation for each situation. (Use a box for the unknown quantity.)

a) There are 9 apples altogether.
Five are outside of a box.
How many are inside?
$9 = 5 + \square$

b) There are 7 apples altogether.
Three are outside of a box.
How many are inside?
____

c) There are 8 pears altogether.
Three are inside a bag.
How many are outside?
____

d) Ten students are at the library.
Two are in the computer room.
How many are outside?
____

4. Tim took some apples from a box. Show how many apples were in the box originally.

a) 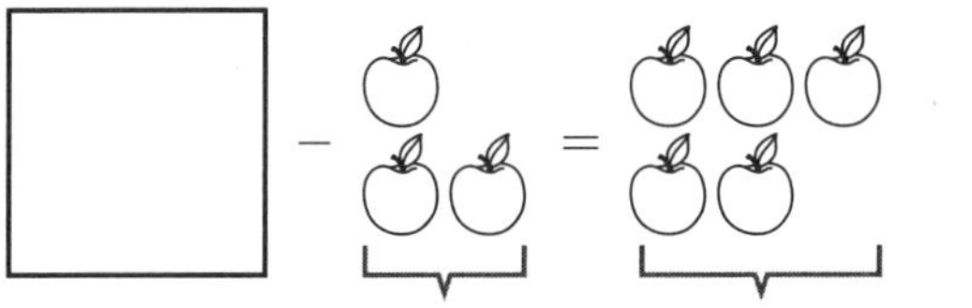

Tim took away this many. *This is how many were left.*

b) 

c) 

d) 

5. Show how many apples were in the box originally. Then write an equation to represent the picture.

a) 

$\square - 3 = 4$

b) 

$\square - 2 = 6$

6. Find the number that makes the equation true and write it in the box.

a) $\square + 4 = 7$

b) $\square + 3 = 6$

c) $\square + 5 = 9$

d) $9 - \square = 6$

e) $17 - \square = 13$

f) $11 - \square = 9$

g) $2 \times \square = 6$

h) $3 \times \square = 15$

i) $3 \times \square = 9$

j) $\square \div 2 = 4$

k) $\square \div 5 = 3$

l) $\square \div 3 = 4$

m) $5 + 4 = 6 + \square$

n) $10 - 4 = \square + 5$

o) $2 = 8 - \square$

BONUS ▶ Put the same number in both boxes to make the equation true.

a) $\square + 2 = 8 - \square$

b) $\square \div 2 = \square - 2$

c) $\square \times \square = 9$

7. Find two different answers for the equation. Put the same number in the same shapes.

$\triangle + \triangle + \bigcirc = 5$

$\square + \square + \diamond = 5$

EE6-3 Variables

1. Look at the sign at right, then write a numerical expression for the cost of renting skates for…

a) 2 hours: 3×2 b) 5 hours: ________

c) 6 hours: ________ d) 8 hours: ________

A **variable** is a letter or symbol (such as x, n, or H) that represents a number.

To make an **algebraic expression**, replace some numbers in a numerical expression with variables.

Examples of algebraic expressions: $x + 1$ $3 + 4 \times T$ $2 + t - 3 \times h$

2. Write an expression for the distance a car would travel at the given speed and time.

a) Speed: 60 mi per hour
Time: 2 hours
Distance: __________ mi

b) Speed: 80 km per hour
Time: 3 hours
Distance: __________ km

c) Speed: 70 km per hour
Time: h hours
Distance: __________ km

In the product of a number and a variable, the multiplication sign is usually dropped.

Examples: $3 \times T$ can be written $3T$ and $5 \times z$ can be written $5z$.

3. Look at the sign at right, then write an algebraic expression for the cost of renting skis for…

a) h hours: $5 \times h$ or $5h$ b) t hours: _______ or _____

c) x hours: _______ or _____ d) n hours: _______ or _____

4. Write an equation that tells you the relationship between the numbers in Column A and Column B.

a)

A	B
1	4
2	5
3	6

$A + 3 = B$

b)

A	B
1	2
2	4
3	6

$2 \times A = B$
or $2A = B$

c)

A	B
1	3
2	4
3	5

____

d)

A	B
1	3
2	6
3	9

____
____

e)

A	B
1	5
2	10
3	15

____
____

5. Circle the tables in Question 4 that are ratio tables.

6. Write an equation. Use the variable x for the number of apples in the box.

a) There are 10 apples altogether. Four are outside of a box.

____

b) There are 12 apples altogether. Seven are outside of a box.

____

> When replacing a variable with a number, we use brackets.
>
> Example: Replacing n with 7 in the expression $3n$ gives $3(7)$, which is another way to write 3×7.

7. Write the number 2 in the brackets and evaluate.

a) $5\,(\,2\,) =$ $\underline{5 \times 2}$ $=$ $\underline{10}$

b) $3\,(\quad) =$ _____ $=$ _____

c) $4\,(\quad) =$ _____ $=$ _____

d) $2\,(\quad) + 5$

$=$ _____ $=$ _____

$=$ _____

e) $4\,(\quad) - 2$

$=$ _____ $=$ _____

$=$ _____

f) $6\,(\quad) + 3$

$=$ _____ $=$ _____

$=$ _____

8. Replace n with 2 in each expression and evaluate.

a) $4n + 3$

$= 4(2) + 3$

$= 8 + 3$

$= 11$

b) $5n + 1$

c) $3n - 2$

d) $2n + 3$

e) $4n - 3$

f) $2n - 4$

9. Replace the variable with the given number and evaluate.

a) $5h + 2, \quad h = 3$

$5\,(3) + 2$

$= 15 + 2$

$= 17$

b) $2n + 3, \quad n = 6$

c) $5t - 2, \quad t = 4$

d) $3m + 9, \quad m = 8$

e) $9 - z, \quad z = 4$

f) $3n + 2, \quad n = 5$

10. Evaluate each expression.

a) $2n + 3, \quad n = 5$

$2(5) + 3$

$= 10 + 3 = 13$

b) $2t + 3, \quad t = 5$

c) $2w + 3, \quad w = 5$

11. What do you notice about your answers to Question 10? ____________________

Why is that so? ____________________

____

EE6-4 Modeling Equations

1. Each bag contains the same unknown number of apples. Let x stand for the number of apples in one bag. Write a mathematical expression for the total number of apples.

a)	b)	c)
 $x + 2$	 ________	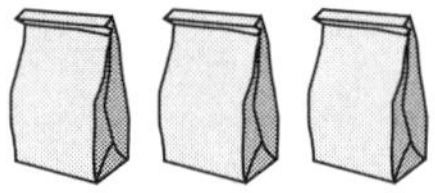 ________

2. Write an **expression** for the total number of apples. Write an **equation** by making the expression equal to the total number of apples.

a) There are **7 apples** in total.

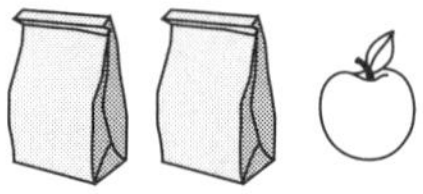

Expression $2x + 1$

Equation $2x + 1 = 7$

b) There are **10 apples** in total.

Expression ________

Equation ________

c) There are **15 apples** in total.

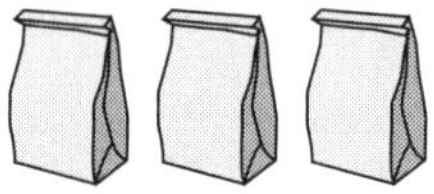

Expression ________

Equation ________

3. Write an equation and find the number of apples in each bag.

a) 9 apples in total

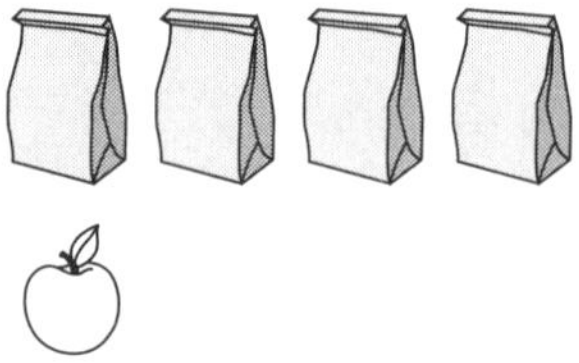

Equation $4x + 1 = 9$

2 apples in each bag

b) 13 apples in total

Equation ________

_____ apples in each bag

c) 17 apples in total

Equation ________

_____ apples in each bag

d) 11 apples in total

Equation ________

_____ apples in each bag

e) 14 apples in total

Equation ________

_____ apples in each bag

f) 31 apples in total

Equation ________

_____ apples in each bag

4. Does this type of model work for the equation $3x - 4 = 14$? Explain in your notebook.

EE6-5 Solving Equations with Balances

1. The scales are balanced. Cross out the same number of apples on each side to find how many apples are in the bag.

a)

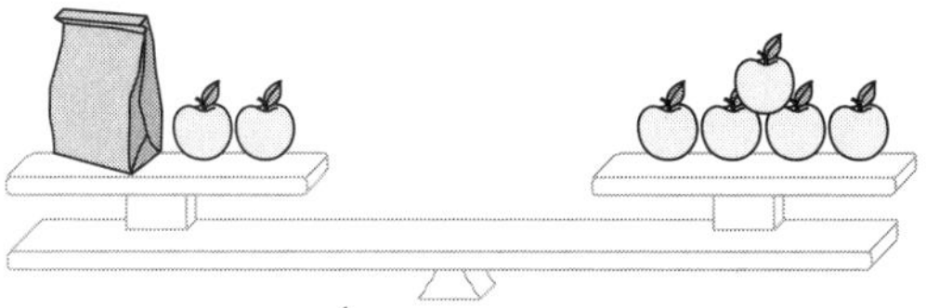

There are _____apples in the bag.

b)

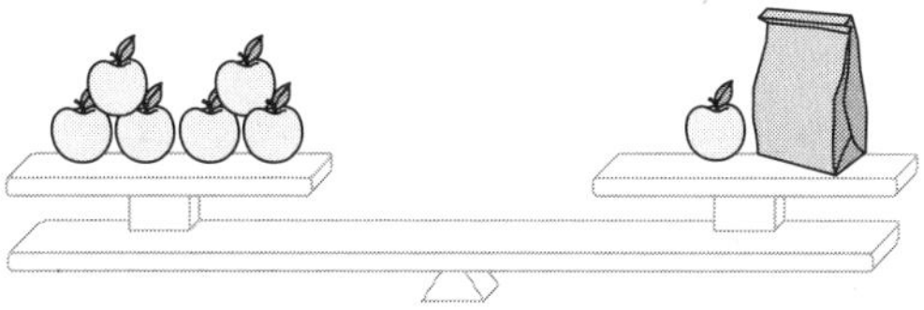

There are _____apples in the bag.

An equation is like balanced scales. An equal sign between the sides shows that they are equal.

To solve $x + 4 = 10$, subtract 4 from both sides of the equation.

$x + 4 = 10$

$\underline{-4 \quad -4}$

$x = 6$

2. Subtract 4 from both sides of the equation.

a) $x + 4 = 12$
$\underline{-4 \quad -4}$
$x =$ [8]

b) $x + 4 = 9$
$\underline{-4 \quad -4}$
$x =$ [ ]

c) $14 = x + 4$
$\underline{-4 \quad -4}$
[ ] $= x$

d) $56 = x + 4$
$\underline{-4 \quad -4}$
[ ] $= x$

3. Subtract the same number from both sides of the equation.

a) $x + 15 = 32$
$\underline{-15 \quad -15}$
$x =$ [ ]

b) $x + 43 = 59$
$\underline{-43 \quad -43}$
$x =$ [ ]

c) $37 = x + 19$
$\underline{-19 \quad -19}$
[ ] $= x$

d) $86 = x + 38$
$\underline{-38 \quad -38}$
[ ] $= x$

4. Which number will you subtract from both sides to solve the equation? Subtract the number and solve the equation.

a) $x + 5 = 12$
$-$ [5] $\quad -$ [ ]
$x =$ [ ]

b) $x + 14 = 29$
$-$ [ ] $\quad -$ [ ]
$x =$ [ ]

c) $14 = x + 8$
$-$ [ ] $\quad -$ [ ]
[ ] $= x$

d) $53 = x + 24$
$-$ [ ] $\quad -$ [ ]
[ ] $= x$

5. Solve the equation by subtracting the same number from both sides.

a) $x + 15 = 33$
$\underline{-15 \quad -15}$
$x = 18$

b) $x + 53 = 75$

c) $44 = x + 8$

d) $42 + x = 64$

6. The scales are balanced. All bags in the same picture have the same number of apples. How many apples are in each bag?

a) 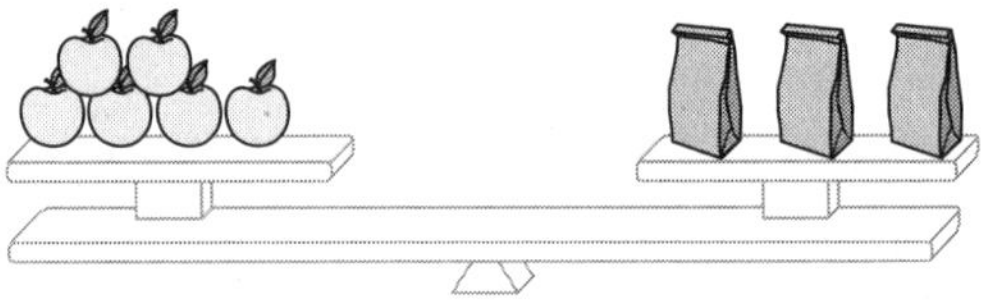

There are ______ apples in each bag.

b) 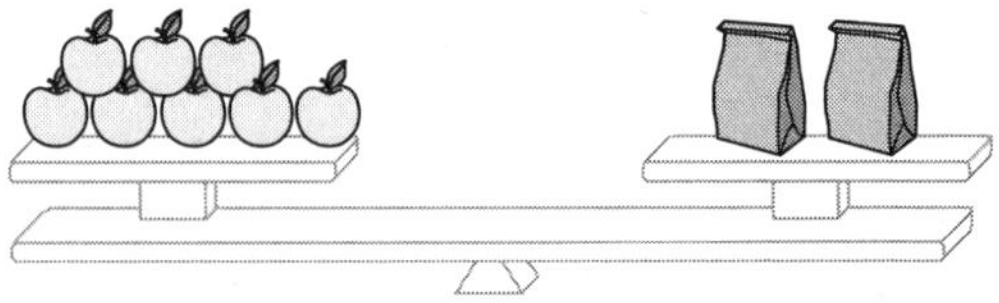

There are ______ apples in each bag.

7. Complete the picture and solve the equation. The first one is started for you.

a) $12 = 3 \times b$

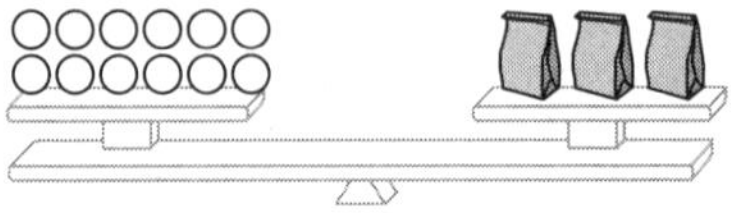

$b =$ ______

b) $2 \times b = 10$

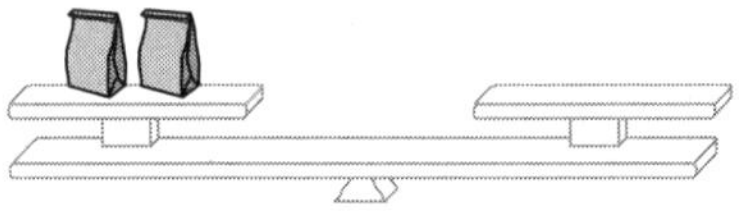

$b =$ ______

c) $4 \times b = 8$

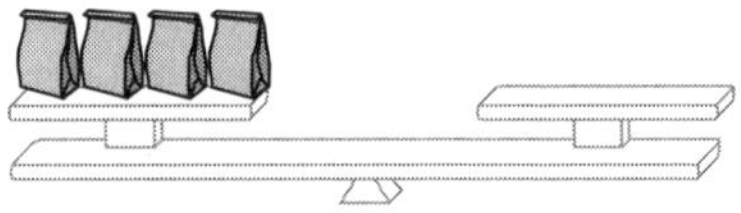

$b =$ ______

8. Evaluate.

a) $(5 \times 3) \div 3$

$=$ ______ $\div 3$

$=$ ______

b) $(3 \times 6) \div 6$

$=$ ______ $\div 6$

$=$ ______

c) $(8 \times 7) \div 7$

$=$ ______ $\div 7$

$=$ ______

Multiplying and dividing by the same number gets you back to the number you started with.

Example: $4 \times 3 = 12$, so $12 \div 3 = 4$ or $(4 \times 3) \div 3 = 4$

You can do the same with unknown numbers and letters.

Example:  $\times 3 =$   $\div 3 =$ 

( $\times 3) \div 3 =$  or $(b \times 3) \div 3 = b$

9. What number will you divide the expression by to get back to b?

a) $(b \times 3) \div$ ______ $= b$

b) $(b \times 8) \div$ ______ $= b$

c) $(b \times 5) \div$ ______ $= b$

10. a) Divide both sides by the same number to solve the equation.

i) $b \times 3 = 15$

$b \times 3 \div 3 = 15 \div 3$

$b = 5$

ii) $b \times 5 = 20$

iii) $b \times 2 = 16$

b) Use the picture to explain why you can divide both sides by 3 to solve the equation $b \times 3 = 6$.

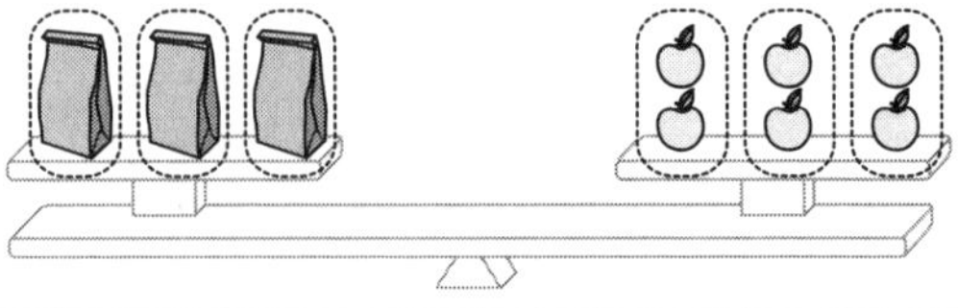

EE6-6 Solving Equations—Guess and Check

Finding the value of a variable that makes an equation true is called solving for the variable. Sindi uses a table to solve $2x + 1 = 7$.

x	$2x + 1$	Is equation true?
1	3	✗
2	5	✗
3	7	✓

So $x = 3$ makes the equation true.

1. Complete the table, then solve for x.

a) $3x + 2 = 14$

x	$3x + 2$	True?
1	*$3(1) + 2 = 5$*	✗
2	*$3(2) + 2 = 8$*	✗

So $x =$ _____

b) $4x + 3 = 23$

x	$4x + 3$	True?
1	*$4(1) + 3 = 7$*	✗

So $x =$ _____

c) $5x - 2 = 13$

x	$5x - 2$	True?

So $x =$ _____

2. Replace n with 5 and say whether 5 is too high or too low.
Then try a lower or higher number.

a) $3n + 2 = 20$

n	$3n + 2$	Answer
5	*$3(5) + 2$*	*17*

5 is *too low*

b) $5n + 1 = 21$

n	$5n + 1$	Answer
5	*$5(5) + 1$*	

5 is ________

c) $2n + 3 = 15$

n	$2n + 3$	Answer
5		

5 is ________

d) $4n + 3 = 27$

n	$4n + 3$	Answer
5		

5 is _____

e) $5n - 6 = 14$

n	$5n - 6$	Answer
5	*$5(5) - 6$*	

5 is _____

f) $3n - 3 = 15$

n	$3n - 3$	Answer
5		

5 is _____

3. Solve for n by guessing small values for n, checking, and revising.

a) $3n + 2 = 14$
b) $5n - 2 = 13$
c) $4n - 1 = 15$
d) $6n - 5 = 31$
e) $7n - 2 = 19$
f) $2n + 3 = 9$

EE6-7 Equations Involving Fractions

There are 6 apples. Some are in a bag and the other 4 are on a table.

David uses the equation $x + 4 = 6$ to find out how many apples are in the bag.
To solve $x + 4 = 6$, subtract 4 from both sides of the equation.

$$\begin{aligned} x + 4 &= 6 \\ -4 &= -4 \\ \hline x &= 2 \end{aligned}$$

← *2 apples are in the bag*

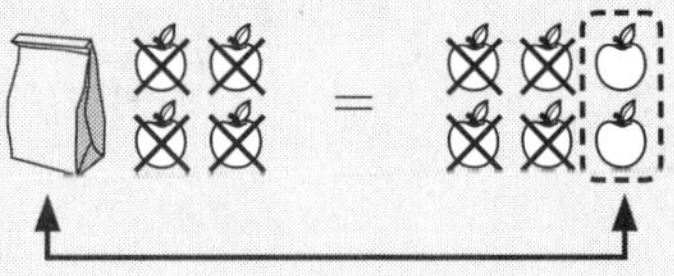

1. Write an equation and then find the number of apples in the bag by solving the equation.

a) 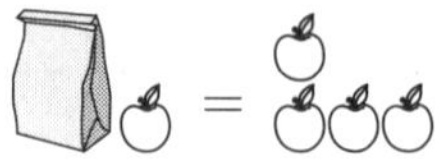

$$\begin{aligned} x + 1 &= 4 \\ -1 &= -1 \\ \hline x &= 3 \end{aligned}$$

b) 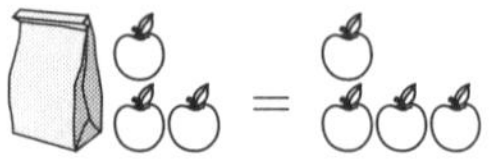

c) 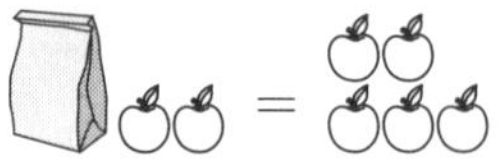

d) 

Diba's mother cut a pizza into 6 pieces. She put away some pieces in the fridge and left 4 pieces on the kitchen table.

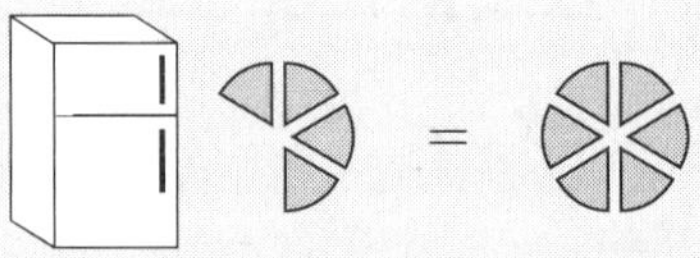

Diba uses the equation $x + \frac{4}{6} = \frac{6}{6}$ to find out what fraction of the whole pizza is in the fridge.

$$\begin{aligned} x + \frac{4}{6} &= \frac{6}{6} \\ -\frac{4}{6} &= -\frac{4}{6} \\ \hline x &= \frac{2}{6} \end{aligned}$$

← $\frac{2}{6}$ *of the whole pizza is in the fridge*

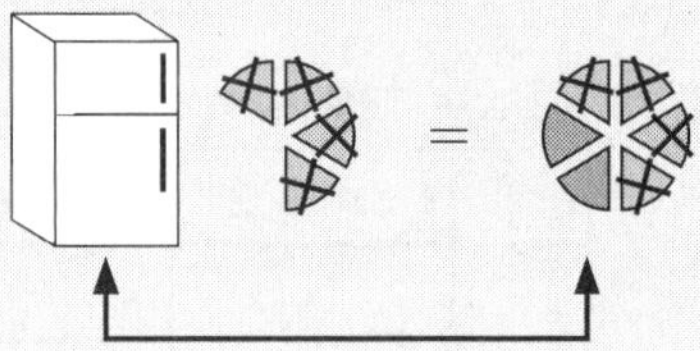

2. Subtract $\frac{1}{6}$ from both sides of the equation.

a) $x + \frac{1}{6} = \frac{6}{6}$

$-\frac{1}{6} \quad -\frac{1}{6}$

$x = \boxed{\frac{5}{6}}$

b) $x + \frac{1}{6} = \frac{3}{6}$

$-\frac{1}{6} \quad -\frac{1}{6}$

$x = \boxed{}$

c) $\frac{4}{6} = x + \frac{1}{6}$

$-\frac{1}{6} \quad -\frac{1}{6}$

$\boxed{} = x$

d) $\frac{5}{6} = x + \frac{1}{6}$

$-\frac{1}{6} \quad -\frac{1}{6}$

$\boxed{} = x$

3. Solve the equation by subtracting the same number from both sides.

a) $x + \frac{1}{5} = \frac{3}{5}$

$-\frac{1}{5} \quad -\frac{1}{5}$

$x = \frac{2}{5}$

b) $x + \frac{3}{7} = \frac{5}{7}$

c) $\frac{8}{10} = x + \frac{7}{10}$

BONUS ▶ $\frac{2}{3} = x + \frac{2}{3}$

4. Replace n with $\frac{1}{4}$ in the expression, then evaluate. Reduce your answer to the lowest terms.

a) $n + \frac{1}{4}$

$= \frac{1}{4} + \frac{1}{4}$

$= \frac{2}{4}$

$= \frac{1}{2}$

b) $n + \frac{3}{4}$

c) $\frac{3}{4} - n$

d) $n - \frac{1}{4}$

5. Replace the variable with the given number, then evaluate.

a) $h + 2\frac{1}{5}$, $h = \frac{2}{5}$

$= \frac{2}{5} + 2\frac{1}{5}$

$= 2\frac{3}{5}$

b) $n + 1\frac{2}{10}$, $n = \frac{3}{10}$

c) $t - \frac{2}{7}$, $t = 3\frac{4}{7}$

d) $m + 2\frac{1}{5}$, $m = \frac{3}{5}$

e) $1\frac{5}{6} - z$, $z = \frac{1}{6}$

f) $n + 5\frac{1}{4}$, $n = 1\frac{3}{4}$

g) $n - 1\frac{1}{10}$, $n = 3\frac{2}{5}$

h) $3\frac{1}{4} - n$, $n = 1\frac{1}{2}$

6. Solve the equation by subtracting or adding the same number to both sides.

a) $x + 1\frac{1}{5} = 4\frac{3}{5}$

$\quad -1\frac{1}{5} \quad -1\frac{1}{5}$

$x = 3\frac{2}{5}$

b) $x + 2\frac{3}{7} = 3\frac{5}{7}$

c) $\frac{3}{4} = x + \frac{1}{2}$

d) $2\frac{1}{5} + x = 4\frac{2}{5}$

e) $x - 3\frac{1}{2} = 1\frac{1}{2}$

f) $x - 2\frac{3}{5} = 3\frac{1}{10}$

g) $\frac{8}{6} = x - \frac{2}{3}$

BONUS ▶ $3\frac{2}{5} + x = 4\frac{3}{10}$

NS6-24 Decimal Fractions

In a **decimal fraction**, the denominator is a power of ten.

10, 100, 1,000, 10,000, ... are **powers of 10.**
Example: $\frac{8}{100}$ is a decimal fraction.

5, 26, 111, 700, ... are **not powers of 10.**
Example: $\frac{8}{700}$ is not a decimal fraction.

1. Circle the decimal fractions.

$\frac{3}{10}$ $\frac{25}{100}$ $\frac{333}{1,000}$ $\frac{7}{29}$ $\frac{1}{100}$ $\frac{100}{13}$ $\frac{4}{1,000}$ $\frac{48}{10}$ $\frac{16}{101}$ $\frac{1}{70}$

There are 100 squares on a **hundredths grid.**

1 column $= \frac{10}{100} = \frac{1}{10} =$ 1 tenth

1 square $= \frac{1}{100} =$ 1 hundredth

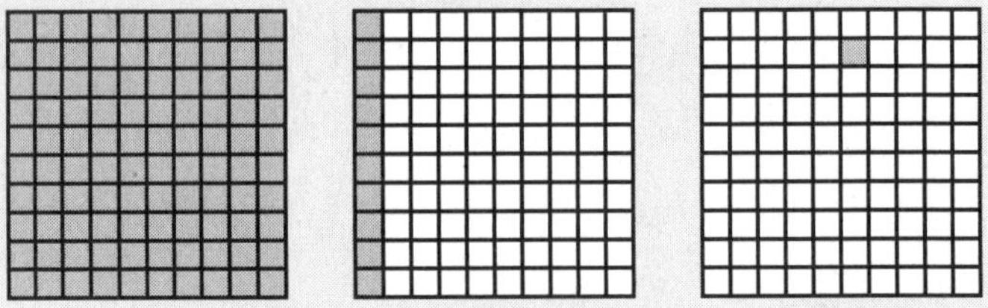

1 one   1 tenth   1 hundredth

2. Write two equivalent fractions for the shaded part of the grid.

a) 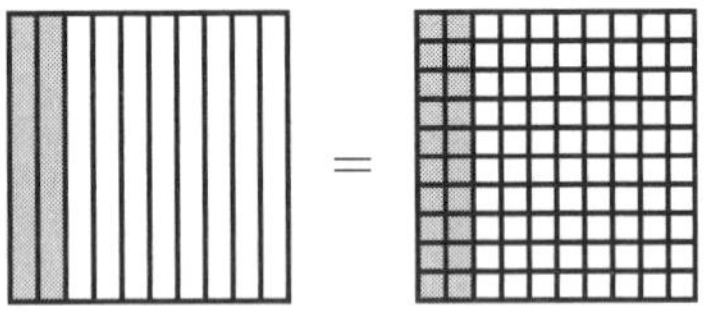

$\frac{2}{10} = \frac{\_\_}{100}$

b) 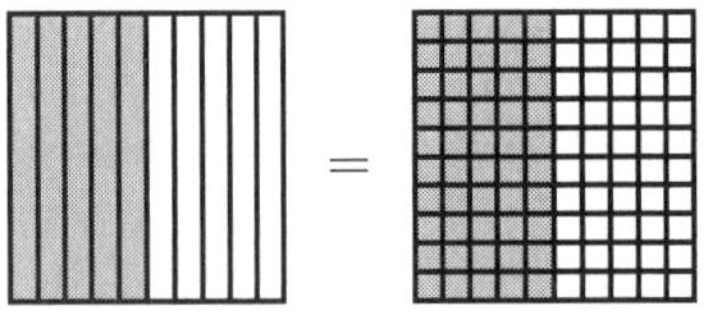

$\frac{\_\_}{10} = \frac{\_\_}{100}$

c) 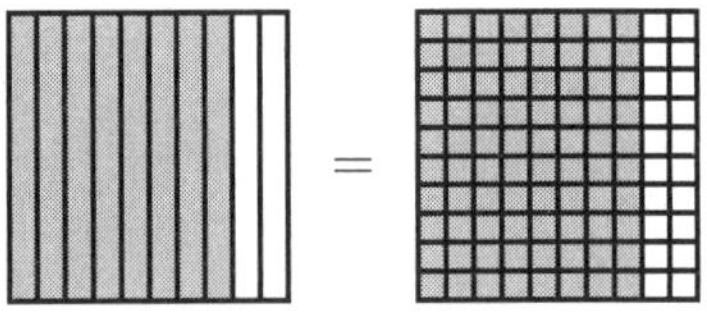

$\frac{\_\_}{10} = \frac{\_\_}{100}$

3. Write an equivalent fraction with denominator 100.

a) $\frac{8 \times 10}{10 \times 10} = \frac{\_\_}{100}$

b) $\frac{7 \times 10}{10 \times 10} = \frac{\_\_}{100}$

c) $\frac{4}{10} = \frac{\_\_}{100}$

d) $\frac{5}{10} = \_\_$

e) $\frac{9}{10} = \_\_$

f) $\frac{2}{10} = \_\_$

4. Write an equivalent fraction with denominator 1,000.

a) $\frac{8 \times 10}{100 \times 10} = \frac{\_\_}{1,000}$

b) $\frac{7}{100} = \frac{\_\_}{1,000}$

c) $\frac{2}{100} = \frac{\_\_}{1,000}$

d) $\frac{9 \times 100}{10 \times 100} = \frac{\_\_}{1,000}$

e) $\frac{7}{10} = \frac{\_\_}{1,000}$

f) $\frac{4}{10} = \frac{\_\_}{1,000}$

g) $\frac{6}{10} = \_\_$

h) $\frac{5}{100} = \_\_$

i) $\frac{1}{100} = \_\_$

5. Write the equivalent hundredths and thousandths.

Tenths	$\frac{7}{10}$	$\frac{3}{10}$	$\frac{8}{10}$	$\frac{2}{10}$	$\frac{9}{10}$	$\frac{10}{10}$
Hundredths						
Thousandths						

1 more zero: $\frac{3}{10} \rightarrow \frac{30}{100}$ (1 more zero)

1 more zero: $\frac{4}{100} \rightarrow \frac{40}{1,000}$ (1 more zero)

2 more zeros: $\frac{7}{10} \rightarrow \frac{700}{1,000}$ (2 more zeros)

6. How many zeros were added to the denominator? Add the same number of zeros to the numerator.

a) $\frac{8}{10} = \frac{\quad}{100}$ b) $\frac{90}{100} = \frac{\quad}{1,000}$ c) $\frac{7}{100} = \frac{\quad}{1,000}$ d) $\frac{4}{10} = \frac{\quad}{1,000}$

e) $\frac{6}{10} = \frac{\quad}{1,000}$ f) $\frac{3}{10} = \frac{\quad}{100}$ **BONUS▸** $\frac{40}{1,000} = \frac{\quad}{10,000,000}$

7. Write the decimal fraction shown by the shaded part of the grid in four ways.

	$\frac{\quad}{\mathbf{100}}$	$\frac{\quad}{\mathbf{10}} + \frac{\quad}{\mathbf{100}}$	____ **hundredths**	____ **tenths** ____ **hundredths**
a) 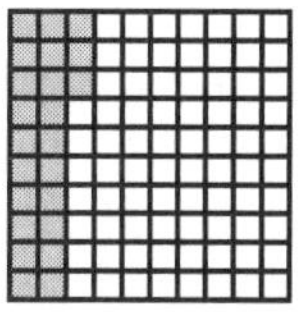	$\frac{23}{100}$	$\frac{2}{10} + \frac{3}{100}$	__23__ hundredths	__2__ tenths __3__ hundredths
b) 			____ hundredths	____ tenths ____ hundredths
c) 			____ hundredths	____ tenths ____ hundredths

To add $\frac{9}{10} + \frac{4}{100} + \frac{8}{1{,}000}$, change all fractions to thousandths.

$$\frac{9 \times 100}{10 \times 100} + \frac{4 \times 10}{100 \times 10} + \frac{8}{1{,}000} = \frac{900}{1{,}000} + \frac{40}{1{,}000} + \frac{8}{1{,}000} = \frac{948}{1{,}000}$$

8. Add. Show your work.

a) $\frac{5 \times 100}{10 \times 100} + \frac{3 \times 10}{100 \times 10} + \frac{7}{1{,}000}$

$= \frac{500}{1{,}000} + \frac{30}{1{,}000} + \frac{7}{1{,}000} = \frac{537}{1{,}000}$

b) $\frac{3 \times 100}{10 \times 100} + \frac{8 \times 10}{100 \times 10} + \frac{6}{1{,}000}$

$= \frac{}{1{,}000} + \frac{}{1{,}000} + \frac{}{1{,}000} = \frac{}{1{,}000}$

c) $\frac{2 \times}{10 \times} + \frac{9 \times}{100 \times} + \frac{4}{1{,}000}$

$= \frac{}{1{,}000} + \frac{}{1{,}000} + \frac{}{1{,}000} = \frac{}{1{,}000}$

d) $\frac{6}{10} + \frac{1}{100} + \frac{5}{1{,}000}$

$= \frac{}{1{,}000} + \frac{}{1{,}000} + \frac{}{1{,}000} = \frac{}{1{,}000}$

9. Write the sum as a sum of fractions with the same denominator.

a) $\frac{1}{10} + \frac{6}{100} + \frac{2}{1{,}000} = \frac{100}{1{,}000} + \frac{60}{1{,}000} + \frac{2}{1{,}000} = \frac{162}{1{,}000}$

b) $\frac{2}{10} + \frac{7}{100} + \frac{5}{1{,}000} =$

c) $\frac{6}{10} + \frac{3}{100} + \frac{4}{1{,}000} =$

10. Add the tenths and hundredths in your head.

a) $\frac{1}{10} + \frac{9}{100} =$ ______

b) $\frac{6}{10} + \frac{7}{100} =$ ______

c) $\frac{7}{10} + \frac{2}{100} =$ ______

d) $\frac{1}{10} + \frac{3}{100} =$ ______

11. Add in your head.

a) $\frac{9}{10} + \frac{6}{100} + \frac{7}{1{,}000} =$

b) $\frac{4}{10} + \frac{4}{100} + \frac{4}{1{,}000} =$

c) $\frac{5}{10} + \frac{6}{1{,}000} =$

d) $\frac{1}{100} + \frac{9}{1{,}000} =$

e) $\frac{9}{100} + \frac{1}{1{,}000} =$

f) $\frac{8}{10} + \frac{8}{1{,}000} =$

NS6-25 Place Value and Decimals

Decimals are a way to record place values based on decimal fractions.

365 → 3 hundreds + 6 tens + 5 ones

0.365 → 3 tenths + 6 hundredths + 5 thousandths

$$\frac{3}{10} + \frac{6}{100} + \frac{5}{1{,}000}$$

1. Write the decimal as a sum of a whole number and decimal fractions.

a) $2.17 = \underline{\ 2\ } + \frac{1}{10} + \frac{7}{100}$

b) $3.24 = \underline{\qquad} + \frac{\quad}{10} + \frac{\quad}{100}$

c) $5.79 = \underline{\qquad} + \frac{\quad}{10} + \frac{\quad}{100}$

d) $6.87 = \underline{\qquad} + \frac{\quad}{10} + \frac{\quad}{100}$

e) $0.38 = \underline{\qquad} + \frac{\quad}{10} + \frac{\quad}{100}$

f) $9.51 = \underline{\qquad} + \frac{\quad}{10} + \frac{\quad}{100}$

g) $3.206 = \underline{\qquad} + \frac{\quad}{10} + \frac{\quad}{100} + \frac{\quad}{1{,}000}$

h) $1.532 = \underline{\qquad} + \frac{\quad}{10} + \frac{\quad}{100} + \frac{\quad}{1{,}000}$

i) $6.521 = \underline{\qquad} + \frac{\quad}{10} + \frac{\quad}{100} + \frac{\quad}{1{,}000}$

j) $7.025 = \underline{\qquad} + \frac{\quad}{10} + \frac{\quad}{100} + \frac{\quad}{1{,}000}$

2. Write the decimal as a sum of a whole number and decimal fractions.
Do not write the fractions with a numerator of 0.

a) $4.017 = 4 + \frac{1}{100} + \frac{7}{1{,}000}$

b) $7.204 = \qquad + \frac{\quad}{10} + \frac{\quad}{1{,}000}$

c) 0.709 =

d) 6.087 =

e) 0.008 =

f) 4.001 =

3. What is the value of the 9 in each decimal? Write the answer two ways.

a) 0.497 $\frac{9}{100}$ or *9 hundredths*

b) 8.439 $\frac{9}{\quad}$ or *9* ______________

c) 1.923 $\frac{9}{\quad}$ or ______________

d) 0.907 $\frac{9}{\quad}$ or ______________

e) 0.479 ______ or ______________

f) 5.491 ______ or ______________

g) 3.904 ______ or ______________

h) 7.609 ______ or ______________

4. Write the decimal fractions in the place value chart, then write the number as a decimal.

a) $\frac{3}{10} = 0.\underline{\ 3\ }$

Ones	Tenths
0 •	3

b) $\frac{6}{10} = 0.\_\_\_$

Ones	Tenths
•	

c) $\frac{6}{10} + \frac{5}{100} = \underline{\ 0\ }.\_\_\_\ \_\_\_$

Ones	Tenths	Hundredths
0 •		

d) $\frac{5}{10} + \frac{4}{100} = \_\_\_.\_\_\_\ \_\_\_$

Ones	Tenths	Hundredths
•		

e) $\frac{1}{10} + \frac{8}{100} = \_\_\_.\_\_\_\ \_\_\_$

Ones	Tenths	Hundredths
0 •		

f) $\frac{2}{10} + \frac{4}{100} + \frac{3}{1,000} = \_\_\_.\_\_\_\ \_\_\_\ \_\_\_$

Ones	Tenths	Hundredths	Thousandths
0 •	2	4	3

g) $\frac{1}{10} + \frac{5}{100} + \frac{4}{1,000} = \_\_\_.\_\_\_\ \_\_\_\ \_\_\_$

Ones	Tenths	Hundredths	Thousandths
0 •			

h) $3 + \frac{1}{10} + \frac{8}{100} = \underline{\ 3\ }.\_\_\_\ \_\_\_$

Ones	Tenths	Hundredths
3 •		

i) $7 + \frac{3}{100} + \frac{5}{1,000} = \_\_\_.\_\_\_\ \_\_\_\ \_\_\_$

Ones	Tenths	Hundredths	Thousandths
•			

j) $30 + 4 + \frac{2}{100} = \_\_\_\ \_\_\_.\_\_\_\ \_\_\_$

Tens	Ones	Tenths	Hundredths
	•		

5. The decimal point is between the ______________ and ______________ place values.

6. Write the decimal in the place value chart.

	Ones	Tenths	Hundredths	Thousandths
a) 0.512	0 •	5	1	2
b) 0.905	•			
c) 0.3	•			
d) 1.536	•			
e) 4.763	•			
f) 0.8	•			
g) 3.48	•			

7. Underline the smallest place value. Write the decimal in words.

a) 0.<u>6</u> = *six tenths* ____________ b) 0.07 = ____________

c) 0.005 = ____________ d) 0.02 = ____________

e) 0.3 = ____________ f) 0.004 = ____________

8. Write the decimal in expanded form.

a) 0.407 = *0* ones + *4* tenths + *0* hundredths + *7* thousandths

b) 5.163 = *5* ones + ____ tenth + ____ hundredths + ____ thousandths

c) 3.08 = ____ ones + ____ tenths + ____ hundredths

d) 0.76 = ____ ones + ____ tenths + ____ hundredths

e) 8.201 = ____ ones + ____ tenths + ____ hundredths + ____ thousandth

9. Write the number in expanded form as a decimal.

a) 0 ones + 3 tenths + 5 hundredths + 2 thousandths = *0* .____ ____ ____

b) 7 ones + 4 tenths + 1 hundredth + 6 thousandths = *7* .____ ____ ____

c) 4 ones + 5 tenths = ____.____

d) 9 ones + 8 tenths + 2 hundredths = ____.____ ____

e) 5 tenths + 3 thousandths = *0* .____ ____ ____

f) 3 hundredths + 5 thousandths = ____.____ ____ ____

A **dime** is **one tenth** of a dollar. A **penny** is **one hundredth** of a dollar.

10. a) Express the value of each decimal in four ways.
Hint: Put a zero in the hundredths place if there are no hundredths.

i) 0.63 ____ dimes ____ pennies
____ tenths ____ hundredths
____ pennies
____ hundredths

ii) 0.8 ____ dimes ____ pennies
____ tenths ____ hundredths
____ pennies
____ hundredths

b) George says that 0.63 is greater than 0.8 because 63 is greater than 8.
Can you explain his mistake?

11. Put a decimal point in each number so that the digit 7 has the value $\frac{7}{10}$.

a) 5 7 2 b) 1 0 7 c) 2 8 7 5 9 d) 1 7

Positive and Negative Decimals

The whole-number part of a decimal is the part **to the left** of the decimal point.

decimal point

7.348

whole-number part fractional part

1. Underline the whole-number part of the decimal.

a) 36.497 b) 196.4 c) 25.76 d) 8.036 e) 0.38

2. Write the number as a decimal.

a) 2 tens + 4 ones + 3 tenths + 5 hundredths + 2 thousandths = ___ ___ . ___ ___ ___

b) 9 ones + 4 tenths + 1 hundredth + 6 thousandths = ____________

c) 4 tens + 8 ones + 7 tenths + 2 hundredths = ____________

3. Write the decimal in the place value chart.

	Hundreds	Tens	Ones	Tenths	Hundredths	Thousandths
a) 17.34		*1*	*7*	*3*	*4*	
b) 8.675						
c) 250.93						
d) 49.007						

4. Write the whole number and how many hundredths or thousandths.

a) 6.45 *six* and *forty-five* hundredths

b) 1.32 __________ and ______________________________ hundredths

c) 86.007 ______________________________ and __________ thousandths

d) 7.052 __________ and ______________________________ thousandths

e) 20.104 __________ and ______________________________ thousandths

5. Write the decimal in words.

a) 6.8 *six and eight tenths*

b) 3.02 ______________________________

c) 25.79 ______________________________

d) 15.285 ______________________________

A decimal can be written as a mixed number. Example: $3.75 = 3\frac{75}{100}$

6. Write the number represented on the grids in three ways.

a) 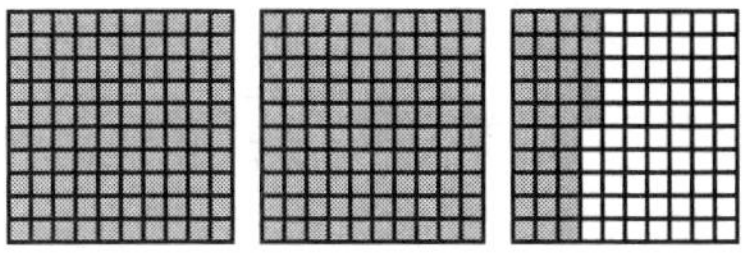

_2_ ones _35_ hundredths   _2_ . _3_ _5_ $2\frac{35}{100}$

b) 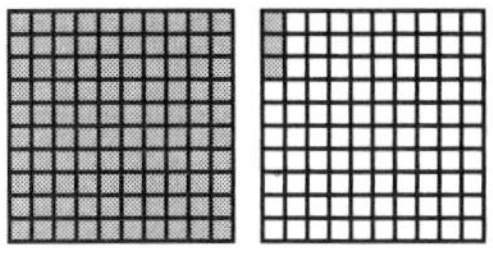

____ one ____ hundredths   ____ . ____ ____   ____ $\frac{}{100}$

c) 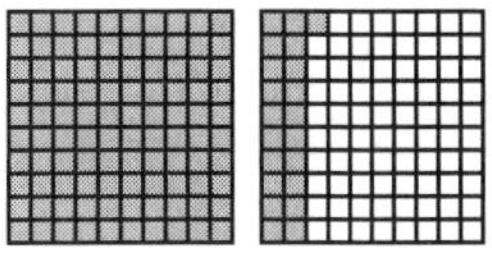

____ one ____ hundredths   ____ . ____ ____   ____ $\frac{}{100}$

7. Write a mixed number for the decimal.

a) $2.8 =$ b) $3.04 =$ c) $7.068 =$

When two numbers are equal, so are their opposites!
Example: $7.4 = 7\frac{4}{10}$ so $-7.4 = -7\frac{4}{10}$

8. Write a negative mixed number for the negative decimal.

a) -3.21 b) -1.62 c) -8.6 d) -9.137 e) -31.76 f) -82.505

$-3\frac{21}{100}$

9. Write a decimal for the mixed number.

a) $+2\frac{17}{100}$ b) $-1\frac{67}{100}$ c) $+76\frac{7}{10}$ d) $-5\frac{375}{1{,}000}$ e) $-3\frac{9}{10}$ f) $29\frac{5}{1{,}000}$

When the whole-number part of the decimal is zero, you don't have to write the 0.
Example: 0.25 can be written as .25.

10. Circle the numbers that are equal to four tenths.

$\frac{4}{1{,}000}$ $\frac{4}{10}$ $\frac{4}{100}$ four hundredths   four tens

.04   0.4   0.04   .4   40   400

11. Write five tenths in at least three ways.

12. Change the improper fraction into a mixed number by shading the correct number of pieces.

a) $\frac{27}{10}$ 

Mixed number:

b) $\frac{31}{10}$ 

Mixed number:

13. Fill in the blanks. Then write the mixed number.

a) $48 \div 10 =$ ____ R ____ so $\frac{48}{10} = 4\frac{8}{10}$

b) $67 \div 10 =$ ____ R ____ so $\frac{67}{10} =$

c) $99 \div 10 =$ ____ R ____ so $\frac{99}{10} =$

d) $745 \div 100 =$ ____ R ____ so $\frac{745}{100} =$

14. Write the improper fraction as a mixed number and then as a decimal.

a) $\frac{23}{10} = \boxed{2\frac{3}{10}} = \underline{\;2.3\;}$

b) $\frac{59}{10} = \boxed{} =$ ____

c) $\frac{121}{100} = \boxed{} =$ ____

d) $\frac{7,452}{100} = \boxed{} =$ ____

To write the improper fraction $\frac{43,725}{100}$ as a decimal:
Write the numerator without the commas.
Then place the decimal point to match the denominator of the fraction.

$$\frac{43,725}{100} = 437.25$$

100: 2 zeros — 437.25: 2 digits

15. Write the improper fraction as a decimal.

a) $\frac{74}{10} = \underline{\;7.4\;}$

b) $\frac{684}{100} =$ ____

c) $\frac{835}{100} =$ ____

d) $\frac{5,374}{10} =$ ____

e) $\frac{1,902}{100} =$ ____

BONUS▶ $\frac{285,376}{10,000} =$ ____

16. Write the negative improper fraction as a negative decimal.

a) $-\frac{89}{10} = \underline{\;-8.9\;}$

b) $-\frac{729}{10} =$ ____

c) $-\frac{642}{100} =$ ____

d) $-\frac{307}{10} =$ ____

e) $-\frac{3,704}{100} =$ ____

BONUS▶ $-\frac{432,095}{10,000} =$ ____

NS6-27 Equivalent Fractions and Decimals

1. Complete the chart.

	Drawing	Fraction	Decimal	Equivalent Decimal	Equivalent Decimal Fraction	Drawing
a)	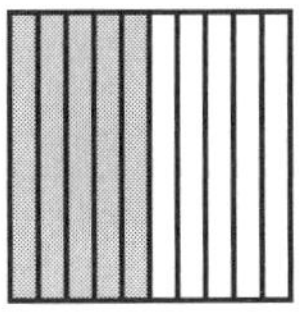	$\frac{5}{10}$	0.5	0.50	$\frac{50}{100}$	
b)	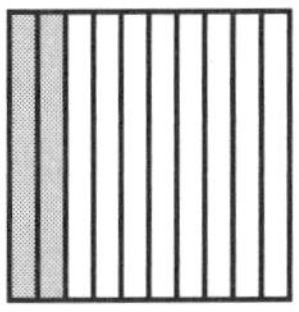	$\frac{\_\_}{10}$	__.__	__.__ __	$\frac{\_\_}{100}$	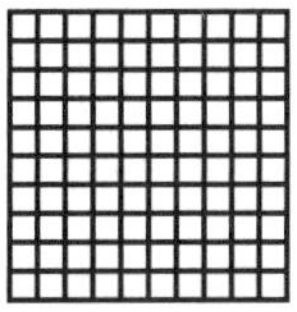
c)	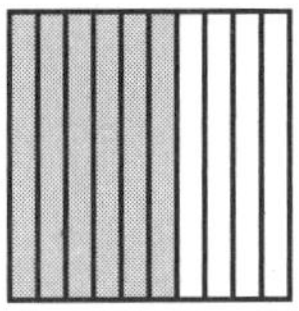					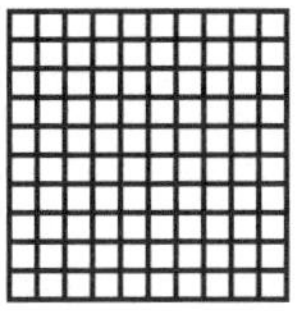

2. Write equivalent decimal fractions for the decimal.

a) $0.3 = \frac{3}{10} = \frac{30}{100} = \frac{300}{1,000}$

b) $.9 = \frac{\_\_}{10} = \frac{\_\_}{100} = \frac{\_\_}{1,000}$

c) $0.04 = \frac{\_\_}{100} = \frac{\_\_}{1,000}$

d) $0.09 = \frac{\_\_}{100} = \frac{\_\_}{1,000}$

3. Fill in the missing numbers. Remember: $\frac{1}{10} = \frac{10}{100} = \frac{100}{1,000}$

a) $0.8 = \frac{8}{10} = \frac{\_\_}{100} = 0.80$

b) $0.5 = \frac{5}{10} = \frac{\_\_}{100} = \frac{\_\_}{1,000} = 0.500$

c) $0.\_\_ = \frac{\_\_}{10} = \frac{40}{100} = 0.\_\_\ \_\_$

d) $0.\_\_ = \frac{\_\_}{10} = \frac{\_\_}{100} = \frac{700}{1,000} = 0.\_\_\ \_\_\ \_\_$

e) $0.03 = \frac{3}{100} = \frac{\_\_}{1,000} = 0.030$

f) $0.\_\_\ \_\_ = \frac{2}{100} = \frac{\_\_}{1,000} = 0.020$

4. Write each decimal as a sum of decimal fractions.

a) $0.27 = \frac{2}{10} + \frac{7}{100} = \frac{27}{100}$

b) $0.40 = \frac{\_\_}{10} + \frac{\_\_}{100} = \frac{\_\_}{100}$

c) $.06 = \frac{\_\_}{10} + \frac{\_\_}{100} = \frac{\_\_}{100}$

d) $0.532 = \frac{\_\_}{10} + \frac{\_\_}{100} + \frac{\_\_}{1,000} = \frac{\_\_}{1,000}$

e) $0.918 = \frac{}{10} + \frac{}{100} + \frac{}{1,000} = \frac{}{1,000}$

f) $.702 = \frac{}{10} + \frac{}{100} + \frac{}{1,000} = \frac{}{1,000}$

g) $0.036 = \frac{}{10} + \frac{}{100} + \frac{}{1,000} = \frac{}{1,000}$

h) $0.003 = \frac{}{10} + \frac{}{100} + \frac{}{1,000} = \frac{}{1,000}$

5. Write the decimal in expanded form and as a fraction with denominator 1,000.

	Decimal	Expanded Form	Fraction with Denominator 1,000
a)	0.382	$\frac{3}{10} + \frac{8}{100} + \frac{2}{1,000}$	$\frac{382}{1,000}$
b)	0.204		
c)	0.086		
d)	0.73		$\frac{}{1,000}$

6. Write the decimal in expanded form using words and write the total number of thousandths.

	Decimal	Expanded Form	Thousandths
a)	0.328	3 tenths 2 hundredths 8 thousandths	328 thousandths
b)	0.409	___ tenths ___ hundredths ___ thousandths	___ thousandths
c)	0.098	___ tenths ___ hundredths ___ thousandths	___ thousandths
d)	0.35	___ tenths ___ hundredths ___ thousandths	___ thousandths

If a decimal is equivalent to a fraction, their opposites are equivalent too.

Example: $0.275 = \frac{275}{1,000}$, so $-0.275 = -\frac{275}{1,000}$

7. Write the equivalent fractions.

a) $0.34 = \frac{34}{100}$, so $-0.34 = -\frac{}{100}$

b) $0.7 = \frac{}{10}$, so $-0.7 = -\frac{}{10}$

c) $0.06 = \frac{}{100}$, so $-0.06 = -\frac{}{100}$

d) $0.804 = \frac{}{1,000}$, so $-0.804 = -\frac{}{1,000}$

e) $-0.5 =$

f) $-0.74 =$

g) $-0.605 =$

h) $-0.004 =$

NS6-28 Ordering Decimals

1. Write an equivalent fraction.

a) $\frac{4}{10} = \frac{\_\_\_}{100}$ b) $\frac{52}{100} = \frac{\_\_\_}{1,000}$ c) $\frac{70}{100} = \frac{\_\_\_}{1,000}$ d) $\frac{7}{100} = \frac{\_\_\_}{1,000}$

e) $\frac{3}{100} = \frac{\_\_\_}{1,000}$ f) $\frac{6}{10} = \frac{\_\_\_}{1,000}$ g) $\frac{9}{10} = \frac{\_\_\_}{1,000}$ h) $\frac{1}{100} = \frac{\_\_\_}{1,000}$

2. Fill in the blank.

a) 3 tenths = ______ hundredths b) 36 hundredths = ______ thousandths

c) 9 tenths = ______ thousandths d) 5 hundredths = ______ thousandths

e) 60 hundredths = ______ thousandths f) 7 tenths = ______ hundredths

3. Change both decimals to fractions with the same denominator.
Then write $<$ (less than) or $>$ (greater than) to show which decimal is greater.

a)

	Decimals	0.6 [$<$] 0.67	0.53 [ ] 0.503	.4 [ ] .376
rough work	**Fractions**	$\frac{6}{10}$ $\frac{67}{100}$		
	Fractions with the same denominator	$\frac{60}{100}$ $\frac{67}{100}$		

b)

	Decimals	0.08 [ ] 0.165	0.5 [ ] 0.007	.8 [ ] .912
rough work	**Fractions**			
	Fractions with the same denominator			

To compare decimals, Rena adds zeros so all numbers have the same number of digits after the decimal point.

Example: .6 and .42 Add a zero to .6: .6 ⟶ .60
60 hundredths are greater than 42 hundredths, so .6 is greater than .42.

4. Add zeros to compare the decimals. Circle the greatest decimal.

a) .76 (.80) b) 0.7 .08 c) .6 .503

d) .49 .623 .5 e) .4 .32 .41 f) 0.720 0.80 .716

g) 3.53 .4573 .66 h) 12.31 .230 .12 i) 2.5 .25 2.05

5. Write the numbers in the place value chart. Order the numbers from greatest to least.

a) 37.03, 3.706, 7.306, 6.73

Tens	Ones	Tenths	Hundredths	Thousandths
3	7	0	3	

_______, _______, _______, _______

b) 0.654, 0.555, 0.655, 0.554

Ones	Tenths	Hundredths	Thousandths

_______, _______, _______, _______

6. Arrange the numbers in increasing order.

a) 3.67, 3.076, 367

_______, _______, _______

b) 0.004, 0.040, 0.041

_______, _______, _______

7. a) Write a decimal between 0.457 and 0.5.

b) Write five decimals between −1.33 and −1.32.

8. Write the numbers in the place value chart. Order the numbers from least to greatest.

a) −6.43, −6.331, −6.33, −6.4

+/−	Ones	Tenths	Hundredths	Thousandths

_______, _______, _______, _______

b) −0.9, −0.09, −0.099, −1.9

+/−	Ones	Tenths	Hundredths	Thousandths

_______, _______, _______, _______

c) −1.999, 2.01, −1.9, 2.0

+/−	Ones	Tenths	Hundredths	Thousandths

_______, _______, _______, _______

d) 14.05, −15.04, −1.04, 5.4

+/−	Tens	Ones	Tenths	Hundredths

_______, _______, _______, _______

NS6-29 Comparing Decimal Fractions and Decimals

The number line is divided into tenths. Point A is at $\frac{8}{10} = 0.8$. Point B is at $-\frac{8}{10} = -0.8$.

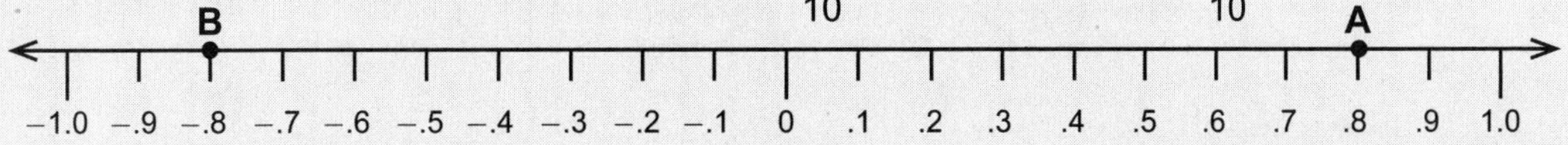

1. Write a decimal and a fraction for each point on the number line.

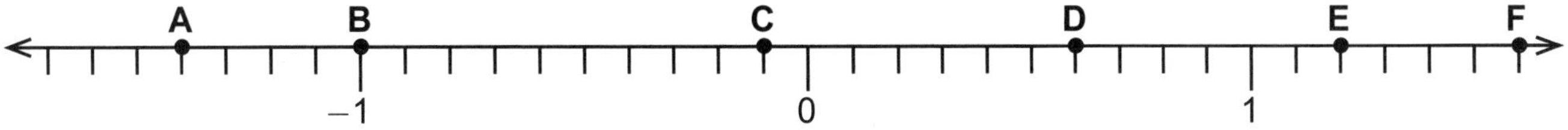

	A	B	C	D	E	F
Decimal	*−1.4*					
Fraction	*$-1\frac{4}{10}$*					

2. Mark each point with a dot and the correct letter. The letters spell the word _______________.

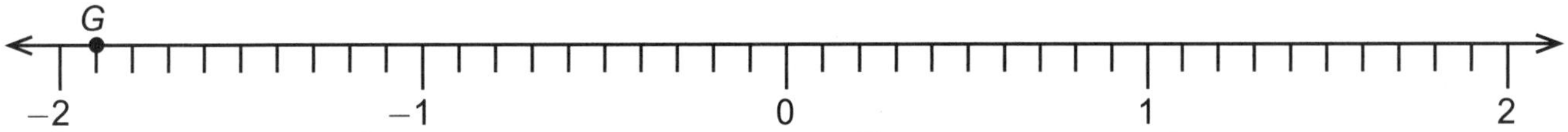

U. −1.3 **A.** $1\frac{3}{10}$ **I.** −.7 **T.** $\frac{7}{10}$ **G.** $-1\frac{9}{10}$ **R.** 1.9

The number line is divided into hundredths. Point A is at $\frac{26}{100} = 0.26$.

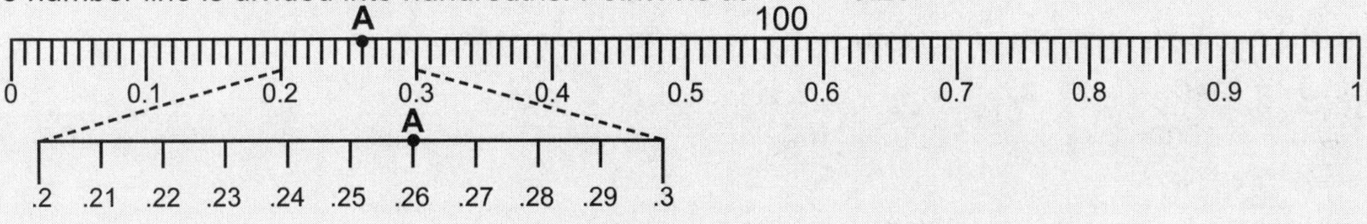

3. Write a decimal fraction and a decimal for each point on the number line

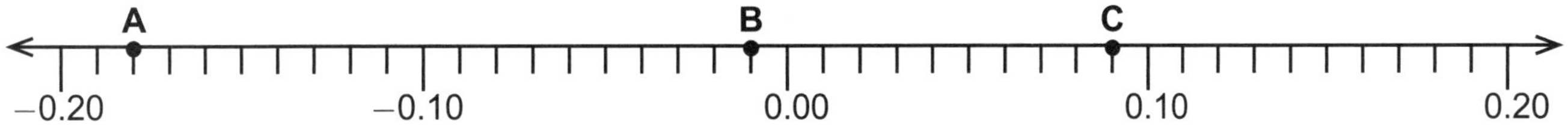

A. ________ ________ **B.** ________ ________ **C.** ________ ________

4. Mark each point on the number line with a dot and the correct letter.

What word do the letters spell? _________________.

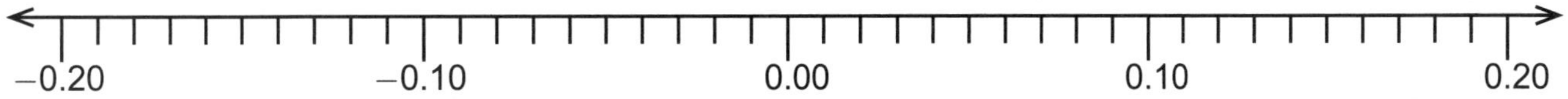

R. .17 **W.** $-\frac{17}{100}$ **I.** $-\frac{10}{100}$ **E.** 0.10 **T.** $\frac{1}{100}$ **N.** −.01

5. Cross out the labels for the points that are incorrect. Write the correct number.

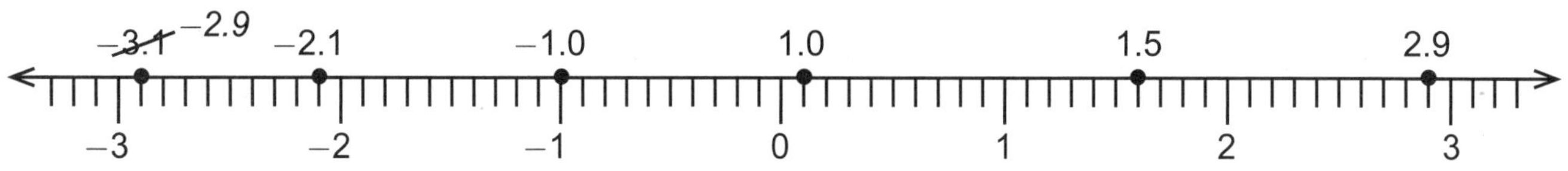

6. Arrange the numbers from least to greatest.

a) $1\frac{15}{1,000}$, $-\frac{15}{1,000}$, $\frac{995}{1,000}$

__________, __________, __________

b) $-\frac{207}{1,000}$, $\frac{27}{100}$, $-\frac{3}{10}$

__________, __________, __________

7. Change all of the decimals to fractions with denominator 100. Then write the numbers in order from greatest to least.

a) .3   –.3 $-\frac{3}{100}$

$\frac{30}{100}$ ______ ______

______ > ______ > ______

b) $-\frac{37}{100}$ .8   –.4

______ ______ ______

______ > ______ > ______

c) –1.4 $1\frac{4}{100}$ $\frac{14}{100}$

______ ______ ______

______ > ______ > ______

8. Use the numbers 100 and 1,000 as denominators to make the statement true.

a) $\frac{7}{100} > \frac{7}{1,000}$ b) $\frac{7}{\_\_\_} < \frac{7}{\_\_\_}$ c) $-\frac{7}{\_\_\_} > -\frac{7}{\_\_\_}$ d) $-\frac{7}{\_\_\_} < -\frac{7}{\_\_\_}$

9. Use the numbers 3 and 40 as numerators to make the statement true.

a) $\frac{3}{10} < \frac{40}{100}$ b) $\frac{\_\_\_}{1,000} > \frac{\_\_\_}{100}$ c) $-\frac{\_\_\_}{100} < -\frac{\_\_\_}{1,000}$ d) $-\frac{\_\_\_}{10} > -\frac{\_\_\_}{100}$

10. a) The American toad hibernates underground during the winter. The colder the weather on average, the deeper the toad burrows. The average winter temperature is –0.5°F where Toad A lives, and –1.5°F where Toad B lives. Which toad's burrow is deeper? __________

b) The American bullfrog hibernates in the water near the bottom of ponds. The western pond turtle digs into the mud under ponds. The bottom of a pond is at –2.53 m. Which animal could be found at each depth?

–2.35 m ____________________ and –3.25 m ____________________

11. Use all the digits 5, 6, 7, and 1 to write a number between the given numbers.

a) 5.617 < __________ < 5.761   b) –57.16 < __________ < –51.76

NS6-30 Comparing Fractions and Decimals

1.

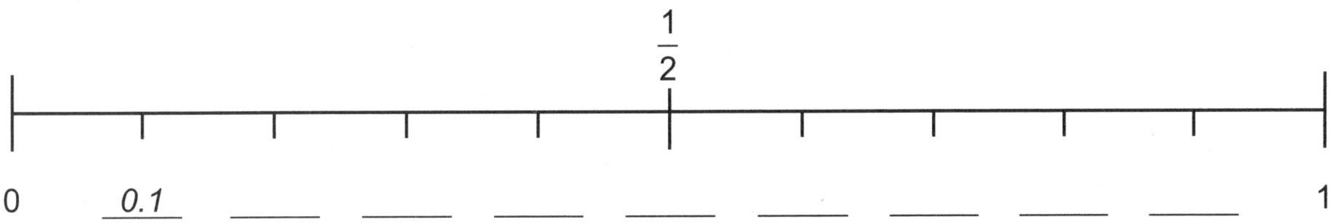

a) Write a decimal for each mark on the number line above.

b) Which decimal is equal to one-half? ___________

c) Use the number line to compare the pair of numbers.
Write $<$ (less than), $>$ (greater than), or $=$ (equal to).

i) 0.9 [$>$] $\frac{1}{2}$ ii) $\frac{1}{2}$ [ ] 0.3 iii) 0.1 [ ] $\frac{1}{2}$

iv) $\frac{1}{2}$ [ ] 0.8 v) 0.5 [ ] $\frac{1}{2}$ vi) $\frac{1}{2}$ [ ] 0.7

2.

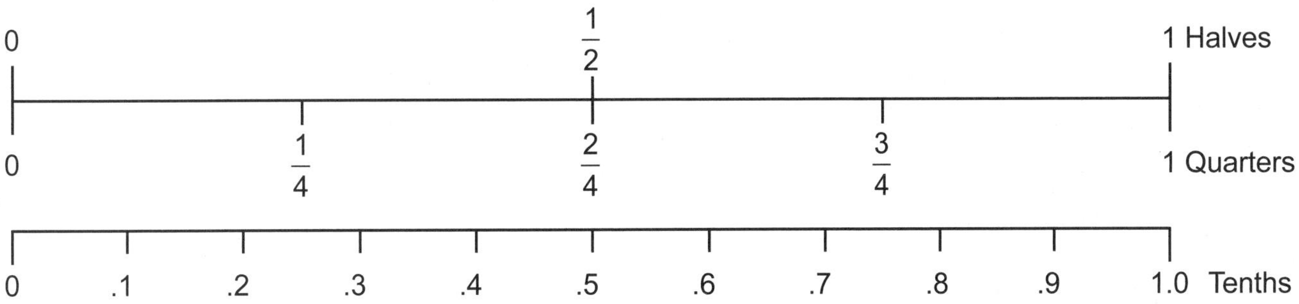

Use the number lines above to compare the pair of numbers. Write $<$ or $>$.

a) 0.7 [ ] $\frac{3}{4}$ b) $\frac{1}{4}$ [ ] .4 c) 0.8 [ ] $\frac{1}{2}$

d) $\frac{1}{2}$ [ ] .6 e) 0.9 [ ] $\frac{3}{4}$ f) $\frac{1}{4}$ [ ] 0.2

3.

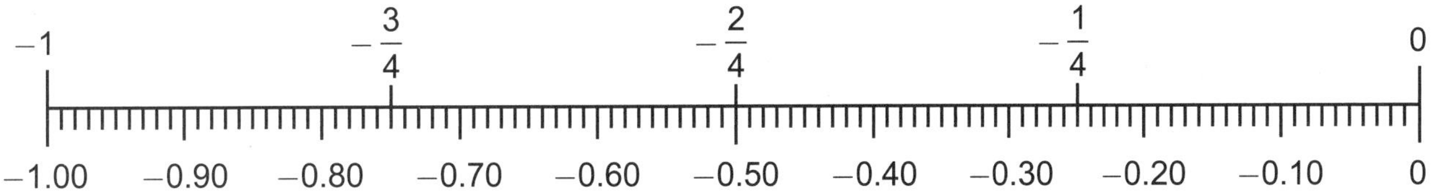

Use the double number line above to compare the pair of numbers. Write $<$ or $>$.

a) $-\frac{3}{4}$ [ ] $-.71$ b) -0.41 [ ] $-\frac{1}{4}$ c) $-\frac{1}{2}$ [ ] -0.25

d) -0.34 [ ] $-\frac{3}{4}$ e) $-\frac{1}{2}$ [ ] $-.67$ f) $-.08$ [ ] $-\frac{1}{4}$

4. Write the equivalent fractions.

a) $\frac{2}{5} = \frac{}{10} = \frac{}{100}$ b) $\frac{3}{5} = \frac{}{10} = \frac{}{100}$ c) $\frac{4}{5} = \frac{}{10} = \frac{}{100}$

5. Shade $\frac{1}{4}$ of the squares. Write a fraction and a decimal for $\frac{1}{4}$ and $\frac{3}{4}$.

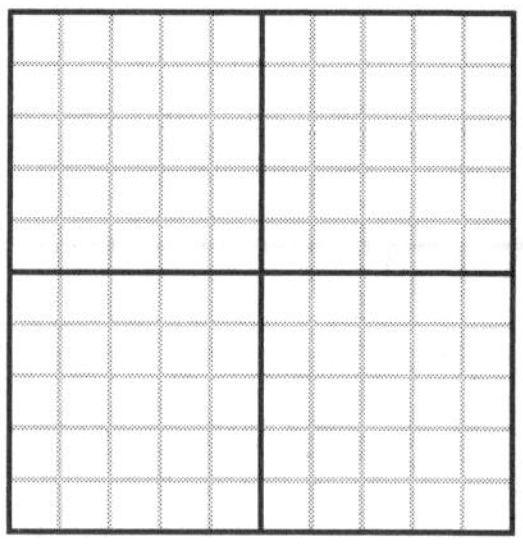

Fraction: $\frac{1}{4} = \frac{}{100}$ Decimal: $\frac{1}{4} = .\_\_\_\_$

Fraction: $\frac{3}{4} = \frac{}{100}$ Decimal: $\frac{3}{4} = .\_\_\_\_$

6. Change both numbers to fractions with denominator 100. Then write > or < in the box.

a) $\frac{3}{4} = \frac{}{100}$ ☐ $.72 = \frac{}{100}$ b) $.53 = \frac{}{100}$ ☐ $\frac{3}{4} = \frac{}{100}$ c) $\frac{3}{5} = \frac{}{100}$ ☐ $.87 = \frac{}{100}$

7. Write the numbers in order from least to greatest. Explain how you found your answer.

a) $\frac{3}{4}$ $-.42$ $.8$ b) $.35$ $-\frac{1}{2}$ $-\frac{4}{5}$ c) $\frac{3}{5}$ $-\frac{1}{2}$ $-.45$

8. Explain how you know that 0.65 is greater than $\frac{1}{2}$.

9. A boat is moving toward a shallow part of the river. The surface of the water is at 0 m. The bottom of the boat is at -1.4 m. The bottom of the shallow part of the river is at $-1\frac{3}{5}$ m. Which picture more accurately shows the situation, A or B? Will the boat pass through safely?

Picture A

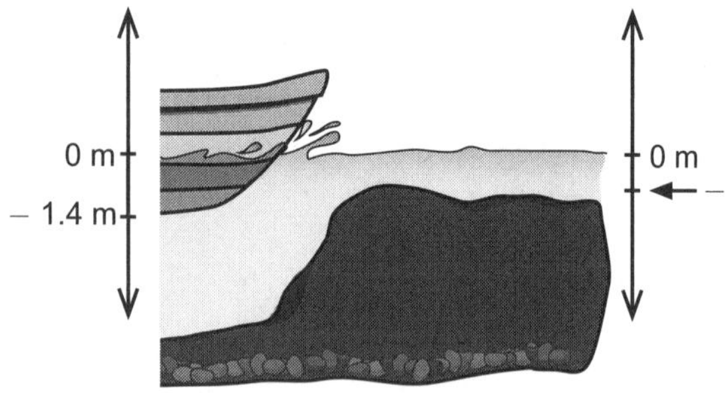

Picture B

Multi-Digit Addition

1. Add the numbers below by drawing base ten materials and by adding the digits. Use the base ten materials to show how to combine the numbers and how to regroup.

a) 26 + 36

	With Base Ten Materials		With Numerals	
	Tens	Ones	Tens	Ones
26			*2*	*6*
36			*3*	*6*
sum		*regroup 10 ones as 1 ten*	*5*	*12*
		after regrouping	*6*	*2*

b) 57 + 27

	With Base Ten Materials		With Numerals	
	Tens	Ones	Tens	Ones

2. Add the ones digits. Show how you would regroup 10 ones as 1 ten.

tens go here

a) *1* / 16 + 17 = *3*
b) 24 + 36
c) 57 + 19
d) 73 + 19
e) 57 + 35

ones go here

3. Use regrouping to add the numbers.

a) *1* / 46 + 25 = *71*
b) 33 + 48
c) 72 + 19
d) 85 + 17
e) 47 + 26

f) 38 + 43
g) 69 + 9
h) 74 + 19
i) 43 + 39
j) 68 + 29

Simon adds 363 + 274 using base ten materials.

363 = 3 hundreds + 6 tens + 3 ones

+ **274** = 2 hundreds + 7 tens + 4 ones

= 5 hundreds + 13 tens + 7 ones

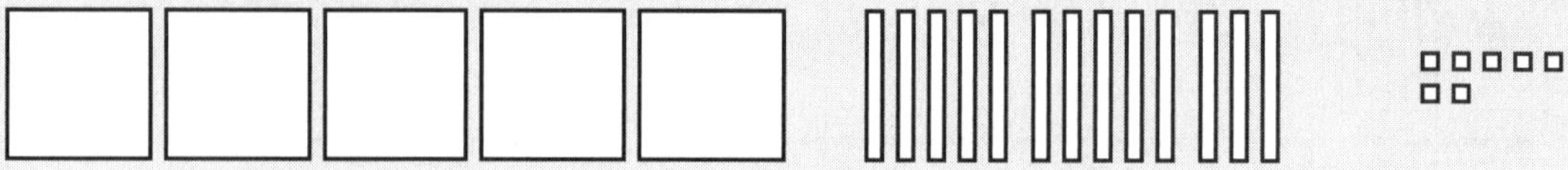

Then, to get the final answer, Simon regroups 10 tens as 1 hundred.

= 6 hundreds + 3 tens + 7 ones

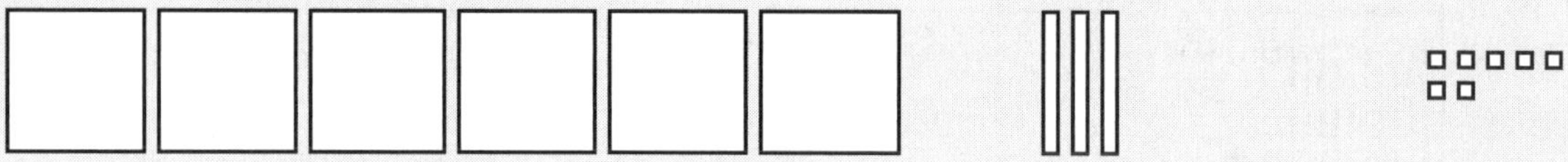

So 363 + 274 = 637.

4. Add the numbers below, either by using base ten materials or by drawing a picture in your notebook. Record your work here.

483		_______ hundreds +		_______ tens +		_______ ones
+ 245	+	_______ hundreds +		_______ tens +		_______ ones
	=	_______ hundreds +		_______ tens +		_______ ones
after regrouping	=	_______ hundreds +		_______ tens +		_______ ones

5. Add. You will need to regroup.

a) [1]
$\begin{array}{r} 364 \\ +\ 253 \\ \hline 17 \end{array}$

b) [ ]
$\begin{array}{r} 571 \\ +\ 255 \\ \hline \end{array}$

c) [ ]
$\begin{array}{r} 652 \\ +\ 94 \\ \hline \end{array}$

d) [ ]
$\begin{array}{r} 362 \\ +\ 482 \\ \hline \end{array}$

6. Add, regrouping where necessary.

a) $\begin{array}{r} 168 \\ +\ 323 \\ \hline \end{array}$

b) $\begin{array}{r} 255 \\ +\ 362 \\ \hline \end{array}$

c) $\begin{array}{r} 395 \\ +\ 123 \\ \hline \end{array}$

d) $\begin{array}{r} 465 \\ +\ 159 \\ \hline \end{array}$

7. Add by lining the numbers up correctly in the grid.

a) 449 + 346

	4	4	9
+	3	4	6

b) 273 + 456

+			

c) 832 + 109

+			

d) 347 + 72

+			

8. Add the numbers below, either by using base ten materials or by drawing a picture in your notebook. Record your work here. (Use  to show a thousand.)

5,486 ______ thousands + ______ hundreds + ______ tens + ______ ones

+ 3,621 + ______ thousands + ______ hundreds + ______ tens + ______ ones

= ______ thousands + ______ hundreds + ______ tens + ______ ones

after regrouping = ______ thousands + ______ hundreds + ______ tens + ______ ones

9. Add. You will need to regroup hundreds as thousands.

a)
```
   [1]
  4 6 8 3
+ 2 7 1 2
---------
  7 3 9 5
```

b)
```
  [ ]
  2 5 3 7
+ 4 6 2 1
---------
```

c)
```
  [ ]
  8 6 5 4
+   7 2 4
---------
```

d)
```
  [ ]
  3 1 7 4
+ 4 9 2 3
---------
```

10. Add. You will need to regroup tens as hundreds.

a)
```
    [ ]
  8 5 6 3
+ 1 3 5 1
---------
```

b)
```
    [ ]
  4 4 8 7
+ 2 3 5 1
---------
```

c)
```
    [ ]
  3 6 8 3
+ 3 1 3 2
---------
```

d)
```
    [ ]
  2 4 7 8
+   2 7 1
---------
```

11. Add, regrouping where necessary.

a)
```
  5 8 4 6
+ 1 1 3 5
---------
```

b)
```
  3 5 6 4
+ 2 8 1 3
---------
```

c)
```
  7 3 2 4 6
+ 1 8 3 8 2
-----------
```

d)
```
  2 3 5 2 7 5
+ 5 1 2 9 1 3
-------------
```

12. a) Camile cycled 2,357 km one year and 5,753 km the next. How many kilometers did she cycle altogether?

b) Two nearby towns have populations of 442,670 and 564,839. What is the total population of both towns?

NS6-32 Multi-Digit Subtraction

Mark subtracts 54 – 17 using base ten materials.

Step 1:
Mark represents 54 with base ten materials.

Tens	Ones
5	4

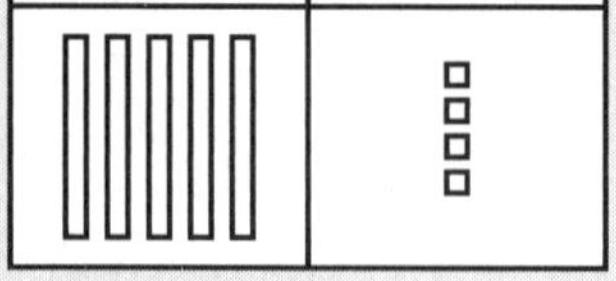

Here is how Mark uses numerals to show his work:

	5	4
–	1	7

Step 2:
7 (the ones digit of 17) is greater than 4 (the ones digit of 54) so Mark regroups a tens block as 10 ones.

Tens	Ones
4	14

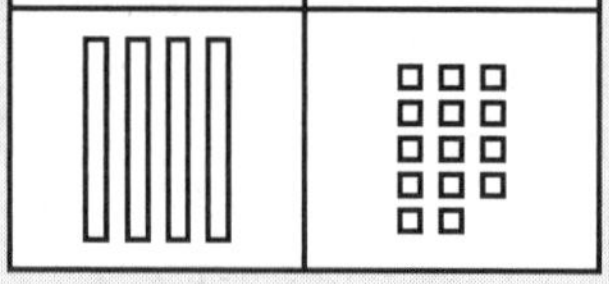

Here is how Mark shows the regrouping.

	4	*14*
	~~5~~	~~4~~
–	1	7

Step 3:
Mark subtracts 17 (he takes away 1 tens block and 7 ones).

Tens	Ones
3	7

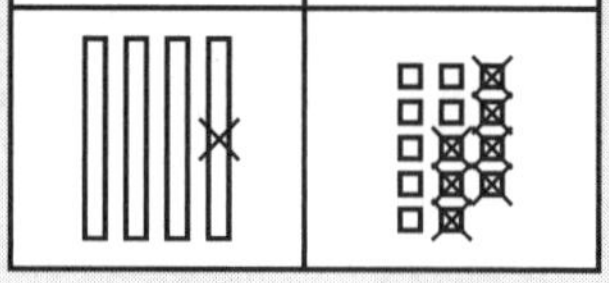

And now Mark can subtract 17.

	4	*14*
	~~5~~	~~4~~
–	1	7
	3	7

1. In these questions, Mark doesn't have enough ones to subtract. Help him by regrouping a tens block as 10 ones. Show how he would rewrite his subtraction statement.

a) 53 – 36

Tens	Ones
5	3

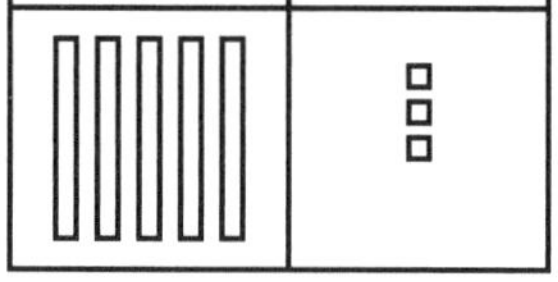

Tens	Ones
4	*13*

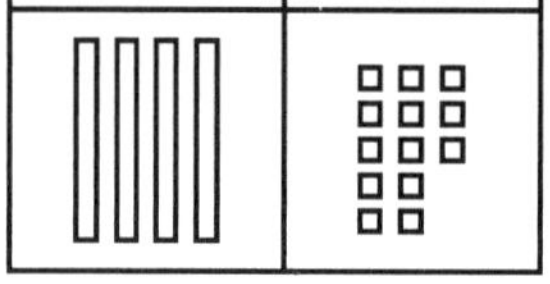

	5	3
–	3	6

	4	*13*
	~~5~~	~~3~~
–	3	6

b) 65 – 29

Tens	Ones
6	5

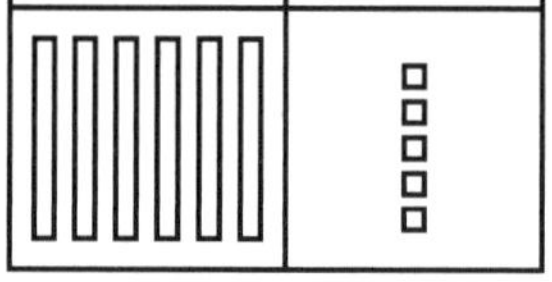

Tens	Ones

	6	5
–	2	9

	6	5
–	2	9

2. Subtract by regrouping.

a)

	7	*12*
	~~8~~	~~2~~
–	3	7
	4	*5*

b)

	5	4
–	2	6

c)

	7	5
–	3	8

d)

	4	1
–	2	3

e)

	6	7
–	4	9

3. Subtract by regrouping 1 hundred as 10 tens.

a)

	5	*13*	
	~~6~~	~~3~~	8
–	4	5	3

b)

	8	5	4
–	3	7	2

c)

	7	5	5
–	3	8	2

d)

	4	2	3
–	1	8	2

4. Subtract by regrouping 1 ten as 10 ones.

a)

		7	14
	7	~~8~~	~~4~~
−	2	4	8

b)

	3	4	3
−	2	1	9

c)

	8	2	5
−	5	1	7

d)

	6	7	1
−	3	1	6

Sometimes you need to regroup twice.

Example:

	Step 1:	Step 2:	Step 3:	Step 4:	Step 5:
			12	12	12
	2 16	2 16	7 ~~2~~ 16	7 ~~2~~ 16	7 ~~2~~ 16
	8 ~~3~~ ~~6~~	8 ~~3~~ ~~6~~	~~8~~ ~~3~~ ~~6~~	~~8~~ ~~3~~ ~~6~~	~~8~~ ~~3~~ ~~6~~
	− 3 5 8	− 3 5 8	− 3 5 8	− 3 5 8	− 3 5 8
		8	8	7 8	4 7 8

5. Subtract, regrouping twice.

a)

	9	3	4
−	4	5	6

b)

	7	4	7
−	2	6	9

c)

	5	3	2
−		5	9

d)

	8	9	2	9
−	4	9	5	8

6. a) The Nile River is about 6,690 km long and the Amazon River is 6,440 km long. How much longer is the Nile River than the Amazon River?

b) A box turtle can live 100 years. A rabbit can live 15 years. How much longer than a rabbit can a box turtle live?

Sometimes you need to regroup three times (regroup 1 ten as 10 ones, 1 hundred as 10 tens, and 1 thousand as 10 hundreds).

Example:

	Step 1:	Step 2:	Step 3:	Step 4:	Step 5:
			11	13 11	13 11
	1 13	1 13	3 ~~1~~ 13	5 ~~3~~ ~~1~~ 13	5 ~~3~~ ~~1~~ 13
	6 4 ~~2~~ ~~3~~	6 4 ~~2~~ ~~3~~	6 ~~4~~ ~~2~~ ~~3~~	~~6~~ ~~4~~ ~~2~~ ~~3~~	~~6~~ ~~4~~ ~~2~~ ~~3~~
	− 3 7 4 6	− 3 7 4 6	− 3 7 4 6	− 3 7 4 6	− 3 7 4 6
		7	7 7	6 7 7	2 6 7 7

7. Subtract, regrouping three times.

a)

	8	7	2	5
−	4	9	5	8

b)

	6	4	3	7
−	2	6	7	8

c)

	4	5	6	3
−	1	7	9	5

d)

	7	8	4	3
−	4	8	6	5

8. In the questions below, you will have to regroup *two*, *three*, or *four* times.

Example:

	Step 1:	Step 2:	Step 3:	Step 4:
		9	9 9	9 9
	0 10	0 ~~10~~ 10	0 ~~10~~ ~~10~~ 10	0 ~~10~~ ~~10~~ 10
	~~1~~ ~~0~~ 0 0	~~1~~ ~~0~~ ~~0~~ 0	~~1~~ ~~0~~ ~~0~~ ~~0~~	~~1~~ ~~0~~ ~~0~~ ~~0~~
	− 7 5 6	− 7 5 6	− 7 5 6	− 7 5 6
				2 4 4

a)

	1	0	0	0
−		4	6	8

b)

	1	0	0
−		3	2

c)

	1	0	0	0	0
−		6	4	8	6

d)

	1	0	0	0	0
−		5	1	1	1

9. A school has 150 students.
Eighty of the students are boys.
How many are girls?

10. Raj has 150 stamps.
Marina has 12 fewer stamps than Raj.
Cedric has 15 more stamps than Raj.
How many stamps do the children have altogether?

11. A grocery store had 480 cans of soup.
In one week, the store sold

- 212 cans of tomato soup
- 57 cans of chicken soup
- 43 cans of mushroom soup

How many cans were left?

12. a) The Washington Monument is 555 ft tall. The Capitol Building is 289 ft tall. How many feet taller than the Capitol is the Washington Monument?

b) The construction of the Capitol building in Washington, DC, started in 1791. How many years ago was that?

c) The population of Washington, DC, in 1900 was 278,718. In 2000, its population was 572,059. How much did the population of Washington, DC, grow over 100 years?

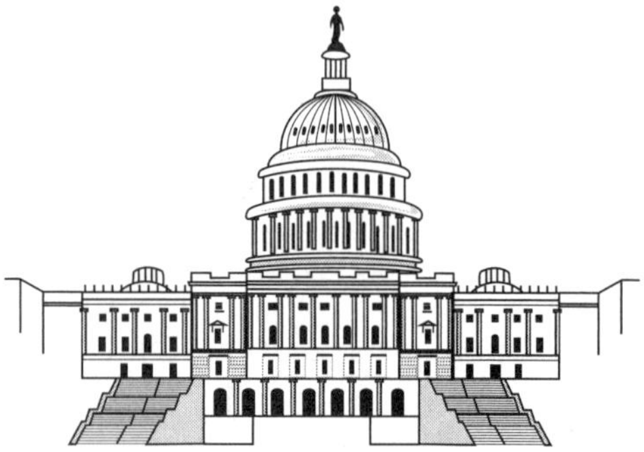

NS6-33 Adding and Subtracting Decimals

A base ten representation for decimal tenths and hundredths

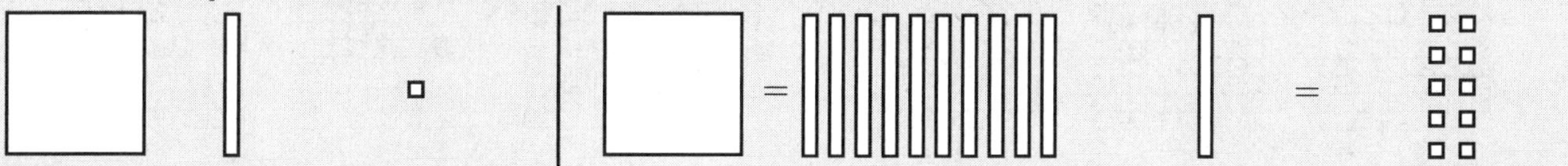

1 one | 1 tenth | 1 hundredth | 1 one = 10 tenths | 1 tenth = 10 hundredths

1. Regroup every 10 tenths as 1 one.

a)

Ones	Tenths	
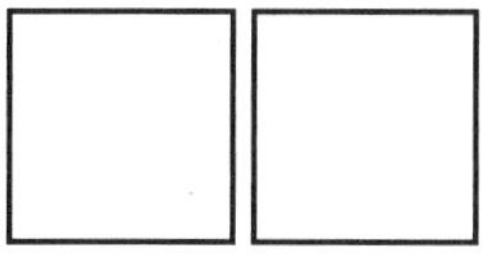	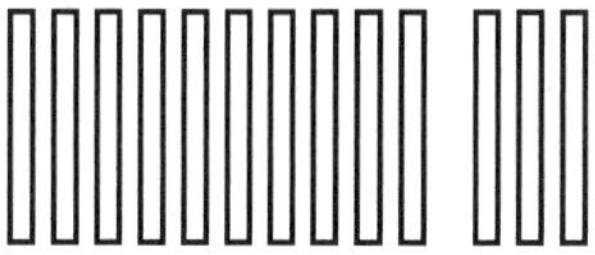	_____ ones + _____ tenths
		_____ ones + _____ tenths

(after regrouping)

b) 27 tenths = _____ ones + _____ tenths

c) 36 tenths = _____ ones + _____ tenths

d) 19 tenths = _____ one + _____ tenths

e) 73 tenths = _____ ones + _____ tenths

2. Regroup so that each place value has a single digit.

a) 2 ones + 14 tenths = __3__ ones + __4__ tenths

b) 6 tenths + 17 hundredths = _____ tenths + _____ hundredths

c) 5 hundredths + 11 thousandths = _____ hundredths + _____ thousandth

d) 3 hundredths + 10 thousandths = _____ hundredths + _____ thousandths

3. Exchange 1 tenth for 10 hundredths or 1 hundredth for 10 thousandths.

a) 6 tenths + 0 hundredths = __5__ tenths + __10__ hundredths

b) 9 tenths + 0 hundredths = _____ tenths + _____ hundredths

c) 7 hundredths + 2 thousandths = _____ hundredths + _____ thousandth

d) 4 tenths + 7 hundredths = _____ tenths + _____ hundredths

e) 9 hundredths + 1 thousandth = _____ hundredths + _____ thousandths

f) 5 hundredths + 0 thousandths = _____ hundredths + _____ thousandths

BONUS▶ 1 tenth + 0 hundredths + 5 thousandths = ___ tenths + ___ hundredths + __15__ thousandths

4. Write a fraction for each shaded part. Then add the fractions, and shade your answer.

a) 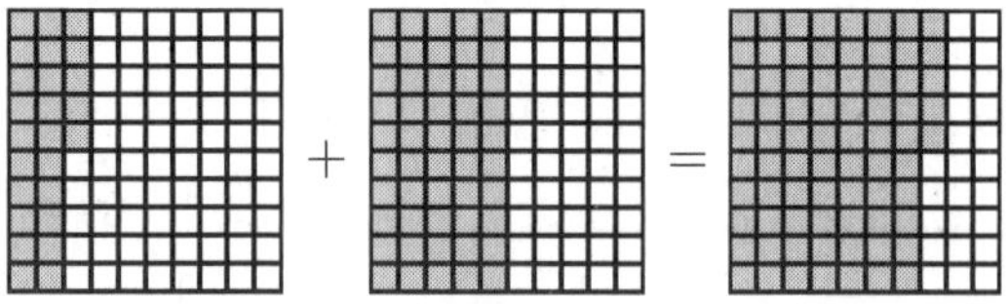

$\frac{25}{100} + \frac{50}{100} = \frac{75}{100}$

b) 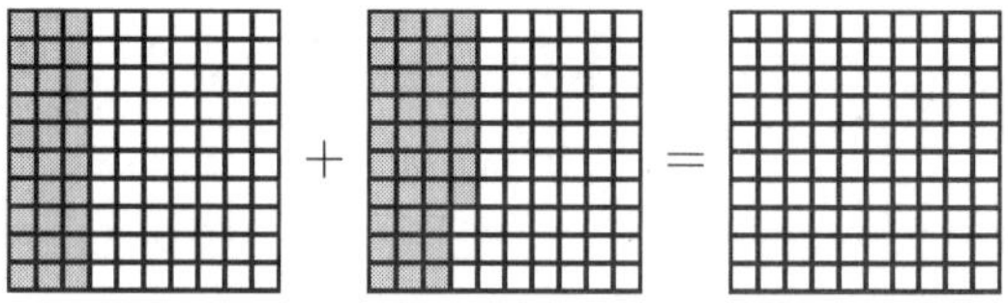

c) 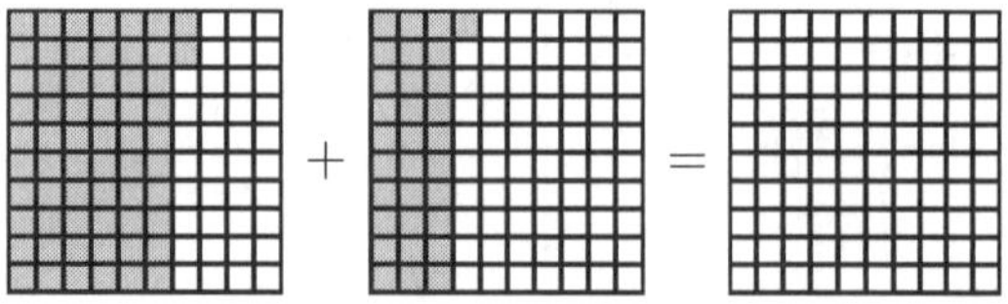

d) 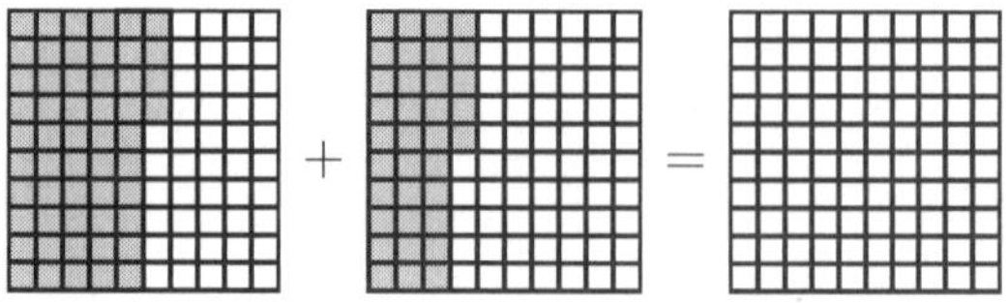

5. Write the decimals that correspond to the fractions in Question 4.

a) *.25 + .50 = .75* ____________

b) ____________

c) ____________

d) ____________

6. Add by adding each place value.

a) 32.1 + 6.48

	Tens	Ones	Tenths	Hundredths
	3	2 .	1	
+		6 .	4	8
	3	*8* .	*5*	*8*

b) 40.53 + 27.2

	Tens	Ones	Tenths	Hundredths
	4	0 .	5	3
+	2	7 .	2	
		.		

7. Add by adding each place value and then regroup.

a) 0.72 + 3.5

	Ones	Tenths	Hundredths
	.		
+	.		
	.		
after regrouping	.		

b) 50.8 + 7.96

	Tens	Ones	Tenths	Hundredths
		.		
+		.		
		.		
after regrouping		.		

8. Add the decimals by lining up the decimal points.

a) 0.32 + 0.57 =

	0	. 3	2
+	0	. 5	7
	0	. 8	9

b) 0.91 + 0.04 =

c) 0.5 + 0.48 =

d) 0.22 + 0.57 =

You can show regrouping on a grid. Example: 6.9 + 2.3

	1	
	6	. 9
+	2	. 3
	9	. **2**

9 tenths + 3 tenths = 12 tenths were regrouped as **1** one and **2** tenths

9. Add the decimals by lining up the decimal points. You will need to regroup.

a) 0.8 + 0.56

b) 0.37 + 0.48

c) 0.81 + 0.58

d) 0.46 + 0.22 + 2.37

10. Line up the decimal points and add the following numbers.

a) 4.32 + 2.17

b) 3.64 + 5.23

c) 4.872 + 3.191

d) 0.675 + 0.52

11. a) Add .65 + .2 by changing the decimals to fractions:

$.65 + .2 = \frac{\quad}{100} + \frac{\quad}{10}$

$= \frac{\quad}{100} + \frac{\quad}{100}$

$=$ ____

b) Add .65 + .2 by lining up the decimal points.

c) Did you get the same answer both ways? If not, find your mistake.

12. Anne made punch by mixing .63 L of juice with .36 L of ginger ale. How many liters of punch did she make?

13. Each wing of a butterfly is 3.72 cm wide. Its body is .46 cm wide. How wide is the butterfly?

14. Subtract by crossing out the correct number of boxes.

a) 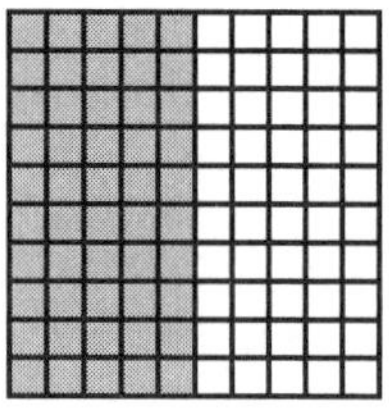

$\frac{50}{100} - \frac{30}{100} =$

b) 

$\frac{38}{100} - \frac{12}{100} =$

c) 

$\frac{69}{100} - \frac{34}{100} =$

d) 

$\frac{57}{100} - \frac{25}{100} =$

15. Write the decimals that correspond to the fractions in Question 14.

a) *.50 – .30 = .20*   b) ________   c) ________   d) ________

16. Subtract the decimals by lining up the decimal points.

a) 0.53 – 0.21

	0 •	*5*	*3*
–	*0* •	*2*	*1*
	0 •	*3*	*2*

b) 0.88 – 0.34

	•		
–	•		
	•		

c) 0.46 – 0.23

	•		
–	•		
	•		

d) 0.75 – 0.21

	•		
–	•		
	•		

17. Subtract the decimals. You will need to regroup.

a) 0.35 – 0.17

		2	*15*
	0 •	~~*3*~~	~~*5*~~
–	*0* •	*1*	*7*
	0 •	*1*	*8*

b) 0.64 – 0.38

	•		
–	•		
	•		

c) 0.92 – 0.59

	•		
–	•		
	•		

d) 0.53 – 0.26

	•		
–	•		
	•		

e) 1.00 – .82   f) 1.00 – 0.36   g) 1.00 – 0.44   h) 1.00 – 0.29

18. Subtract the decimals.

a) .82 – .45   b) .97 – .38   c) .72 – .64   d) .31 – .17

e) .58 – .3   f) .62 – .6   g) .987 – .125   h) .530 – .172

19. Find the missing decimal.

a) 1 = .35 + ☐   b) 1 = .72 + ☐   c) 1 = .41 + ☐   d) 1 = .07 + ☐

NS6-34 Rounding

1. Underline the digit you wish to round to. Then say whether you would round up or down.

a) thousands

2	7	3	2	5

round up / round down

b) ten thousands

6	8	4	1	1

round up / round down

c) hundreds

7	4	5	0	8

round up / round down

d) tens

4	0	8	1	2	3

round up / round down

e) thousands

1	9	6	7	8	2

round up / round down

f) thousands

3	0	0	5	2	7

round up / round down

To round...

Step 1: Round the underlined digit up or down.

To round up, add 1 to the digit.
To round down, keep the digit the same.

hundreds

4	5	7	3	2	5
			3		

up / down

Step 2: The digits to the right of the rounded digit become zeros.

The digits to the left remain the same.

hundreds

4	5	7	3	2	5
4	5	7	3	0	0

up / down

2. Round to the indicated place value.

a) thousands

1	0	0	7	2	3
1	0	1	0	0	0

up / down

b) ten thousands

9	8	6	4	5	1

up / down

c) hundreds

3	1	7	2	2	6

up / down

d) hundred thousands

2	1	5	9	3	2	7

up / down

e) tens

3	8	5	7	2	0	6

up / down

f) hundred thousands

6	6	7	8	9	5	2

up / down

Sometimes in rounding you have to regroup.

Example: Round 37,952 to the nearest hundred.

3	7	9	5	2
		10		

Round 9 hundreds up to 10 hundreds.

3	7	9	5	2
	8	0		

Regroup the 10 hundreds as 1 thousand. Add it to the 7 thousands to make 8 thousands.

3	7	9	5	2
3	8	0	0	0

Complete the rounding.

BONUS ▶ Round each number, regrouping if necesary.

a) 395,721 to the ten thousands b) 427,296 to the tens c) 20,963 to the hundreds

Mathematicians use the sign $\approx$ to mean **approximately equal to**.

3. Estimate the sums and differences by rounding to the nearest hundreds or thousands.

a) $290 \to 300$, $+360 \to +400$, $= 700$

b) $390 \to \square$, $+460 \to +\square$, $= \square$

c) $6{,}301 \to \square$, $-1{,}708 \to -\square$, $= \square$

d) $680 \to \square$, $+160 \to +\square$, $= \square$

e) $470 \to \square$, $-220 \to -\square$, $= \square$

f) $5{,}610 \to \square$, $+7{,}240 \to +\square$, $= \square$

g) $941 - 463 \approx$ ________

h) $1{,}267 + 5{,}679 \approx$ ________

i) $5{,}232 - 2{,}854 \approx$ ________

4. Estimate. Then add or subtract. Hint: Which digit will you round to? It may not be the leading digit.

a) $273{,}572 + 675{,}215$

b) $20{,}273 - 15{,}723$

c) $80{,}278 - 42{,}325$

d) $1{,}275{,}382 + 5{,}385{,}273$

5. a) The Everglades National Park in Florida covers 1,509,000 acres. The Boundary Waters Canoe Area Wilderness in Minnesota covers 810,087 acres. Estimate the total by rounding to the hundred thousands. Then add to find the exact answer.

b) In 2010, the population in Truth or Consequences, New Mexico, was 6,475 and in Sulphur, Louisiana, it was 20,410. Estimate the difference by rounding to the thousands.

c) To estimate the difference $1{,}875 - 1{,}432$, should you round the numbers to the nearest thousands or the nearest hundreds? Explain.

6. A supermarket sold 472 apples, 783 oranges, 341 pears, and 693 bananas. How many pieces of fruit in total did the supermarket sell? Use estimation to check your solution. Explain your estimation strategy.

7. Round 628,315 to the nearest...

a) tens

b) hundreds

c) thousands

d) ten thousands

e) hundred thousands

BONUS ▶ millions

NS6-35 Rounding Decimals

1. Draw an arrow to 0 or 1 to show whether the circled number is closer to 0 or 1.

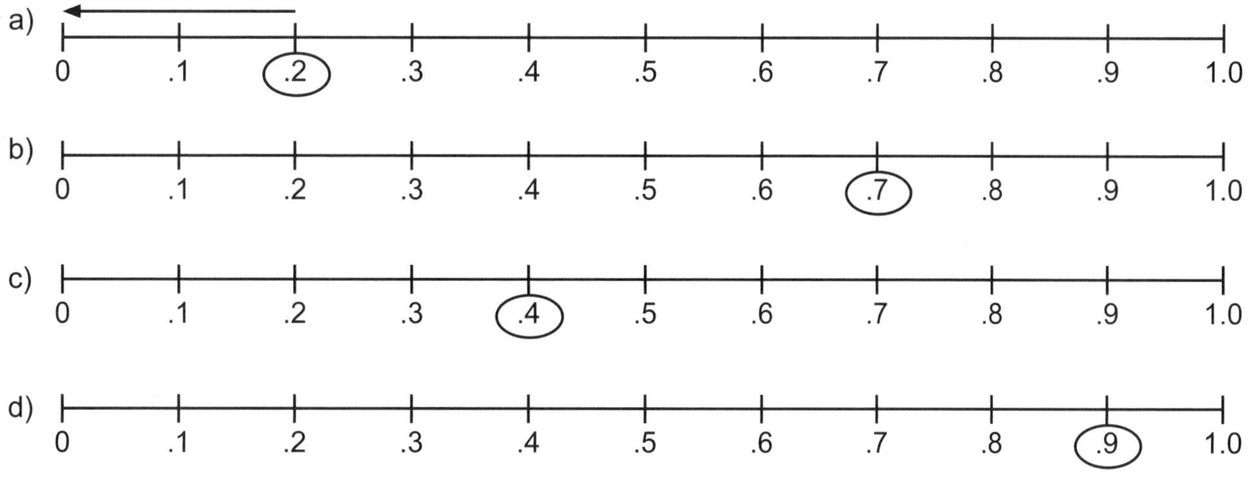

2. Draw an arrow to show which whole number you would round to.

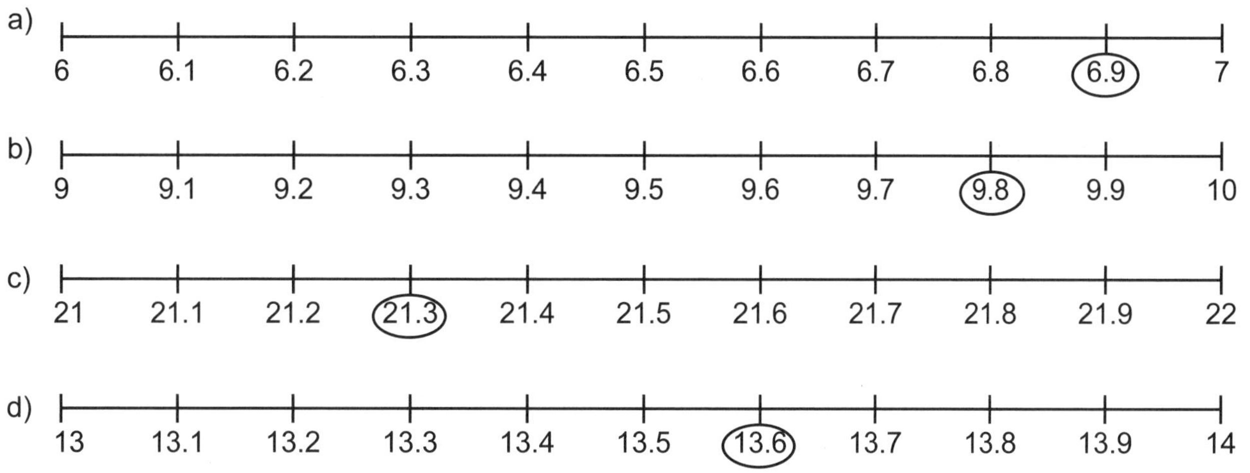

3. Circle the correct answer.

a) 8.2 is to closer to 8 or 9

b) 5.7 is closer to 5 or 6

c) 18.6 is closer to 18 or 19

d) 57.2 is closer to 57 or 58

4. Draw an arrow to show which number (to the nearest tenth) you would round to.

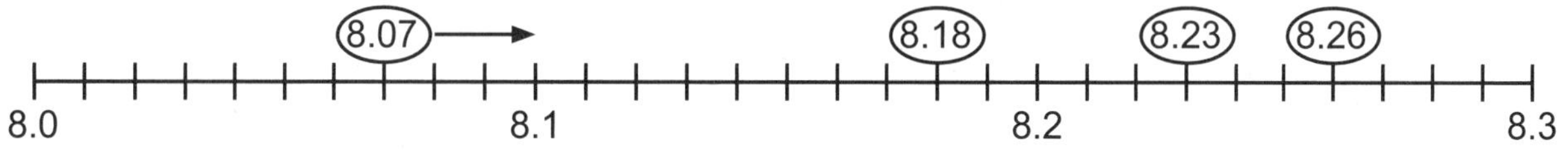

5. Circle the correct answer.

a) 7.12 is closer to 7.1 or 7.2

b) 4.37 is closer to 4.3 or 4.4

c) 25.64 is closer to 25.6 or 25.7

d) 39.83 is closer to 39.8 or 39.9

To round to a place value less than 1:

Step 1: Round the underlined digit up or down.

To round up, add 1 to the digit.
To round down, keep the digit the same.

hundredths

4	5.	7	<u>3</u>	2	5	up
			3			(down)

Step 2: The digits to the right of the rounded digit are dropped.

The digits to the left remain the same.

hundredths

4	5.	7	<u>3</u>	2	5	up
4	5.	7	3			(down)

6. Round to the given place value.

a) tenths

2.	3	7	5

b) hundredths

3.	1	4	2

c) tenths

4	2.	5	6	2

d) ones

9	8.	0	2

e) tenths

3.	2	7	0	6

f) ones

1.	1

g) tenths

3.	3	1

h) hundredths

4	2.	7	3	1

i) thousandths

3.	2	7	0	6

j) tenths

9	2.	1	5	7

k) hundredths

3	6.	2	8	3

l) ones

1.	5	3	2

7. Is the number closer to 0 or 1? Round to the nearest whole number.

a) $0.9 \approx$ _1_ b) $0.3 \approx$ _0_ c) $0.8 \approx$ ____ d) $0.43 \approx$ ____ e) $0.55 \approx$ ____

8. Round to the given place values.

		Round to the tenths	Round to the hundredths	Round to the thousandths
a)	0.1234	0. ___	0. ___ ___	0. ___ ___ ___
b)	4.6789	4. ___	4. ___ ___	4. ___ ___ ___
c)	5.1774	5. ___	5. ___ ___	5. ___ ___ ___
d)	7.008	7. ___	7. ___ ___	7. ___ ___ ___
	BONUS ▶ 0.9936	___. ___	___. ___ ___	___. ___ ___ ___

9. Write a decimal for each description. Some questions have more than one answer.

a) between 3.52 and 3.57: □.□□

b) between 1.70 and 1.80: □.□□

c) between 2.6 and 2.7: □.□□

d) between 12.65 and 12.7: □□.□□

10. Use the numerals 5, 6, 7, and 0 to write a number between the given numbers:

a) $0.567 <$ ________________ < 0.675

b) $5.607 <$ ________________ < 5.760

11. Estimate the sum or difference using the whole number parts of the decimals.

Example: For **32**.456 + **6**.71 + **0**.253, estimate **32** + **7** + **0** = 39.
So, the sum is close to 39.

a) $2.785 + 3.76$

≈ ______ + ______ = ______

b) $12.348 - 4.97$

≈ ______ − ______ = ______

c) $12.75 + 10.603 + 0.24$

≈ ______ + ______ + ______ = ______

d) $9.345 + 0.13 + 6.019$

≈ ______ + ______ + ______ = ______

12. Estimate by rounding to the nearest 100 and 1,000.

		Round to the hundreds	Round to the thousands
a)	7,652.73 + 6,281.56	≈ ________ + ________ = ________	≈ ________ + ________ = ________
b)	9,702.76 − 9,564.82	≈ ________ − ________ = ________	≈ ________ − ________ = ________

13. For each question below, estimate the answer before calculating.

a) Anika wants to buy three items that cost \$14.79, \$12.25, and \$37.50. If she has \$65 with her, does she have enough money to buy all three items?

b) Mars is 227.94 million kilometers from the Sun. Earth is 148.64 million kilometers from the Sun. How much farther from the Sun is Mars?

c) The average high temperature in Anchorage, AK, is 42.92°F. It is 48.66°F hotter in Fort Worth, TX. What is the average high temperature in Fort Worth?

d) There are approximately 19.61 million people living in Beijing, China. Approximately 65.83 million people live in Hunan, China. How many more people live in Hunan?

14. The decimal hundredths that could be rounded off to 5.3 are from 5.25 to 5.34. Which decimal hundredths could be rounded off to 7.2? Explain.

NS6-36 Decimals Review

1. Fill in the missing numbers on the number line.

   a) 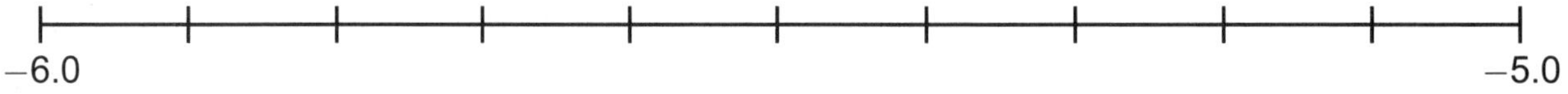

   b) 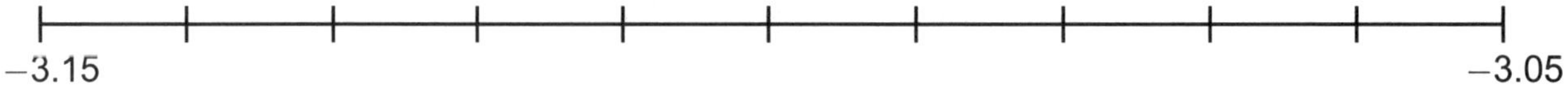

   c) 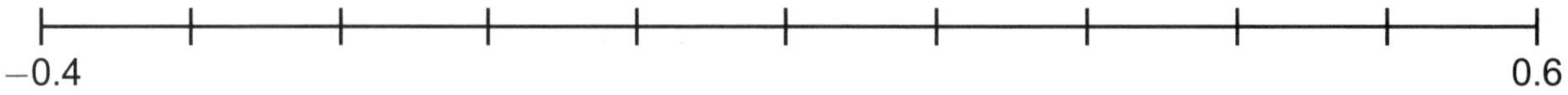

2. How far apart are the numbers? Use the number lines in Question 1 to find the answer.

   a) −3.14 and −3.07 ________ b) 0.5 and −0.3 ________

3. Continue the pattern.

   a) −.3, −.4, −.5, ______, ______, ______ b) −9.6, −9.5, −9.4, ______, ______, ______

   c) 4.34, 4.36, 4.38, ______, ______, ______ d) −1.23, −1.26, −1.29, ______, ______, ______

4. Write a decimal between the two given decimals. There are several correct answers.

   a) −4.34 and −4.31 − ☐.☐☐ b) −2.70 and −2.60 − ☐.☐☐

   c) −3.8 and −3.75 − ☐.☐☐ d) −19.8 and −19.7 − ☐☐.☐☐

5. Explain why rounding to the nearest dollar is not helpful for the following question: Gad has $39.47. Prya has $38.74. About how much more money than Prya does Gad have? To answer this question, what should you round to?

6. The average high temperature at the South Pole is −71.14°F in April and −59.98°F in October. In which month is it colder at the South Pole: April or October? __________

7. A research submarine is 212.5 m below sea level.

   a) The submarine is filming a fish at −213.06 m.

   Is the fish below or above the submarine? ______________

   b) The submarine goes down 10 m. Which number gives its new position? Draw a diagram to explain.

   A. −202.5 m **B.** −222.5 m **C.** −212.15 m **D.** −112.5 m

8. Write a decimal between the two given decimals. There are several correct answers.

a) 5.31 and 5.34 □.□□

b) 0.6 and 0.7 □.□□

c) 4.55 and 4.6 □.□□

d) 98.96 and 99 □□.□□

9. Fill in the boxes. Use the digits 1, 2, 3, and 4 once in each sum or difference.

a)
```
   □.□
 + 2.□
 -----
   □.6
```

b)
```
   □.□
 - □.□
 -----
   1.1
```

c)
```
   □.□
 + □.□
 -----
   5.5
```

d)
```
   □.2
 - □.□
 -----
   □.9
```

10. A slice of cheese pizza has 9.41 grams of fat, and a slice of pepperoni pizza has 9.82 grams of fat.

a) Which slice has less fat: the cheese slice or the pepperoni slice? How much less fat?

b) Ryan ate one slice of pepperoni pizza and one slice of cheese pizza. How much fat was in his meal?

11. a) How many degrees warmer, on average, is Honolulu than New York City?

b) How many degrees colder, on average, is Anchorage than Honolulu?

c) The average high temperature in Phoenix, AZ, is 41.41°F greater than in Anchorage. What is the average high temperature in Phoenix?

City	Average High Temperature
Anchorage, AK	42.92°F
Honolulu, HI	84.67°F
New York City, NY	62.17°F

12. Mercury is 57.6 million kilometers from the Sun. Earth is 148.64 million kilometers from the Sun. How much farther from the Sun is Earth?

13. Juanita paid for a telescope that costs $275.50 with three $100 bills. Calculate her change.

14. Mark has $50.00. He wants to buy a pair of shoes for $23.52 and a pair of pants for $39.47. How much more money does he need to buy the pants and the shoes?

Fractions of a Whole Number

There are 3 equal groups of dots, so each group is $\frac{1}{3}$ of 6.

There are 2 dots in each group, so $\frac{1}{3}$ of 6 is 2.

There are 4 dots in two groups, so $\frac{2}{3}$ of 6 is 4.

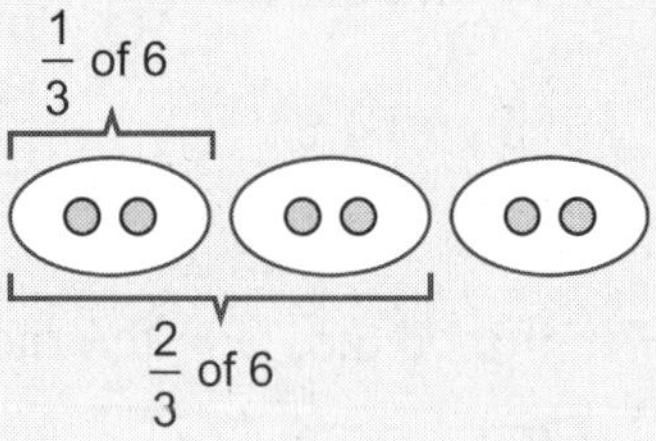

1. Write a fraction for the amount of dots shown.

a) 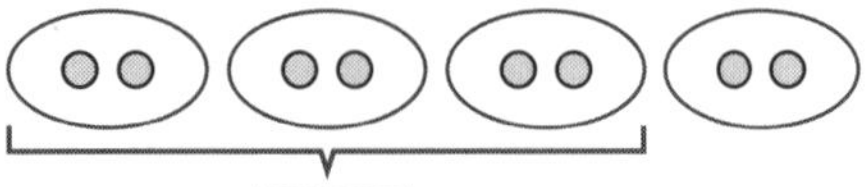

$\boxed{\frac{3}{4}}$ of 8

b) 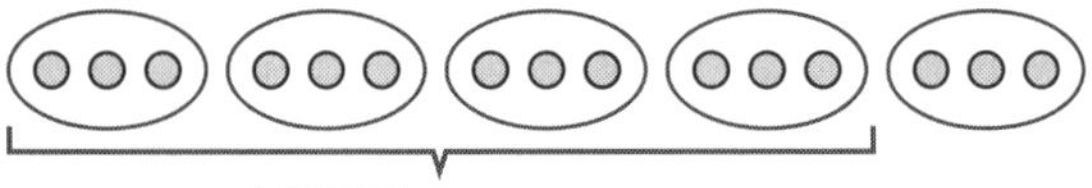

[ ] of 15

2. Fill in the missing numbers.

a) $\boxed{\frac{1}{3}}$ of 6 = ____

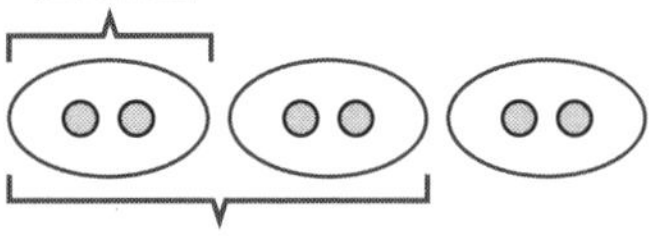

[ ] of ____ = ____

b) [ ] of 8 = ____

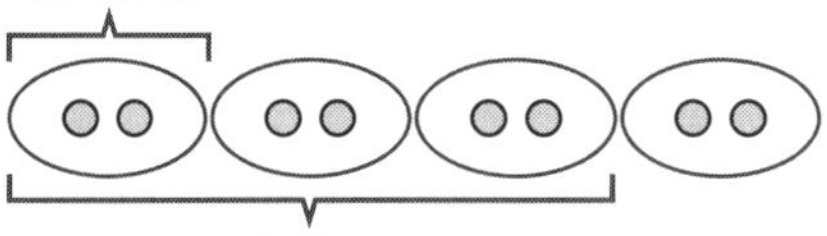

[ ] of ____ = ____

c) [ ] of 9 = ____

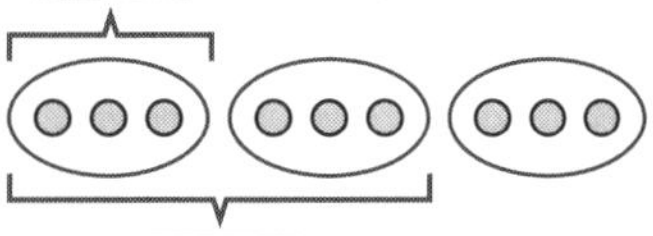

[ ] of ____ = ____

d) 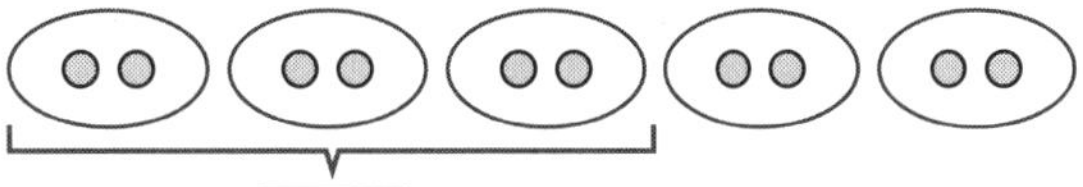

[ ] of ____ = ____

e) 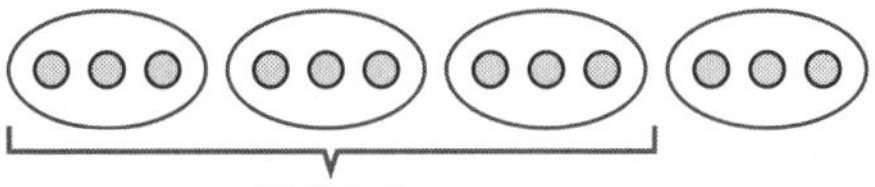

[ ] of ____ = ____

3. Circle the given amount.

a) $\frac{2}{3}$ of 6 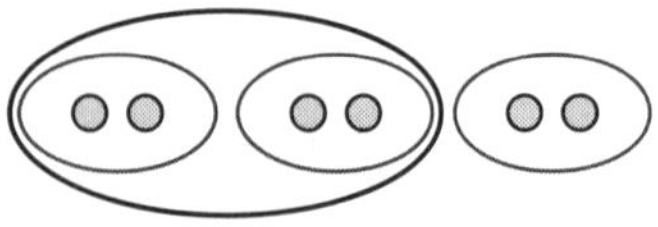

b) $\frac{3}{4}$ of 8 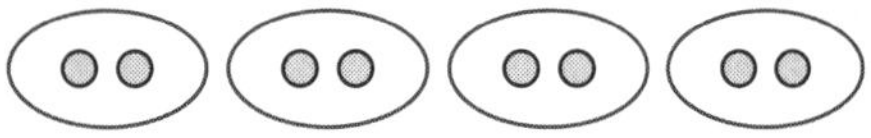

4. Draw the correct number of dots in each group, then circle the given amount.

a) $\frac{3}{4}$ of 16 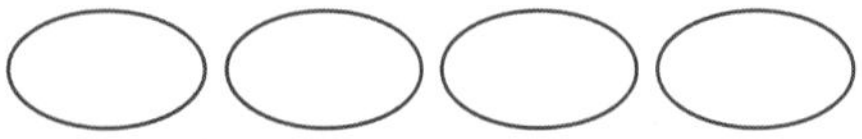

b) $\frac{2}{3}$ of 15 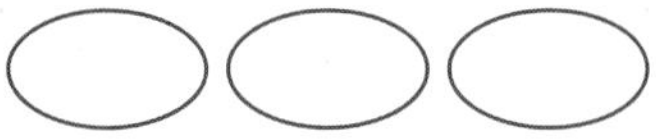

5. Find the fraction of the whole amount by drawing the correct number of groups and then filling in the correct number of dots in each group.

a) $\frac{2}{3}$ of 9 is ____________.

b) $\frac{3}{5}$ of 10 is ____________.

Andy finds $\frac{2}{3}$ of 12 as follows:

Step 1: He finds $\frac{1}{3}$ of 12 by dividing 12 by 3.

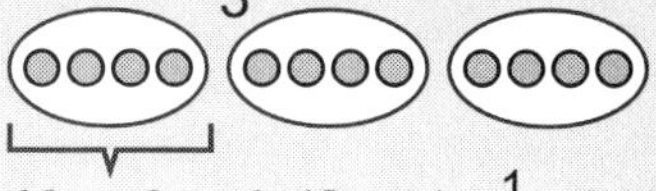

12 ÷ 3 = 4 (So 4 is $\frac{1}{3}$ of 12.)

Step 2: Then he multiplies the result by 2:

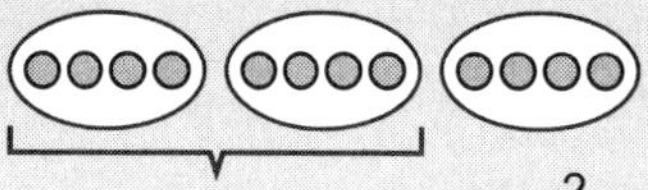

4 × 2 = 8 (So 8 is $\frac{2}{3}$ of 12.)

6. Find the following amounts using Andy's method.

a) $\frac{1}{3}$ of 9 = ____ so $\frac{2}{3}$ of 9 = ____

b) $\frac{1}{4}$ of 8 = ____ so $\frac{3}{4}$ of 8 = ____

c) $\frac{1}{3}$ of 15 = _____ so $\frac{2}{3}$ of 15 = _____

d) $\frac{1}{5}$ of 25 = _____ so $\frac{3}{5}$ of 25 = _____

e) $\frac{1}{5}$ of 20 = _____ so $\frac{2}{5}$ of 20 = _____

f) $\frac{1}{7}$ of 21 = _____ so $\frac{3}{7}$ of 21 = _____

7. Twenty students are on a bus. $\frac{3}{5}$ are boys. How many boys are on the bus? ________

8. A store had 15 watermelons. They sold $\frac{2}{3}$ of the watermelons. How many watermelons were sold? ____________ How many were left? ____________

9. Shade $\frac{1}{4}$ of the squares. Draw stripes in $\frac{1}{6}$ of the squares. How many squares are blank? ____________

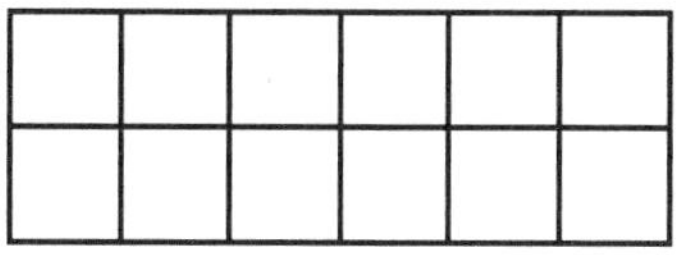

10. Alan started studying at 8:15. He studied history for $\frac{1}{3}$ of an hour and math for $\frac{2}{5}$ of an hour. At what time did he stop studying?

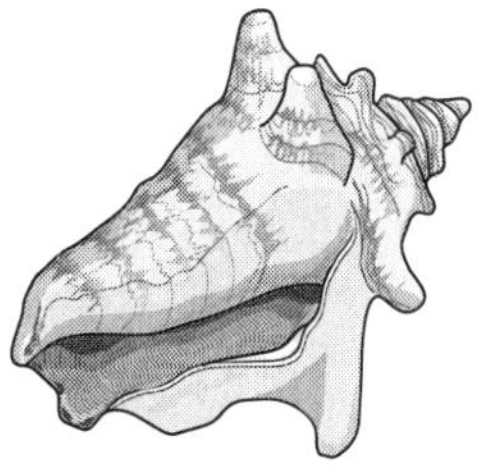

11. Ed has 20 sea shells: $\frac{2}{5}$ are turret shells, $\frac{1}{4}$ are scallops, the rest are conchs. How many shells are conchs?

12. Which is longer, 21 months or $1\frac{5}{6}$ of a year?

BONUS▸ There were 108 grapes. Sara ate $\frac{1}{2}$ of them, Jeff ate $\frac{1}{3}$ of them, and Ron ate $\frac{1}{6}$ of them. How many were left over?

NS6-38 Multiplying Fractions by Whole Numbers

REMINDER ▶ Multiplication is a short form for addition.

$3 \times 4 = 4 + 4 + 4$ $\quad$ $5 \times 7 = 7 + 7 + 7 + 7 + 7$ $\quad$ $2 \times 9 = 9 + 9$

1. Write the product as a sum.

a) $3 \times \frac{1}{4} = \frac{1}{4} + \frac{1}{4} + \frac{1}{4}$ $\quad$ b) $2 \times \frac{3}{7} =$ $\quad$ c) $4 \times \frac{5}{11} =$

2. Write the sum as a product.

a) $\frac{1}{2} + \frac{1}{2} + \frac{1}{2} =$ $\quad$ b) $\frac{5}{9} + \frac{5}{9} =$ $\quad$ c) $\frac{3}{4} + \frac{3}{4} + \frac{3}{4} + \frac{3}{4} + \frac{3}{4} =$

3. Find the product by first writing it as a sum.

a) $4 \times \frac{3}{5} = \frac{3}{5} + \frac{3}{5} + \frac{3}{5} + \frac{3}{5} = \frac{12}{5}$ $\quad$ b) $2 \times \frac{4}{7} =$

c) $6 \times \frac{4}{11} =$ $\quad$ d) $5 \times \frac{3}{7} =$

To multiply a fraction by a whole number, multiply the numerator by the whole number and leave the denominator the same. Example: $3 \times \frac{2}{9} = \frac{2}{9} + \frac{2}{9} + \frac{2}{9}$

$$= \frac{2+2+2}{9}$$

$$= \frac{6}{9} \leftarrow 3 \times 2$$

4. Multiply the fraction by the whole number. Write your answer as a mixed number.

a) $4 \times \frac{3}{7} = \frac{12}{7} = 1\frac{5}{7}$ $\quad$ b) $3 \times \frac{4}{5} = \frac{}{5} =$ $\quad$ c) $2 \times \frac{7}{10} = \frac{}{10} =$

d) $7 \times \frac{3}{8} = \frac{}{8} =$ $\quad$ e) $5 \times \frac{2}{3} = \frac{}{3} =$ $\quad$ f) $6 \times \frac{3}{7} = \frac{}{7} =$

5. Find the product. Simplify your answer. (Show your work in your notebook.)

a) $3 \times \frac{4}{6} = \frac{12}{6} = 2 \leftarrow 12 \div 6$ $\quad$ b) $8 \times \frac{3}{4} =$ $\quad$ c) $5 \times \frac{4}{10} =$

d) $12 \times \frac{2}{8} =$ $\quad$ e) $3 \times \frac{6}{9} =$ $\quad$ f) $7 \times \frac{4}{7} =$

g) $9 \times \frac{2}{3} =$ $\quad$ h) $12 \times \frac{5}{6} =$ $\quad$ i) $15 \times \frac{6}{10} =$

In mathematics, the word "of" can mean multiply. Examples:

"2 groups of 4" means $2 \times 4 = 8$ "$\frac{1}{2}$ of a group of 6" means $\frac{1}{2} \times 6 = 6 \div 2 = 3$

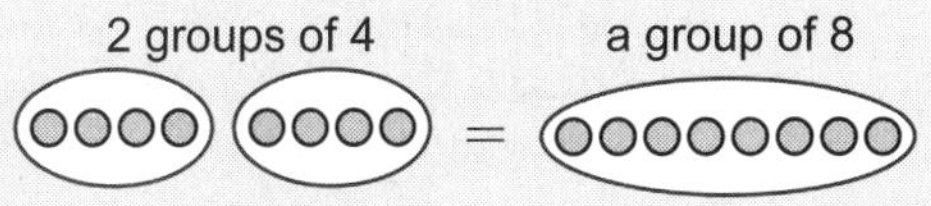

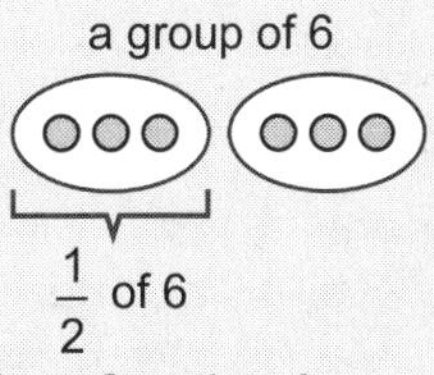

You can use Andy's method from the previous lesson to multiply a fraction by a whole number.

6. Calculate the product by calculating the fraction of the whole number.

a) $\frac{2}{3} \times 9 = \frac{2}{3}$ of $9 =$ _6_ ← $2 \times (9 \div 3)$ b) $\frac{1}{2} \times 8 = \frac{1}{2}$ of $8 =$ _____

c) $\frac{3}{5} \times 10 =$ _____ d) $\frac{1}{4} \times 20 =$ _____ e) $\frac{5}{6} \times 12 =$ _____ f) $\frac{3}{4} \times 16 =$ _____

Sohrab and Julie multiply the same numbers, but in a different order.

Sohrab: $\frac{2}{3} \times 6 = 2 \times (6 \div 3)$
$= 2 \times 2$
$= 4$

Julie: $6 \times \frac{2}{3} = (6 \times 2) \div 3$
$= 12 \div 3$
$= 4$

They get the same answer, 4.

7. a) Multiply the same numbers, but in a different order.

i) $\frac{2}{3} \times 9$ and $9 \times \frac{2}{3}$

$= 2 \times (9 \div 3)$ $= (9 \times 2) \div 3$

$=$ $=$

$=$ $=$

ii) $\frac{3}{5} \times 10$ and $10 \times \frac{3}{5}$

$=$ $=$

$=$ $=$

$=$ $=$

iii) $\frac{1}{4} \times 8$ and $8 \times \frac{1}{4}$

iv) $\frac{5}{6} \times 12$ and $12 \times \frac{5}{6}$

b) Do both products have the same answer? If not, find your mistake.

8. To make 1 pie, a recipe calls for $\frac{3}{4}$ of a cup of blueberries.
How many cups of blueberries are needed for 4 pies?

9. Diba's exercise routine takes $\frac{3}{5}$ of an hour. She exercises 5 days a week.
How many hours a week does she exercise?

NS6-39 Multiplying Decimals by Powers of 10

If a hundreds block represents 1 whole, then a tens block represents 1 tenth (or 0.1).

10 tenths make 1 whole:
10 × 0.1 = 1.0

1. Multiply the number of tens blocks by 10. Draw the number of hundreds blocks you would have, then complete the multiplication sentence.

a) 10 × 

10 × 0.2 = _2_

b) 10 ×  =

10 × 0.3 = _____

c) 10 × 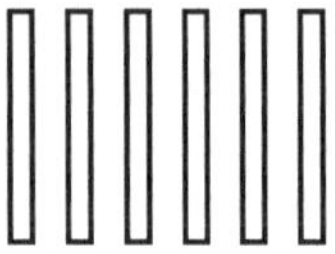 =

10 × 0.6 = _____

REMINDER ▶ hundreds ← × 10 — tens ← × 10 — ones ← × 10 — tenths ← × 10 — hundredths

2. Use place value to multiply by 10.

a) 5 hundredths × 10 = _5 tenths_

b) 7 tenths × 10 = ____________

c) 8 ones × 10 = ____________

d) 3 hundredths × 10 = ____________

e) 9 tenths × 10 = ____________

f) 8 hundredths × 10 = ____________

3. Use place value to multiply by 10.

	Tens	Ones	Tenths	Hundredths
0.04 =			*0*	*4*
0.04 × 10 =		*0*	*4*	
0.5				
0.5 × 10 =				
2.37				
2.37 × 10 =				

4. Multiply by 10.

a) $0.5 \times 10 =$ _____ b) $0.08 \times 10 =$ _____ c) $0.003 \times 10 =$ _____ d) $0.6 \times 10 =$ _____

e) $0.07 \times 10 =$ _____ f) $0.004 \times 10 =$ _____ g) $0.2 \times 10 =$ _____ h) $0.09 \times 10 =$ _____

5. Write the number in expanded form, then multiply by 10.

a) $34.5 =$ *30 + 4 + 0.5*

So $34.5 \times 10 =$ *300 + 40 + 5*

$=$ *345*

b) $7.12 =$ __________

So $7.12 \times 10 =$ __________

$=$ _____

c) $80.04 =$ __________

So $80.04 \times 10 =$ __________

$=$ _____

d) $70.36 =$ __________

So $70.36 \times 10 =$ __________

$=$ _____

6. To multiply by 10, shift the decimal point one place to the right.

a) $10 \times 1.7 =$ _____ b) $1.6 \times 10 =$ _____ c) $18.2 \times 10 =$ _____ d) $17.3 \times 10 =$ _____

e) $10 \times 23.5 =$ _____ f) $10 \times 1.72 =$ _____ g) $10 \times 42.6 =$ _____ h) $5.36 \times 10 =$ _____

7. 10×3 can be written as a sum: $3 + 3 + 3 + 3 + 3 + 3 + 3 + 3 + 3 + 3$.
Write 10×0.3 as a sum and skip count by 0.3 to find the answer.

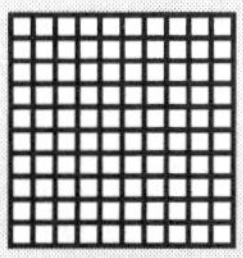 = 1.0 □ = 0.01 → 100 × □ = 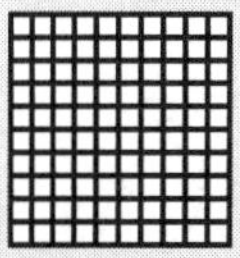

If a hundreds block represents 1 whole, then a ones block represents 1 hundredth (or 0.01).

100 hundredths make 1 whole: $100 \times 0.01 = 1.0$

8. Write a multiplication equation for the picture.

a) 100 × □□ = 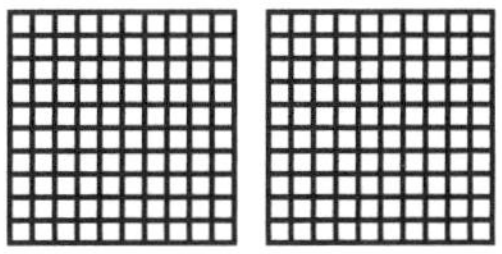

100 × 0.02 = __________

b) 100 × □□□ = 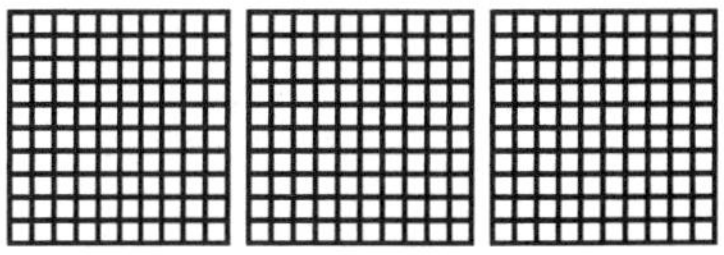

_____ = __________

c) 100 × □□□□□ = 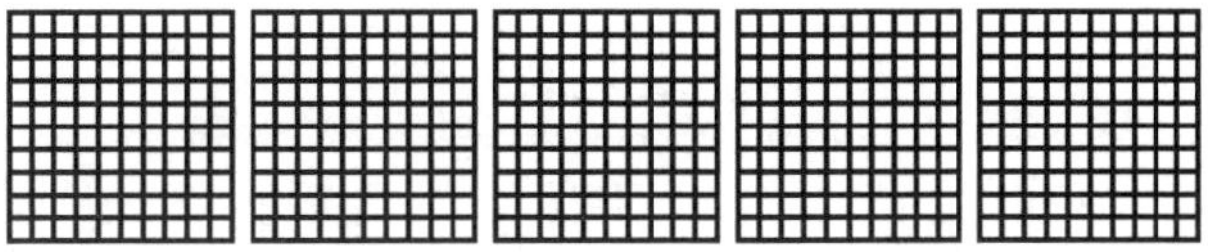

_____ = __________

REMINDER ▶ Each place value is 100 times greater than the place value two positions over.

Example: 1 thousandth × 100 = 1 tenth, so 0.001 × 100 = 0.1

hundreds   tens   ones   tenths ⟵ hundredths ⟵ thousandths

9. Multiply the place value by 100.

a) 100 × 1 tenth = *1 ten*   b) 100 × 1 one   c) 100 × 1 hundredth   d) 100 × 1 thousandth

10. Use place value to multiply by 100.

a) 8 thousandths × 100 = *8 tenths*

b) 9 ones × 100 = ________

c) 7 tenths × 100 = ________

so 0.7 × 100 = ________

d) 6 hundredths × 100 = ________

so 0.06 × 100 = ________

11. Write the number in expanded form, then multiply by 100.

a) 3.45 = *3 + 0.4 + 0.05*

so 3.45 × 100 = *300 + 40 + 5 = 345*

b) 80.04 × 100   c) 70.006 × 100

d) 20.3 × 100   e) 2.03 × 100

12. To multiply by 100 or 1,000, shift the decimal point two or three places to the right.

a) 1.7 × 100

I move the decimal point _____ places right.

		1.	7					rough work
								final answer

b) 1,000 × 0.83

I move the decimal point _____ places right.

		0.	8	3				rough work
								final answer

c) 12.0408 × 1,000

I move the decimal point _____ places right.

	1	2.	0	4	0	8		rough work
								final answer

d) 100 × 0.95

I move the decimal point _____ places right.

		0.	9	5				rough work
								final answer

13. a) Multiply the fraction by 10. Write your answer in lowest terms.

i) $10 \times \frac{2}{10}$ ii) $10 \times \frac{3}{100}$ iii) $10 \times \frac{16}{10}$ iv) $10 \times \frac{5}{1,000}$

b) Multiply the decimal by 10.

i) 10 × 0.2   ii) 10 × 0.03   iii) 10 × 1.6   iv) 10 × 0.005

c) Are your answers to parts a) and b) the same? Why is this the case?

NS6-40 Multiplying and Dividing by Powers of 10

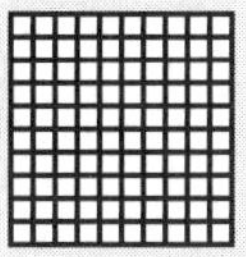 $\div$ 10 = 

Divide 1 whole into 10 equal parts; each part is 1 tenth.
1.0 $\div$ 10 = 0.1

 $\div$ 10 = ▫

Divide 1 tenth into 10 equal parts; each part is 1 hundredth.
0.1 $\div$ 10 = 0.01

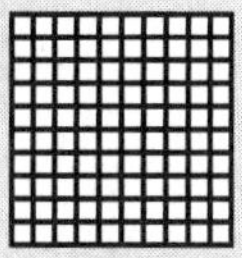 $\div$ 100 = ▫

Divide 1 whole into 100 equal parts; each part is 1 hundredth.
1.0 $\div$ 100 = 0.01

1. Complete the picture and write a division equation.

a) 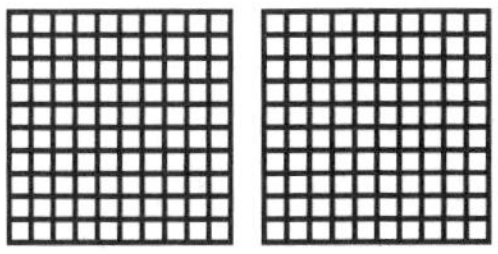 $\div$ 10 = 

2.0 $\div$ 10 = *0.2*

b) 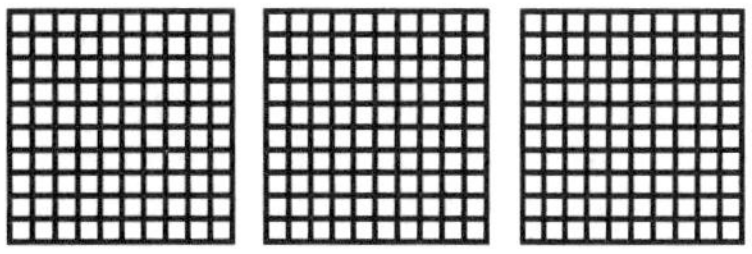 $\div$ 10 =

______ = ______

c)  $\div$ 10 = 

0.3 $\div$ 10 = ______

d)  $\div$ 10 =

______ = ______

e) 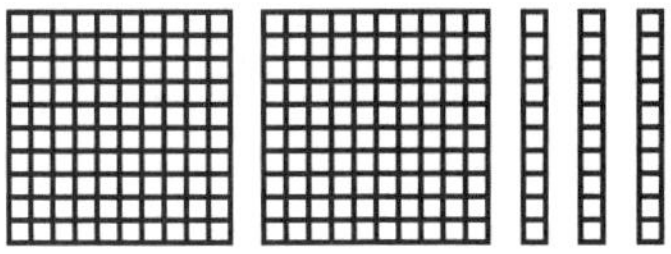 $\div$ 10 = 

______ = ______

f) 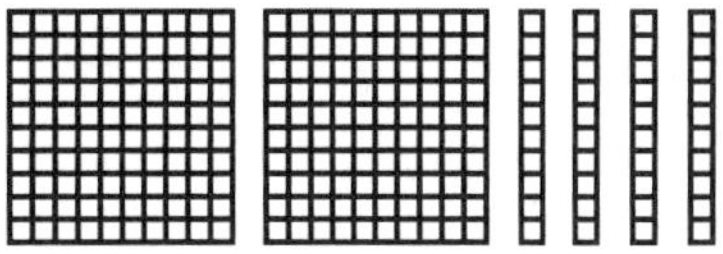 $\div$ 10 =

______ = ______

To divide by 10, 100, or 1,000, shift the decimal point one, two, or three places to the left.

3.84 × 10 = 38.4
38.4 $\div$ 10 = 3.84

2.87 × 100 = 287
287 $\div$ 100 = 2.87

0.0352 × 1,000 = 35.2
35.2 $\div$ 1,000 = 0.0352

2. Shift the decimal point one or two places to the left by drawing an arrow, as shown in the box.
Hint: If there is no decimal point, add one to the right of the number first.

a) 0.3 $\div$ 10 = *.03*
b) 0.5 $\div$ 10 = ______
c) 0.7 $\div$ 10 = ______
d) 1.3 $\div$ 10 = ______
e) 7.6 $\div$ 10 = ______
f) 12.0 $\div$ 10 = ______
g) .9 $\div$ 10 = ______
h) 27.3 $\div$ 10 = ______
i) 3.0 $\div$ 100 = ______
j) 6 $\div$ 100 = ______
k) .7 $\div$ 100 = ______
l) 17.2 $\div$ 100 = ______

3. Explain why 1.00 $\div$ 100 = .01 using dollar bills as wholes.

4. A wall 3.5 m wide is painted with 100 stripes of equal width. How wide is each stripe?

5. 5 × 3 = 15 and 15 $\div$ 5 = 3 are in the same fact family.
Write a division equation in the same fact family as 10 × 0.1 = 1.0.

6. a) To multiply by 10, I move the decimal point __1__ place(s) to the __right__.

b) To multiply by 1,000, I move the decimal point _____ place(s) to the ______________.

c) To divide by 100, I move the decimal point _____ place(s) to the ______________.

d) To divide by 10, I move the decimal point _____ place(s) to the ______________.

e) To ______________ by 1,000, I move the decimal point _____ places to the left.

f) To ______________ by 10, I move the decimal point _____ place to the left.

g) To ______________ by 100, I move the decimal point _____ places to the right.

h) To divide by 10,000,000, I move the decimal point _____ places to the ______________.

i) To multiply by 100,000, I move the decimal point _____ places to the ______________.

7. Fill in the blanks. Next, draw arrows to show how you would shift the decimal point. Then write your final answer in the grid.

a) 7.325 × 100

Move the decimal point __2__ places __right__.

		7.	3	2	5			rough work
		7	3	2.	5			final answer

b) 5.3 ÷ 1,000

Move the decimal point __3__ places __left__.

				5.	3			rough work
		.0	0	5	3			final answer

c) 247.567 × 1,000

Move the decimal point ____ places _________.

	2	4	7.	5	6	7		rough work
								final answer

d) 100.45 ÷ 100

Move the decimal point ____ places _________.

	1	0	0.	4	5			rough work
								final answer

e) 0.602 × 10,000

Move the decimal point ____ places _________.

				.6	0	2		rough work
								final answer

f) 24.682 ÷ 10,000

Move the decimal point ____ places _________.

		2	4.	6	8	2		rough work
								final answer

8. Copy the numbers onto grid paper. Show how you would shift the decimal point in each case.

a) 2.65 × 1,000 b) 47.001 × 100 c) 0.043 × 10 d) 20.06 × 1,000 e) 0.07 × 10,000

f) 0.643 ÷ 10 g) 170.45 ÷ 100 h) 36.07 ÷ 1,000 i) 17.35 ÷ 10,000 j) 0.05 ÷ 1,000

NS6-41 Multiplying Decimals by Whole Numbers

The picture shows how to multiply a decimal by a whole number.

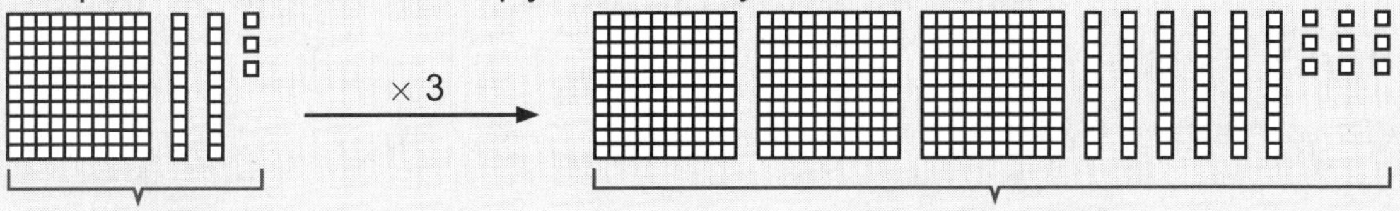

1. Multiply mentally. Multiply each digit separately.

a) 3 × 1.32 = ______ b) 2 × 2.4 = ______ c) 6 × 1.01 = ______ d) 3 × 3.2 = ______

e) 4 × 2.12 = ______ f) 5 × 3.1 = ______ g) 2 × 4.21 = ______ h) 7 × 4.11 = ______

2. Multiply by exchanging tenths for ones.

a) 7 × 1.3 = *7* ones + *21* tenths = *9* ones + *1* tenth = *9.1*

b) 3 × 3.4 = ______ ones + ______ tenths = ______ ones + ______ tenths = ______

c) 4 × 4.7 = ______ ones + ______ tenths = ______ ones + ______ tenths = ______

d) 3 × 2.9 = ____

3. Multiply by exchanging tenths for ones or hundredths for tenths.

a) 3 × 3.51 = *9* ones + *15* tenths + *3* hundredths
= ______ ones + ______ tenths + ______ hundredths = ______

b) 4 × 2.14 = ______ ones + ______ tenths + ______ hundredths
= ______ ones + ______ tenths + ______ hundredths = ______

4. Multiply. In some questions you will have to regroup twice.

a)

	2.	4	2
×			4
		.	

b)

	6.	3	5
×			3
		.	

c)

	7.	2	1
×			6
		.	

d)

	2.	0	9
×			3
		.	

5. Find the product.

a) 5 × 3.6 b) 3 × 0.4 c) 6 × 4.2 d) 9 × 2.27 e) 7 × 34.6 f) 8 × 4.3

g) 4 × 2.7 h) 5 × 9.52 i) 7 × 5.98 j) 8 × 6.29 k) 3 × 46.92 l) 4 × 36.75

6. You can rewrite the product 80 × 3.6 as 10 × 8 × 3.6. Use this method to find these products.

a) 40 × 2.1 b) 60 × 0.7 c) 30 × 9.68 d) 200 × 7.5 e) 500 × 0.2

RP6-11 Equivalent Ratios

In this picture, the ratio of bananas to apples is

3 bananas to every 4 apples, **3 : 4** OR

6 bananas to every 8 apples, **6 : 8**.

1. Group the fruit to show two equivalent ratios.

a) 

__________ to every __________

or __________ to every __________

b) 

__________ to every __________

or __________ to every __________

2. a) Talia created a sequence of equivalent ratios. She started with the ratio 2 triangles to every 3 rectangles. Fill in the missing figures and ratios.

Triangles	△ △	△ △ △ △	△ △ △ △ △ △	
Rectangles	▭ ▭ ▭	▭ ▭ ▭ ▭ ▭ ▭		▭ ▭ ▭ ▭ ▭ ▭ ▭ ▭ ▭ ▭ ▭ ▭
Ratio	*2 : 3*	*4 : 6*		

b) Talia records the equivalent ratios in a table. Fill in the missing ratios.

Is this a ratio table? _____ Explain how you know.

____

____

Triangles	**Rectangles**
2	3

3. Fill in the ratio table. Then write a sequence of four equivalent ratios.

a)

3	4
6	*8*

3 : 4 = *6* : *8* = ___ : ___ = ___ : ___

b)

2	5

2 : 5 = ______ = ______ = ______

4. Find the missing term(s).

a) 3 : 7 = _____ : 14 b) 5 : 6 = 10 : _____ = _____ : 18 c) 2 : 5 = _____ : 20

RP6-12 Finding Equivalent Ratios

A recipe for granola calls for 2 cups of raisins for every 3 cups of oats.

How many cups of raisins will Eschi need for 12 cups of oats?

She writes a sequence of equivalent ratios to find out.

She multiplies both terms in the ratio 2 : 3 by 2, then by 3, then by 4.

2 : 3 = 4 : 6 = 6 : 9 = 8 : 12

Eschi needs 8 cups of raisins.

1. Solve the problem by writing a sequence of equivalent ratios. The first one is started for you.

   a) A recipe calls for 5 cups of oats for every 3 cups of raisins. How many cups of oats are needed for 12 cups of raisins?

   5 : 3 = 10 : 6 = ___ : ___ = ___ : ___

   b) Two centimeters represent 11 km. How many kilometers does 8 cm on the map represent?

   ____

   c) Six bus tickets cost $5. How much will 18 tickets cost?

   ____

   d) There are 3 red fish for every 5 blue fish in an aquarium. If there are 24 red fish, how many blue fish are there?

   ____

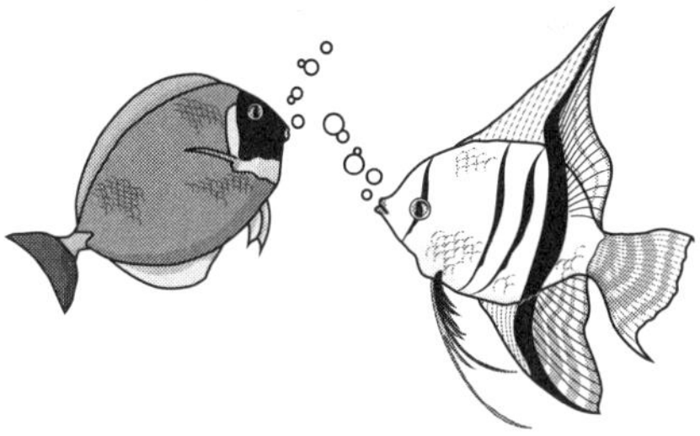

2. Find the missing number in the ratio table. Hint: You can use skip counting or multiplication.

a) ×2 (arrows from top row to bottom row)

3	5
6	*10*

b)

3	4
15	

c)

3	2
	6

d)

4	5
20	

e)

4	9
24	

f)

6	2
	6

g)

3	2
27	

h)

5	2
15	

Sometimes, the arrow may point from bottom to top.

i) ×3 (arrows from bottom row to top row)

12	*15*
4	5

j)

12	
4	9

k)

	8
3	2

l)

3	7
12	

m)

	20
7	5

n)

15	
3	8

o)

5	1
	5

p)

8	
4	5

Three subway tickets cost $5. Kyle wants to know how many tickets he can buy for $20. He finds an equivalent ratio using a ratio table:

Step 1: He makes a ratio table showing the cost for each amount of tickets. He writes a question mark (?) for the missing number.

Tickets	Costs ($)
3	5
?	20

Step 2: He finds the number being multiplied by in the second column. Then he multiplies by that number in the first column to find the missing number.

Tickets	Costs ($)
3	5
12	20

×4 (first column) ×4 (second column)

Therefore 3 : 5 = 12 : 20 and 12 tickets cost $20.

Use ratio tables to solve the following questions.

3. There are 2 apples in a bowl for every 3 oranges.
If there are 9 oranges, how many apples are there?

4. Five bus tickets cost $3.
How many bus tickets can you buy with $9?

5. To make fruit punch, you mix 1 liter of orange juice with 2 liters of pineapple juice.
If you have 3 liters of orange juice, how many liters of pineapple juice do you need?

6. Nora can run 3 laps in 4 minutes.
At that rate, how many laps could she run in 12 minutes?

7. A basketball team won 2 out of every 3 games they played.
The team played a total of 15 games.
How many games did the team win?
Hint: The quantities are "games won" and "games played."

8. The ratio of boys to girls in a class is 4 : 5.
If there are 20 boys, how many girls are there?

9. Two centimeters on a map represents 5 km in real life.
If a lake is 6 cm long on the map, what is its actual size?

10. In a pet shop, there are 3 cats for every 2 dogs.
If there are 12 cats in the shop,
how many dogs are there?

RP6-13 Percentages

A **percentage** is a ratio that compares a number to 100.

The term percentage means "per 100" or "for every 100" or "out of 100." For example, 84% on a test means 84 out of 100.

You can think of a percentage as a short form for a fraction with denominator 100. Example: $45\% = \frac{45}{100}$

1. Write the percentage as a fraction.

a) 7% b) 92% c) 5% d) 15%

e) 50% f) 100% g) 2% h) 17%

2. Write the fraction as a percentage.

a) $\frac{2}{100}$ b) $\frac{31}{100}$ c) $\frac{52}{100}$ d) $\frac{100}{100}$

e) $\frac{17}{100}$ f) $\frac{88}{100}$ g) $\frac{7}{100}$ h) $\frac{1}{100}$

3. Write the decimal as a fraction and then a percentage.

a) $0.72 = \frac{72}{100} = 72\%$ b) $0.27 =$ c) $0.04 =$

4. Write the fraction as a percentage by first changing it to a fraction over 100.

a) $\frac{3 \times 20}{5 \times 20} = \frac{60}{100} = 60\%$ b) $\frac{2}{5}$

c) $\frac{4}{5}$ d) $\frac{1}{4}$

e) $\frac{3}{4}$ f) $\frac{1}{2}$

g) $\frac{3}{10}$ h) $\frac{7}{10}$

i) $\frac{17}{25}$ j) $\frac{17}{20}$

k) $\frac{3}{25}$ l) $\frac{19}{20}$

m) $\frac{23}{50}$ n) $\frac{47}{50}$

5. Write the decimal as a percentage.

a) $0.2 = \dfrac{2 \times 10}{10 \times 10} = \dfrac{20}{100} = 20\%$

b) 0.5

c) 0.7

d) 0.9

6. What percentage of the figure is shaded?

a) 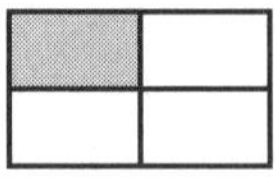

b) 

c) 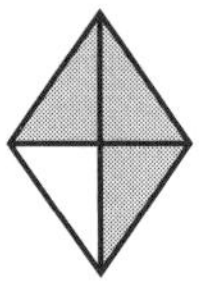

d) 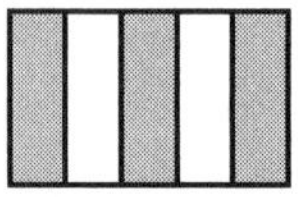

7. Change the fraction to a percentage by first reducing it to lowest terms.

a) $\dfrac{9 \div 3}{15 \div 3} = \dfrac{3}{5} = \dfrac{3 \times 20}{5 \times 20} = \dfrac{60}{100} = 60\%$

b) $\dfrac{12}{15}$

c) $\dfrac{3}{6}$

d) $\dfrac{7}{35}$

e) $\dfrac{21}{28}$

f) $\dfrac{1}{2}$

g) $\dfrac{12}{30}$

h) $\dfrac{10}{40}$

i) $\dfrac{20}{40}$

j) $\dfrac{16}{40}$

k) $\dfrac{60}{150}$

l) $\dfrac{45}{75}$

RP6-14 Visual Representations of Percentages

1. Fill in the chart. The first column has been done for you.

Drawing	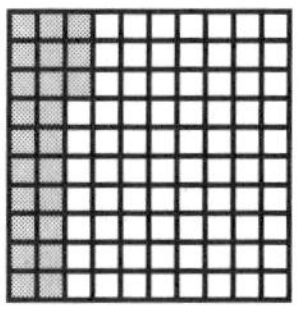	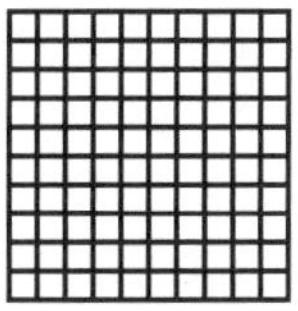	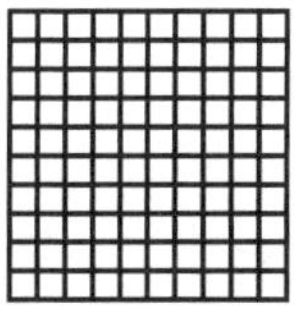	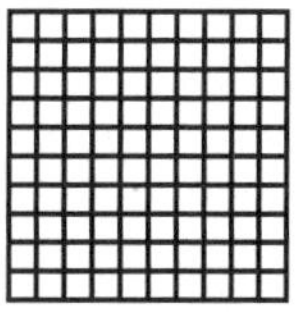
Fraction	$\frac{23}{100}$	$\frac{\_\_\_}{100}$	$\frac{45}{100}$	$\frac{\_\_\_}{100}$
Decimal	0.23	0.___	0.___	0.81
Percentage	23%	63%	___%	___%

Use a ruler for Questions 2–4.

2. Shade 50% of the shape.

a) 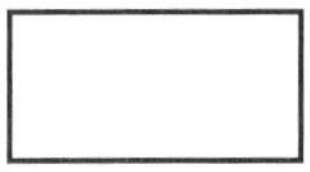

b) 

c) 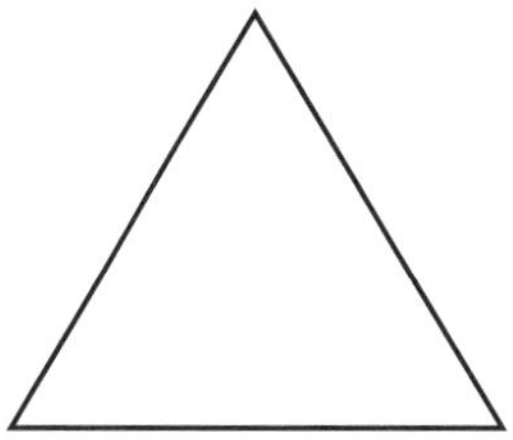

3. Shade 25% of the box.

a) 

b) 

c) 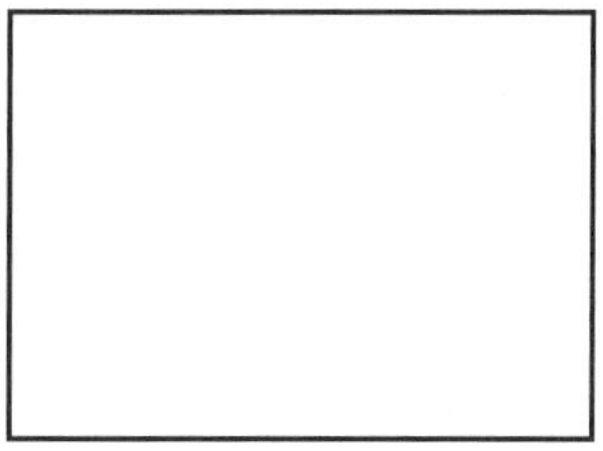

4. Color 50% of the rectangle blue, 40% red, and 10% green.

5. a) Write a fraction for the shaded part: ☐

b) Write the fraction with a denominator of 100: ☐

c) Write a decimal and percentage for the shaded part: _____ _____

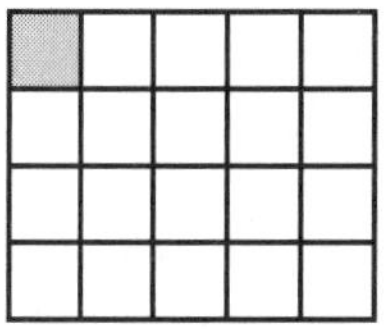

6. Write a fraction and a percentage for each division of the number line.

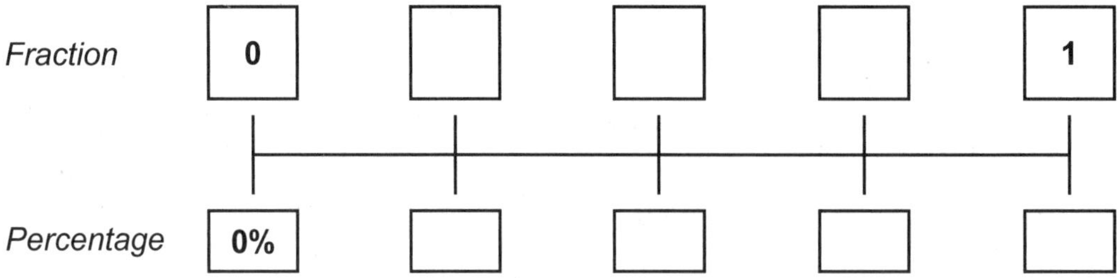

7. Draw marks to show 25%, 50%, and 75% of the line segment.

a) b)

c) d)

8. Extend the line segment to show 100%.

a) 50%

b) 25%

c) 20%

d) 75%

e) 0% 60%

f) 0% 80%

g) 0% 10%

9. Estimate the percentage of the line segment to the left of the mark.

a) 0% 100%

b) 0% 100%

10. Draw a rough sketch of a floor plan for a museum.

The different collections should take up the following amounts of space:

- Dinosaurs 40%
- Animals 20%
- Rocks and Minerals 10%
- Ancient Artifacts 20%

Washrooms should take up the final 10% of the floor space.

11. Asia covers 30% of the world's landmass.
Using a globe, compare the size of Asia to the size of Australia.
Approximately what percentage of the world's landmass does Australia cover?

RP6-15 Comparing Decimals, Fractions, and Percentages

1. From the list below, choose the percentage closest to the fraction.

10%	25%	50%	75%

a) $\frac{3}{5}$ ____ b) $\frac{4}{5}$ ____ c) $\frac{2}{5}$ ____ d) $\frac{2}{10}$ ____

e) $\frac{1}{10}$ ____ f) $\frac{4}{10}$ ____ g) $\frac{9}{10}$ ____ h) $\frac{4}{25}$ ____

i) $\frac{11}{20}$ ____ j) $\frac{16}{20}$ ____ k) $\frac{37}{40}$ ____ l) $\frac{1}{12}$ ____

2. Write $<$, $>$, or $=$ between each pair of numbers. Change the numbers in each pair to fractions with the same denominator first.

a) $\frac{1}{2}$ □ 47% b) $\frac{1}{2}$ □ 53% c) $\frac{1}{4}$ □ 23% d) $\frac{3}{4}$ □ 70%

$\frac{50 \times 1}{50 \times 2}$ □ $\frac{47}{100}$ □ □ □

$\frac{50}{100}$ $>$ $\frac{47}{100}$ □ □ □

e) $\frac{2}{5}$ □ 32% f) 0.27 □ 62% g) 0.02 □ 11% h) $\frac{1}{10}$ □ 10%

□ □ □ □

□ □ □ □

i) $\frac{19}{25}$ □ 93% j) $\frac{23}{50}$ □ 46% k) 0.9 □ 10% l) $\frac{11}{20}$ □ 19%

□ □ □ □

□ □ □ □

3. Write the set of numbers in order from least to greatest by first changing each number to a *fraction.*

a) $\frac{3}{5}$, 42% , .73 b) $\frac{1}{2}$, .73 , 80%

c) $\frac{1}{4}$, .09 , 15% d) $\frac{2}{3}$, 57% , .62

RP6-16 Long Multiplication (Review)

To multiply 37 × 20, first multiply 37 × 2, then multiply by 10.
This is how to record your answer on a grid:

	1	
	3	7
×		2
	7	4

× 10 →

	1	
	3	7
×	2	0
7	4	0

1. Multiply.

a)

	6	3
×		5

→

		6	3
	×	5	0
			0

b)

	4	9
×		3

→

		4	9
	×	3	0
			0

c)

		3	5
	×	8	0

d)

		5	2
	×	9	0

e)

		3	6
	×	5	0

f)

		5	3
	×	6	0

To multiply 37 × 25, split 25 into two numbers that are easier to multiply by. The picture shows why this works.

a multiple of 10 → **20**; a 1-digit number → **5**

$37 \times 25 = 37 \times \mathbf{20} + 37 \times \mathbf{5}$

$= 740 + 185$

$= 925$

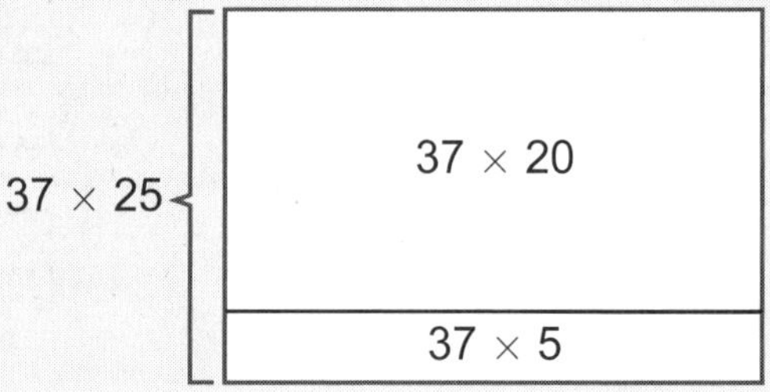

2. Multiply. Do your rough work in your notebook.

a) 34 × 27

34 × 20 = _____

34 × 7 = _____

so 34 × 27 = _____

b) 56 × 32

56 × 30 = _____

56 × 2 = _____

so 56 × 32 = _____

c) 83 × 26

83 × 20 = _____

83 × 6 = _____

so 83 × 26 = _____

d) 78 × 45

78 × 40 = _____

78 × 5 = _____

so 78 × 45 = _____

You can record the steps in multiplying 2-digit numbers on a grid.

Example: Find 37 × 25.

Step 1: Calculate 37 × 5.

Step 2: Calculate 37 × 20.

Step 3: Add the results.

1	*3*	
	3	7
×	2	5
1	*8*	*5* ← 37 × 5
7	*4*	*0* ← 37 × 20
9	*2*	*5*

3. Practice Step 1.

a)

	1	
	2	4
×	1	3
	7	*2* = 24 × 3

b)

	3	3
×	3	9

c)

	5	2
×	4	4

d)

	1	6
×	3	5

4. Practice Step 2.

a)

		1	
		3	4
	×	4	3
	1	*0*	*2*
			= 34 × 40

b)

		1	
		6	9
	×	5	2
	1	*3*	*8*

c)

		1	
		5	2
	×	3	6
	3	*1*	*2*

d)

		3	
		6	7
	×	2	5
	3	*3*	*5*

5. Practice Steps 1 and 2.

a) Regrouping 35 × 20; Regrouping for 35 × 6

		3	5
	×	2	6
			= 35 × 6
			0 = 35 × 20

b)

		3	2
	×	5	4

c)

		4	5
	×	3	5

d)

		1	6
	×	4	2

6. Multiply.

a)

			3	7
		×	2	5
+				*0*

b)

			6	9
		×	5	3
+				*0*

c)

			7	4
		×	5	2

d)

			5	4
		×	3	2

Finding Percentages

If you use a thousands cube to represent 1 whole, you can see that taking $\frac{1}{10}$ of a number is the same as dividing the number by 10—the decimal shifts one place left.

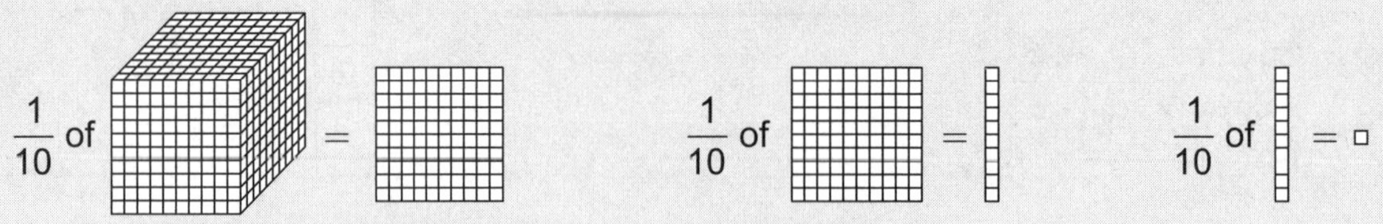

$\frac{1}{10}$ of 1 = 0.1 $\qquad$ $\frac{1}{10}$ of 0.1 = 0.01 $\qquad$ $\frac{1}{10}$ of 0.01 = 0.001

1. Find $\frac{1}{10}$ of the number by shifting the decimal. Write your answer in the box provided.

a) 4 (= 4.0) [*0.4*] b) 7 [ ] c) 32 [ ] d) 120 [ ] e) 3.8 [ ] f) 2.5 [ ]

2. 10% is short for $\frac{1}{10}$. Find 10% of the number.

a) 9 [ ] b) 5.7 [ ] c) 4.05 [ ] d) 6.35 [ ] e) 0.06 [ ] f) 21.1 [ ]

You can find percentages that are multiples of 10.

Example: To find 30% of 21, find 10% of 21 and multiply the result by 3.

Step 1: 10% of 21 = [2.1]

Step 2: 3 × [2.1] = 6.3 ⟶ 30% of 21 = 6.3

3. Find the percentage using the method above.

a) 40% of 15
i) 10% of *15* = [ ]
ii) *4* × [ ] = ____

b) 60% of 25
i) 10% of ____ = [ ]
ii) ___ × [ ] = ____

c) 90% of 2.3
i) 10% of ____ = [ ]
ii) ___ × [ ] = ____

d) 60% of 35
i) 10% of ____ = [ ]
ii) ___ × [ ] = ____

e) 40% of 24
i) 10% of ____ = [ ]
ii) ___ × [ ] = ____

f) 20% of 1.3
i) 10% of ____ = [ ]
ii) ___ × [ ] = ____

RP6-18 Finding Percentages Using Multiplication

Remember: 35% is short for $\frac{35}{100}$. To find 35% of 27, Sadie finds $\frac{35}{100}$ of 27.

Step 1: She multiplies 27 by 35.

2	3	
	2	7
×	3	5
1	3	5
8	1	0
9	4	5

Step 2: She divides the result by 100.

945 ÷ 100 = 9.45

So 35% of 27 is 9.45.

1. Find the percentage using Sadie's method.

a) 45% of 32

Step 1:

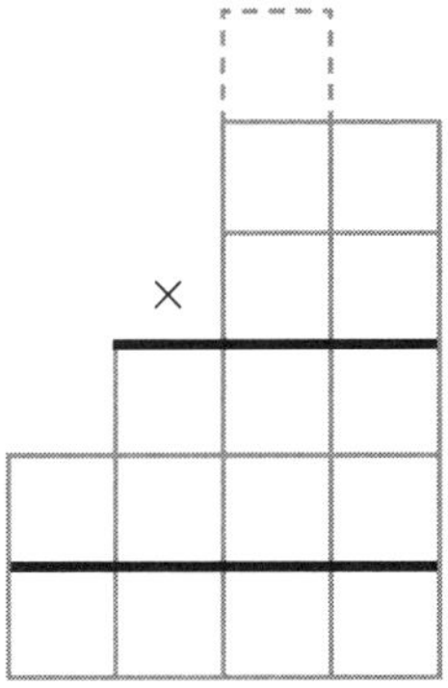

Step 2:

_____ ÷ 100 =

So _____ of _____ is _____ .

b) 28% of 63

Step 1:

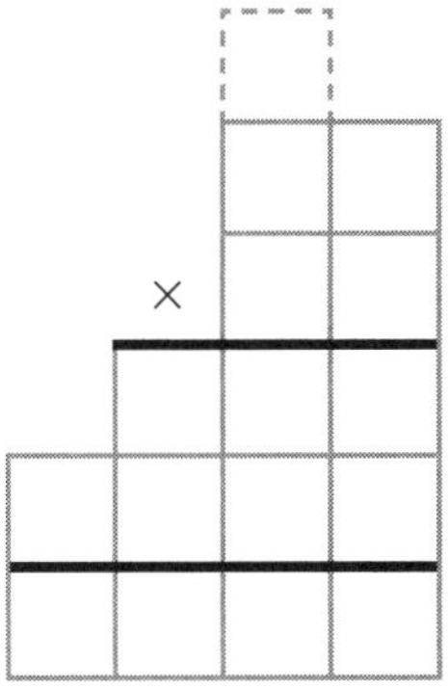

Step 2:

_____ ÷ 100 =

So _____ of _____ is _____ .

2. Find the percentage using Sadie's method.

a) 13% of 9 b) 52% of 7 c) 65% of 8 d) 78% of 9

e) 23% of 42 f) 17% of 68 g) 37% of 80 h) 62% of 75

3. 25% is equal to $\frac{1}{4}$ and 75% is equal to $\frac{3}{4}$. Find...

a) 25% of 80. b) 25% of 280. c) 25% of 12. d) 75% of 20. e) 75% of 320.

Percentages: Word Problems

1. Find the percentage of each child's stamp collection that comes from "other" countries.
Hint: Change all fractions to percentages.

a) Anne's collection:

USA	Canada	Other
40%	$\frac{1}{2}$	
= 40%	*= 50%*	*= 10%*

b) Brian's collection:

USA	England	Other
80%	$\frac{1}{10}$	

c) Juan's collection:

Mexico	USA	Other
$\frac{1}{2}$	40%	

d) Lanre's collection:

USA	Nigeria	Other
22%	$\frac{3}{5}$	

e) Faith's collection:

Jamaica	USA	Other
$\frac{3}{4}$	15%	

f) Carlo's collection:

France	Italy	Other
$\frac{3}{4}$	10%	

2. A painter spends $500.00 on art supplies. Complete the chart.

	Fraction of Money Spent	Percentage of Money Spent	Amount of Money Spent
Brushes			$50.00
Paint	$\frac{4}{10}$		
Canvas		50%	

3. Indra spent 1 hour doing homework. The chart shows the time she spent on each subject.

a) Complete the chart.

b) How did you find the amount of time spent on math?

Subject	Fraction of 1 Hour	Percent of 1 Hour	Decimal	Number of Minutes
English	$\frac{1}{4}$		.25	15
Science	$\frac{1}{20}$	5%		
Math		50%		
French			.20	

4. Roger wants to buy a deck of cards that costs $8.00. The taxes are 15%. How much did he pay in taxes?

5. There are 15 boys and 12 girls in a class.
$\frac{3}{4}$ of the girls have black hair, and 60% of the boys have black hair.
How many children have black hair?

Fractions, Ratios, and Percentages

1. Write the number of boys (**b**), girls (**g**), and children (**c**) in each class.

a) There are 8 boys and 5 girls in a class. **b:** _8_ **g:** _5_ **c:** _13_

b) There are 4 boys and 7 girls in a class. **b:** ____ **g:** ____ **c:** ____

c) There are 12 boys and 15 girls in a class. **b:** ____ **g:** ____ **c:** ____

d) There are 9 girls in a class of 20 children. **b:** ____ **g:** ____ **c:** ____

e) There are 7 boys in a class of 10 children. **b:** ____ **g:** ____ **c:** ____

2. Write the number of boys, girls, and children in each class.
Then write the fraction of children who are boys and the fraction who are girls.

a) There are 5 boys and 6 girls in a class. **b:** _5_ $\frac{5}{11}$ **g:** _6_ $\frac{\square}{\square}$ **c:** ____

b) There are 15 children in the class. 8 are boys. **b:** ____ $\frac{\square}{\square}$ **g:** ____ $\frac{\square}{\square}$ **c:** ____

3. Write the fraction of children in the class who are boys and the fraction who are girls.

a) There are 5 boys and 17 children in the class. **b:** $\frac{5}{17}$ **g:** $\frac{\square}{\square}$

b) There are 3 boys and 2 girls in the class. **b:** $\frac{\square}{\square}$ **g:** $\frac{\square}{\square}$

c) There are 9 girls and 20 children in the class. **b:** $\frac{\square}{\square}$ **g:** $\frac{\square}{\square}$

d) The ratio of boys to girls in the class is 5 : 9. **b:** $\frac{\square}{\square}$ **g:** $\frac{\square}{\square}$

e) The ratio of girls to boys in the class is 7 : 8. **b:** $\frac{\square}{\square}$ **g:** $\frac{\square}{\square}$

f) The ratio of boys to girls in the class is 10 : 11. **b:** $\frac{\square}{\square}$ **g:** $\frac{\square}{\square}$

g) The ratio of boys to students in the class is 11 : 23. **b:** $\frac{\square}{\square}$ **g:** $\frac{\square}{\square}$

h) The ratio of students to girls in the class is 25 : 13. **b:** $\frac{\square}{\square}$ **g:** $\frac{\square}{\square}$

4. Fill in the missing numbers for each classroom.

	Ratio of				What Fraction	
	girls to students	boys to students	girls to boys	boys to girls	are girls?	are boys?
a)	2 : 5	*3 : 5*	*2 : 3*	*3 : 2*	$\frac{2}{5}$	$\frac{3}{5}$
b)	4 : 7					
c)						$\frac{1}{4}$
d)		23 : 50				
e)				9 : 16		
f)						$\frac{1}{2}$
g)			7 : 10			
h)					$\frac{12}{15}$	
i)				25 : 31		

5. Fill in the missing numbers for each classroom.

	Percent that Are Girls	Percent that Are Boys	Fraction that Are Girls	Fraction that Are Boys	Ratio of Girls to Boys
a)	40%	*60%*	$\frac{40}{100}$	$\frac{60}{100}$	*40 : 60*
b)		35%			
c)				$\frac{3}{4}$	
d)					10 : 15
e)			$\frac{1}{2}$		
f)	65%				
g)					23 : 27

There are 3 boys for every 2 girls in a class of 20 students. How many boys are in the class?

Method 1: Julie writes a sequence of equivalent ratios.

3 boys : 2 girls = 6 boys : 4 girls = 9 boys : 6 girls = 12 boys : 8 girls

There are 12 boys in the class.

Stop when the terms of the ratio add to 20.

Method 2: Sally uses different equivalent ratios to find the answer. There are 3 boys for every 5 students in the class.

3 boys : 5 students = 6 boys : 10 students = 9 boys : 15 students = 12 boys : 20 students

There are 12 boys in the class.

Stop when you reach 20.

Method 3: Karen uses fractions. The ratio of boys to girls is 3 : 2.

So the fraction of boys in the class is $\frac{3}{5}$.

$\frac{3}{5} \times 20 = 12$

So there are 12 boys in the class.

6. From the information given, determine the number of girls and boys in each class.

a) There are 20 children in a class. $\frac{2}{5}$ are boys.

b) There are 42 children. $\frac{3}{7}$ are girls.

c) There are 15 children.
The ratio of girls to boys is 3 : 2.

d) There are 24 children.
The ratio of girls to boys is 3 : 5.

7. Which classroom has more girls?

a) In Classroom A, there are 40 children. 60% are girls.

In Classroom B, there are 36 children. The ratio of boys to girls is 5 : 4.

b) In Classroom A, there are 28 children. The ratio of boys to girls is 5 : 2.

In Classroom B, there are 30 children. $\frac{3}{5}$ of the children are boys.

8. Look at the word "California."

a) What is the ratio of vowels to consonants?

b) What fraction of the letters are vowels?

c) What percentage of the letters are consonants?

9. Write the amounts in order from least to greatest: $\frac{1}{20}$, 20% , 0.2. Show your work.

10. Kevin has 360 hockey cards. Thirty percent are New York Rangers cards, and half are Detroit Red Wings cards. The rest are Los Angeles Kings cards. How many cards from each team does Kevin have?

Long Division (Review)

Linda needs to divide 95 objects into 4 equal groups.
She uses long division and a model to solve the problem.

95 = 9 tens + 5 ones

Step 1: Write the numbers like this:

the number of groups ⟶ $4\overline{)95}$ ⟵ the number of objects to be divided

1. Fill in the blanks for the division expression.

a) $2\overline{)53}$ ___ groups ___ tens ___ ones

b) $5\overline{)71}$ ___ groups ___ tens ___ ones

c) $4\overline{)97}$ ___ groups ___ tens ___ ones

d) $5\overline{)88}$ ___ groups ___ tens ___ ones

Step 2: How many tens can be put in each group?

2 tens in each group ⟶ **2**

4 groups ⟶ $4\overline{)95}$

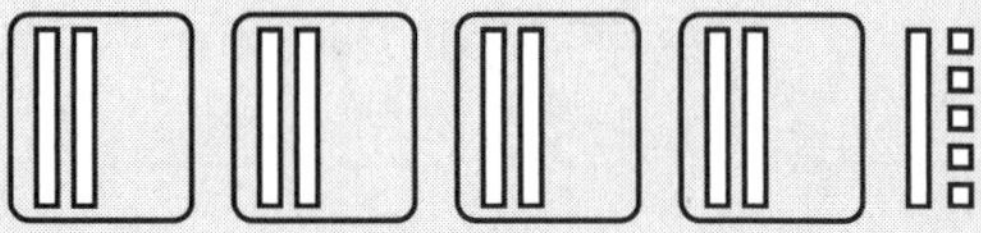

2. How many tens can be put in each group?

a) $\begin{array}{r} 2 \\ 4\overline{)87} \end{array}$

b) $\begin{array}{r} \\ 3\overline{)94} \end{array}$

c) $\begin{array}{r} \\ 6\overline{)74} \end{array}$

d) $\begin{array}{r} \\ 2\overline{)98} \end{array}$

3. For the division expression, write how many groups are being made and how many tens can be put in each group.

a) $4\overline{)55}$

groups _____

number of tens in each group _____

b) $5\overline{)97}$

groups _____

number of tens in each group _____

c) $3\overline{)76}$

groups _____

number of tens in each group _____

d) $3\overline{)89}$

groups _____

number of tens in each group _____

Step 3: How many tens have been placed in the groups altogether?

$\begin{array}{r} \times\ 2 \\ 4\overline{)95} \\ \mathbf{8} \end{array}$

2 ⟵ 2 tens in each group

4 groups ⟶ 4

8 ⟵ 2 × 4 = 8 tens have been placed

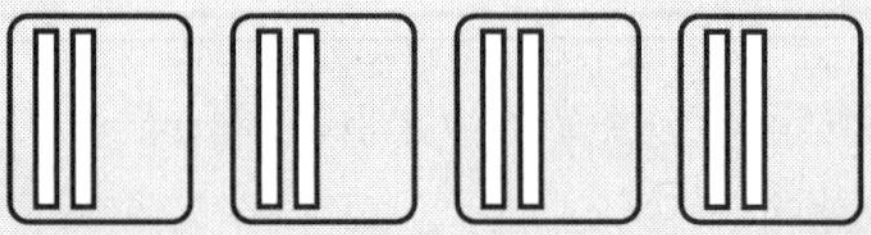

4. Multiply to decide how many tens have been placed altogether.

a) $\begin{array}{r} \times\ 2 \\ 3\overline{)87} \\ 6 \end{array}$

b) $\begin{array}{r} 2 \\ 4\overline{)99} \end{array}$

c) $\begin{array}{r} 3 \\ 2\overline{)79} \end{array}$

d) $\begin{array}{r} 4 \\ 2\overline{)89} \end{array}$

5. Use skip counting to find out how many tens can be placed in each group. Then use multiplication to find out how many tens have been placed altogether.

a) $8\overline{)94}$ b) $5\overline{)94}$ c) $2\overline{)88}$ d) $7\overline{)95}$ e) $3\overline{)87}$

f) $4\overline{)85}$ g) $4\overline{)92}$ h) $5\overline{)63}$ i) $2\overline{)98}$ j) $6\overline{)90}$

Step 4: How many tens are left over?

There are 9 tens.

Linda has placed 8.

9 – 8 = 1 ten is left over →

2	
4) 9	5
– 8	
1	

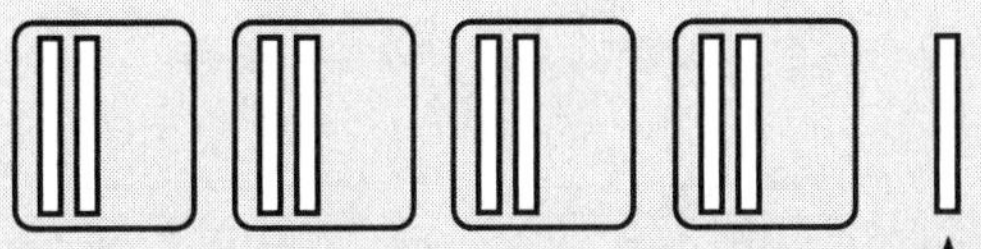

1 ten left over ↑

6. Carry out the first four steps of long division. Use grid paper for parts f) to j).

a) $7\overline{)97}$ b) $3\overline{)74}$ c) $2\overline{)63}$ d) $4\overline{)73}$ e) $6\overline{)89}$

f) $7\overline{)85}$ g) $7\overline{)84}$ h) $3\overline{)87}$ i) $5\overline{)71}$ j) $4\overline{)52}$

Step 5: There are 1 ten and 5 ones left over.
So there are 15 ones left over.

Write 5 beside the 1 to show this.

2	
4) 9	5
– 8	↓
1	**5**

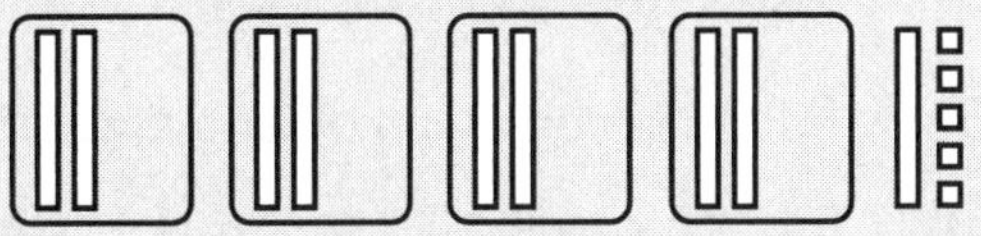

← There are 15 ones still to place

7. Carry out the first five steps of long division. Use grid paper for parts f) to j).

a) $5\overline{)75}$ b) $7\overline{)87}$ c) $4\overline{)93}$ d) $2\overline{)73}$ e) $2\overline{)74}$

f) $8\overline{)97}$ g) $4\overline{)76}$ h) $3\overline{)94}$ i) $7\overline{)91}$ j) $9\overline{)94}$

Step 6: How many ones can be placed in each group?

Divide to find out.

	2	**3**	← 15 ÷ 4 = 3 R?
4)	9	5	
−	8	↓	
	1	**5**	

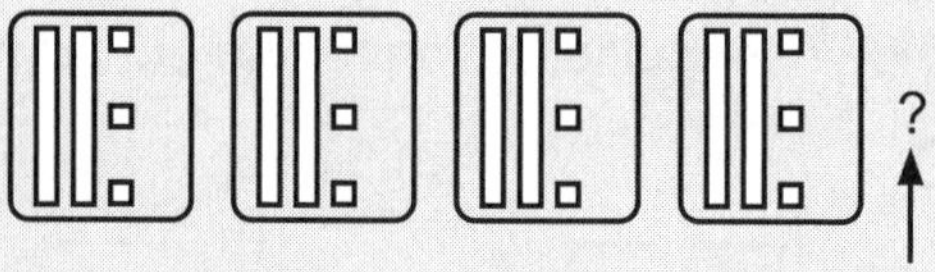

8. Carry out the first six steps of long division.

a) $5\overline{)94}$ b) $4\overline{)87}$ c) $2\overline{)75}$ d) $3\overline{)51}$ e) $5\overline{)72}$

f) $7\overline{)85}$ g) $2\overline{)95}$ h) $8\overline{)96}$ i) $3\overline{)92}$ j) $2\overline{)93}$

Step 7: How many ones are left over?

×	2	**3**	← 3 ones in each group
4)	9	5	← 4 groups
−	8		
	1	**5**	
−	**1**	**2**	← 4 × 3 = 12 ones were placed
		3	← 15 − 12 = 3 ones are left over

95 ÷ 4 = 23 with 3 left over

9. Carry out all seven steps of long division. Use grid paper for parts f) to j).

a) $4\overline{)71}$ b) $5\overline{)84}$ c) $6\overline{)96}$ d) $7\overline{)85}$ e) $9\overline{)95}$

f) $4\overline{)65}$ g) $6\overline{)78}$ h) $3\overline{)84}$ i) $3\overline{)75}$ j) $3\overline{)96}$

RP6-22 Long Division and Unit Rates

Divide 334 objects into 2 groups using long division and a base ten model: 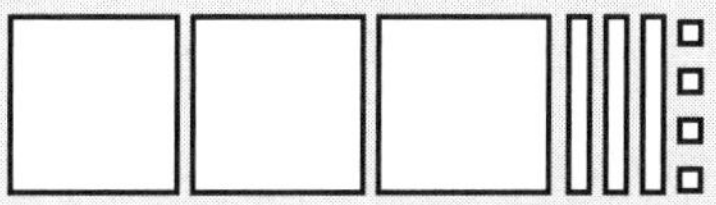

Step 1: Divide the hundreds into 2 groups.

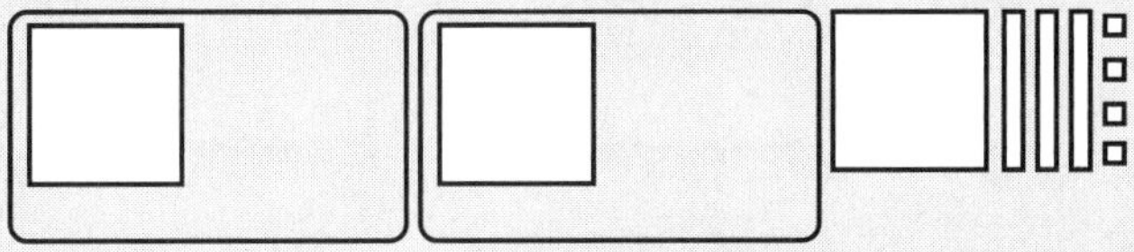

	1			← 1 hundred in each group
2)	3	3	4	
−	**2**			← 2 hundreds placed
	1			← 1 hundred left over

Step 2: Regroup the remaining hundreds as tens.

	1			
2)	3	3 ↓	4	
−	2			
	1	**3**		← 13 tens

1. Carry out the first two steps of long division.

a)

	1		
2)	3	1	6
−	*2*		

b)

3)	8	1	5
−			

c)

2)	7	4	6
−			

d)

5)	9	3	7
−			

e)

4)	9	5	1
−			

Step 3: Divide the tens into 2 groups.

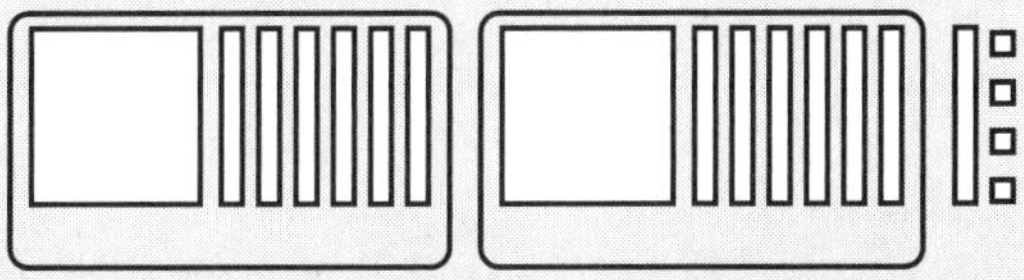

	1	**6**		← 6 tens in each group
2)	3	3	4	
−	2			
	1	3		
	1	**2**		← 12 tens placed
		1		← 1 ten left over

Step 4: Regroup and divide the remaining ones.

	1	6	**7**	← 7 ones in each group
2)	3	3	4	
−	2			
	1	3		
	1	2		
		1	**4**	← 1 ten + 4 ones = 14 ones
		1	**4**	← 14 ones placed
			0	← 0 left over

So **334** ÷ **2** = **167**

2. Divide. Use grid paper.

a) 5) 7 8 6

b) 4) 7 8 1

c) 3) 8 3 5

d) 6) 8 7 5

e) 8) 9 9 5

3. In each question below, there are fewer hundreds than the number of groups. Write a "0" in the hundreds place to show that no hundreds can be placed in equal groups. Then perform the division as if the hundreds had been exchanged for tens.

a)

	0	***4***	3	*4 tens in each group*
8)	3	4	6	
–	***3***	***2***		*32 tens placed*
		2	6	*2 tens are left over*
–		2	*4*	
			2	

b)

5)	4	7	5
–			
–			

c)

9)	2	9	9
–			
–			

d)

7)	3	6	7
–			
–			

e) 3)115 f) 4)341 g) 8)425 h) 6)379 i) 9)658

4. In each question below, there are not enough tens to divide into the groups. Write a "0" in the tens place to show that no tens can be placed, then continue the division, regrouping tens as ones.

a)

	2	***0***	8	*0 tens in each group*
3)	6	2	5	
–	*6*			
	0	***2***		*2 tens to place in 3 groups*
–		***0***		*0 tens placed*
		2	*5*	
–		*2*	*4*	
			1	

b)

4)	8	3	5
–			
–			
–			

c)

2)	8	1	5
–			
–			
–			

d)

7)	7	5	3
–			
–			
–			

5. Divide.

a) 3)417 b) 4)821 c) 8)725 d) 6)973 e) 9)639

6. Divide to find the missing information.

a) 5 jackets cost $75

1 jacket costs _____

b) 6 tickets cost $138

1 ticket costs _____

c) 148 miles per 4 gallons

_____ miles per 1 gallon

7. Find the unit rate.

a) 3 boxes for 72 cans

1 box for _____ cans

b) 236 miles in 4 hours

_____ miles in 1 hour

c) $104 for 8 hours

_____ per hour

8. Which is the best deal for renting skates? **A.** $30 for 2 hours, **B.** $48 for 4 hours, or **C.** $39 for 3 hours

G6-1 Polygons (Review)

Polygons are named according to how many sides they have.

3 sides: triangle 4 sides: quadrilateral 5 sides: pentagon 6 sides: hexagon

1. Count the sides. Then name the shape.

a) 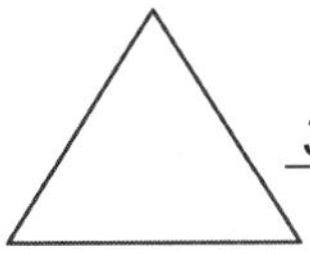 3 sides

triangle

b) 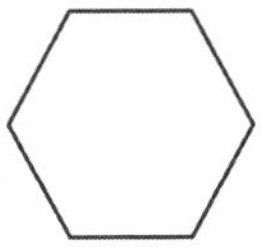 ___ sides

____

c) 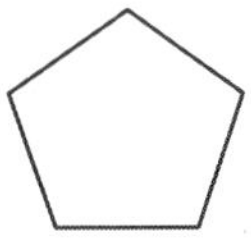 ___ sides

____

d) 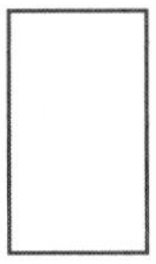 ___ sides

____

2. Complete the chart. Find as many shapes as you can for each shape name.

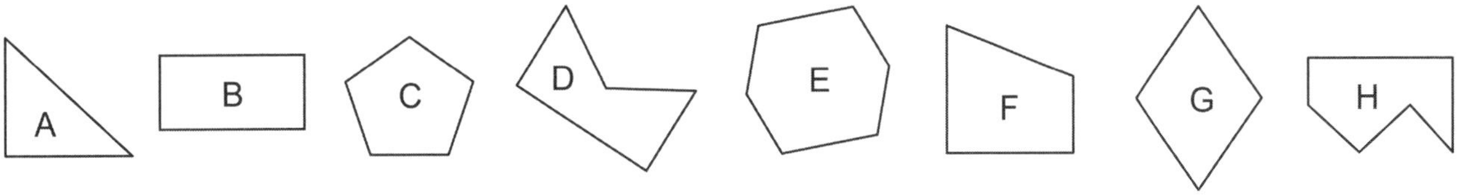

Shapes	Letters
Triangles	
Quadrilaterals	

Shapes	Letters
Pentagons	
Hexagons	

In mathematics, square corners are called **right angles**.

A rectangle has 4 right angles.

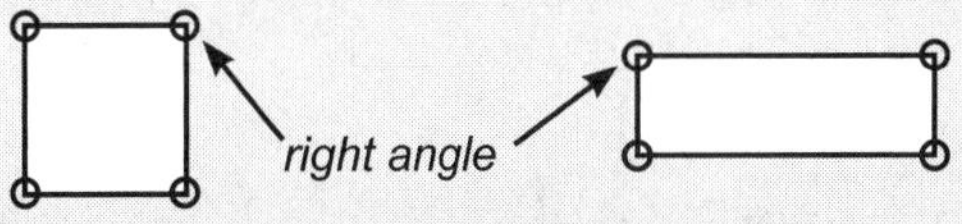

To check if an angle is a right angle, compare it with a corner of a piece of paper.

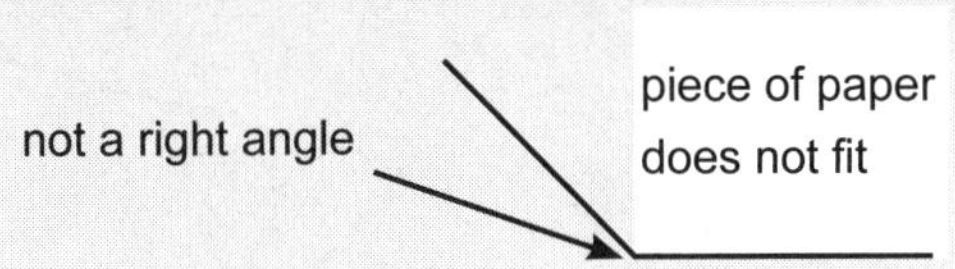

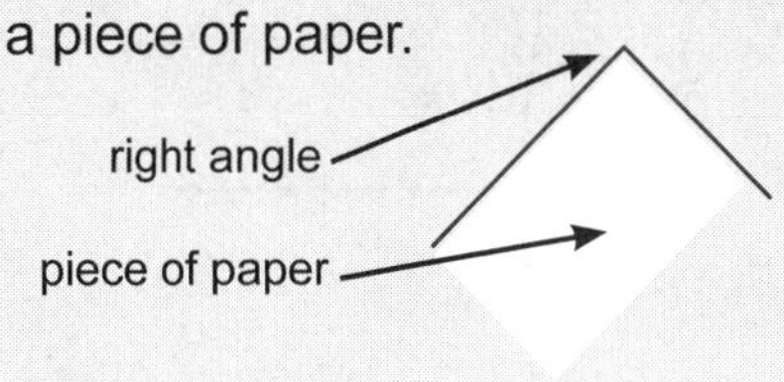

3. Circle the right angles. Check your answers with the corner of a piece of paper.

a) 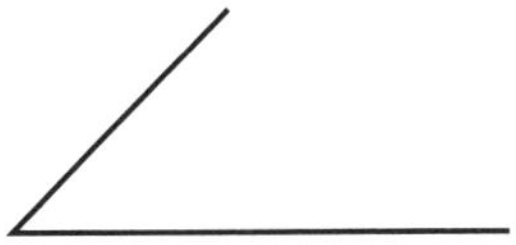

b) 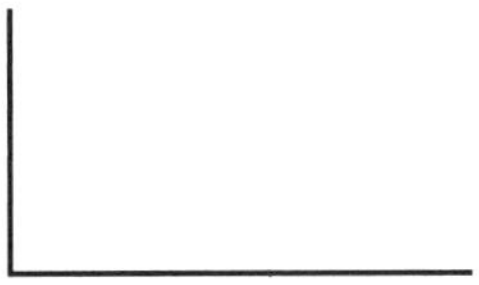

c) 

d) 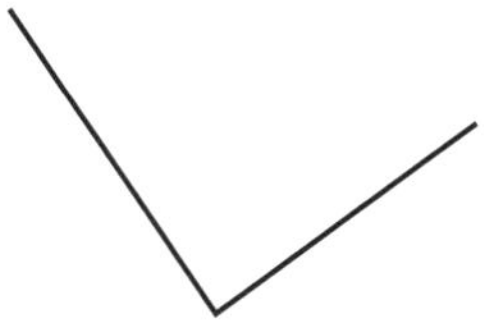

e) 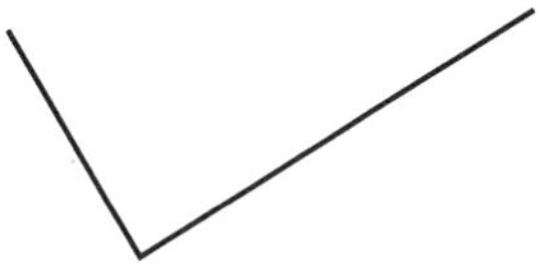

f) 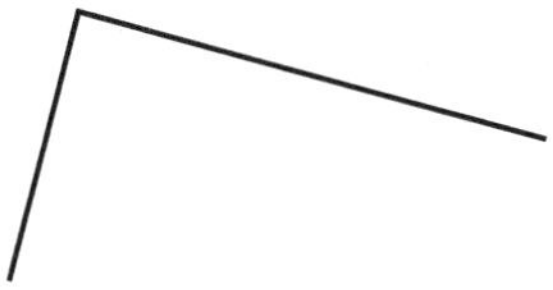

g) 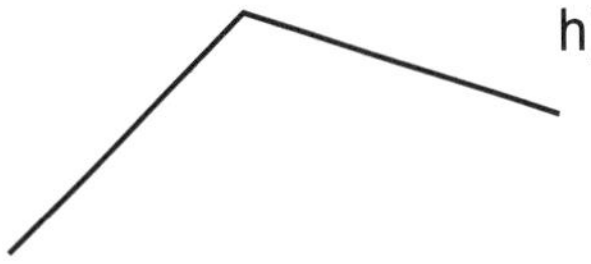

h) 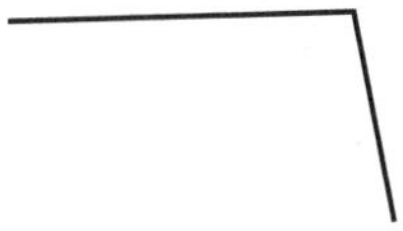

Mathematicians use a small square to mark right angles.

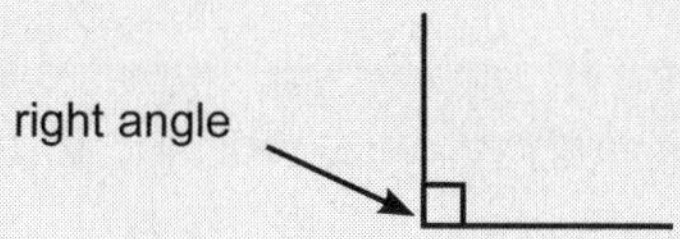

4. Mark the right angles with a small square.

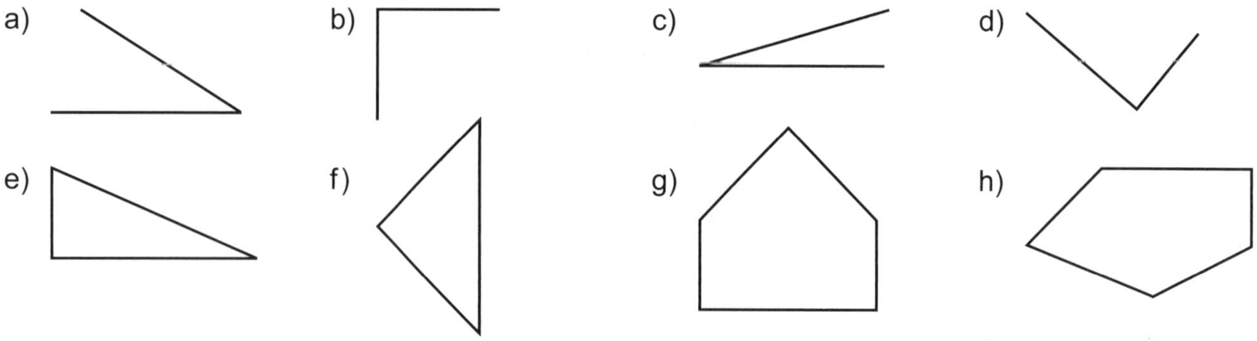

5. Circle the shape that has no right angle.

When two lines make a right angle, they are called **perpendicular lines**.

6. Which lines are perpendicular? Check for right angles and mark them.

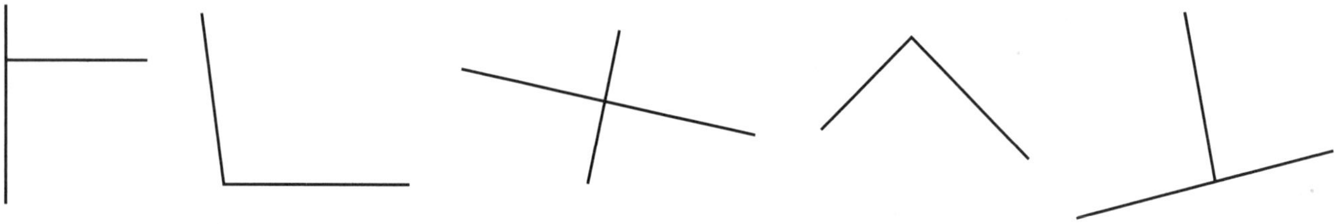

7. Which polygons have pairs of perpendicular sides? Mark the right angles with small squares.

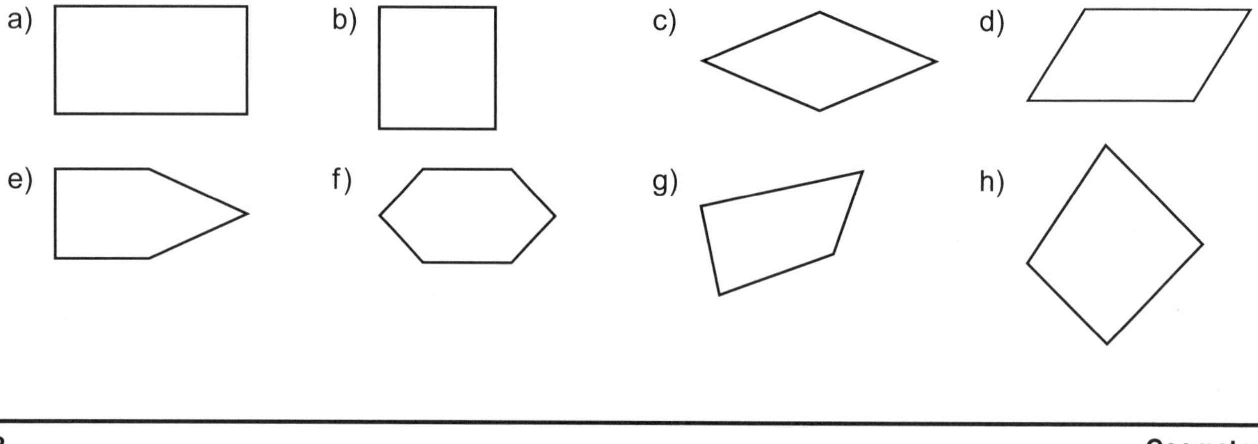

G6-2 Special Quadrilaterals

Parallel lines are like the long, straight rails on a railroad track.
Parallel lines are:

- Straight
- Always the same distance apart

You can extend lines in both directions as much as you want.
No matter how long they are, parallel lines will **never** meet.

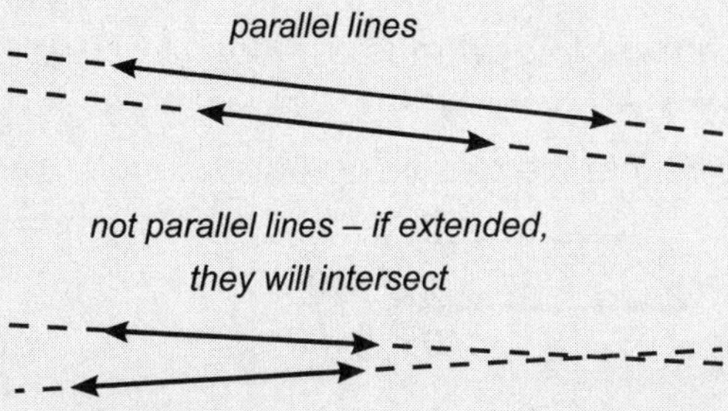

1. Extend the lines to check if they intersect. Then circle parallel lines.

a)

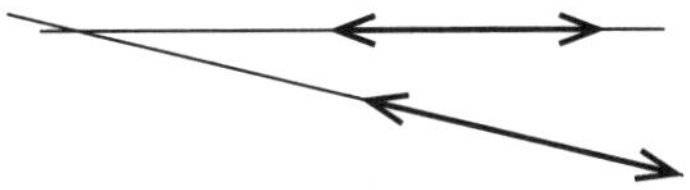

b)

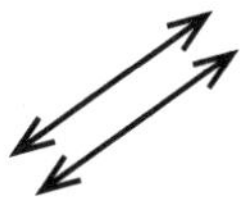

c)

d)

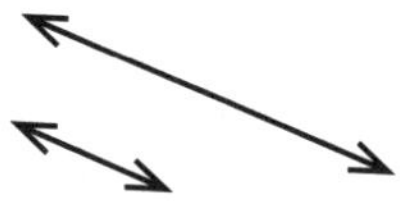

2. Each shape below has one pair of parallel sides. Mark opposite sides that are not parallel with an "X."

a)

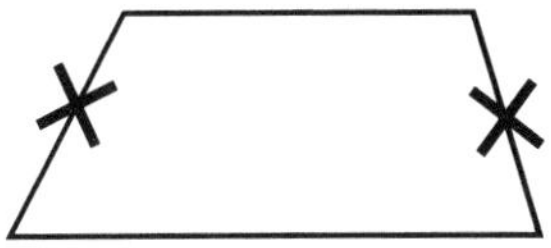

b)

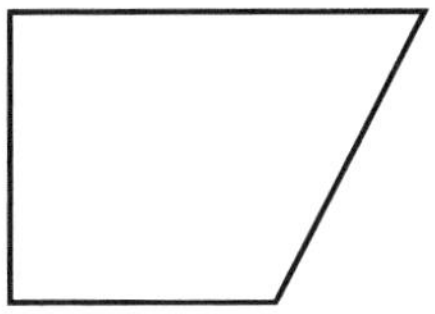

c)

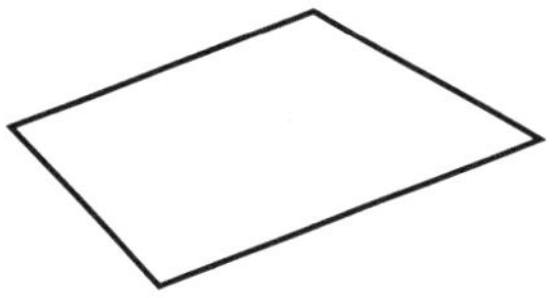

d)

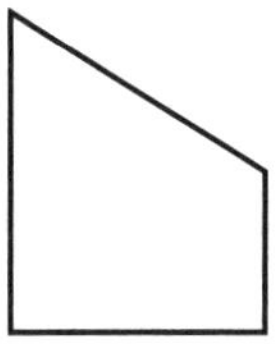

We use arrows to mark parallel sides. If there is more than one pair of parallel sides in a shape, use a different number of arrows for each pair.

Example:

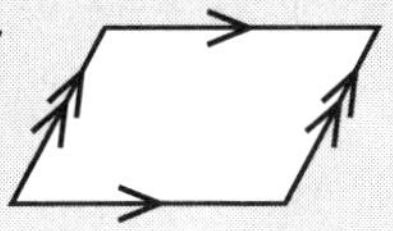

3. Mark all the pairs of parallel sides in each shape. Write the number of pairs in the blank.

a)

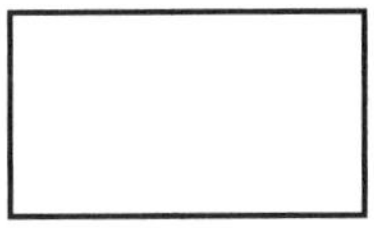

_____ pairs

b)

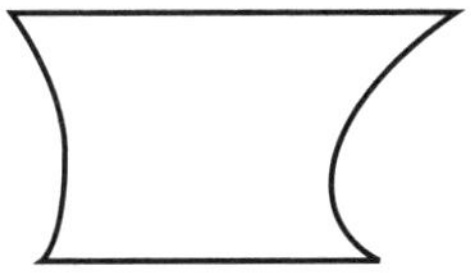

_____ pair

c)

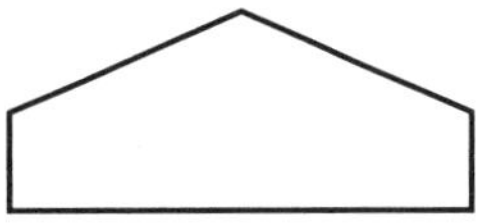

_____ pair

d)

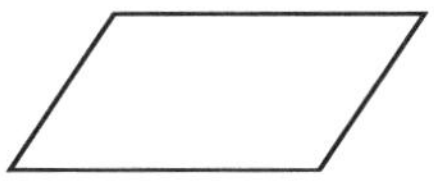

_____ pairs

e)

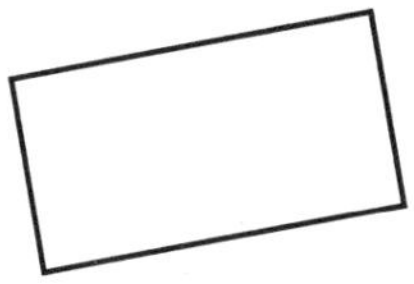

_____ pairs

f)

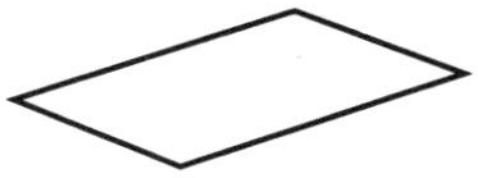

_____ pairs

g)

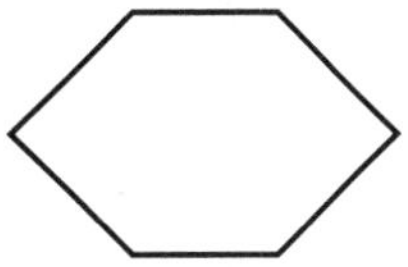

_____ pairs

BONUS ▶

_____ pairs

Some quadrilaterals (polygons with 4 sides) have special names.

A **parallelogram** is a quadrilateral with 2 pairs of parallel sides.

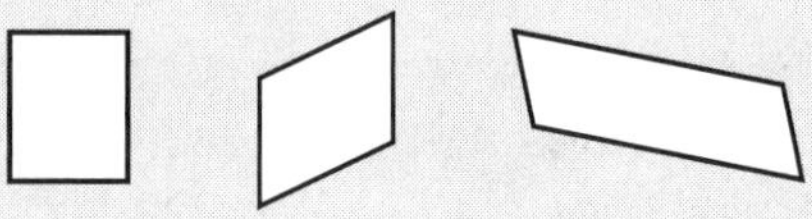

4. Circle the parallelograms.

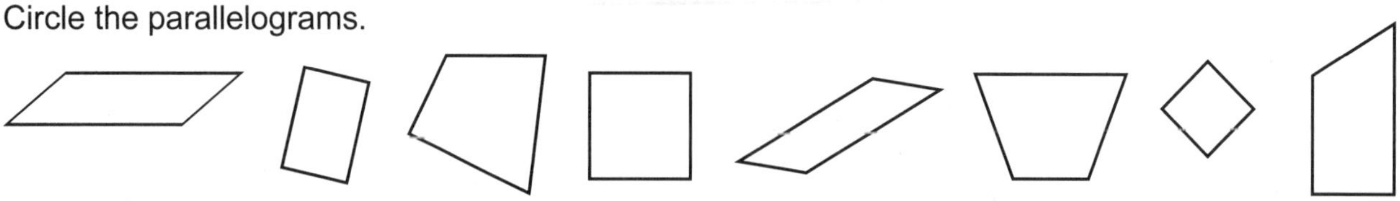

A **rhombus** is a parallelogram with 4 equal sides.

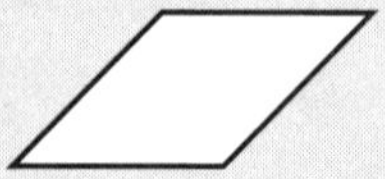

A **rectangle** is a parallelogram with 4 right angles.

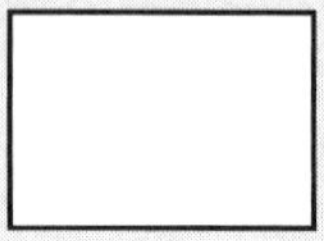

A **square** is a parallelogram with 4 right angles and 4 equal sides.

A **trapezoid** is a quadrilateral with exactly one pair of parallel sides.

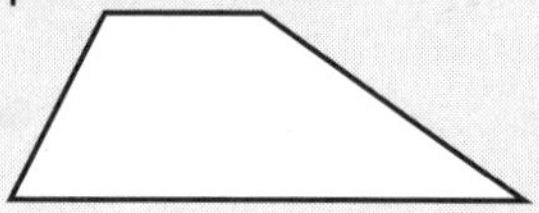

5. Mark all right angles in the quadrilaterals and measure the length of each side. Then choose the best (most specific) name for each quadrilateral.

a) ______ cm

______ cm  ______ cm

______ cm

Name: ______________________

b) ______ cm

______ cm 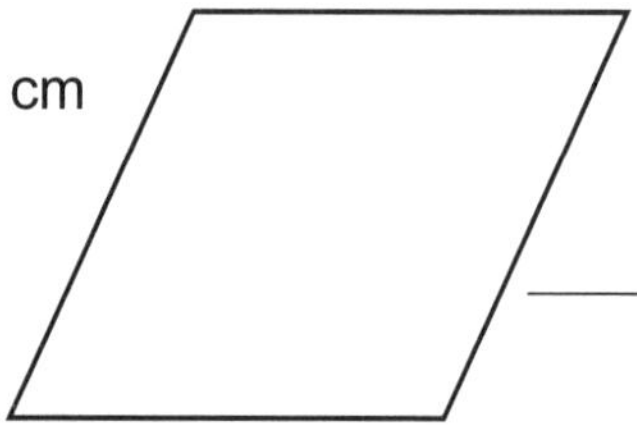 ______ cm

______ cm

Name: ______________________

6. Name the shapes. Use the words "rhombus," "square," "parallelogram," and "rectangle."

a) 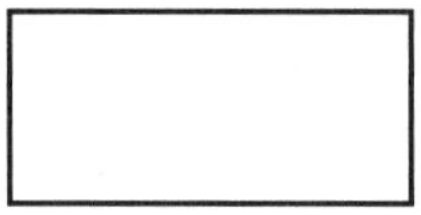

____

b) 

____

c) 

____

d) 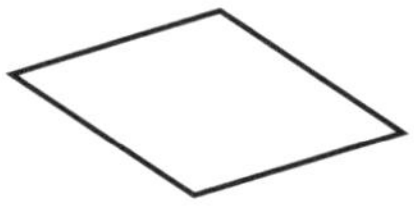

____

e) 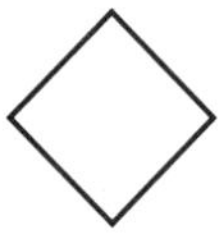

____

f) 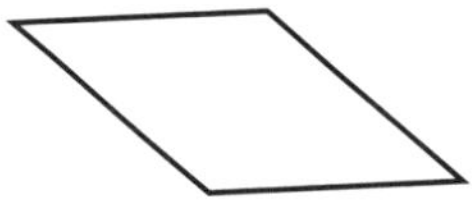

____

g) 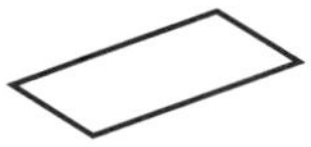

____

h) 

____

7. For each quadrilateral, write how many *pairs* of sides are parallel.
Then identify the quadrilateral.

a) 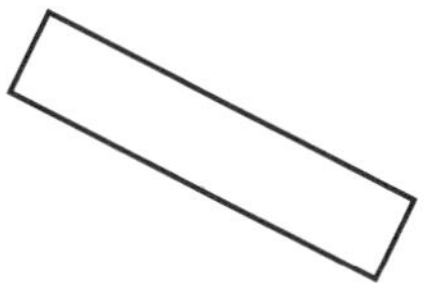

b) 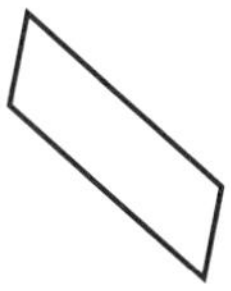

c) 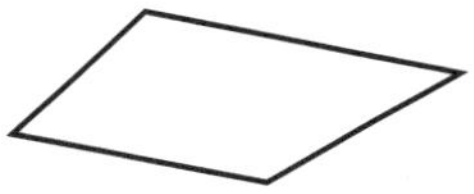

d) 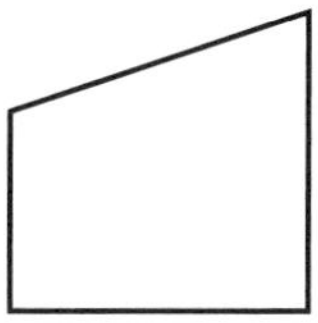

8. Sketch a quadrilateral with …

a) no parallel sides.

b) one pair of parallel sides.

c) two pairs of parallel sides and no right angles.

9. Use the words "all," "some," or "no" for each statement.

a) _______ squares are rectangles.

b) _______ trapezoids are parallelograms.

c) _______ parallelograms are trapezoids.

d) _______ parallelograms are rectangles.

10. a) A shape has four right angles. Which two special quadrilaterals might it be?

_________________ or _________________

b) A quadrilateral has all equal sides. Which two special quadrilaterals might it be?

_________________ or _________________

c) Write three different names for a square.

_________________, _________________, and _________________

11. Describe any similarities or differences between …

a) a rhombus and a parallelogram.

b) a rhombus and a square.

c) a trapezoid and a parallelogram.

d) a rhombus and a rectangle.

BONUS ▶ Explain one of your answers in Question 11.

G6-3 Parallel Lines on a Grid

1. How many units **right** (⟶) or **left** (⟵) did the dot slide from position 1 to position 2?

a) 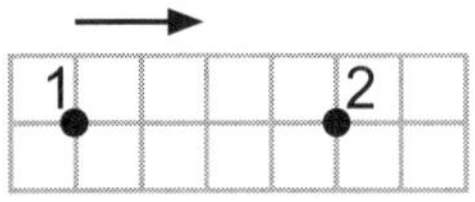

________ units right

b) 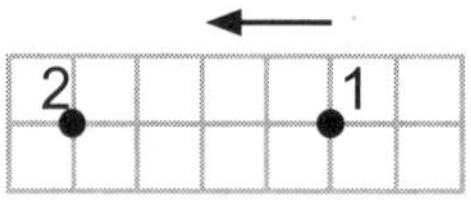

____

c) 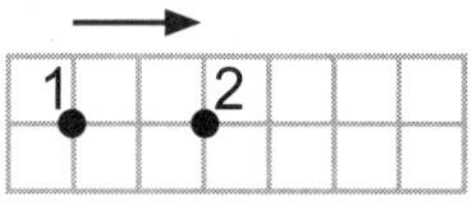

____

2. How many units **right** or **left** and how many units **up** or **down** did the dot slide from position *A* to position *B*?

a) 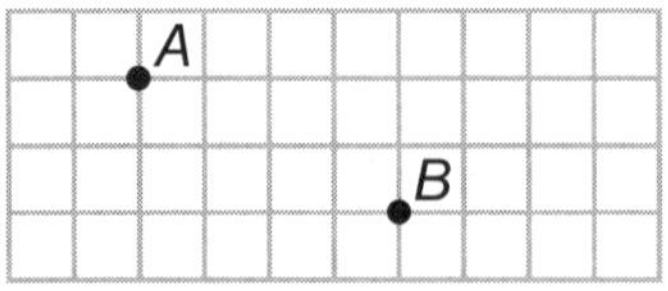

___ units right ___ units down

b) 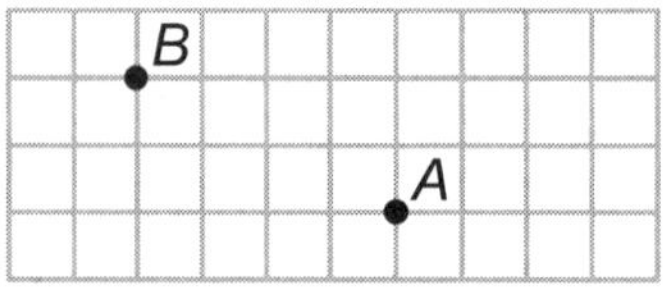

___ units left___ units up

c) 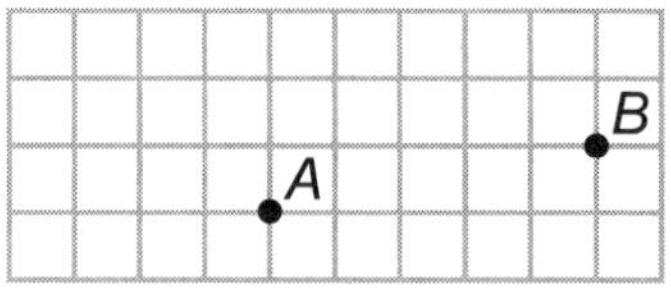

___ units right ___ unit up

3. Slide the dot.

a) 5 units right; 2 units down

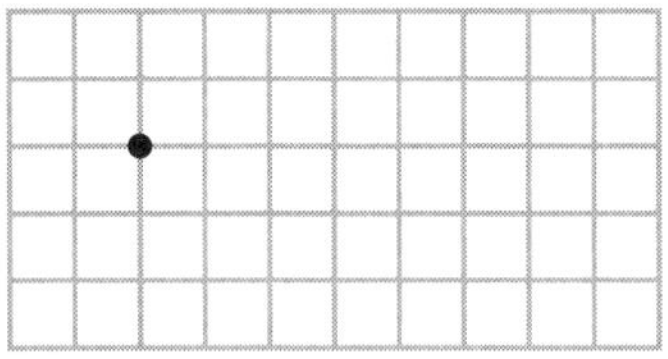

b) 6 units left; 3 units up

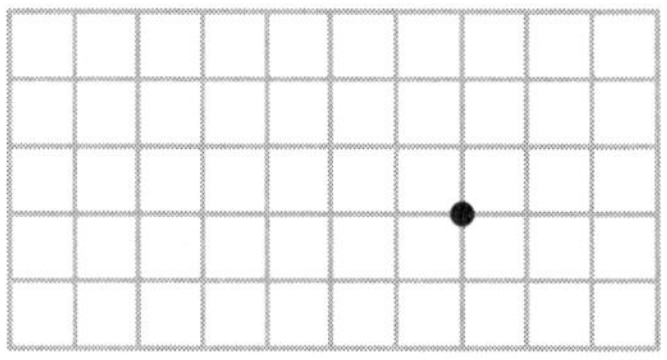

c) 3 units left; 4 units down

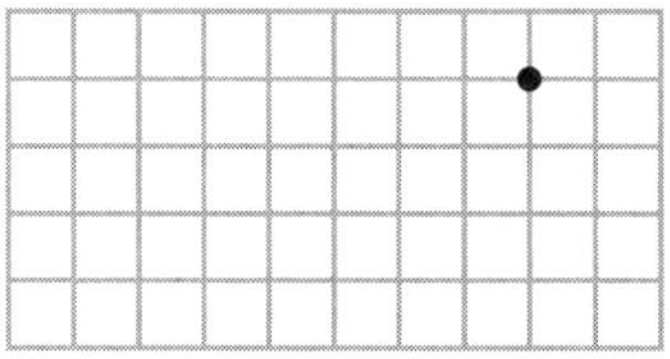

4. a) Slide both dots using the directions given. Draw a line segment between each dot and its image.

i) 3 units right; 1 unit down

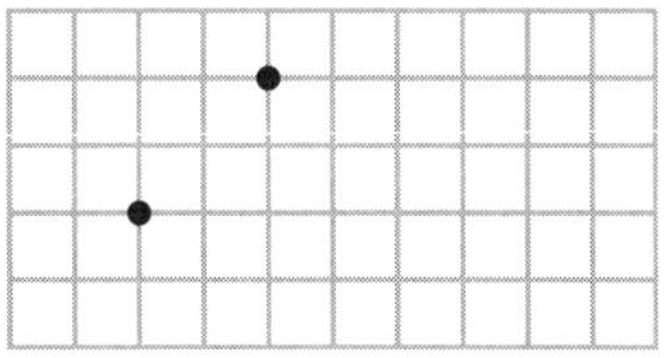

ii) 5 units left; 2 units up

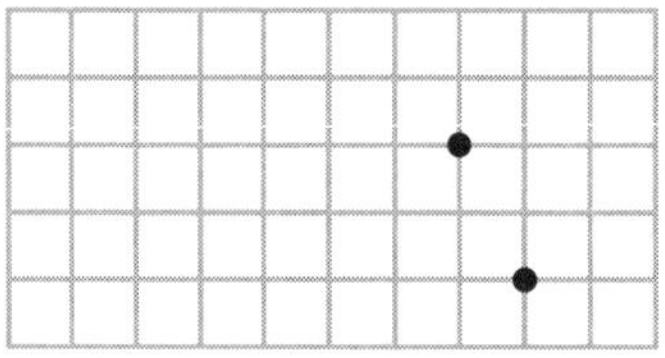

iii) 6 units left; 2 units down

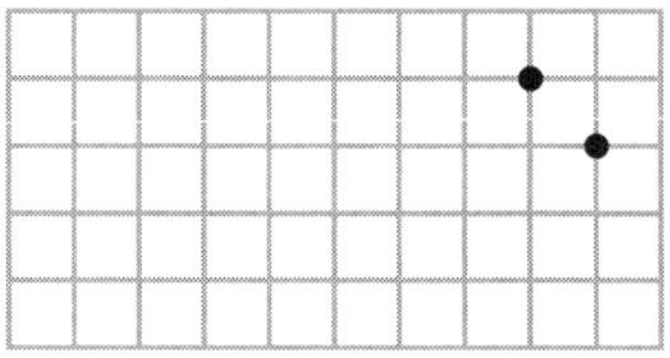

b) Are the line segments you drew parallel? ________________________________

5. a) Line segments *AB* and *CD* are parallel and equal. Describe the slide from *A* to *B* and from *C* to *D*. What do you notice?

b) Join *B* to *D* and *A* to *C*. How many pairs of parallel sides does the quadrilateral *ABDC* have?

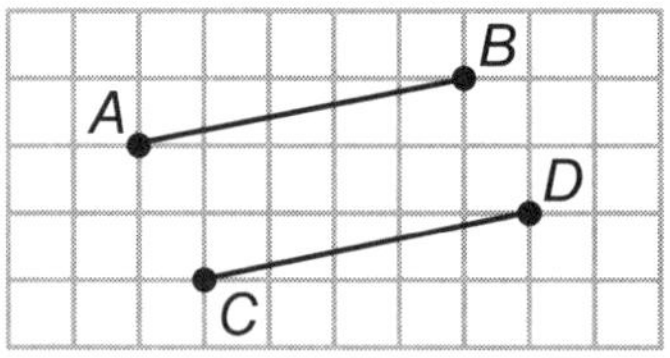

G6-4 Coordinate Systems

1. Join the dots in the given column, row, or both.

a) Column 2

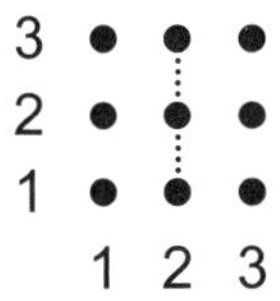

b) Row 3

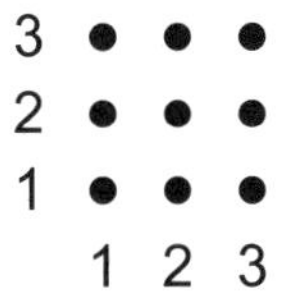

c) Column 3, Row 1

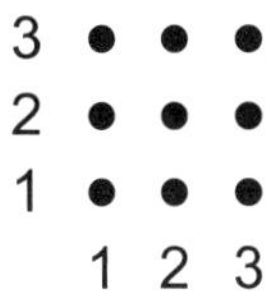

d) Column 1, Row 2

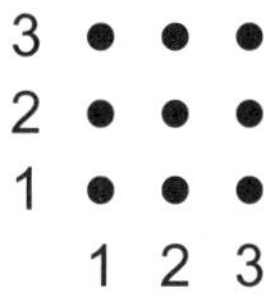

2. Circle the dot in the given position.

a) Column 2, Row 1

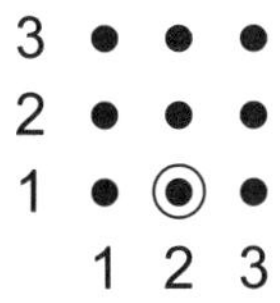

b) Column 3, Row 2

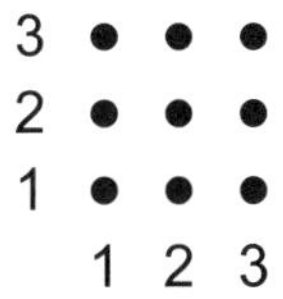

c) Column 3, Row 1

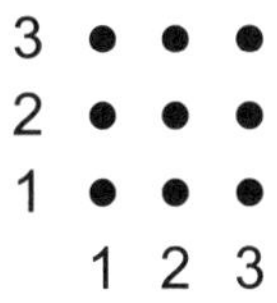

d) Column 2, Row 2

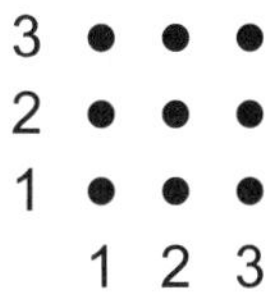

The row and the column for a point can be written in brackets.
The column is always written first.

(5, 3)
column ↗ ↖ row

3. Circle the dot in the given position.

a) (2, 1)

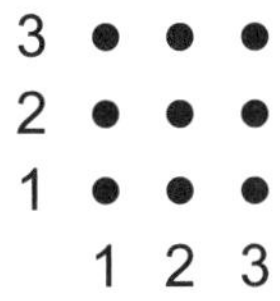

b) (3, 3)

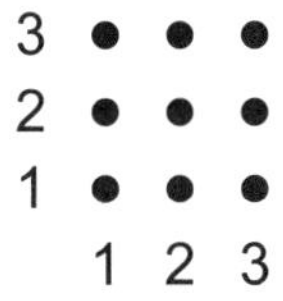

c) (1, 2)

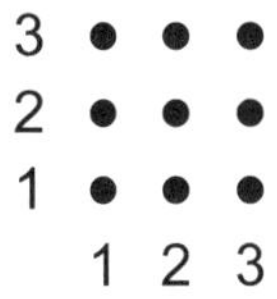

d) (2, 3)

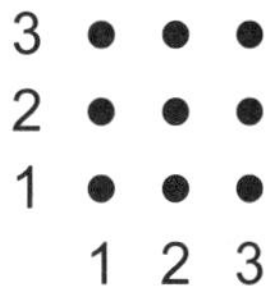

You can use letters instead of numbers to label rows and columns.

4. Circle the given point.

a) (A, 3)

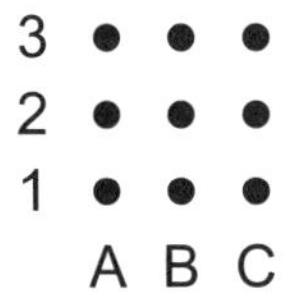

b) (Y, B)

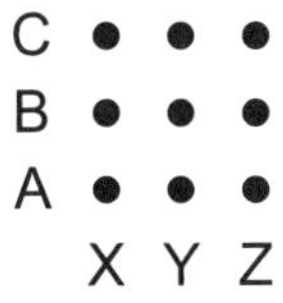

c) (0, 2)

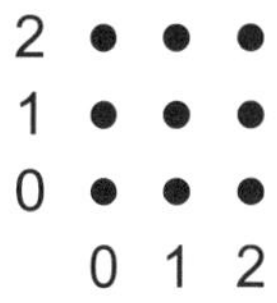

d) (0, 0)

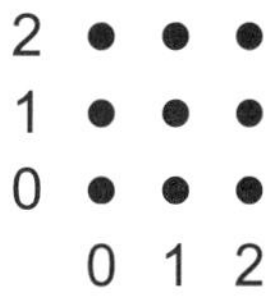

e) (A, C)

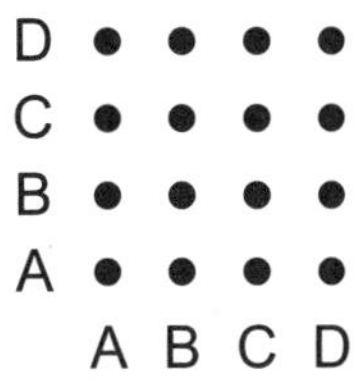

f) (2, X)

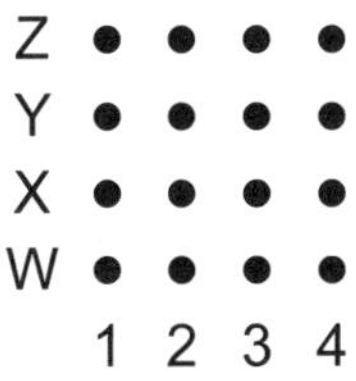

g) (4, 1)

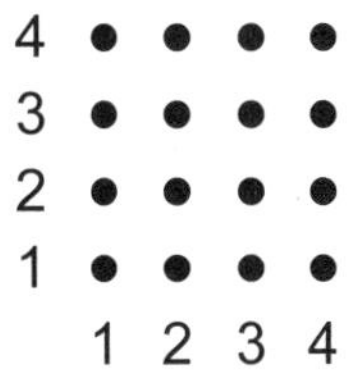

h) (3, 4)

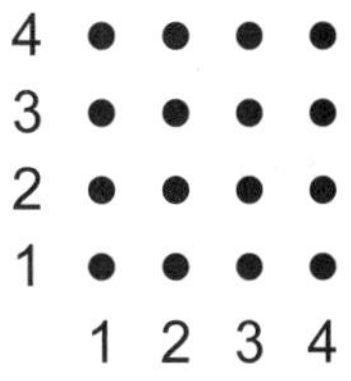

Two numbers in brackets in order are called an **ordered pair.** The ordered pair that gives the position of a point on a grid is called the **coordinates** of the point.

5. a) Plot and label the points on the coordinate grid. Cross out the points as you go.

~~*A* (1, 5)~~ *B* (1, 7) *C* (3, 7) *D* (6, 4)

E (7, 4) *F* (8, 3) *G* (7, 3) *H* (5, 1)

I (5, 0) *J* (4, 1) *K* (4, 2)

b) Join the points in alphabetical order. Then join *A* to *K*.

c) What does the picture you've got look like?

____

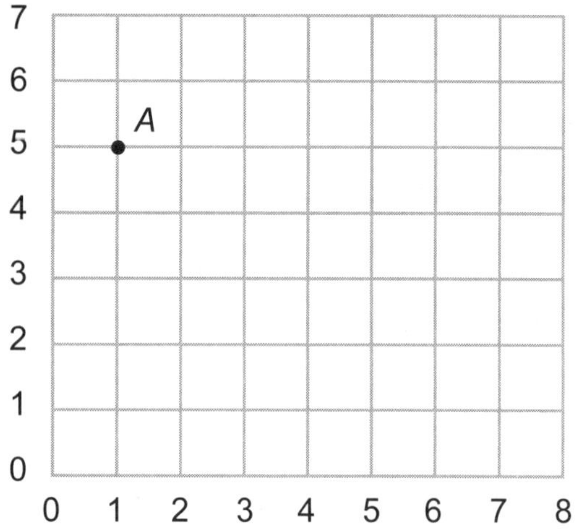

6. Graph each set of ordered pairs and join the dots to form a polygon. Identify the special quadrilateral drawn. The special quadrilaterals are parallelogram, rectangle, rhombus, trapezoid, square.

a) *A* (1, 2) *B* (4, 4) *C* (3, 2) *D* (0, 0)

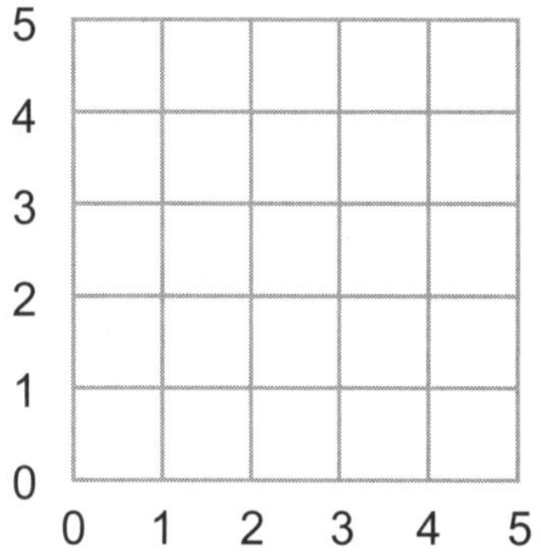

ABCD is a ____________________.

b) *E* (3, 0) *F* (3, 5) *G* (1, 3) *H* (1, 1)

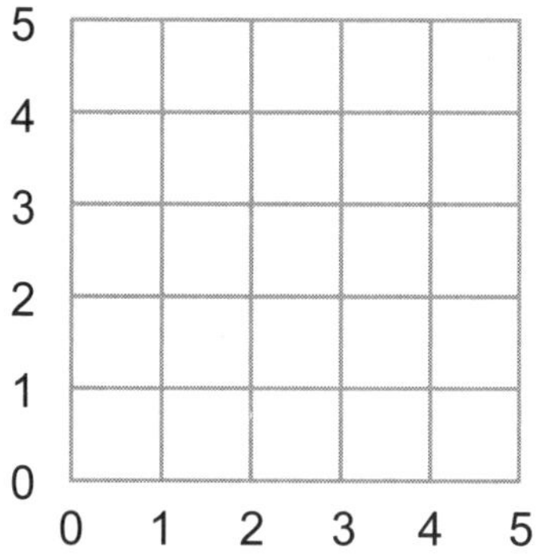

EFGH is a ____________________.

7. a) Plot and label the points on the coordinate grid. Cross out the points as you go.

~~*A* (2, 1)~~ *B* (5, 1) *C* (5, 4) *D* (2, 4)

E (9, 5) *F* (7, 6) *G* (0, 0) *H* (0, 3)

b) Join the correct points to make each quadrilateral, then identify it.

ABCD ____________________

BEFC ____________________

ADHG ____________________

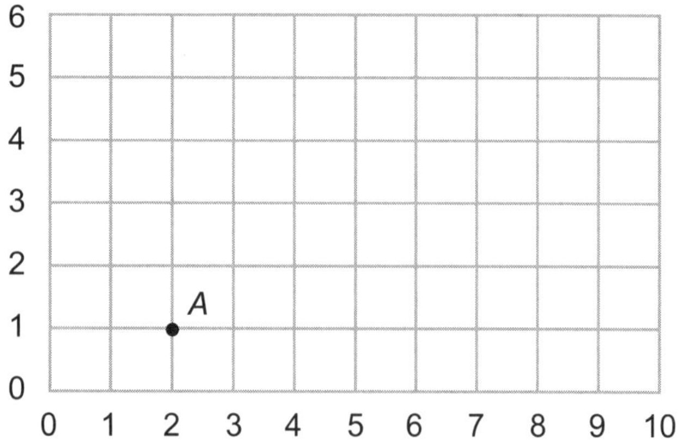

8. Write the coordinates of each point.

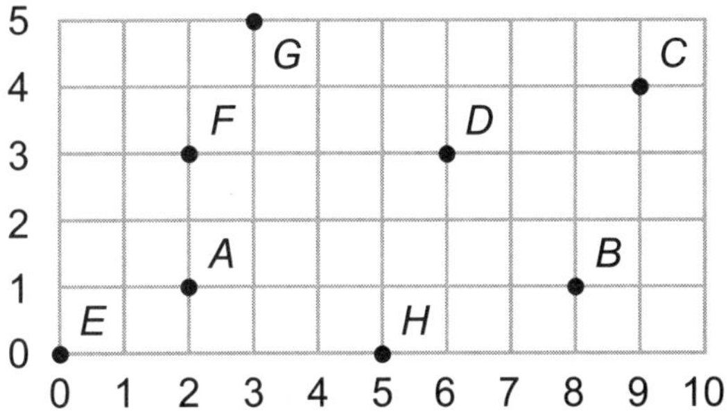

A (,) *B* (,)
C (,) *D* (,)
E (,) F (,)
G (,) *H* (,)

9. Add a point *D* so that the four points become the vertices of the given quadrilateral *ABCD*. Then write the coordinates of the vertices.

a) rectangle

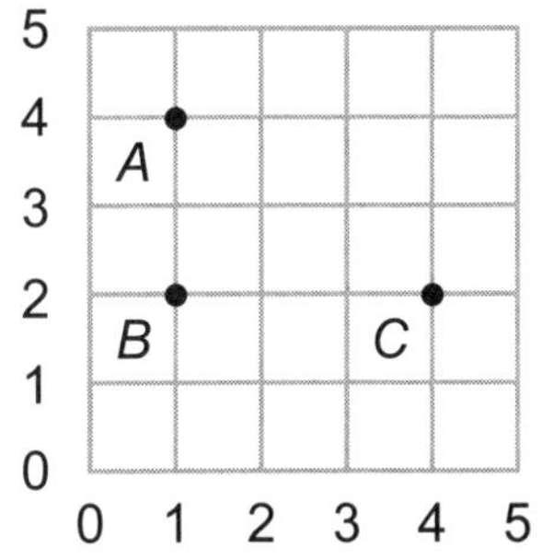

A (,), *B* (,),
C (,), *D* (,)

b) a parallelogram

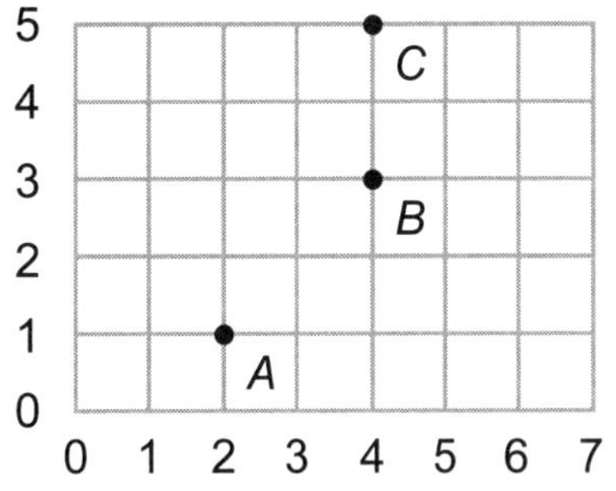

A (,), *B* (,),
C (,), *D* (,)

10. Draw a quadrilateral of the given type on the grid. Write the coordinates of the vertices.

a) a trapezoid

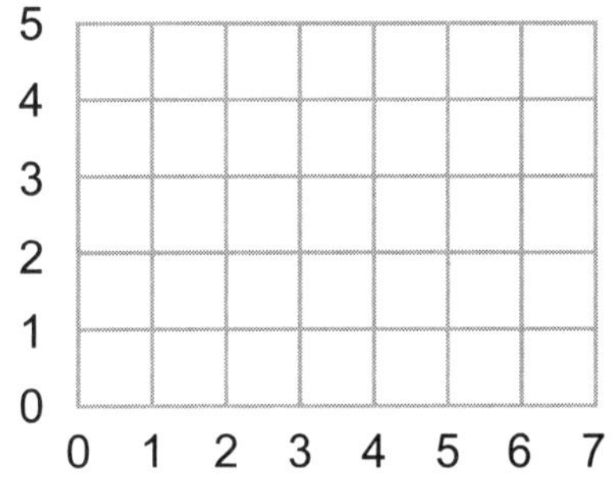

A (,), *B* (,),
C (,), *D* (,)

b) a rhombus

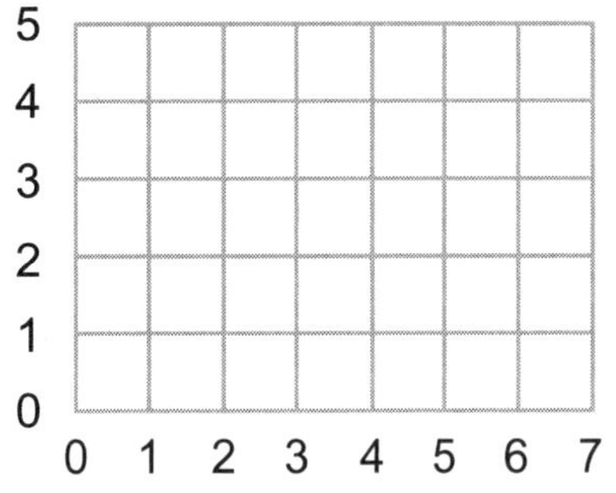

A (,), *B* (,),
C (,), *D* (,)

BONUS ▶ Draw a polygon on a coordinate grid (use grid paper). Tell a partner the coordinates of the vertices of your polygon. Have your partner name the polygon.

G6-5 Horizontal and Vertical Distance

1. a) Find the horizontal distance between the points.

   i) (2, 0) and (7, 0): ___5___ units

   ii) (2, 1) and (7, 1): ______ units

   iii) (2, 3) and (7, 3): ______ units

   iv) (2, *y*) and (7, *y*): ______ units

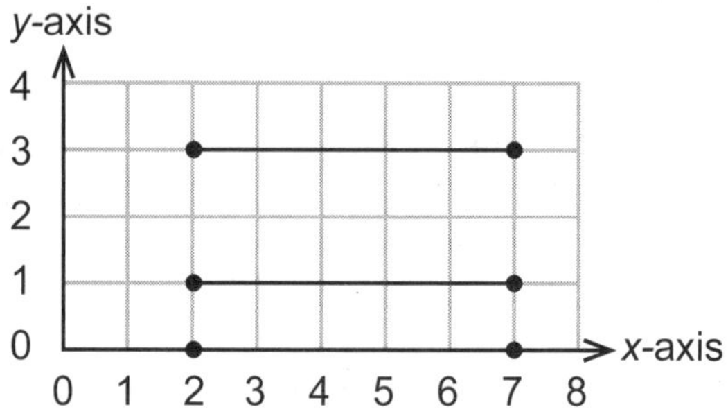

   b) How do you get the horizontal distance between the points from their first coordinates?

   ____

2. Find the difference between the first coordinates to find the horizontal distance between the points.

   a) (3, 0) and (1, 0): ______ units

   b) (5, 0) and (2, 0): ______ units

   c) (1, 10) and (8, 10): ______ units

   d) (8, 126) and (2, 126): ______ units

3. a) Find the vertical distance between the points.

   i) (0, 2) and (0, 5): ______ units

   ii) (1, 2) and (1, 5): ______ units

   iii) (2, 2) and (2, 5): ______ units

   iv) (*x*, 2) and (*x*, 5): ______ units

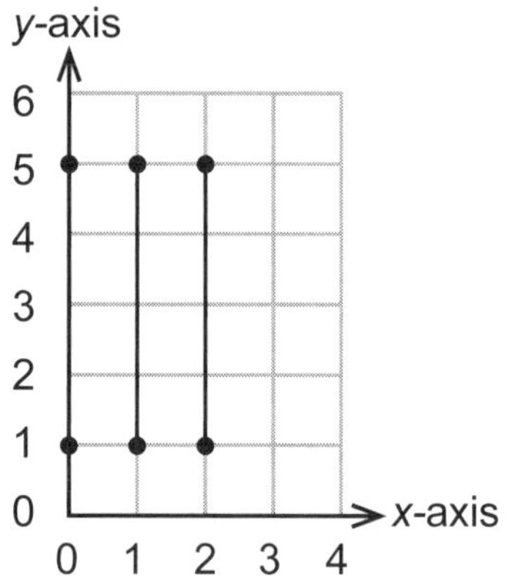

   b) How do you get the vertical distance between the points from their second coordinates?

   ____

   ____

4. Find the difference between the second coordinates to find the vertical distance between the points.

   a) (1, 3) and (1, 2): ______ units

   b) (1, 5) and (1, 2): ______ units

   c) (10, 10) and (10, 2): ______ units

   d) (4, 5) and (4, 2): ______ units

   e) (14, 2) and (14, 7): ______ units

   f) (561, 2) and (561, 5): ______ units

5. The diagram at right shows a coordinate grid with some lines and labels left out. *A* is at (5, 5). The vertical distance between *A* and *D* is 5.

   Write the coordinates of *B*, *C*, and *D*:

   B (,   )   *C* (,   )   *D* (,   )

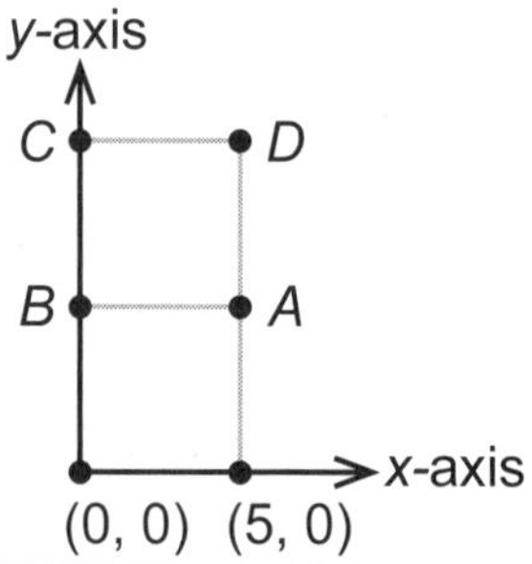

G6-6 Ratios and Coordinate Systems

1. Make a ratio table for each ratio.

a) 3:5

3	*5*
6	*10*
9	*15*

b) 7:2

c) 4:9

BONUS ▶ 12:7

2. Make a ratio table. Then write a list of ordered pairs for each table.

a) 3:7

3	*7*	*(3, 7)*
6	*14*	*(6, 14)*
9	*21*	(,)

b) 11:5

c) 5:6

3. a) Write a list of ordered pairs for each ratio table.

i)

1	2	*(1, 2)*
2	4	(,)
3	6	(,)
4	8	(,)

ii)

1	1	
2	2	
3	3	
4	4	

iii)

3	1	
6	2	
9	3	
12	4	

b) Mark the ordered pairs on the graph and connect the points.

i)

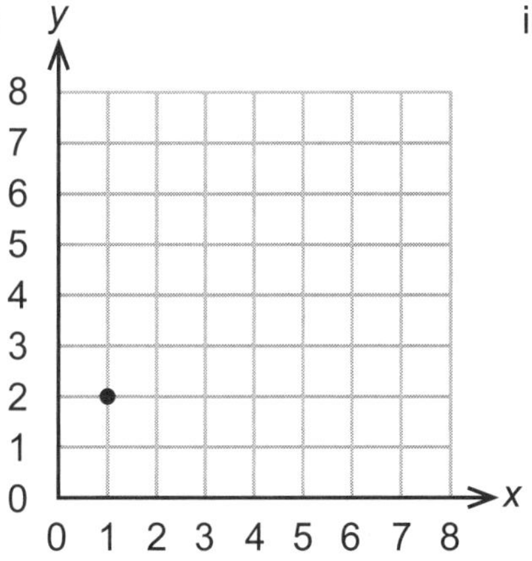

ii)

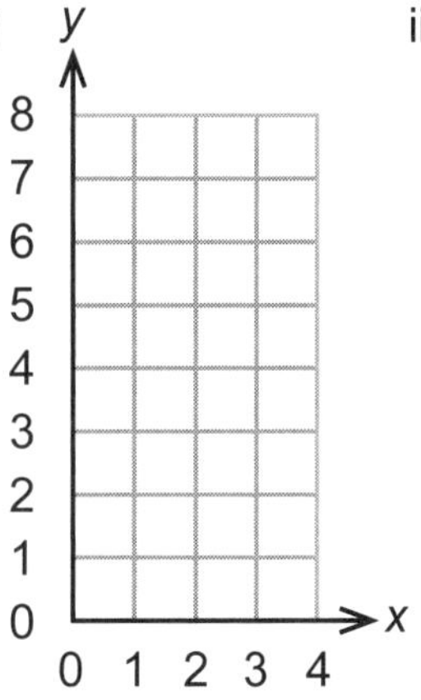

iii)

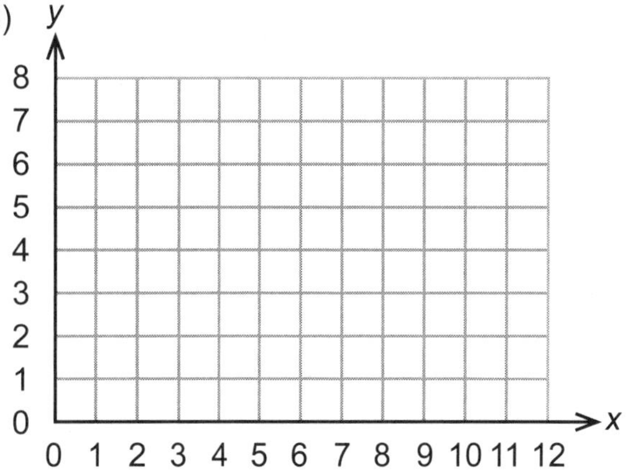

c) What do you notice about the points in each graph? ______________________

d) Extend the line to the edges of the grid. What is the lowest point on the line that is on the grid?

i) (,) ii) (,) iii) (,)

What do you notice? ______________________

When you plot the ordered pairs from a ratio table, connect the dots, and extend the line, the line will always pass through (0, 0).

4. a) Finish the ratio table. Then plot the ordered pairs. Pay attention to the scale!

i)

x	***y***
4	3

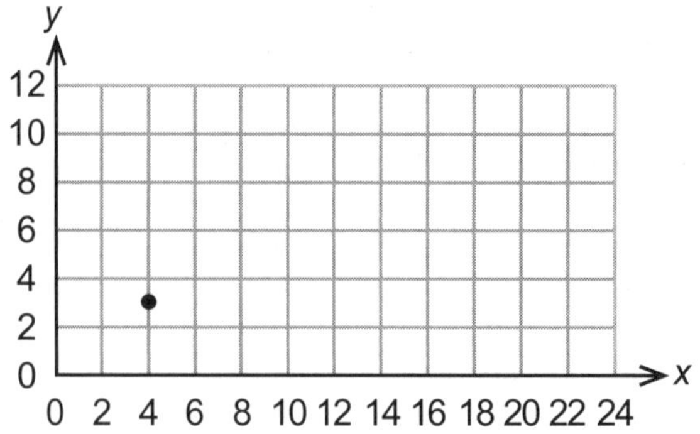

ii)

x	***y***
5	2

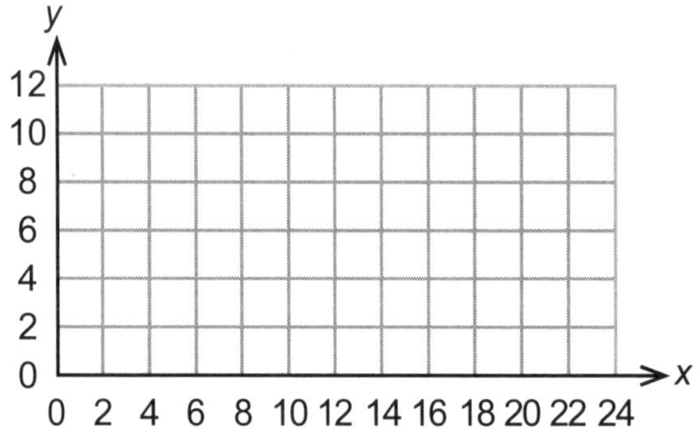

iii)

x	***y***
6	4

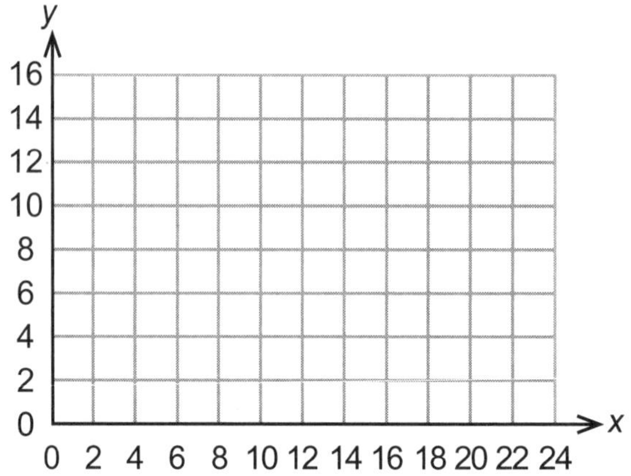

b) Join the points on each graph with a line. Extend the line to make sure the lines go through (0, 0).

5. a) Plot the ordered pairs from each table. Connect the points and extend the line.

i)

Input	Output
1	1
2	3
3	5

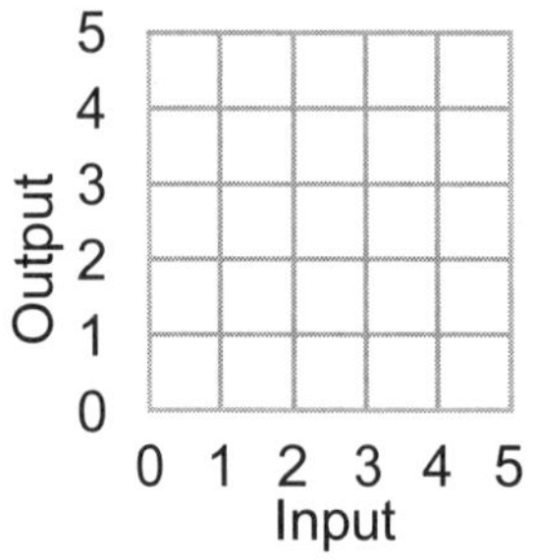

ii)

Input	Output
1	2
2	3
3	4

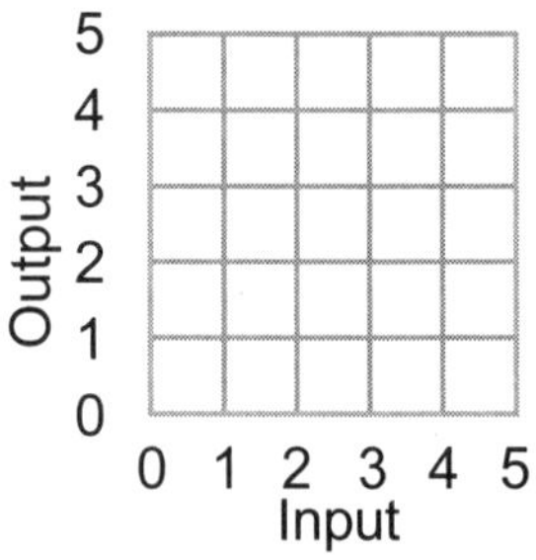

b) How can you tell from the graph that these are not ratio tables?

G6-7 Area of Rectangles

1. Write an addition equation and a multiplication equation for the number of boxes in the rectangle.

a) 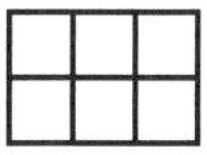

$2 + 2 + 2 = 6$ ________

$3 \times 2 = 6$ ________

b) 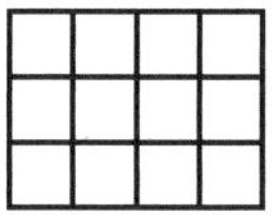

____

____

c) 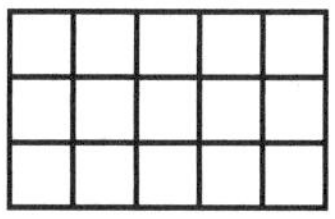

____

____

d) 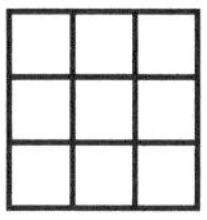

____

____

e) 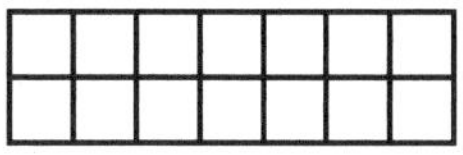

____

____

f) 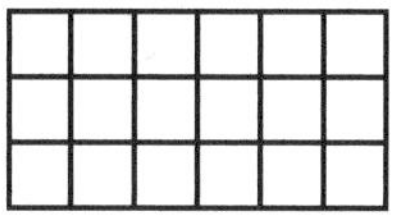

____

____

2. Write the number of boxes along the width and the length of the rectangle. Then write a multiplication equation for the area of the rectangle (in square units).

a) 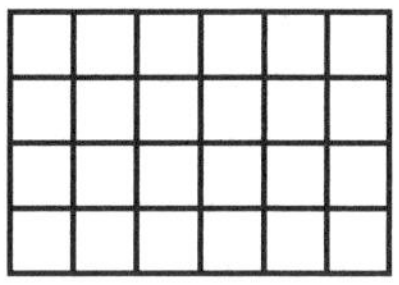

Width = ______

Length = ______

____

b) 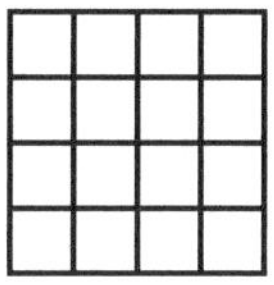

Width = ______

Length = ______

____

c) 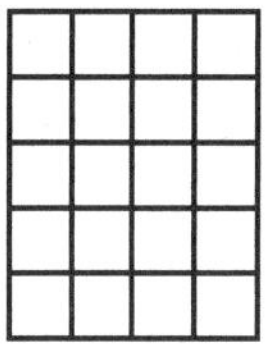

Width = ______

Length = ______

____

3. Using a ruler, join the marks to divide the rectangle into square centimeters. Write a multiplication equation for the area of the rectangle in square centimeters.

a) 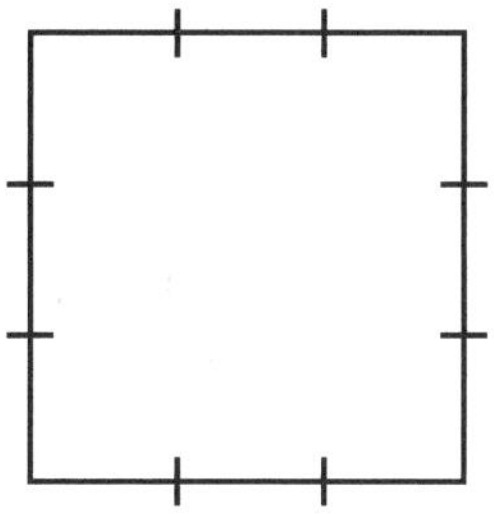

Area = ______

b) 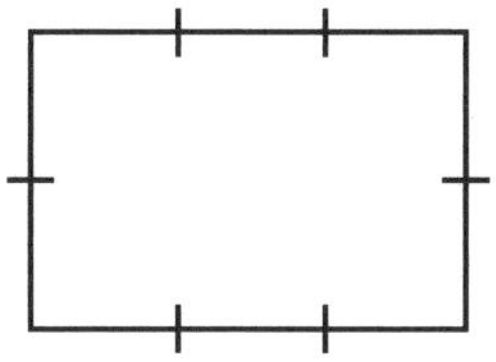

Area = ______

c) 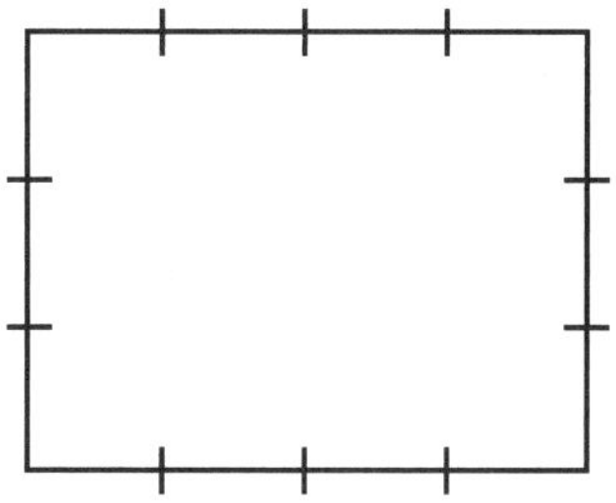

Area = ______

4. Write a formula for the area of a rectangle using its length and width.

____

Area of rectangle = length × width or $A = l \times w$

5. Measure the length and width of the rectangle in centimeters. Find the area.

a) 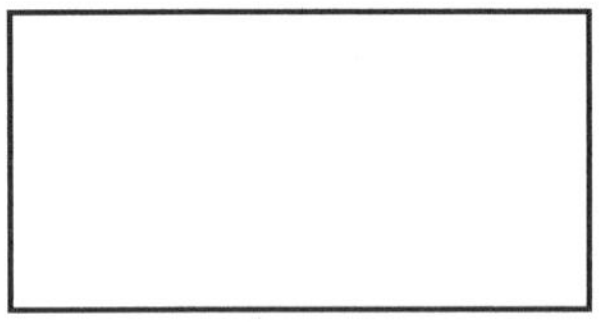

____

b) 

____

c) 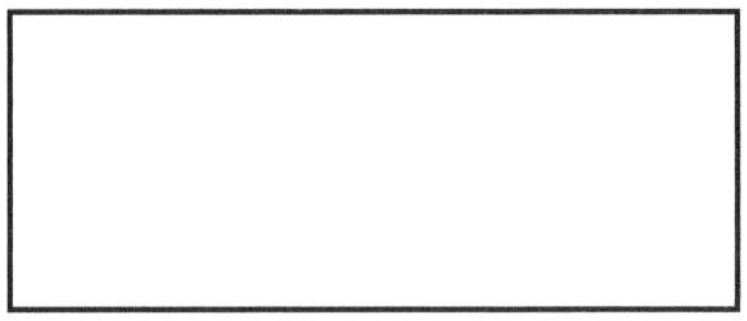

____

6. a) Calculate the area of each rectangle (include the units). The rectangles are not drawn to scale.

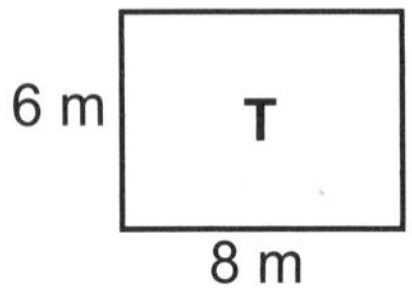

Area = _______

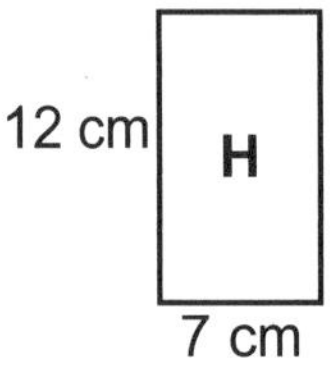

Area = _______

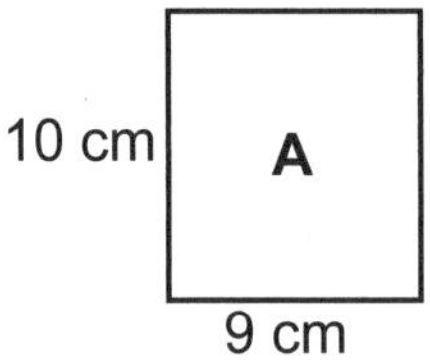

Area = _______

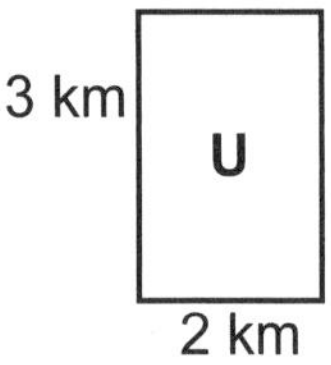

Area = _______

b) List the rectangles from greatest to least area: _____ , _____ , _____ , _____

What state do the letters spell? ____________

7. Find the area of the rectangle using the length and the width.

a) Width = 5 m Length = 7 m

Area = *35 m²*

b) Width = 3 m Length = 9 m

Area = _______

c) Width = 7.5 cm Length = 8 cm

Area = _______

d) Width = 9 in Length = 11 in

Area = _______

e) Width = 5 ft Length = 12 ft

Area = _______

f) Width = 3.7 ft Length = 10 ft

Area = _______

8. a) A rectangle has length 6 ft and width 4 ft. What is its area?

b) A rectangle has width 2 cm and length 5 cm. What is its area?

c) A square has length 9 cm. What is its area?

9. A rectangle with width 3 cm and length 4 cm has area 12 cm^2.

a) Find a different pair of numbers that multiply to equal 12.

b) Draw a rectangle with width and length equal to your numbers.

$3 \times 4 = 12$ (3 ↑ *width*, 4 ↑ *length*, 12 ↑ *area*)

G6-8 Area and Perimeter

1. a) Measure the length and the width of each rectangle in centimeters. Find the perimeter and area of each rectangle. Write the answers in the table.

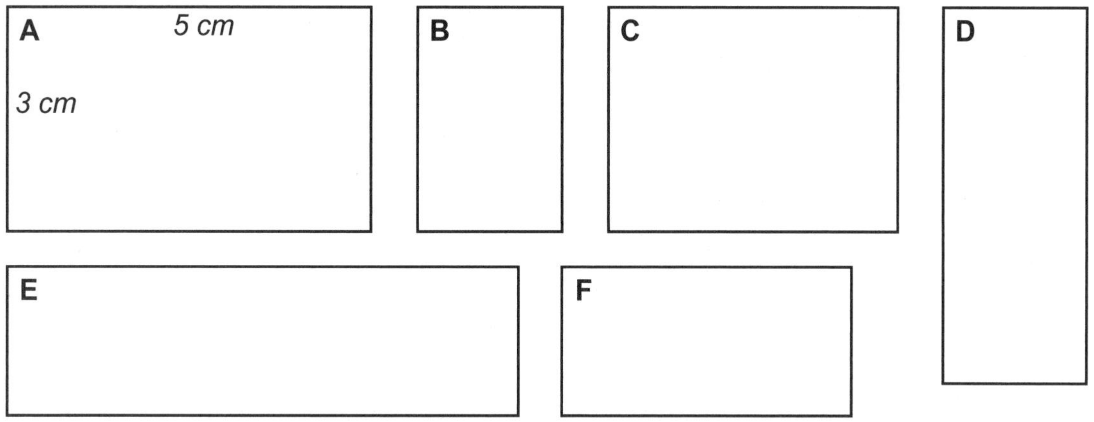

Shape	Perimeter	Area
A	*3 cm + 5 cm + 3 cm + 5 cm = 16 cm*	*3 cm × 5 cm = 15 cm²*
B		
C		
D		
E		
F		

b) Shape E has a greater perimeter than Shape A. Does it also have a greater area? _______

c) Name two rectangles that have the same perimeter and different areas. _______ and _______

d) Write the shapes in order from greatest to least perimeter. ______________________________

e) Write the shapes in order from greatest to least area. ______________________________

f) Are the orders in parts d) and e) the same? _______

g) How are perimeter and area different?

2. Do you need to find the area or the perimeter to find ...

a) the amount of paper needed to cover a bulletin board? ______________________________

b) the distance around a field? ______________________________

c) the amount of carpet needed for a room? ______________________________

d) the amount of ribbon needed to make a border for a picture? ______________________________

G6-9 Area of Composite Shapes

1. a) Calculate the area of each figure.

b) Draw a line to show how Shape C can be divided into rectangles A and B.

i) 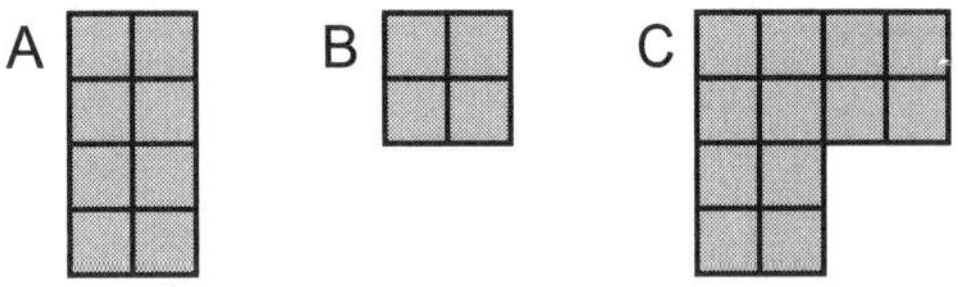

Area of A = _______

Area of B = _______

Area of C = _______

ii) 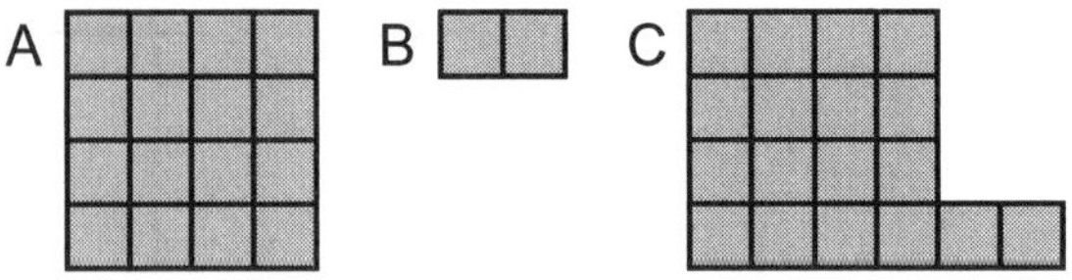

Area of A = _______

Area of B = _______

Area of C = _______

iii) 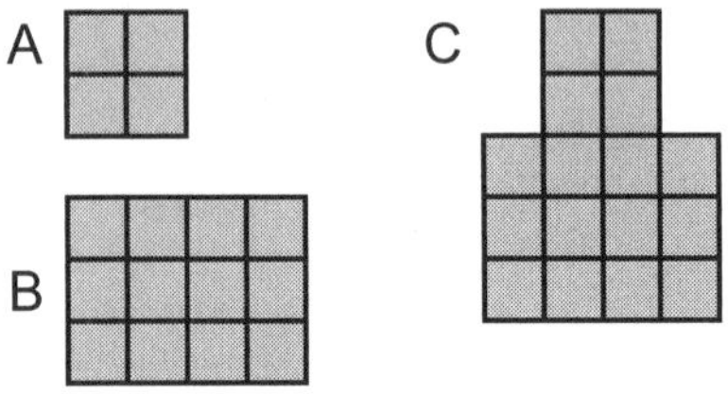

Area of A = _______

Area of B = _______

Area of C = _______

iv) 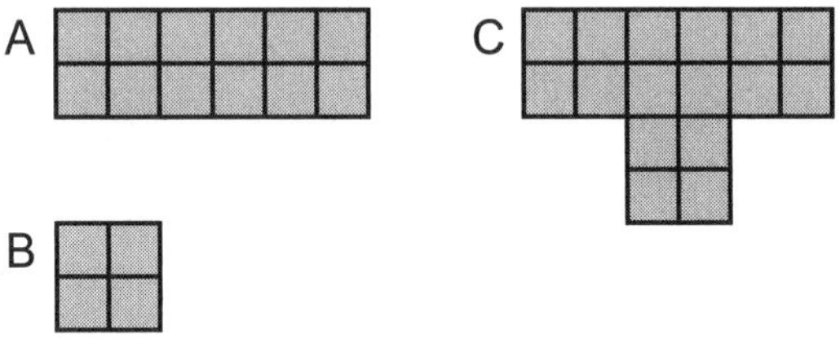

Area of A = _______

Area of B = _______

Area of C = _______

c) How can you get the area of C from the areas of A and B? Write an equation.

Area of C = ____

2. Draw a line to divide the figure into two rectangles.
Use the areas of the rectangles to find the total area of the figure.

a) 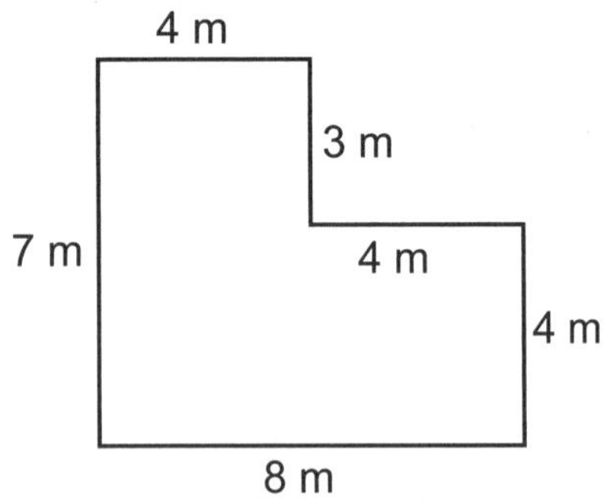

b) 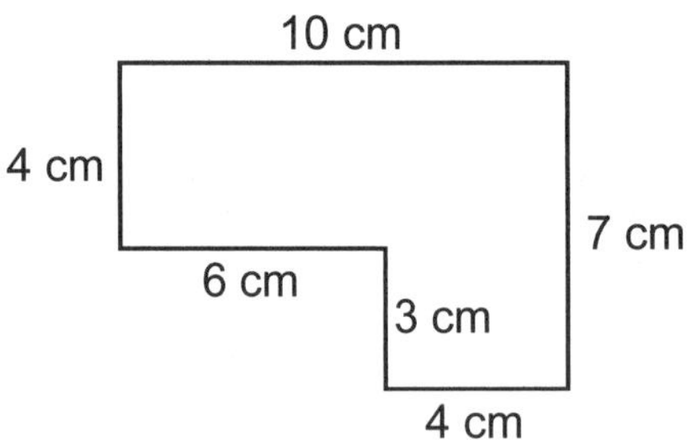

c) 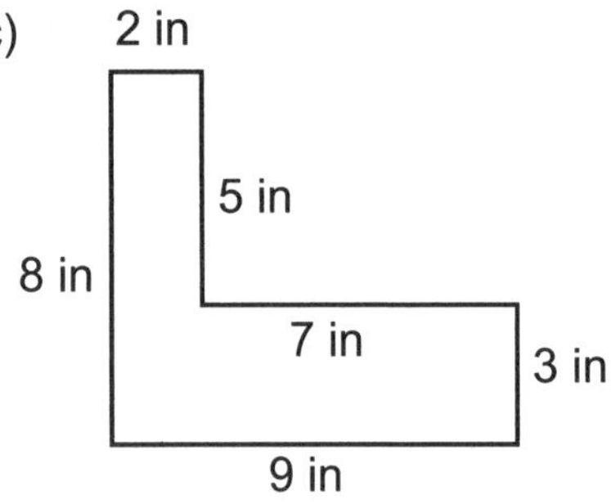

a) Area of Rectangle 1 = _____

Area of Rectangle 2 = _____

Total area = _______

b) Area of Rectangle 1 = _____

Area of Rectangle 2 = _____

Total area = _______

c) Area of Rectangle 1 = _____

Area of Rectangle 2 = _____

Total area = _______

3. a) A building is 8 stories high. The wing is 5 stories high. How many stories high is the tower?

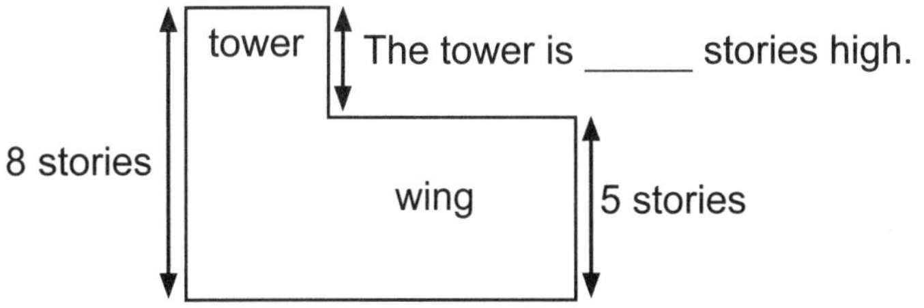

b) The tower of a building is 10 m wide. The base is 50 m wide. How wide is the wing?

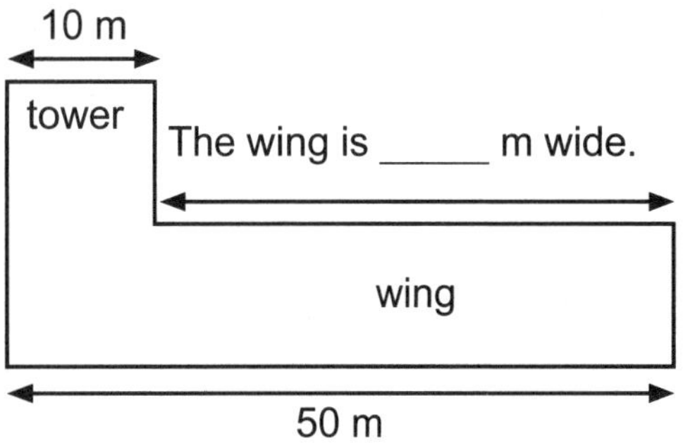

4. Find the missing side lengths. Divide the figure into two rectangles and find their areas. Then find the total area of the figure.

a)

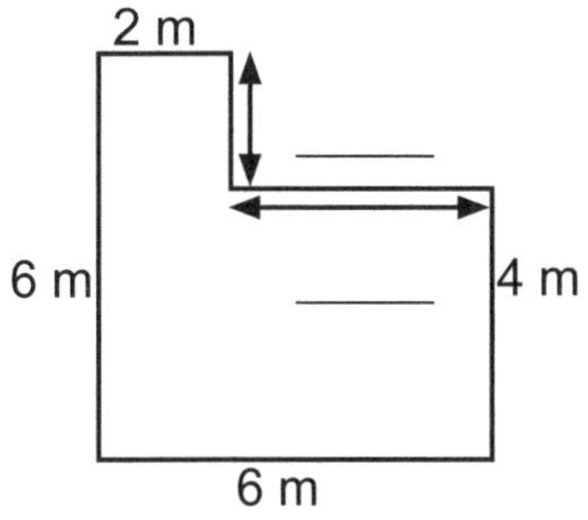

Area of Rectangle 1 = _______

Area of Rectangle 2 = _______

Total area = _______

b)

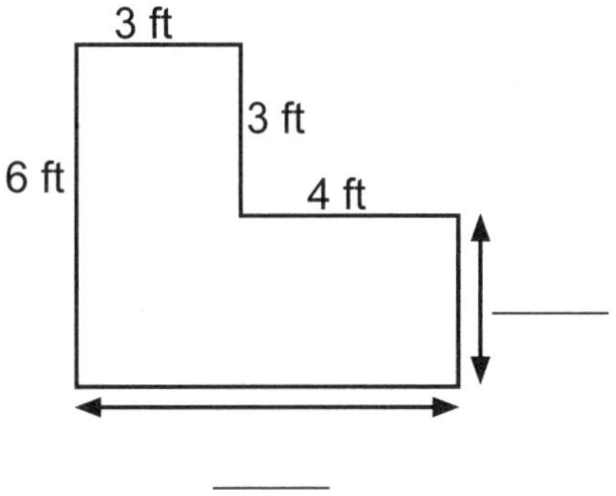

Area of Rectangle 1 = _______

Area of Rectangle 2 = _______

Total area = _______

5. The picture shows plans for two flowerbeds. Find the area and the perimeter of each flowerbed.

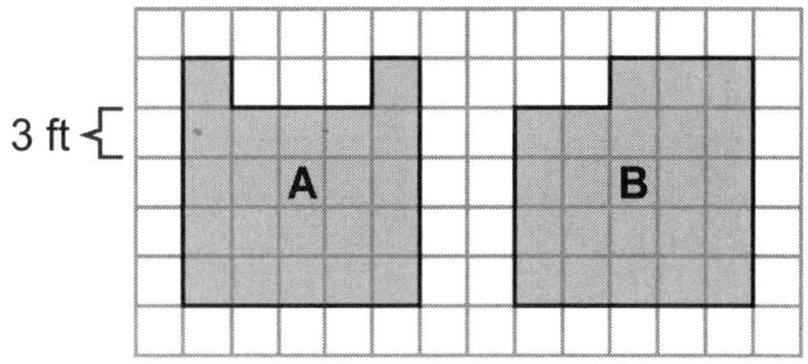

Flowerbed A

Area = _______

Perimeter = _______

Flowerbed B

Area = _______

Perimeter = _______

Which flowerbed has greater area? _______

Which has greater perimeter? _______

6. The picture shows plans for two parks. Find the area and the perimeter of each park.

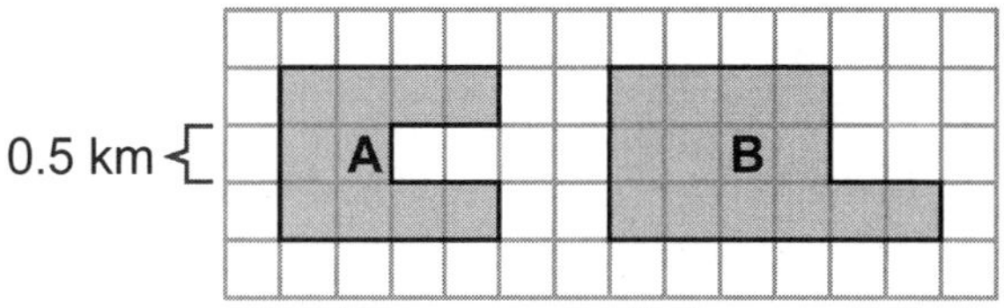

Park A

Area = _______

Perimeter = _______

Park B

Area = _______

Perimeter = _______

Area of Parallelograms

1. Move the shaded triangle to make a rectangle with the same area as the parallelogram. Find the base and the height of the parallelogram and the width and the height of the rectangle.

a)

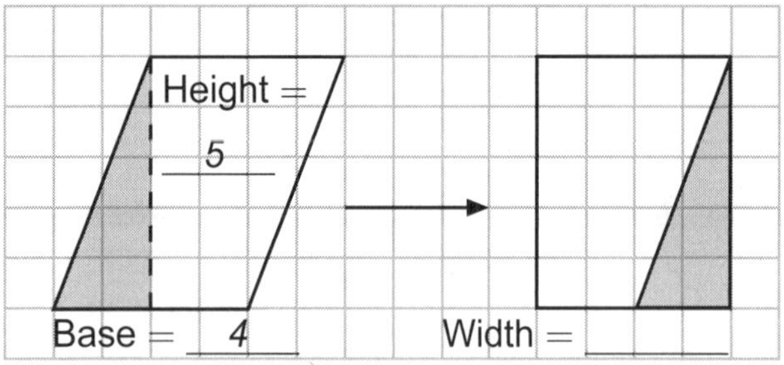

Height = ______

b)

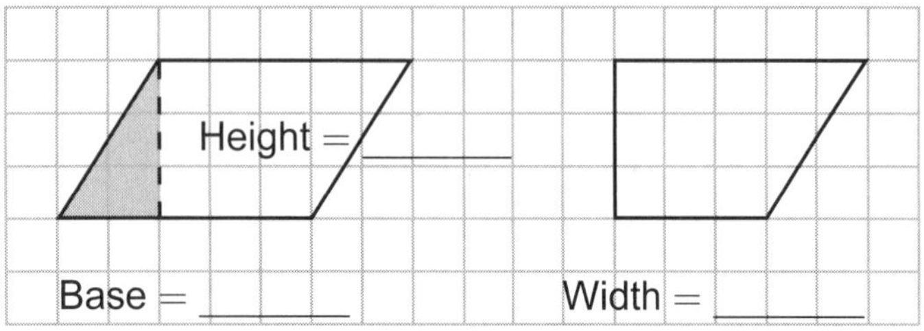

Height = ______

c)

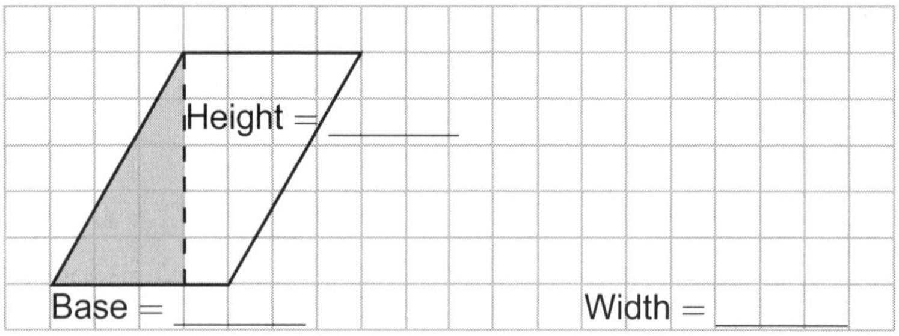

Height = ______

d)

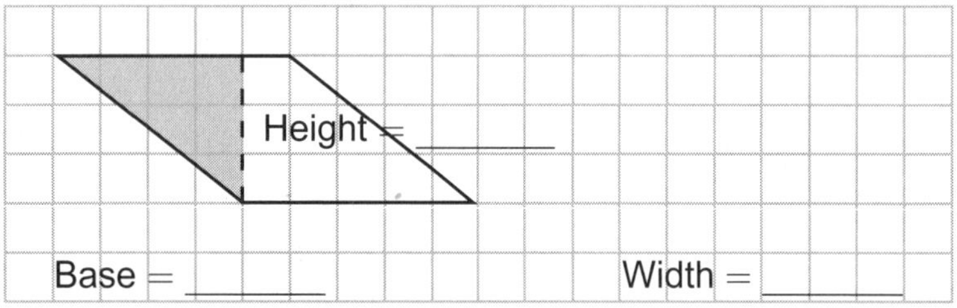

Height = ______

2. a) Look at your answers in Question 1. Complete each sentence with the word "base" or "height."

The height of the rectangle is the same as the ______________ of the parallelogram.

The width of the rectangle is the same as the ______________ of the parallelogram.

b) Area of rectangle = width × height. What is the formula for the area of a parallelogram?

Area of parallelogram = ______________ × ______________

Area of parallelogram = base × height or $A = b \times h$

3. Find the area of the parallelogram given the base and height.

a) Base = 5 cm
Height = 7 cm
Area = _______

b) Base = 4 cm
Height = 3 cm
Area = _______

c) Base = 8 cm
Height = 6 cm
Area = _______

d) Base = 3.7 cm
Height = 6 cm
Area = _______

Any side of a parallelogram can be used as a base. The height is always perpendicular to the base.

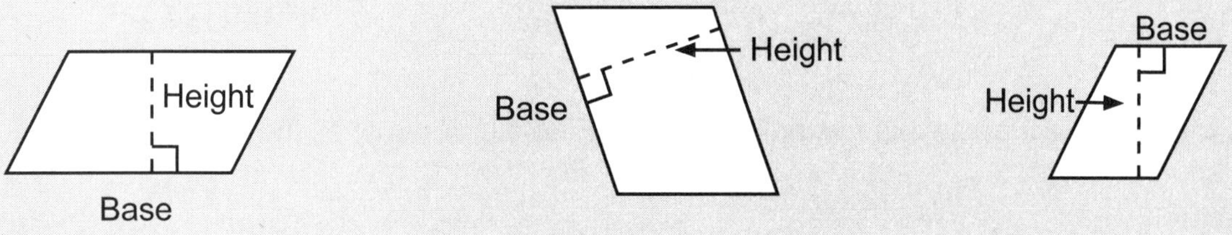

4. Find the area in two ways, by using different sides as base. Use a ruler.

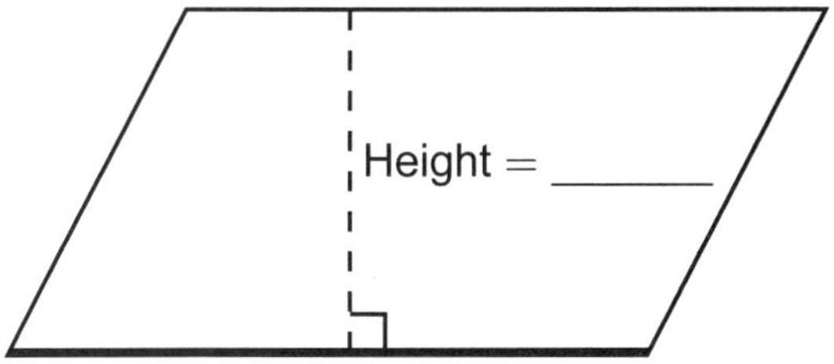

Base = _______

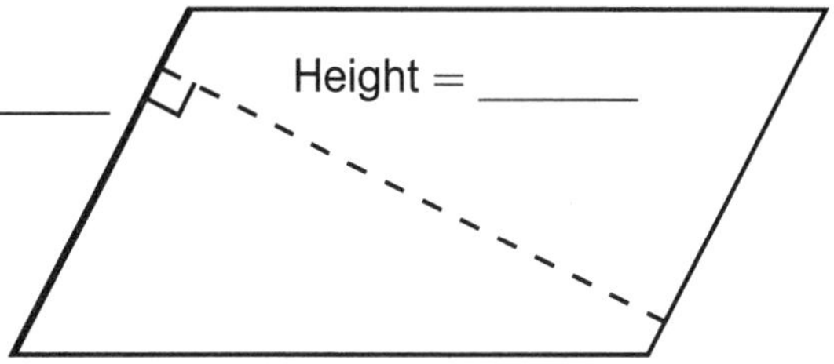

Base = _______

Area = _______

Area = _______

5. Draw a perpendicular to the base of each parallelogram (thick line) using a protractor or a square corner.

Measure the height and the base of the parallelogram. Find the area of the parallelogram.

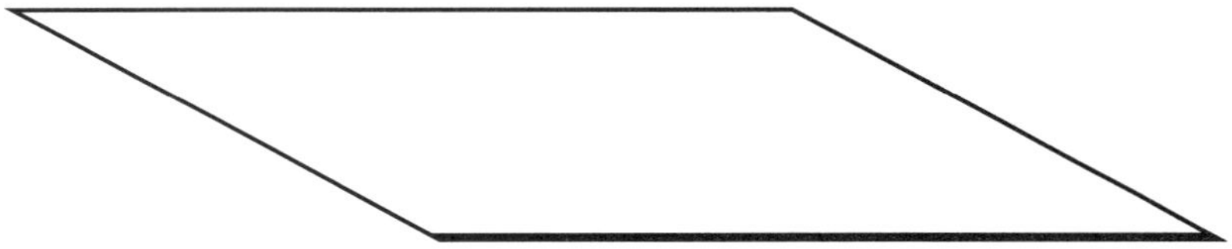

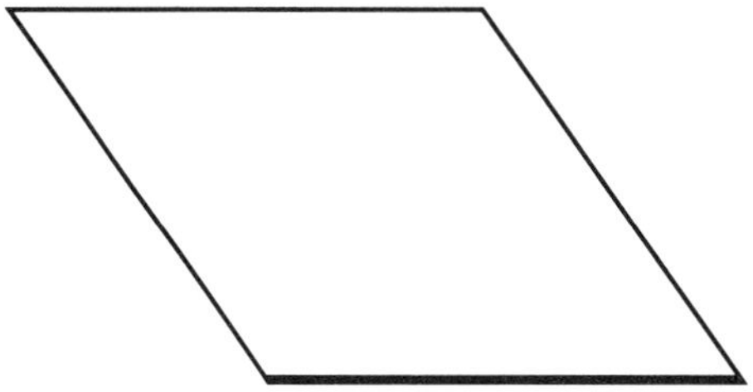

Area = _______

Area = _______

6. A bus has ten windows that are parallelograms with height 1 m and base 1.3 m. Glass costs $23 for each 1 m^2. How much will it cost to replace the glass in all ten windows?

G6-11 Area of Triangles

Two identical right triangles make a rectangle.

Area of right triangle = Area of rectangle ÷ 2

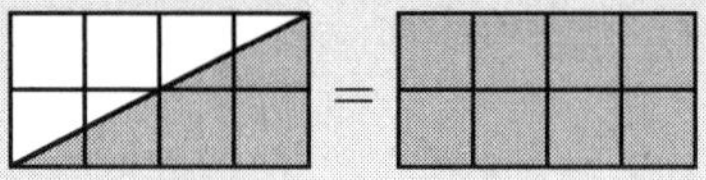

1. Find the area of the triangle in square units.

a) 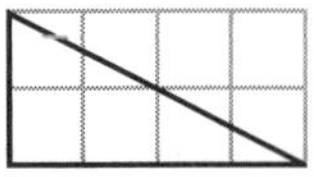 Area = _______

b) 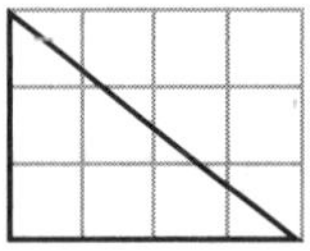 Area = _______

c) 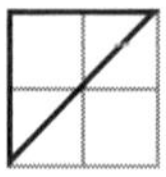 Area = _______

d) 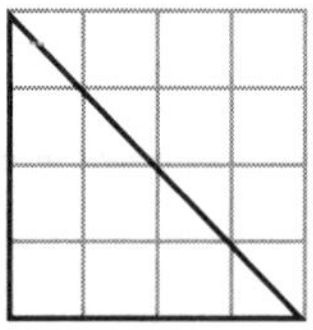 Area = _______

2. Draw a line to divide the triangle into two right triangles. Find the areas of all the triangles in square units.

a) 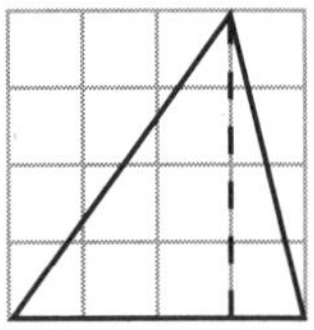

Triangle 1 = *6*

Triangle 2 = *2*

Total area = *8*

b) 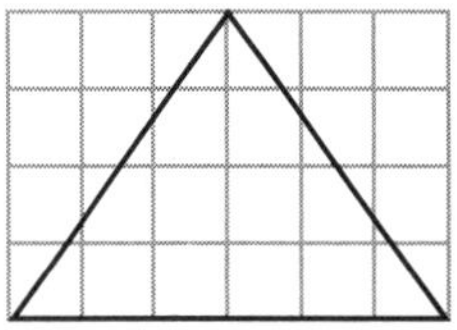

Triangle 1 = _______

Triangle 2 = _______

Total area = _______

c) 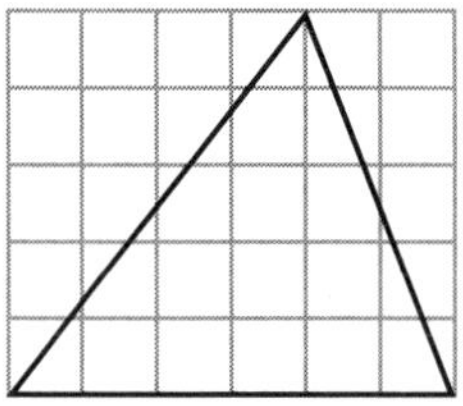

Triangle 1 = _______

Triangle 2 = _______

Total area = _______

d) 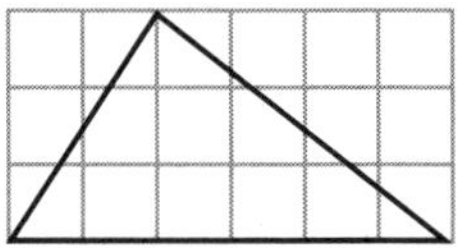

Triangle 1 = _______

Triangle 2 = _______

Total area = _______

3. Rectangle C is made of rectangles A and B. Triangle C is made of triangles A and B.

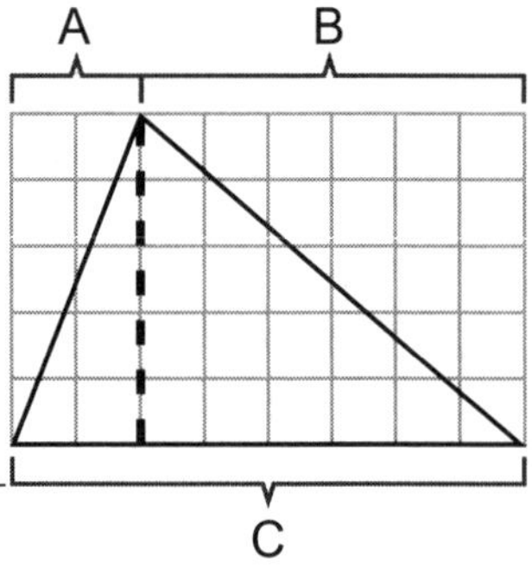

a) Find the areas.

Area of Rectangle A = _______ Area of Triangle A = _______

Area of Rectangle B = _______ Area of Triangle B = _______

Area of Rectangle C = _______ Area of Triangle C = _______

b) What fraction of the area of Rectangle C is the area of Triangle C? _______

4. Juan says: The area of Triangle T is half of the area of the rectangle.

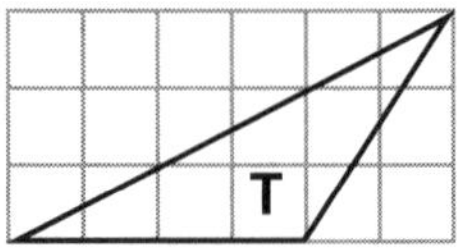

Is he correct? Explain. ______________________________

____

____

Triangles have **base** and **height**. Height is measured along a perpendicular to the base.

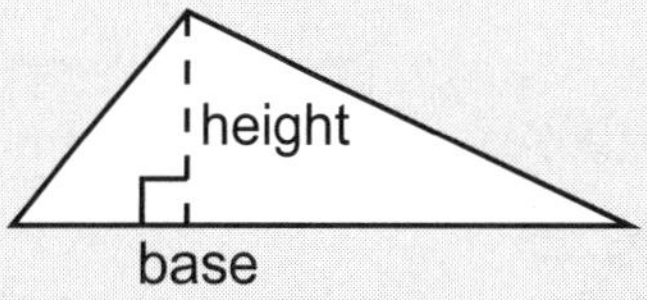

5. a) Find the base and the height of each triangle. Then fill in the table.

	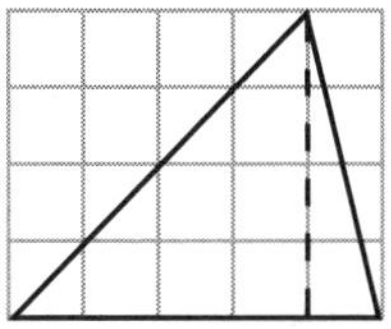	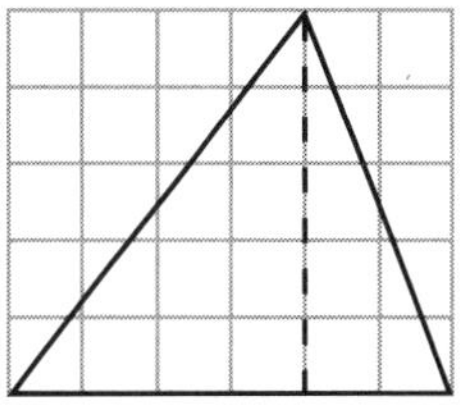	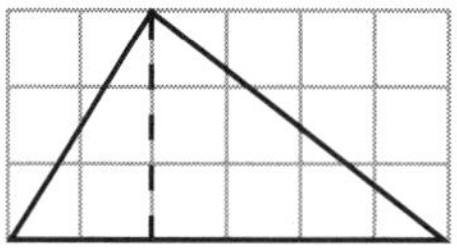
Base of triangle	*5*		
Height of triangle	*4*		
Width of rectangle	*5*		
Height of rectangle	*4*		
Area of rectangle	*20*		
Area of triangle	*10*		

b) Look at the table in part a). Complete each sentence with the word "base" or "height."

The height of the rectangle is the same as the ________________ of the triangle.

The width of the rectangle is the same as the ________________ of the triangle.

Area of triangle = base × height ÷ 2 or $A = b \times h \div 2$

6. Find the area of the triangle given the base and height. Do not forget the units.

a) Base = 5 cm
Height = 8 cm
Area = ______

b) Base = 4 cm
Height = 3 cm
Area = ______

c) Base = 8 cm
Height = 6 cm
Area = ______

d) Base = 3.7 cm
Height = 6 cm
Area = ______

7. Find the area of the triangle.

a) 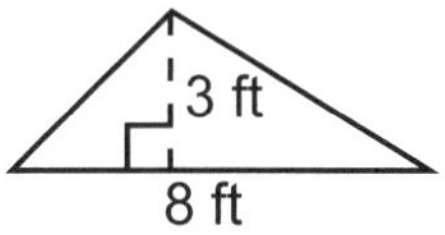

Area = ______

b) 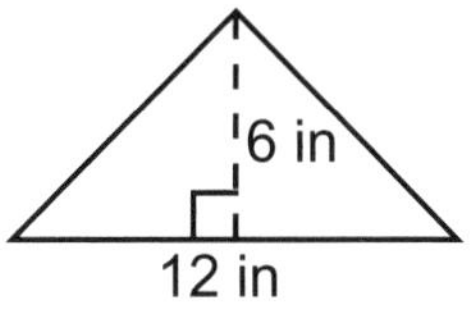

Area = ______

c) 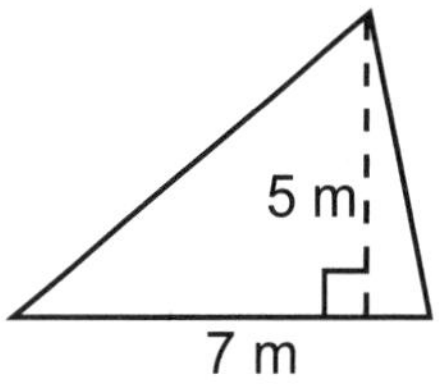

Area = ______

d) 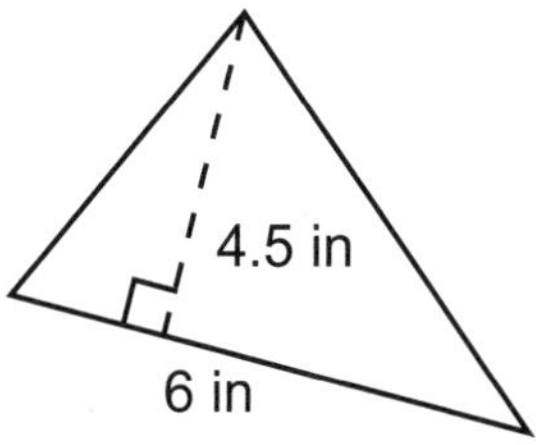

Area = ______

G6-12 Area of Triangles and Parallelograms

REMINDER ▶ Area of parallelogram = base × height or $A = b \times h$

1. Hank joined two copies of Triangle A together to make Parallelogram B.

a) What should he do to find the area of Triangle A from the area of Parallelogram B?

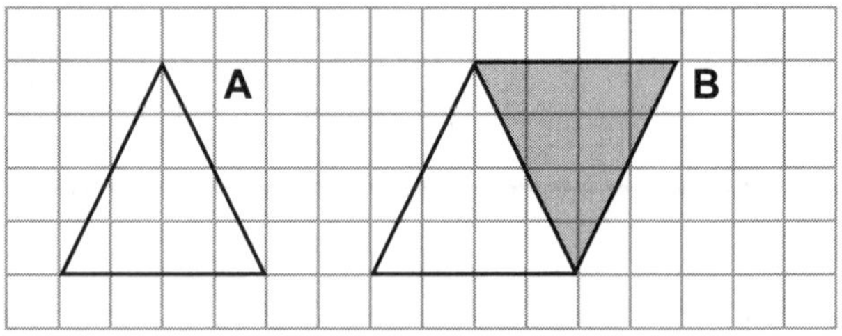

____

Area of B = ______

Area of A = Area of B ÷ ______ = ______

b) Find the area of triangles C and D using Hank's method.

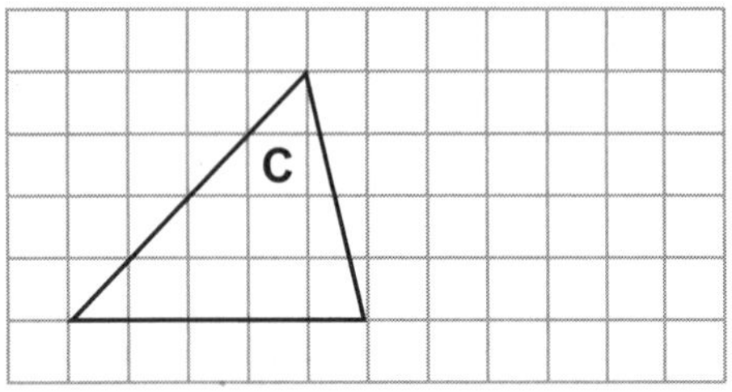

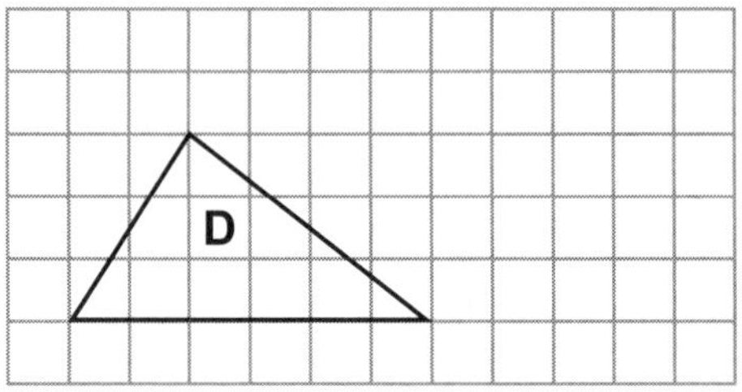

Area of parallelogram = ______

Area of C = ______

Area of parallelogram = ______

Area of D = ______

c) Look at your answers in parts a) and b). Complete each sentence with the word "base" or "height."

The height of the triangle is the same as the ______________ of the parallelogram.

The base of the triangle is the same as the ______________ of the parallelogram.

d) Write the formula for the area of a triangle using the base and the height of the triangle.

Area of triangle = ______________________________

2. Measure the base and height of the triangle. Then find the area of the triangle.

a)

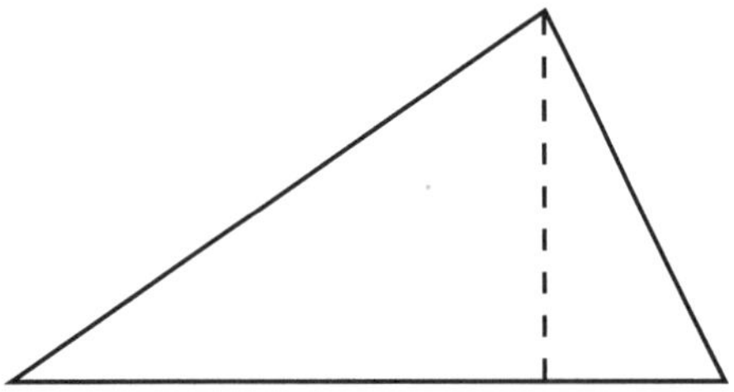

Base = ______

Height = ______

Area = ______

b)

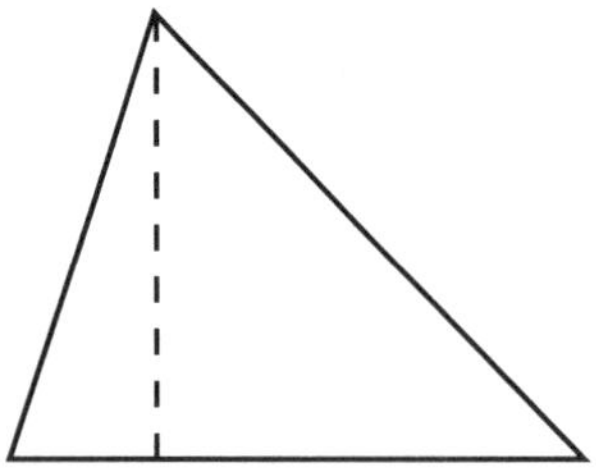

Base = ______

Height = ______

Area = ______

c)

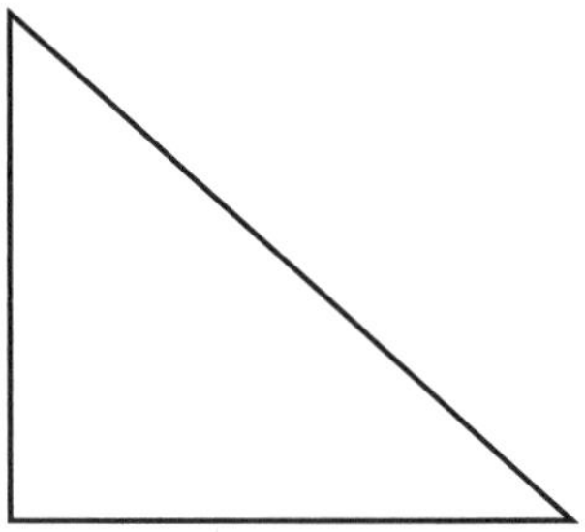

Base = ______

Height = ______

Area = ______

3. Find the area of the triangle with these dimensions.

a) Base = 6 cm
Height = 2 cm
Area = _______

b) Base = 4 in
Height = 6 in
Area = _______

c) Base = 6 ft
Height = 3 ft
Area = _______

d) Base = 3.2 cm
Height = 8 cm
Area = _______

4. In each triangle, the thick line is the base. Use a square corner or a protractor to draw the height. Then measure the bases and the heights and fill in the table.

	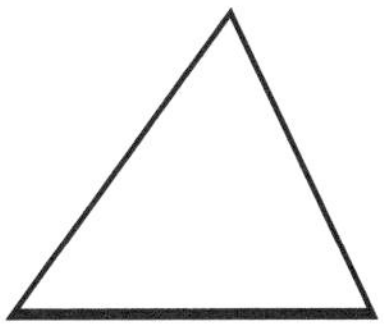	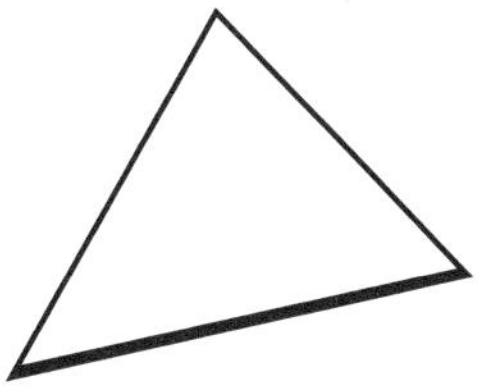	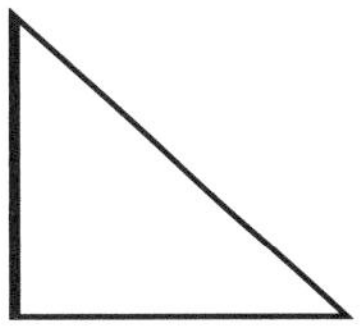	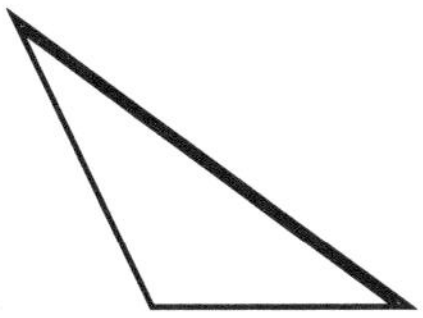
Base				
Height				
Area				

5. a) A company's logo is a triangle with base 6 ft and height 4 ft. What is its area?

b) A park is a right triangle with base 2 km and height 1.5 km. What is its area?

c) A plot of land is a triangle with base 37 yd and height 40 yd. What is its area?

6. Plot the points on the grid, then find the area of the Triangle *ABC.*

a) *A* (1, 1), *B* (5, 1), *C* (4, 5)

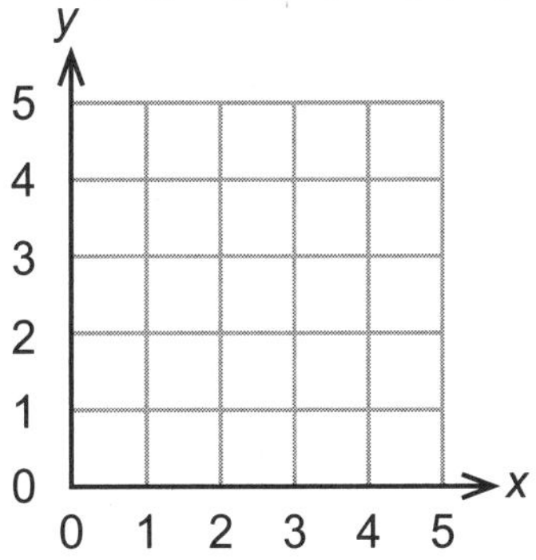

b) *A* (1, 0), *B* (5, 0), *C* (4, 2)

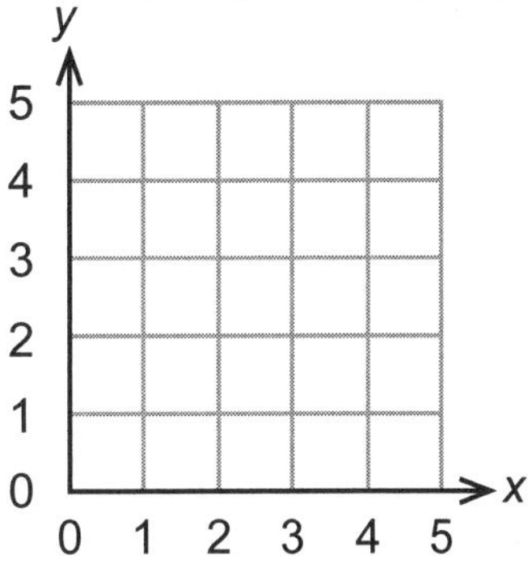

c) *A* (0, 4), *B* (8, 0), *C* (8, 4)

d) *A* (6, 2), *B* (6, 5), *C* (2, 4)

7. a) Find the base, the height, and the area of each triangle. What do you notice?

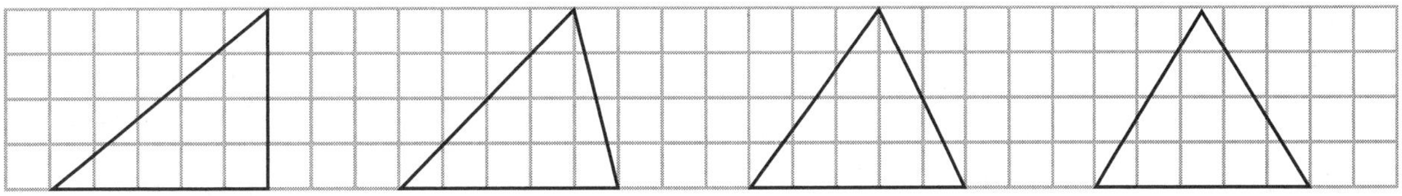

b) On grid paper, draw two different triangles with the same base and height. What do you know about their areas?

G6-13 Area of Trapezoids and Parallelograms

A **trapezoid** is a quadrilateral with exactly one pair of parallel sides. These sides are both called bases.

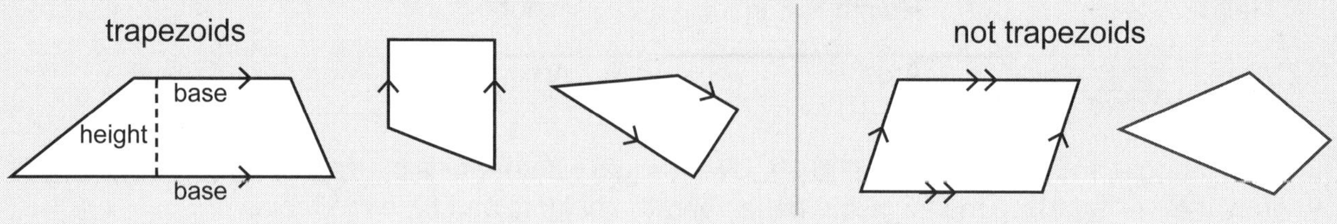

1. Split the trapezoid into a triangle and a rectangle, then find the area of each shape in square units.

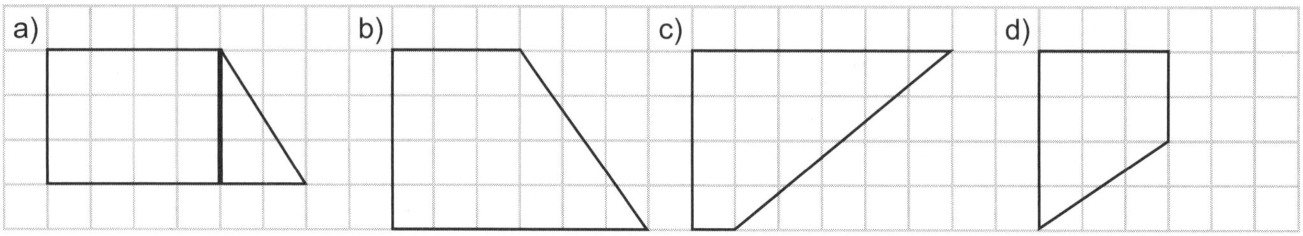

Area of…

a) rectangle = 12
triangle = 3
trapezoid = 15

b) rectangle = _____
triangle = _____
trapezoid = _____

c) rectangle = _____
triangle = _____
trapezoid = _____

d) rectangle = _____
triangle = _____
trapezoid = _____

2. Split the trapezoid into two triangles and a rectangle, then find the area of each shape in square units.

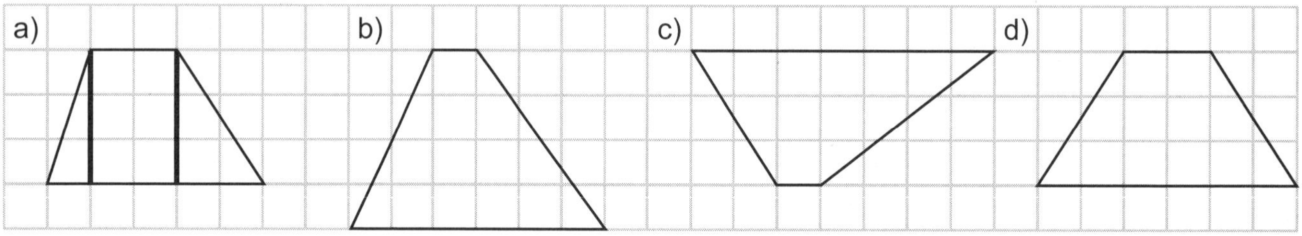

Area of…

a) rectangle = 6
triangle 1 = 1.5
triangle 2 = 3
trapezoid = 10.5

b) rectangle = _____
triangle 1 = _____
triangle 2 = _____
trapezoid = _____

c) rectangle = _____
triangle 1 = _____
triangle 2 = _____
trapezoid = _____

d) rectangle = _____
triangle 1 = _____
triangle 2 = _____
trapezoid = _____

3. a) What is the base of the triangle? ______________________

b) What is the area of the trapezoid? ______________________

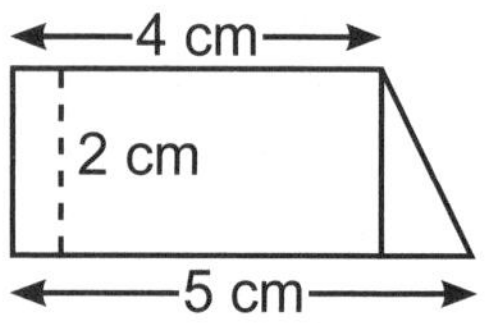

4. Draw an upside down copy of each trapezoid, as shown in part a), to create a parallelogram. Then fill in the blanks for each parallelogram.

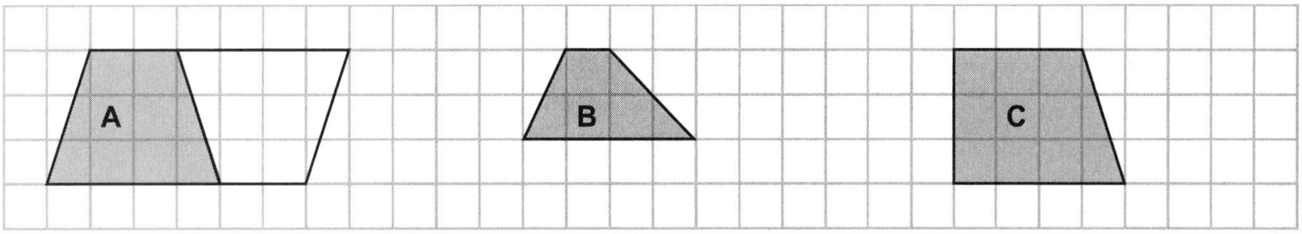

a) length of base = 6 ←4 + 2   b) length of base = _____   c) length of base = _____

height = 3   height = _____   height = _____

5. A trapezoid has the bases given. If you make a parallelogram as in Question 4, what will the base of the parallelogram be?

a) bases of trapezoid = 2 cm and 3 cm   base of parallelogram = ________ *cm*

b) bases of trapezoid = 5 m and 7 m   base of parallelogram = __________

c) bases of trapezoid = 4 in and 6 in   base of parallelogram = __________

REMINDER ▶ Area of parallelogram = base × height   or $A = b \times h$

6. Find the areas of the parallelograms in Question 4.

a) Area of parallelogram = _____ b) Area of parallelogram = _____ c) Area of parallelogram = _____

7. a) How many trapezoids make up each parallelogram in Question 4? __________

b) Area of trapezoid = area of parallelogram ÷ __________

c) Write an equation for the area of each trapezoid in Question 4.

sum of bases *height*

A: (4 + 2) × 3 ÷ 2   **B:** (____ + ____) × ____ ÷ 2   **C:** (____ + ____) × ____ ÷ 2

= 6 × 3 ÷ 2 = ____   = ____ × ____ ÷ 2 = ____   = ____ × ____ ÷ 2 = ____

8. Finish writing a formula for the area of a trapezoid:

Area of trapezoid = (base 1 + base 2) × ______________ ÷ _____

9. Find the area of the trapezoid.

a)
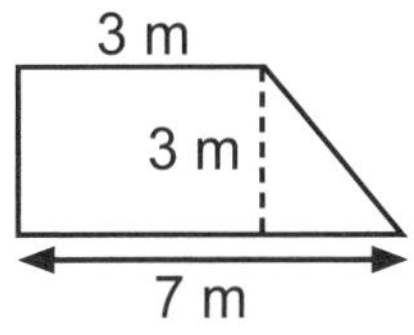

b)
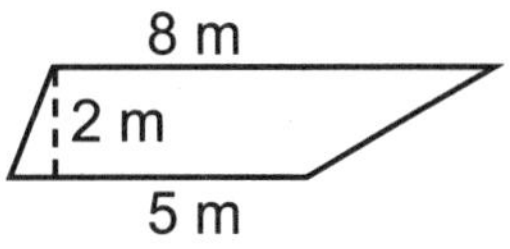

c)
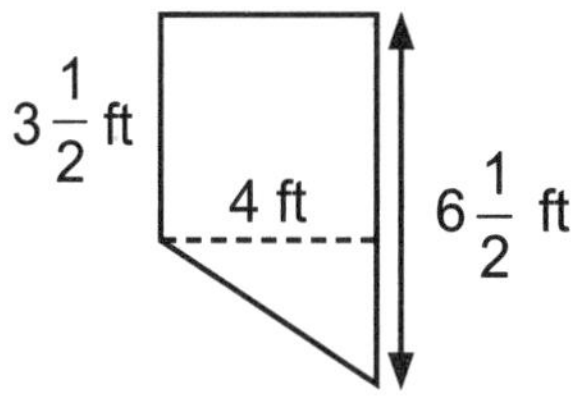

G6-14 Organizing Data

1. Match each area formula to a shape: rectangle, triangle, or parallelogram.

Area of ____________________ = base $\times$ height

Area of ____________________ = length $\times$ width = width $\times$ height

Area of ____________________ = base $\times$ height $\div$ 2

2. Which formula from Question 1 would you use to find the area of the shape?

a) square *area of rectangle = length $\times$ width*

b) rhombus ____________________

3. Write the shape whose area you need to find and the formula for that area.

a) A square has sides 5 cm long. What is its area?

Given: width = 5 cm | Find: area of *rectangle*

length = 5 cm | Formula: *Area = length $\times$ width*

b) A book cover is 30 cm long and 20 cm wide. What is the area of the cover?

Given: length = 30 cm | Find: area of ____________________

width = 20 cm | Formula: ____________________

c) Find the area of a rhombus with base 3 in and height 2.5 in.

Given: base = 3 in | Find: area of ____________________

height = 2.5 in | Formula: ____________________

d) A parking lot is a parallelogram with two sides 200 ft long. It measures 75 ft between these sides. What is the area of the parking lot?

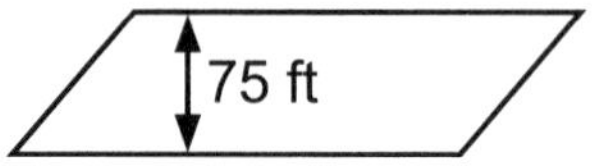

Given: base = 200 ft | Find: area of ____________________

width = 75 ft | Formula: ____________________

e) A traffic island is a triangle with perpendicular sides 5 ft and 10 ft. How many square feet of grass are needed to cover the traffic island?

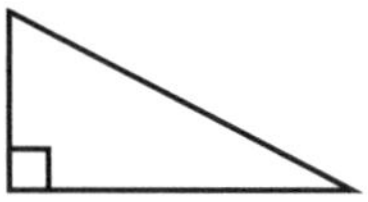

Given: base = 10 ft | Find: area of ____________________

height = 5 ft | Formula: ____________________

4. Solve each problem in Question 3.

5. Organize the data. Write the formula for the area you need to find. Substitute the data into the formula to find the area.

a) A park has the shape of a parallelogram. It has two sides 200 m long that run parallel to each other, and the sides are 135 m apart. How much space does the park take up?

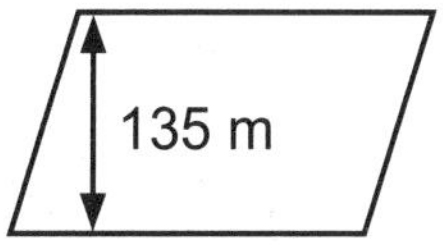

Given: *base = 200 m*　　　Formula: *Area = base × height*

height = 135 m　　　*Area = 200 m × 135 m*

Find: area of *parallelogram*　　　$= 27{,}000\ m^2$

b) Find the area of a triangle with base 2 in and height 3 in.

Given: ______________　　　Formula: ______________

____

Find: area of ______________

c) A rectangular curtain is 3 m wide and 1.8 m long. How many square meters of cloth is the curtain made from?

Given: ______________　　　Formula: ______________

____

Find: area of ______________

d) A flowerbed is a parallelogram with base 4 ft and height 1.75 in. How much space does the flowerbed take up?

Given: ______________　　　Formula: ______________

____

Find: area of ______________

e) A triangular pin has a horizontal top side 27 mm long. Its height is 30 mm. How much space does the pin take up?

Given: ______________　　　Formula: ______________

____

Find: area of ______________

f) A square window has sides 75 cm. How much glass is in the window?

Given: ______________　　　Formula: ______________

____

Find: area of ______________

G6-15 Variables and Area

1. a) Fill in the measurements you are given. Use a variable for what you do not know.

	Problem	Base or Width	Height	Area
i)	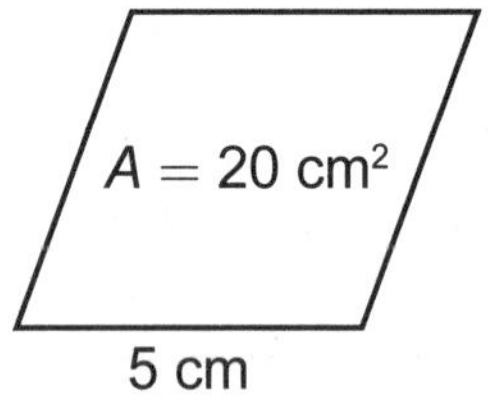	*5 cm*	*h*	*20 cm^2*
ii)	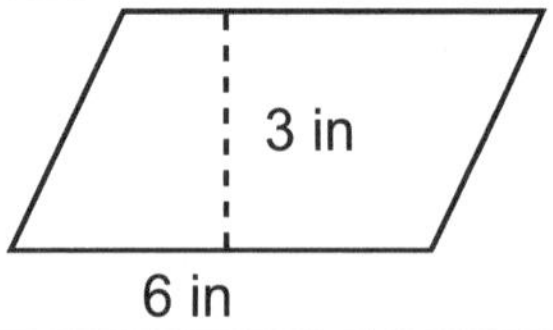			
iii)	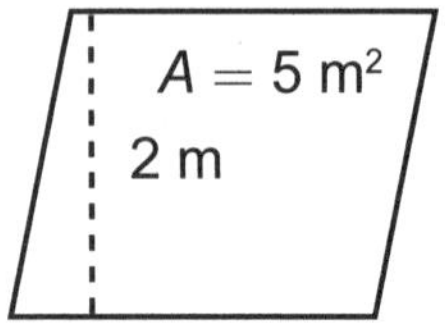			
iv)	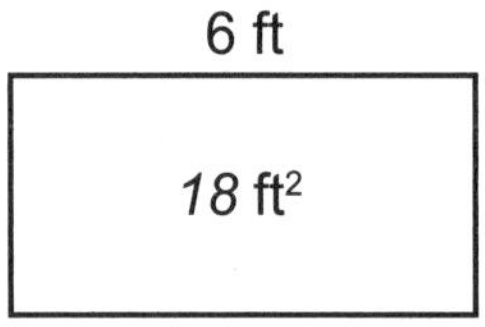			
v)	A rectangle with area 24 cm^2 has height 3 cm. What is its width?			
vi)	A triangle has base 43 mm and height 36 mm. What is its area?			
vii)	A parallelogram with base 4 km has area 20 km^2. What is the height of the parallelogram?			
viii)	A rectangle has width 7 yd and height 6 yd. What is its area?			

b) For each problem in the table use the area formula to write an equation. Then solve the equation.

i) $5\text{ cm} \times h = 20\text{ cm}^2$

$h = 20\text{ cm}^2 \div 5\text{ cm}$

$= 4\text{ cm}$

ii)

iii)

iv)

v)

vi)

vii)

viii)

2. Organize the data. Write the formula you could use and an equation. Then solve the equation.

a) A parallelogram has base 5 cm and area 35 cm^2. What is its height?

Given: *base = 5 cm*

area = 35 cm^2

Find: *height of parallelogram*

Formula: *Area = base × height*

Equation: $5 \text{ cm} \times h = 35 \text{ cm}^2$

$h = 35 \text{ cm}^2 \div 5 \text{ cm}$

$= 7 \text{ cm}$

b) What is the height of a parallelogram with base 3 m and area 12 m^2?

Given: ____________________

____

Find: ____________________

Formula: ____________________

Equation: ____________________

c) A cereal bar wrapper is a rectangle 4 in wide, with area 48 in^2.
What is the length of the wrapper?

Given: ____________________

____

Find: ____________________

Formula: ____________________

Equation: ____________________

d) A flowerbed is a rectangle that covers 24 ft^2. It is 8 ft long. How wide is it?

Given: ____________________

____

Find: ____________________

Formula: ____________________

Equation: ____________________

e) A company logo is a parallelogram with height 80 cm. It covers an area of 6,000 cm^2. How long is the horizontal side of the logo?

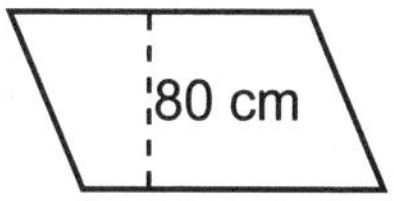

f) Roni's bedroom has area 85.5 ft^2. The room is 9 ft long. What is the width of the room?

BONUS ▶ A hexagon with sides 8 cm and area 158 cm^2 is made of three identical rhombuses. What is the area of each rhombus?
What is the height of each rhombus?

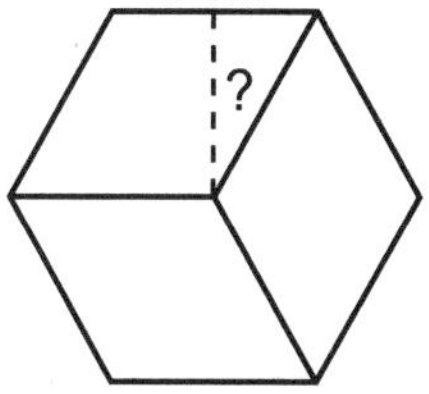

G6-16 Comparing Units of Length

1. a) Complete the table by following the pattern.

m	1	2	3	4	5	6
dm	10	20				
cm	100	200				
mm	1,000	2,000				

b) To convert a measurement from meters to centimeters, you multiply by ______________.

c) To convert a measurement from centimeters to millimeters, you multiply by ______________.

d) To convert a measurement from meters to millimeters, you multiply by ______________.

2. Convert the measurements.

a)

m	cm
8	
10	
75	

b)

m	mm
5	
10	
17	

c)

cm	mm
4	
7	
121	

3. Convert the measurement in centimeters to a mixed measurement.

a) 423 cm = _4_ m _23_ cm b) 514 cm = ____ m _____ cm c) 627 cm = ____ m _____ cm

d) 673 cm = ____ m _____ cm e) 381 cm = ____ m _____ cm f) 203 cm = ____ m _____ cm

4. Convert the mixed measurement to a measurement in centimeters.

a) 3 m = _300_ cm

so 3 m 7 cm

=

	3	0	0	cm
+			7	cm
	3	0	7	cm

b) 4 m = _______ cm

so 4 m 51 cm

=

				cm
+				cm
				cm

c) 5 m = _______ cm

so 5 m 5 cm

=

				cm
+				cm
				cm

d) 8 m 12 cm = _______ cm e) 9 m 27 cm = _______ cm f) 7 m 3 cm = _______ cm

5. Convert the measurement in centimeters to meters.

a) 23 cm = _0.23_ m b) 51 cm = ______ m c) 27 cm = ______ m

d) 67 cm = ______ m e) 3 cm = ______ m f) 2 cm = ______ m

6. Change the measurement in centimeters to a mixed measurement and then to decimal notation.

a) 546 cm = _5_ m _46_ cm = _5.46_ m

b) 217 cm = ____ m ____ cm = ______ m

c) 783 cm = ____ m ____ cm = ______ m

d) 608 cm = ____ m ____ cm = ______ m

e) 72 cm = ____ m ____ cm = ______ m

f) 7 cm = ____ m ____ cm = ______ m

7. Why can we use the same decimal notation for dollars and cents that we use for meters and centimeters?

8. Michelle says that to change 6 m 80 cm to centimeters, you multiply the 6 by 100 and then add 80. Is Michelle correct? Why does Michelle multiply by 100?

9. Convert the measurement in meters to centimeters.

a) 2.35 m = _235_ cm

b) 5.21 m = ______ cm

c) 2.97 m = ______ cm

d) 6.77 m = ______ cm

e) 2.03 m = ______ cm

f) 0.32 m = ______ cm

10. Marko thinks that 3.2 m = 32 cm. Is he correct? Explain why or why not.

11. Find the perimeter of the rectangle on the right.

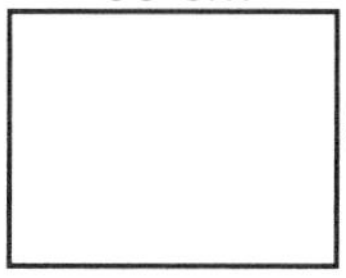

Perimeter = ______ cm = ______ m

Is the perimeter of the rectangle greater or less than 2.4 m? ______

12. a) Write the length and width of each square in centimeters. The squares are not drawn to scale.

i) 1 m = ________ cm

1 m = ________ cm

ii) 2 m = ________ cm

2 m = ________ cm

iii) 3 m = ________ cm

3 m = ________ cm

b) Find the area of each square in square meters and in square centimeters.

i) Area = ______ m^2 = __________ cm^2

ii) Area = ______ m^2 = __________ cm^2

iii) Area = ______ m^2 = __________ cm^2

c) To convert square meters to square centimeters you multiply by _______________.

G6-17 Changing Units of Length

REMINDER ▶

To multiply 2.14 by 10, shift the decimal 1 place to the right: $2.14 \times 10 = 21.4$

To multiply 2.14 by 100, shift the decimal 2 places to the right: $2.14 \times 100 = 214$

To multiply 2.14 by 1,000, shift the decimal 3 places to the right: $2.14 \times 1{,}000 = 2{,}140$

1. a) $11.1 \times 10 =$ ________ b) $32.1 \times 100 =$ ________ c) $43.5 \times 1{,}000 =$ ________

d) $3.78 \times 10 =$ ________ e) $3.41 \times 100 =$ ________ f) $4.52 \times 1{,}000 =$ ________

g) $0.329 \times 10 =$ ________ h) $0.198 \times 100 =$ ________ i) $0.789 \times 1{,}000 =$ ________

BONUS ▶ $23.678 \times 1{,}000{,}000 =$ ______________

REMINDER ▶

To divide 32.1 by 10, shift the decimal 1 place to the left: $32.1 \div 10 = 3.21$

To divide 32.1 by 100, shift the decimal 2 places to the left: $32.1 \div 100 = 0.321$

To divide 32.1 by 1,000, shift the decimal 3 places to the left: $32.1 \div 1{,}000 = 0.0321$

2. a) $11.1 \div 10 =$ ________ b) $37.1 \div 100 =$ ________ c) $43.5 \div 1{,}000 =$ ________

d) $3.78 \div 10 =$ ________ e) $3.41 \div 100 =$ ________ f) $124.52 \div 1{,}000 =$ ________

g) $329 \div 10 =$ ________ h) $198 \div 100 =$ ________ i) $789 \div 1{,}000 =$ ________

BONUS ▶ $23{,}678 \div 1{,}000{,}000 =$ ______________

3. a) Measure the line segment in millimeters, centimeters, and decimeters.

________ mm ________ cm ________ dm

b) Which of the units (mm, cm, or dm) is the largest? ________ The smallest? ________

c) Which unit did you need more of to measure the line, the *largest* unit or the *smallest* unit?

____

d) Write "more" or "fewer" in the blank.

To change a measurement from a *larger* unit to a *smaller* unit,

you need ____________ of the smaller units.

Units become smaller as you go down the stairs.

- 1 step down = 10 times smaller
- 2 steps down = 100 times smaller
- 3 steps down = 1,000 times smaller

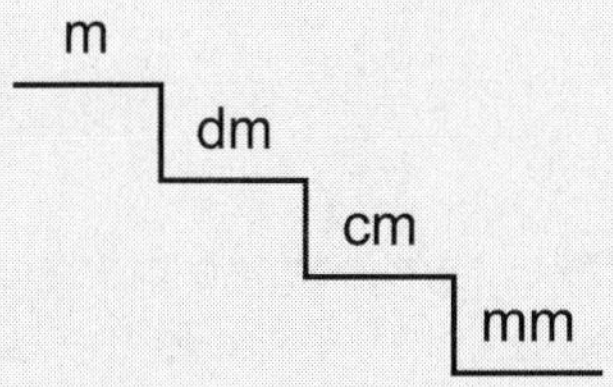

4. Fill in the missing number.

a) 1 cm = _______ mm b) 1 dm = _______ cm c) 1 dm = _______ mm

d) 1 m = _______ dm e) 1 m = _______ cm f) 1 m = _______ mm

5. Change the measurement by following the steps.

a) Change 3.5 cm to mm

The new units are *10* times *smaller* ,

so I need *more* units.

I *multiply* by *10* .

3.5 cm = *35* mm

b) Change 7.2 cm to mm

The new units are _____ times _________,

so I need _________ units.

I ______________ by _____.

7.2 cm = _______ mm

c) Change 2.6 dm to cm

The new units are _____ times _________,

so I need _________ units.

I ______________ by _____.

2.6 dm = _______ cm

d) Change 7.53 cm to mm

The new units are _____ times _________,

so I need _________ units.

I ______________ by _____.

7.53 cm = _______ mm

e) Change 3.4 mm to cm

The new units are _____ times _________,

so I need _________ units.

I ______________ by _____.

3.4 mm = _______ cm

f) Change 8.53 m to cm

The new units are _____ times _________,

so I need _________ units.

I ______________ by _____.

8.53 m = _______ cm

g) Change 5.2 m to cm

h) Change 214 cm to m

i) Change 4 m to dm

j) Change 1.3 dm to mm

k) Change 2.04 cm to mm

l) Change 0.05 m to mm

G6-18 Changing Units and Using Formulas

1. Organize the data. Use geometric and mathematical terms. Then write the formula you could use.

a) A parallelogram-shaped piece of cake has two parallel sides, each 75 mm long, and area 30 cm^2. What is the distance between the parallel sides?

Given: *base = 75 mm* Find: *height of parallelogram*

area = 30 cm^2 Formula: *area = base × height*

b) A rectangle is 0.6 m wide, with area 720 cm^2. What is the height of the rectangle?

Given: ____________ Find: ____________

____________ Formula: ____________

c) Find the area of a triangle with height 25 mm and base 8 cm.

Given: ____________ Find: ____________

____________ Formula: ____________

d) A parking spot has two sides 5 m long. The distance between the sides is 325 cm. What is the area of the parking spot?

Given: ____________ Find: ____________

____________ Formula: ____________

e) A rectangular flowerbed covers 12 m^2. It is 200 cm wide. How long is it?

Given: ____________ Find: ____________

____________ Formula: ____________

2. A parallelogram has base 2 m and height 80 cm.

a) Linh thinks its area is $2 \times 80 = 160$ cm^2. Is she correct? ______ Explain. ____________

____

b) Chu thinks its area is $2 \times 80 = 160$ m^2. Is he correct? ______ Explain. ____________

____

c) Convert the height of the parallelogram to meters. Height = ______ m

Area of parallelogram = ______ m^2

d) Convert the base of the parallelogram to centimeters. Base = ______ cm

Area of parallelogram = ______ cm^2

e) Remember: 1 m^2 = 100 cm × 100 cm = 10,000 cm^2. Is your area in part c) equal to your area in part d)? If not, find your mistake.

3. Convert the measurement. Replace the parts of the formula with the given information. Then solve the equation for the unknown.

a) Base = 45 mm = *4.5* cm

Area = 18 cm^2

Find: height of parallelogram

Formula: area = base × height

18 cm^2 = 4.5 cm × height

Height = 18 cm^2 ÷ 4.5 cm = 4 cm

b) Height = 0.3 m = ______ cm

Area = 1,200 cm^2

Find: base of parallelogram

Formula: area = base × height

c) Base = 0.8 cm = ______ mm

Height = 218 mm

Find: area of parallelogram

Formula: area = base × height

d) Height = 2 m

Base = 120 cm = ______ m

Find: area of triangle

Formula: area = base × height ÷ 2

e) Width = 0.7 cm = ______ mm

Area = 224 mm^2

Find: length of rectangle

Formula: area = length × width

f) Height = 300 cm = ______ m

Area = 21 m^2

Find: base of parallelogram

Formula: area = base × height

4. a) The area of a rectangle is 25 m^2. It is 250 cm long. What is the width of the rectangle?

b) A triangular traffic island has base 125 cm and height 1.4 m. The traffic island needs to be covered in grass. How much grass roll is needed?

c) A bus window is 0.8 m tall and has the shape of a parallelogram. The area of the window is 9,600 cm^2. What is the length of the bottom side of the window?

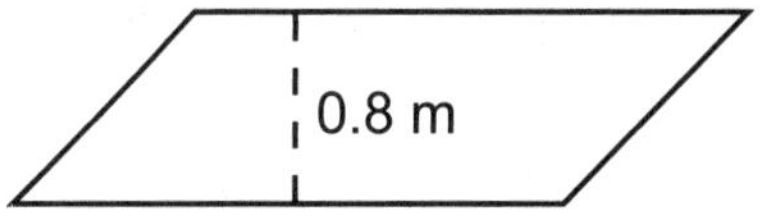

G6-19 Problems with Area

1. A parallelogram is made of a square and two right triangles as shown. The base of each triangle is only half as wide as the square.

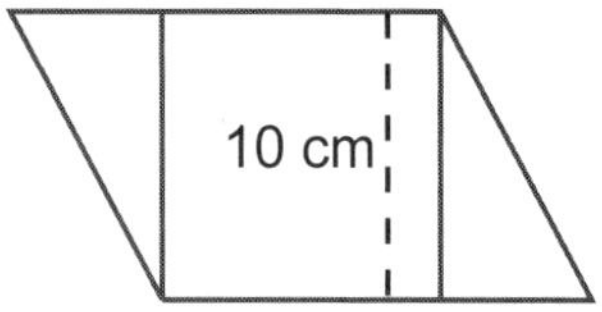

   a) Width of the square = ________

   Base of the triangles = ________

   Area of the square = ________

   Area of each triangle = ________

   Area of the parallelogram = area of the square + _____ × area of the triangle

   = _____ + _____ = _____ cm^2

   b) Use the formula for the area of a parallelogram to solve the same problem.

   Write the formula: Area of parallelogram = ____________________

   Base of parallelogram = ________

   Height of parallelogram = ________

   Area of the parallelogram = ________

   c) Are your answers in parts a) and b) the same? If not, find your mistake.

2. Julie cuts a square into two equal rectangles and rearranges the parts to make another rectangle. The short side of her new rectangle is 6 cm. What is the area of her rectangle?

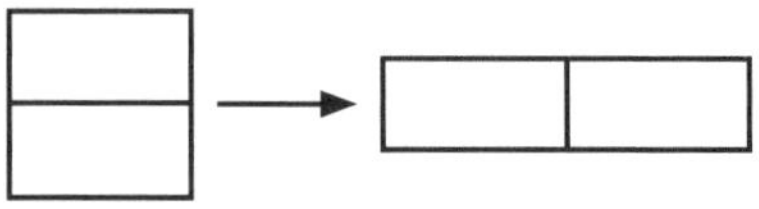

REMINDER ▶ Area of trapezoid = (base 1 + base 2) × height ÷ 2 or $A = (b_1 + b_2) \times h \div 2$

3. Find the area of these trapezoids.

a) 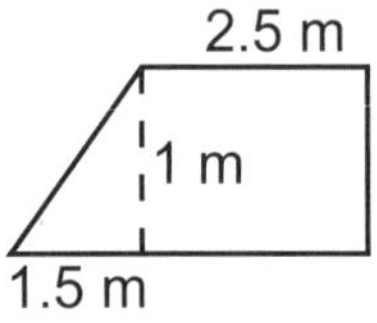

b) 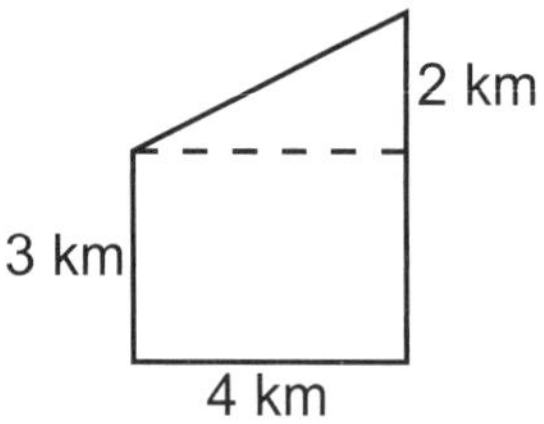

c) 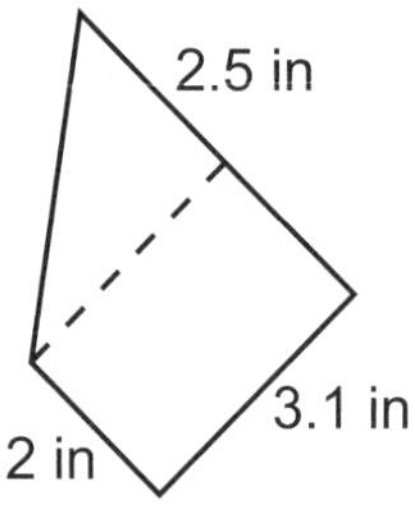

4. Find the area of the shaded part. Then say what fraction of the grid is shaded.
Hint: Use the area of the unshaded part and the area of the grid.

a) 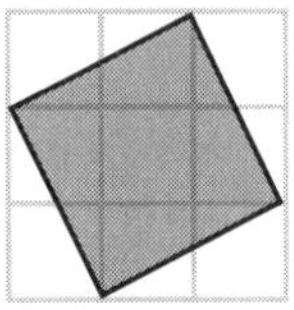

Area = ________

Fraction:

b) 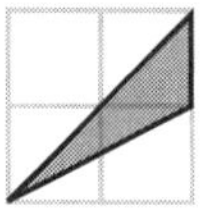

Area = ________

Fraction:

c) 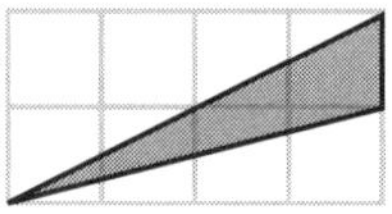

Area = ________

Fraction:

5. Find the area of the shaded shape.

a) 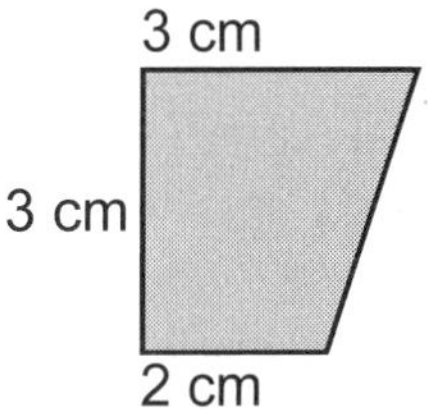

b) 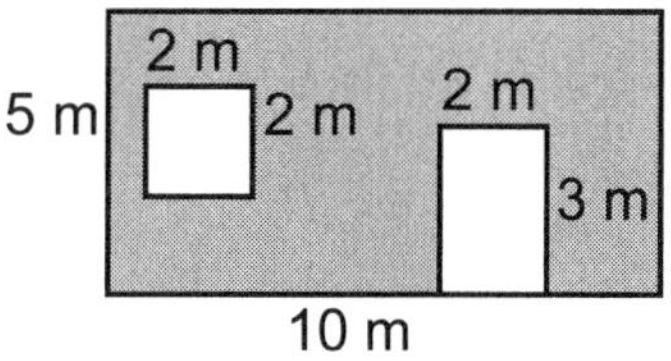

c) 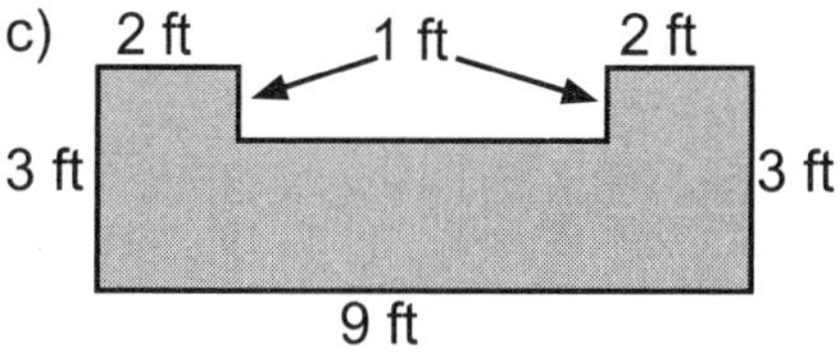

d) 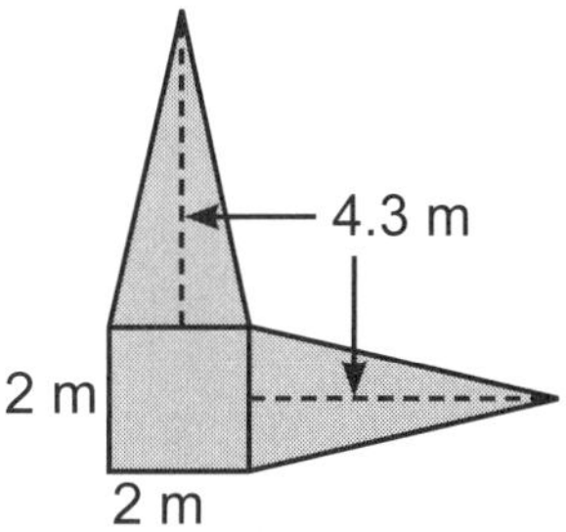

e) 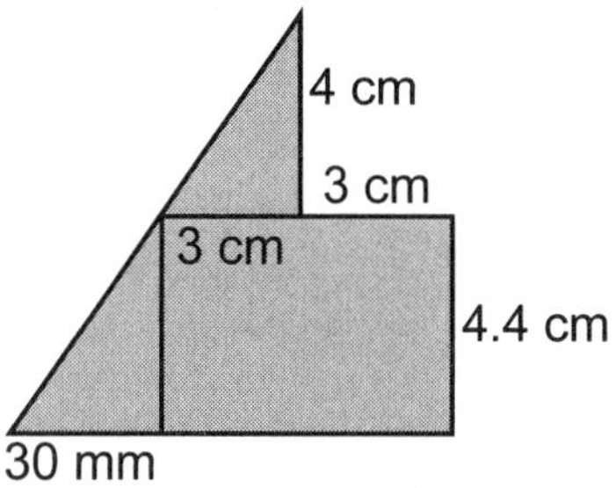

f) 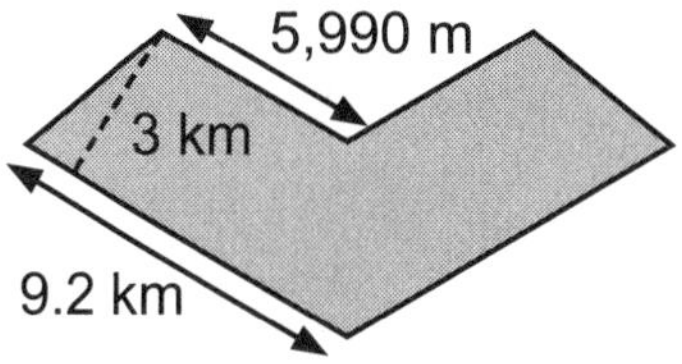

6. A garden has a path in the shape of a parallelogram. The shaded areas are flowerbeds.

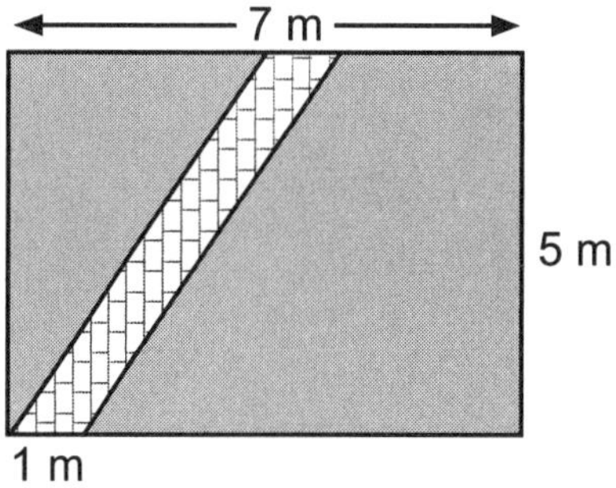

a) What is the height of the path?

b) The base of the path is 1 m. What is the area of the path?

c) What is the total area of the flowerbeds? Show your work.

d) The path is covered in tiles. It cost $3 per square meter to lay the tiles. It cost $5 per square meter to plant the flowerbeds. How much did it cost to create the garden?

7. What is the area of the shaded part in the figure at right?

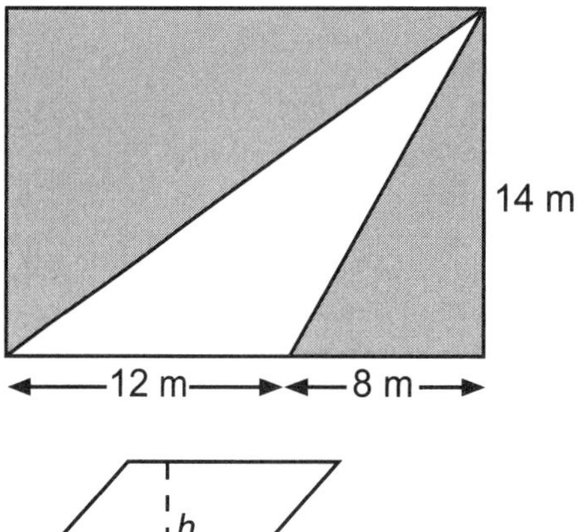

8. A triangle has area 12 cm². Its base is 4 cm.

a) What is the height of the triangle?

b) On grid paper, draw three different triangles with area 12 cm² and base 4 cm.

9. The shape on the right is made from two parallelograms. Its area is 32.5 m². What is the height of the larger parallelogram?

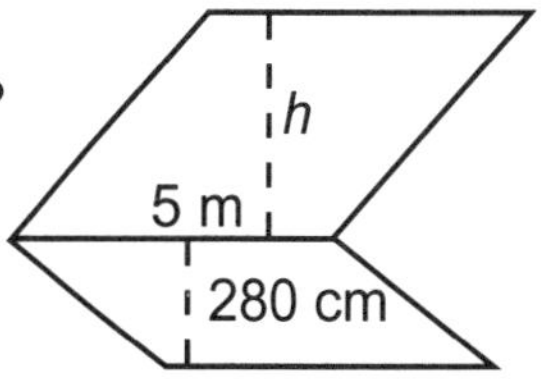

BONUS ▶

The ancient Maya used units of length called kaans. An ancient Mayan field is rhombus-shaped. Its area is 20 square kaans. Each side of the field is 5 kaans long. What is the height of the rhombus-shaped field? Hint: A rhombus is a parallelogram.